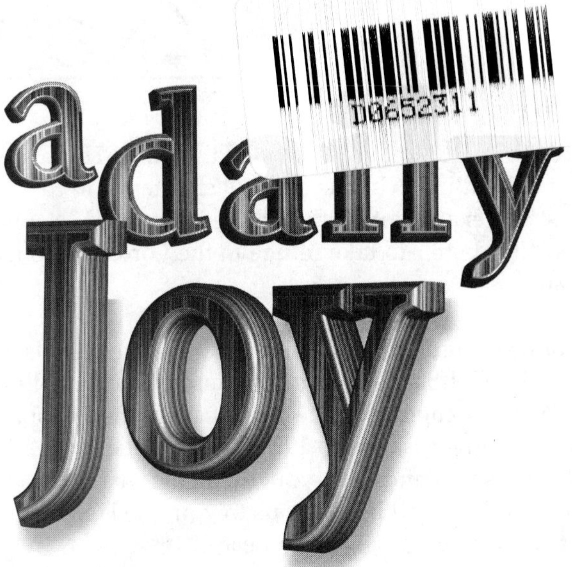

By Ron Hembree

A Quick
Study
Guide
Through
God's
Word

Did You Know?

There are nearly 774,000 words in the Bible. These are contained within 66 books of 1,189 chapters and 31,173 verses. The exact center of the Bible is Psalm 118:8 which states: "It is better to take refuge in the Lord than to trust in man."

The oldest fragment of Biblical text that we have is dated from 587 B.C. It is the Blessing of Aaron found in Numbers 6:24-26 and is engraved on a pair of silver medallions discovered in Jerusalem in 1979. The passage says: "The LORD bless you and keep you; the LORD make his face shine upon you and be gracious to you; the LORD turn his face toward you and give you peace."

The longest word in the Bible is Maher-shalal-hash-baz, who was the son of Isaiah (Isaiah 8:1).

The most common name in the Bible is Zachariah, with over 30 entries. The second most common name is Azariah, while third place goes to the unlikely name of Meshullam (over 20 times).

Did you know that God's name changes?

The creation story in Genesis 1 simply calls the Creator "God." However, in Genesis 2 He is referred to as "Lord God." The word "Lord" stands for *Yahweh,* the Hebrew name for God. This sacred name was represented by the four consonants in *Yahweh* and thus always appeared as *YHWH.*

Devout Jews believe God's name is too sacred to be uttered in human speech. That is why they made the designation *YHWH* so it could not be pronounced. They substitute the word *Adonai* when reading aloud from the Bible. *Adonai* means "My Lord."

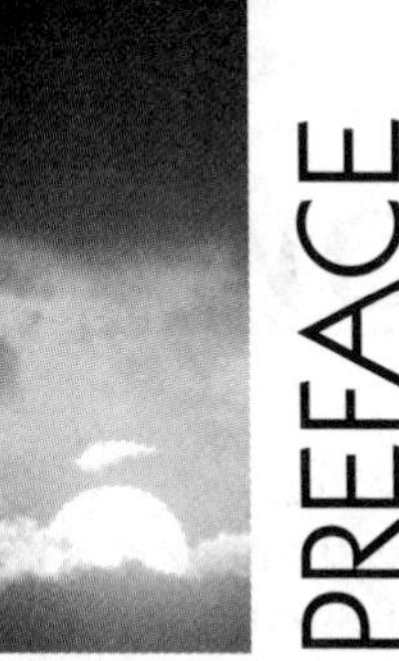

PREFACE

A DAILY JOY

Ancient kings of Israel were instructed: "That copy of the laws (God's Word) shall be his constant companion. He must read from it every day of his life..." Then the king was told why he must do this: "So that he will learn to respect the Lord his God by obeying all of his commands. This regular reading of God's laws will prevent him from feeling that he is better than his fellow citizens. It will also prevent him from turning away from God's laws in the slightest respect and will ensure his having a long, good reign. His sons will then follow him upon the throne" (Deuteronomy 17:19-20 TLB).

It seems to me that we modern day "kings and priests unto God" (Revelation 1:6 and 5:10 KJV) should be just as serious about establishing a habit of daily Bible-reading. This book is intended to help do just that by providing a daily Bible-reading schedule, interesting historical information, and a practical application of each day's reading to our lives.

Each day's reading contains four headings for quick and easy study. They are: **Looking Back, Looking In, Looking Out,** and **Looking Up. Looking Back** reviews an interesting event that occurred on that date in history. **Looking In** makes the transition from that event to the reading of the day. **Looking Out** contains five "Life Lessons" we learn from the daily reading and how they can apply to our lives. **Looking Up** is a suggested prayer for the day that relates to the daily Bible-reading assignment.

My prayer is that your task of daily Bible-reading becomes a real joy, not merely an onerous chore. The result will be just as God promised:

"As the rain and the snow come down from heaven, and do not return to it without watering the earth and making it bud and flourish, so that it yields seed for the sower and bread for the eater, so is my word that goes out from my mouth: It will not return to me empty, but will accomplish what I desire and achieve the purpose for which I sent it. You will go out in joy and be led forth in peace; the mountains and hills will burst into song before you, and all the trees of the field will clap their hands. Instead of the thorn bush will grow the pine tree, and instead of briers the myrtle will grow. This will be for the Lord's renowm, for an everlasting sign, which will not be destroyed" (Isaiah 55:10-13 NIV).

Ron Hembree
Goodyear, AZ

Did You Know?

The word "Bible" comes from a Greek word meaning "books." The Bible is made up of 66 books divided into two sections - the Old Testament and the New Testament. It was written by 40 different authors over a period of 1600 years and written in three languages; yet, from beginning to end, it is one unfolding story. The fact of the Bible's unity is confirmation of God's involvement. God's Holy Spirit influenced the Bible writers to write only the words that came from the mind of God while retaining the personality and writing style of each author.

The Bible we know today is called the "canon of Scripture." The word "canon" means "rule" or "a measuring device" and when used in relation to the Bible means the collections of books that have passed a test of authenticity or authority. In the Hebrew Bible, Genesis is the first book and 2 Chronicles is the last. The 27 books of the New Testament came together based on the test of apostleship. Documents were accepted if they were written by an apostle or someone close to and recognized by an apostle, such as Mark or Luke. By AD 200, Matthew, Mark, Luke, and John were the only accepted Gospels. At the Council of Hippo (in AD 393) and the Council of Carthage (AD 397), the 27 books that make up our New Testament were officially accepted as the canon of Scripture.

The collection of other writings called the "Apocrypha" was written between 200 BC and AD 100. Some consider these important religious and historical documents valuable for study. But they did not become part of the canon of Scripture for several reasons, two of the facts being they did not appear in any Hebrew canon and none of their content is quoted in the New Testament.

JANUARY............

An Interesting Month with Two Different Faces

January is a month with two faces. In the northern half of the world, January is usually the coldest month of the year. Nature is quiet. Birds travel less, and animals such as bears and woodchucks sleep both day and night. Plants rest in preparation for the next growing season. However, in the southern half of the world, January is usually the warmest month of the year. Plants grow and animals are active. The world comes alive with new growth. The voice of the turtledove is heard in the land. In the Northern Hemisphere, the snowdrop is the special flower for the month because it often blooms in the snow.

January is the first month of the year according to the Gregorian calendar, which is used in almost all the world today. The month is named for Janus, a Roman god. According to Roman legend, the ruler Numa Pompilius added January and February to the end of the 10-month Roman calendar in about 700 B.C. He gave the month 30 days. Later, the Romans made January the first month of the year. In 46 B.C., the Roman statesman Julius Caesar added a day to January, making it 31 days long. The Anglo-Saxons called the first month "Wolfmonth," because it was then that wolves came into the village in search of food.

During January, we read Genesis and most of Exodus. These first two Bible books introduce us to the beginning of our world and the start of God's dealing with humanity through a "chosen" people. The Biblical stories present a unique idea of one benevolent God, an ordered universe, and humanity that has goodness at its core. Genesis introduces the story of the Israelite people, but the actual history of Israel as a nation begins in Exodus. The book presents the idea of a God Who brings freedom to the downtrodden and forms a lasting relationship with them. We learn much about the character of God through these two remarkable books.

NEW BEGINNINGS

JANUARY 1

Genesis 1-2

LOOKING BACK New Year's Day has been called "Everyman's Birthday" because it is a time of new beginnings. In some countries, a year is added to everyone's age on January 1 rather than on the anniversary of each person's birth. Ever since 1751, January 1 has been observed as the beginning of the year in most English-speaking countries. That was the year the British Calendar Act was passed. Prior to this date, New Year always began on March 25, approximately at the time of the vernal equinox. Traditionally, New Year's Day is a time for personal introspection and for making resolutions to change some behavioral habits.

LOOKING IN *God's Word starts by taking us back to the beginning, letting us know God's plans for us in our world. Tragically, our first parents failed in fulfilling these plans, but even then God gave them hope they could have a new beginning. Just as each fresh New Year offers opportunity for correction and change, so God gives His children a chance to start over when they turn to Him. However, unlike the New Year's offer, God also gives the strength needed so we can make correction and lasting change. The Bible says: "But as many as received him, to them gave he power to become the sons of God, even to them that believe on his name..." (John 1:12).*

LOOKING OUT

1. **Creation always comes out of chaos. The world was without form and void when God stepped in to bring order. He does the same for us when we turn to Him for help.**
2. **Our problems do not magically disappear. Rather, there is a sensible sequence in solving them. The creation story shows us how God creates order carefully step-by-step.**
3. **God wants to form a partnership with us in fulfilling our purpose. Adam and Eve were to be involved in bringing order to chaos. God gave them wisdom and inspiration.**
4. **God is exceedingly fair. He spelled out the consequences of their choices long before Adam and Eve sinned. Like us, their real problem was not ignorance, but rebellion.**
5. **God has given us all we need for effective and joyful living. Everything that God made was good. Man now was given a choice whether to enjoy creation or to rebel.**

LOOKING UP *Lord, help me to remember you can, and will, bring creation out of the chaos around me. I trust in you!*

RESTRICTIONS

JANUARY 2

Genesis 3-5

LOOKING BACK President Richard Nixon signed a bill on this day, in 1974, requiring states to limit highway speeds to a maximum of 55 miles per hour. This measure was meant to conserve energy during the crisis precipitated by the embargo imposed by the Arab oil-producing countries. A plan, used by some states, limited sales of gasoline on odd-numbered days for cars whose plates ended in odd numbers, and even-numbered days for even-numbered plates. Some states limited purchases to $2-$3 per auto, and lines as long as six miles resulted in some locations. The embargo was lifted on March 13, 1974, five months after it started.

LOOKING IN *The highway speed bill was necessary because man's selfish nature is such that he will not voluntarily limit his excesses. Our first parents' sin unleashed all the selfishness and evil that now plagues our planet. It soon became apparent that laws restricting bad behavior would be necessary. Eating the forbidden fruit had far more consequences than Adam and Eve anticipated. God had emphatically told them to stay away from the tree of the knowledge of good and evil, but they refused to believe their loving Creator. Soon man's sin multiplied, and Cain became the world's first killer. The earth was plunged into a chaos that lasts to this very day.*

LOOKING OUT

1. **Sin is disobeying the revealed Word of God. Adam and Eve did not sin out of ignorance but out of sheer rebellion.**
2. **Sin is believing Satan's lie. The evil one always tries to question God's character. We must turn a deaf ear to him.**
3. **Sin is placing our will above God's. Adam and Eve decided they, alone, knew what would make them happy.**
4. **God's love is seen in judgment. Though God is deeply hurt by man's sin, He still makes clothes for him.**
5. **Judgment is always an act of mercy. Banning man from the tree of life kept him from an eternal state of alienation.**

LOOKING UP *Lord, help me to remember that I am vulnerable to the pull of the flesh. Keep me pure and true to You.*

IMMORALITY

JANUARY 3

Genesis 6-9

LOOKING BACK Marion Davies, renowned lover of William Randolph Hearst, was born on this date in 1897. She was born Marion Cecillia Douras, and made her first film appearance in 1917. Her romantic and professional involvement with Hearst ensured the type of publicity that would launch her into stardom. Her films included *When Knighthood Was in Flower* and *Patsy and Show People*. Davies and Hearst scandalized society with their public illicit affair, in spite of the fact that Hearst was married and the father of several children. Hearst reportedly built his famous California castle so he could carry on his involvement with Davies away from his family.

LOOKING IN *Immorality is never pretty and is even more ugly when it is flaunted in the public's face. In Noah's day, sin was so rampant "that every inclination of the thoughts of his heart was only evil all the time." The Bible says that God was greatly grieved over the blatant sin of mankind and determined to destroy His creation. However, there was a man who was righteous. Noah found grace in the eyes of the Lord. God told Noah to build an ark and warn others of coming judgment. Noah became a laughing stock in that sin-saturated society. However, the day came when Noah and his family were safe in the ark. All others were lost.*

LOOKING OUT

1. While God is exceedingly patient, there is an end to His endurance of evil. God had given man centuries to repent, but they continued in blatant rebellion. Then the flood came.
2. Even in the darkest hour, God provides a way of escape. Noah preached repentance for decades, giving people every opportunity to change. God's mercy is great and long lasting.
3. All discipline from God is directive, not punitive. The flood was actually an act of mercy. Rampant sin-causing disease would have soon wiped out all of creation.
4. There is always an ark of safety, if we will just opt for it. Noah tried to persuade others to be saved, but they would not listen. However, Noah and his family were spared.
5. God gives us a chance to start over again. The flood did not last forever. Noah and his family were given the opportunity to build a better world, just as we are after our conversion.

LOOKING UP *Lord, help me never to trivialize evil. Make me abhor it, and, in You, build a better world around me.*

COMMUNICATION

JANUARY 4

Genesis 10-11

LOOKING BACK Louis Braille, the inventor of a widely used touch system of reading and writing for the blind, was born on this day in 1809. Braille had been permanently blinded at the age of three by a leather- working awl in his father's saddle making shop. He developed a system of writing that uses, ironically, an awl-like stylus to punch marks in paper that can be felt and interpreted by the blind. The system was largely ignored until after Braille died in poverty, suffering from tuberculosis, at the age of 43. Today, the blind can communicate freely by using the Braille system. Public facilities often use the system to identify facilities and conveniences.

LOOKING IN *Communication is one of the greatest keys to success in any venture. When evil sinners determined to defy God by building the Tower of Babel, God solved their arrogance in a very simple way: He disrupted their ability to communicate. God had wonderful plans for His creation, but the people of Babel put their own pleasure before their responsibility. Such rebellion had to be stopped lest God's will for our earth be thwarted. Often we wonder if the arrogant of our world will ever be stopped. We need not fear because God is still on the throne. He knows how to stop those who continue to violate His will and ways.*

LOOKING OUT

1. Pride is a subtle temptress, turning us away from God and the task He has for us. At Babel, pride had driven the builders to abandon God's agenda for one of their own.
2. While there is great power in unity, we must be certain our purposes please God. No weapon formed against God will ultimately prosper. He brings the arrogant low.
3. Defiance will be defeated because God's agenda is bigger than our own. Mankind is part of a divine drama, and that action will be played out regardless of man's opposition.
4. Sin's seeds always bloom, shortening the quality and quantity of our lives. The genealogies following man's rebellion disclose an ever-shortening life span for man.
5. God's stories have happy endings because He never gives up on us. Abraham comes on the scene. This remarkable man starts another chapter in God's patient dealing with us.

LOOKING UP *God, help me to know Your great love. And, Lord, deal with any pride that would separate me from You.*

REBEL

JANUARY 5

Genesis 12-14

LOOKING BACK Edmund Ruffin has never received the accolades his work deserves. He was the early American agriculturist, born on this day in 1794, whose discoveries about crop rotation and fertilizer greatly influenced farm productivity. But, he was also a rebel who advocated Southern secession. As a member of the Palmetto Guards of Charleston, Ruffin was given the honor of firing the first shot on Fort Sumter, April 12, 1861, which touched off the bloody Civil War. According to legend, after the South's defeat, Ruffin became despondent and, wrapping himself in the Confederate flag, took his own life on June 18, 1865.

LOOKING IN *Rebels seldom succeed and often come to a bitter end. The rebels at Babel had their dreams destroyed, but God's work marched on. Abraham now enters the stage of history. He will become the father of a nation through which God's only begotten Son will be introduced to the world. God had been dealing with the world at large but now chose to communicate through a single family. Abraham's family would become a clan and then a nation. His "chosen" people were to live by God's laws and prove that lifestyle to be the highest, healthiest, and holiest way to live. They would also be given the awesome responsibility of communicating these laws to the whole world.*

LOOKING OUT

1. It's never too late, nor are we ever too old, to catch the current of God's move in history. God promised a son to Abraham, but it would be long years before Isaac was born.
2. God uses imperfect people to do his perfect work; we need only respond rightly to His discipline. Abraham's faith had failed in Egypt, but God used him anyway.
3. Conflicts are inevitable and must not be ignored; they must be resolved, using God's ways and wisdom. Abraham and Lot worked out their differences in a godly way.
4. What may appear appealing can be disastrous. Careful prayer helps us choose what is best. Lot greedily grabbed the fertile plains and lived to regret his selfish decision.
5. Giving to God is not a task or a tax; it is a warm and wonderful way to show gratitude. Abraham paid tithe to Melchizedek because he wanted to give thanks to God.

LOOKING UP *Help me, Lord, to choose according to Your will, not according to my wants. May I always be grateful.*

TWELFTHTIDE

Genesis 15-17

LOOKING BACK Today is known as Old Christmas or Twelfthtide because, 12 days after Christmas, some celebrate the visit of the Magi, the first Gentile recognition of Christ. Also, La Befana is observed today in Italy. According to ancient European tradition this is the Epiphany festival in which the "Befana," a kindly witch, bestows gifts on children—toys and candy for those who have been good, but a lump of coal or a pebble for those who have been naughty. The festival begins on the night of January 5– with much noise and merrymaking– when the Befana is supposed to come down the chimney on her broom, leaving gifts in children's stockings.

LOOKING IN *Unlike Befana, God doesn't look to see if we are good before He visits us with His presence and gifts. God didn't call Abram because he was good but because God wanted to bless the world through his seed. God gave us Jesus, His Son, not because we deserved it, but because He is love! Abram will have a special relationship with God, becoming known as a "friend of God." His name will be changed to Abraham to identify the good plans God has for His chosen vessel. God always gives those He loves far more than they ever dreamed. Abraham would have been satisfied with a single son, but God promised him He would make him a father of nations.*

LOOKING OUT

1. **When our faith is fragile, our Heavenly Father repeats His promises. Abraham's faith was stretched many times. In those days of doubt, God reassures him of His promise.**
2. **God knows how to confirm His Word so we really know we have heard from Him. God told Abraham to participate in a dramatic covenant ceremony he could not forget.**
3. **We must hold on to what God has told us, or others will turn us to turmoil. Sarai convinced Abram that he should help God out in bringing about the birth of a son.**
4. **What seems a solution can become a shame when we go our way rather than God's. Sarai lived to regret her prodding Abram into an illicit relationship with her handmaiden.**
5. **God stretches us to what seems like the breaking point before we see His promises fulfilled. Abram was getting older by the moment. It seemed God's promises would fail.**

LOOKING UP *Help me to hold on, Lord, even though it seems such a long time before I see You answering my prayer.*

OVERTHROW

JANUARY 7

Genesis 18-19

LOOKING BACK Pol Pot, one of the most diabolical leaders of this century, was overthrown on this day in 1979. His Cambodian government fell to combined forces of Cambodian rebels and Vietnamese soldiers. The Khmer Rouge Communists, led by Pol Pot, took full control of the Cambodian government and began to supervise the lives of the people closely. The government took over all businesses and farms, killing large numbers of Cambodians. The sharp decline in agricultural production in Cambodia caused severe food shortages in the 1970's. At least one million Cambodians died as a result of execution, starvation, disease, or hard labor.

LOOKING IN *Evil does come too early and stays too long; however, it doesn't last forever. Judgment will come, and evil will end—just as it did for Pol Pot. Sodom and Gomorrah were cities of extreme brutality, sexual perversion, and other incredible evils. Their day of judgment also came. God considered Abraham such a good friend that He wanted Abraham to know what He planned to do with the sinful cities. Abraham's nephew, Lot, resided in Sodom with his family. When God told Abraham about His plan, one of the most remarkable exchanges between God and man followed. Abraham interceded for the city. His concern spared Lot and his two daughters.*

LOOKING OUT

1. **God opens His heart to those He finds as friends. Abraham's relationship with God was so intimate that God could share His plans and secrets with him.**
2. **Fervent prayer works and is encouraged by our Lord. No doubt one of the reasons God told Abraham about His plans was so the patriarch would intercede for the wicked city.**
3. **Sin, stripped of its shiny veneer, is raw, rotten, and dehumanizing. The despicable behavior of Sodom's residents shows the ugly underbelly of lustful rebellion.**
4. **We always lose when we invest too much in this world. Lot, his wife, and family had given too much of themselves to Sodom and Gomorrah. They lost their loved ones.**
5. **We must run from sin and never look back. Lot's wife paused to look back longingly at the burning cities. She was destroyed by an avalanche of molten rock and salt.**

LOOKING UP *Let me be your friend, Lord, so that You might share Your plans and secrets with me. Let me always run from sin.*

PROVEN

JANUARY 8

Genesis 20-22

LOOKING BACK Using a device now known as" Foucault's pendulum," on this day in 1851, a French physicist demonstrated conclusively, for the first time, that the earth really does rotate. Jean Foucault was well-known for his measurements, having used a revolving mirror to measure the speed of light in 1850, proving that light travels more slowly in water than in air, and that the speed varies inversely with the index of refraction. Foucault silenced skeptics by demonstrating the rotation of the earth on its axis with a pendulum experiment and by using a gyroscope that maintained its axis in a fixed direction, while the earth turned relative to that direction.

LOOKING IN *Wisely, men often insist on proof before they believe. God knew and believed Abraham's faith but still demanded proof from His friend. This would be the hardest test Abraham ever had to face. After many years, God had given Abraham a son. Now God demanded Isaac to be sacrificed. The demand must have confused Abraham, but He loved and trusted God so much that he did not question the order. Rather, he headed for the place of sacrifice with the confidence that, somehow, some way, God would make things right. On that sacred mountain so long ago, Abraham successfully proved His faith, and God proved His faithfulness.*

LOOKING OUT

1. Even good men act badly at times, but God will forgive and put them back on the right path. Abraham had great faith, but when it came to protecting his wife, he failed the test.
2. God's promises may be delayed but are never denied; God does what He says He will do. Abraham waited many years for a son, and, finally, Isaac was born.
3. Even though we don't always make the right decisions, God can make those decisions right. Abraham and Sarah dealt badly with Hagar, but God picked up the pieces.
4. Our faith will be tested, but if we go to the wall with God, we find He always provides a way out. At the last moment, God provided the ram in the bushes for Abraham.
5. Testing strengthens our faith, making us ready for what the future holds. God knew Abraham would stand true, and now Abraham knew he loved God more than anything.

LOOKING UP *Help me, Lord, to stand true no matter what test of my faith I face. I know You will always provide.*

LOVE STORY

JANUARY 9

Genesis 23-24

LOOKING BACK "Blondie's" creator was born on this day in 1901. Murat Bernard "Chic" Young created the long-running comic strip in 1930. Originally about a jazz-age flapper who married a playboy from a socially prominent family, "Blondie" soon changed its direction. Two children were added to the cast, along with a dog and her puppies. Dagwood became a working man, and the strip focused on middle-class family situations and problems. "Blondie"introduced America to the "dagwood," an enormous sandwich made during Dagwood's late-night forays to the refrigerator. "Blondie" has maintained a high family standard and is still loved by millions.

LOOKING IN *Family is vital for society to exist and for man to feel fulfilled. The family was God's idea in the first place. The Bible says, "God sets the lonely in families" (Psalm 68:6). Abraham knew Isaac needed a family of his own, and in the custom of the day, Abraham sent his servant to get a wife for his son. Isaac didn't have opportunity to try to impress his bride-to-be. Rather, his father selected Rebekah for him. She didn't even meet her boyfriend until their wedding, yet the marriage worked out well because Abraham, Isaac, and Rebekah knew some spiritual principles we often forget in our modern society. We would do well to consider them.*

LOOKING OUT

1. **It is more important to become the right kind of mate than find the right kind of mate. Abraham selected a wife for his son because he knew this spiritual principle.**
2. **We must follow God, not our emotions. Abraham told his servant to abandon the project if the wife he selected would not come to Isaac. God's call must always have priority.**
3. **Prayer must be our priority. At every juncture, the servant prayed he would be led to the lady God had for Isaac. God is vitally interested in whom we marry.**
4. **God always works on both ends of the problem. Even before the servant finished praying, Rebekah showed up at the well. God had been preparing her heart for these events.**
5. **We must reinvest our love. Isaac had been grieving over his mother's death. However, after he reinvested his love in Rebekah, the Bible says, "Isaac was comforted."**

LOOKING UP *Lead me, Lord, to the relationships You want me to have. May I be careful where I invest my love. Teach me how to better love the ones You bring to me.*

COMMON SENSE

JANUARY 10

Genesis 25-26

LOOKING BACK *Common Sense*, the controversial tract written by Thomas Paine, was published on this day in 1776. More than any other publication, *Common Sense* influenced the authors of the United States' Declaration of Independence, put forth on July 4, 1776. The 50-page pamphlet sold more than 500,000 copies within a few months of its first printing. Paine was a revolutionary leader who made his living as a corset-maker. In addition to *Common Sense*, Paine also wrote *The Age of Reason* and *The Crisis*. Ten years after Paine's death, his remains were moved to England for reburial. However, reburial was refused because of his revolutionary writings.

LOOKING IN *The thing Esau lacked most was "common sense." He let his stomach dictate his actions with regard to his birthright. He lived to deeply regret that foolish decision. Esau wasn't alone in his lack of common sense. It seems Isaac's whole family was cursed with the same deficit. Isaac unwisely preferred one son over another, while Rebekah conspired with Jacob to grab the blessing. Jacob was more than willing to deceive his aging father, in spite of the risks. This tragic incident would split the little family apart, with Esau plotting to murder Jacob and Jacob having to flee in terror from his angry brother. Rebekah would never see her favorite son again.*

LOOKING OUT

1. Each generation has to learn faith. Isaac waited twenty years before Rebekah gave birth to Esau and Jacob.
2. Sometimes God does not answer the "Why" question. Rebekah asked God why the boys were fighting in her womb, but God did not tell her.
3. Showing partiality sets the stage for heartbreak and bitterness. Isaac favored Esau, while Rebekah expressed favoritism toward Jacob.
4. When we just follow feelings, we get into trouble. Esau made his decisions by what he felt at the moment, resulting in a lifetime of regret.
5. Contempt for holy things sets us up for disaster. Esau "despised" his birthright. That is, he didn't take it seriously- a mistake that would cost him dearly.

LOOKING UP *Help me, Lord, to stay away from those things that would divide and destroy the family You have given me. Keep me true to You and Your Word.*

PHILOSOPHY

Genesis 27-28

LOOKING BACK

William James, the most widely-read American philosopher of the 1900's, was born on this day in 1842. Although highly educated, James struggled to find his life's work. He became convinced that a man could devote his life to finding new answers to such questions as: Can human effort change the course of events? Does God exist, and what difference would His existence make to man? What is the good life, and how does man's conviction about what is good affect his behavior? One of his foundational thoughts was expressed in his book, *Varieties of Religious Experience*. He wrote, "There is no worse lie than a truth misunderstood by those who hear it."

LOOKING IN

Contrary to James' idea, lies are lies—there are no better or worse lies. Jacob lied to his father to obtain the birthright. The consequence of that behavior tore the family apart and created pain for Jacob that would last a lifetime. Though forgiven, Jacob reaped the consequences of his deception. Tragically, Jacob could not trust God enough to wait for the birthright, though it had been promised to him at his birth. Jacob's problem is not unlike our own. We often fail God's time test. Even Abraham gave up on having a son with Sarah and took Hagar. Jacob's story underlines the fact that we bring great pain to ourselves when we refuse to wait on God.

LOOKING OUT

1. **There is a right way, and a wrong way, to do the right thing. Deception destroys. God had promised Jacob the birthright, but he was wrong to grab it as he did.**
2. **Pain and alienation always follow disobedience, putting distance between God and us, and others and us. Things were never again the same between Esau and Jacob.**
3. **Sin destroys families. Jacob's sin of deception put an end to his close family. It not only adversely affected him for years but also hurt all of those he cared about the most.**
4. **It is always better to do the right thing than to try to make things right. Esau married girls his parents opposed. He made matters worse in trying to correct his mistake.**
5. **God's mercy moves beyond our bungling and sin, restoring us again to Himself. God didn't cast Jacob aside because of his sin. Rather, God met Jacob in a dream.**

LOOKING UP

Forgive me, Lord, for my sins and bungling. Restore me again to Your presence and to Your will. Give me wisdom to carefully watch my ways that I might not sin against You.

FAMILY

Genesis 29-30

LOOKING BACK "All in the Family," the controversial sitcom created by Norman Lear, premiered on this day in 1971. Based on the success of the British comedy, *Till Death Us Do Part,* Lear's series was the first of its kind to realistically portray the prevailing issues and taboos of its time with a wicked and humorous bent. From bigotry to birth control, few topics were considered too sacred to discuss. Bigoted Archie Bunker held court in his recliner, spewing invective at any who disagreed with him. The sitcom was the forerunner of other "realistic" programs that seem to delight in shocking viewers and presenting views that are questionable.

LOOKING IN *All in the Family may have been the first TV sitcom to portray family realism, but it certainly was not the first communication to do so. The Bible is brutally honest about the very real problems families face as they live together. Jacob's stealing of his brother's birthright forced him to flee for his life. He ran to his mother's relatives, only to enter another highly dysfunctional family. Laban deceives the deceiver, forcing him to take Leah in order to get Rachel. This move would create many problems and heartbreaks in the years to come. Jacob is cheated by his greedy father-in-law and has to deal with the intense jealousy and rivalry between his two wives.*

LOOKING OUT

1. God leads us, even when we are not aware of His direction. It was not by chance that Jacob found his bride and future even while fleeing from his brother's wrath.
2. Coincidences stop happening when we stop praying. Just as Jacob asks about Laban, Rachel shows up at the well. Jacob is immediately struck by her great beauty and grace.
3. Love makes labor light. Jacob was so much in love with Rachel that his years of service for her seemed but a short time, and the sacrifice little, to get the woman of his dreams.
4. We reap what we sow. Jacob, the deceiver, is now deceived by one more sneaky than he. We are always paid back for what we have done—either good or evil.
5. When we are honest, God protects us from those who would cheat us. God gave Jacob special wisdom to handle Laban, who continually wanted to take advantage of Jacob.

LOOKING UP *Lord, help me to do right no matter what others do. I know this pleases You, my Protector. Help me to make my family what You want it to be.*

CORRIDOR OF DEATH

JANUARY 13

Genesis 31-32

LOOKING BACK The suffering of the people of Leningrad, during the German siege of that city, was one of the greatest tragedies of World War II. More than half the population of Russia's second largest city died during the winter of 1942. On this day in 1943, Soviet troops broke through the German lines and opened a 10-mile wide corridor south of Lake Lagoda. Within a week, supplies were arriving in the city by way of the narrow opening. Because fierce German bombardment of the passage continued for another year, the pass came to be called the "Corridor of Death." The siege finally ended on January 27, 1944, after 880 days.

LOOKING IN *Jacob had his own "corridor of death." After many years he was to meet his angry brother once more. In great anxiety and uncertain about the reception, Jacob prepared for the very worst. Jacob was sure his angry brother had not forgiven him. He anticipated Esau killing him, or at least harming some of his family. It was a crisis that never need have happened if Jacob would have waited on God to give him the birthright, rather than greedily grabbing it before God's time. In spite of Jacob's sin, God had worked on Esau's heart so that the fate Jacob feared did not come to pass. The feared reunion became a time of reconciliation and joy.*

LOOKING OUT

1. While God never endorses bad behavior, He continues to work with us. This speaks volumes of His patience and love. Imperfect Jacob was still God's chosen vessel.
2. We can run, but we can't hide; the past will catch up to us. Jacob had fled in fear years before, but he now had to face the brother he cheated. We always do reap what we sow.
3. Our will must be broken if we are to accomplish God's will. Jacob wrestled all night with the heavenly visitor. That encounter would forever change Jacob's character.
4. Once we encounter God, we never forget the experience. Jacob was forever marked by his encounter with the Divine. We are never the same after encountering Jesus Christ.
5. We can only be changed when we submit totally to the will of God. Jacob was now in a position where God could use him. He now would do things God's way, not his way.

LOOKING UP *Lord, help me submit my will to You, knowing that when I do, You will use me for Your great plans.*

TREACHERY

JANUARY 14

Genesis 33-36

January

LOOKING BACK Benedict Arnold's name is synonymous with treachery. He became the most famous traitor in U.S. history. Born on this day in 1741, Arnold first served as major general in the American army but deserted to the British during the Revolutionary War. He became bitter because he had not received credit for his battle bravery and was passed over for promotion by Congress. Arnold constantly brooded over what he considered his country's ingratitude and injustice, and corresponded with the enemy for 16 months. In his anger, Arnold planned to surrender West Point to the enemy, but the plot was exposed. Arnold defected to the British.

LOOKING IN *Levi and Simeon also earned the title of "treacherous." They had brooded over the rape of their sister until it drove them to awful vengeance. Their bloody and brutal act appalled Jacob and brought shame on his family. They had blatantly betrayed the principles of the God Jacob served. Jacob was deeply ashamed of the bad behavior of his boys. It was a deed Jacob would not forget. Years later, while on his death bed, Jacob would recall this despicable act and again condemn Simeon and Levi. They had been in line to receive the birthright, but Jacob would never give them this special blessing because of that angry deed done so long before.*

LOOKING OUT

1. **We set our world on fire when we sin. Shechem burned with lust toward Dinah and then took what he wanted. His awful action would soon have disastrous consequences.**
2. **Our words can incite others to destructive behavior; we must be careful what we say. Jacob told his sons about the rape but offered no instruction about the right response.**
3. **Pampering parents invite destruction. Shechem's father so doted on his son that he wanted to give him everything the boy wanted. That was a tragic decision.**
4. **Deception destroys relationships. Jacob's sons deceived Shechem's clan. This became a pattern in behavior that later resulted in Joseph being sold into slavery.**
5. **Justifying evil is a further evil. When Jacob confronted his sons about their wrong, they excused their behavior saying, "Should he have treated our sister like a prostitute?"**

LOOKING UP *Help me, O Lord, to remember that returning evil for evil is destructive. I must leave vengeance to You.*

SYMBOLS

JANUARY 15

Genesis 37-38

LOOKING BACK Thomas Nast was the maker of symbols. The popular political cartoonist introduced the donkey as the symbol of the Democratic Party in the United States on this day in 1870. He had also created the symbol of the elephant for the Republican Party, as well as the Tammany Tiger. His caricatures of the Tammany Tiger helped break up the notorious political organization headed by William "Boss" Tweed in New York City. Nast's cartoons also contributed to the defeat of Horace Greeley for president in 1872. On a lighter side, in 1860, Nast also introduced the present-day image of Santa Claus in Harper's Weekly.

LOOKING IN *Symbols are used because they easily convey a distinct idea. Unfortunately, Judah became a symbol of deceit and unchecked passion in his dealings with the widow of his sons. His broken promises and lustful nature precipitated a most unpleasant experience in his life and family. Judah thought he could pacify Tamar by making her promises he had no intention of keeping. When Tamar realized that Judah would not keep his word, she determined to get what she wanted and hurt him at the same time. Her ploy worked, and soon Judah had to admit his sin and broken promises. He acknowledged his sin and corrected his bad behavior.*

LOOKING OUT

1. **When we pull up anchor, we tend to drift. Judah moved away from the godly influence of his father's house. Before long, he and his family drifted into questionable behavior.**
2. **Sin shortens one's life. Er was struck down by God because he was so wicked. Sin always has a devastating impact on one's health and well-being.**
3. **Pleasure without responsibility is immoral. God was displeased with Onan because he took the pleasure of sex but wouldn't accept the responsibility accompanying it.**
4. **You can't dabble in sin and not be hurt. Judah thought there would be no consequences to his dalliance with an unknown prostitute. He was dead wrong.**
5. **Facing one's sin is the first step to rehabilitation. Judah acknowledged his evil and did not repeat the behavior. He soon moved back to his father's house and influence.**

LOOKING UP *Lord keep me close to You and Your house. It is there I find the anchor that keeps me from drifting.*

PROHIBITION

JANUARY 16

Genesis 39-41

LOOKING BACK The famous 18th amendment became reality on this day in 1919. Nebraska became the 36th state to ratify the prohibition amendment, making the proposal part of the United States Constitution. One year later, on January 16, 1920, the 18th Amendment took effect, and the sale of alcoholic beverages became illegal in the U.S., with the Volstead Act providing enforcement. This is the first time an amendment to the Constitution dealt with a social issue. The 21st Amendment, repealing the 18th Amendment, went into effect on December 6, 1933. Most agree that the well-intentioned 18th Amendment created more social problems than it solved.

LOOKING IN *Often, when we try to solve problems, we make matters worse. This is exactly what happened when Jacob's sons sold Joseph into slavery. They were fed up with Joseph's dreams and position. They thought the answer to their problem was to sell him into slavery. However, they only made matters worse for themselves. Their aged father grieved so greatly that they despaired for his life. In addition, they would carry the guilt of their actions for many years. It would always be on their minds. Whenever they faced adversity, they presumed it was because of what they had done to Joseph. However, God took this mess they had made and brought something beautiful out of it.*

LOOKING OUT

1. **Satan may delay our destiny, but he cannot defeat it. Joseph was chosen by God to preserve God's people when crisis came. All hell could not stop this divine plan.**
2. **Bitterness cannot change circumstance, but it can change us. Joseph resisted the temptation to become bitter over the hard things that happened to him. God honored his decision.**
3. **God can–and will–wipe out the pain of the past with His unique blessings. A happy marriage and two children caused Joseph to rejoice. His sons' names reflects this thanksgiving.**
4. **Praise for God's goodness should always follow God's provision. Joseph named his sons Manasseh and Ephraim, that all would know how God had turned his life around.**
5. **God always provides for those He has called. Just as Joseph had said, seven years of plenty were followed by severe famine. However, God had already provided a place for His chosen.**

LOOKING UP *Help me, Lord, to resist bitterness and see the hand of God in all things He permits to come to me.*

EDITED

JANUARY 17

Genesis 42-44

LOOKING BACK "Elder statesman of the American Revolution," Benjamin Franklin, is remembered on this day, the anniversary of his birth in 1706. The brilliant inventor-printer lived to be 84. However, some 19 years before he died, Franklin wrote his own epitaph. It said: "The Body of BENJAMIN FRANKLIN/Printer/ Like a Covering of an Old Book/ Its contents torn out/ And script of its Lettering and Gilding/ Lies here, Food for Worms;/ But the work shall not be lost,/ It will (as he believ'd) appear once more/ In a new and more beautiful Edition/ Corrected and amended/ By the Author." Franklin, obviously, was a believer in our Lord Jesus Christ.

LOOKING IN *God is indeed the Master-Editor. Perhaps this is never so clearly seen as in the life of Joseph. Others introduced circumstances in Joseph's life that could have destroyed him. But God edited the script so that what they had planned for evil, He meant for good. All things do work together for good for those who love God. Now, those heartless brothers, who had so long ago contemptuously discarded Joseph, have to face him and what they had done. Joseph is careful to test them before he reveals himself. He wants to know if they have changed their behavior or still are the rascals they once were.*

LOOKING OUT

1. All choices have consequences, and sooner or later we must face the music. Joseph's brothers, tormented by their guilt many years old, now had to face their awful deed.
2. Character is displayed more in prosperity than in poverty and pain. Joseph, with the full power of vengeance in his hand, refused to hurt those who had hurt him so deeply.
3. Difficulties reveal our character. Joseph put pressure on his brothers so he could see how they would respond. What they were would be clearly revealed by this adversity.
4. Pressures intensify until we are willing to face our wrongs. Joseph kept the intense pressure on his brothers, insisting they bring their youngest brother back.
5. When we are truly sorry for our sins we are forgiven and restored. Joseph discovers his brothers are repentant. He invites them to come and live with him in Egypt.

LOOKING UP *Help me, Lord, to exercise a grace that is beyond myself. Let me, like Joseph, be forgiving and restoring.*

INVINCIBLE

JANUARY 18

Genesis 45-47

January

LOOKING BACK French President Raymond Poincare formally opened the World War I Peace Conference at Versailles, France, on this day in 1919. It proceeded under the chairmanship of Georges Clemenceau. The Conference disposed of Germany's colonies and delivered a treaty to the German delegates on May 7, 1919, the fourth anniversary of the sinking of the Luisitania. Final treaty-signing ceremonies were completed at the Palace of Versailles on June 28, 1919. The harsh stipulations of the Versailles Treaty, along with a hard refusal to forgive, set the stage for the bloody second World War. Bitterness breeds bloodshed.

LOOKING IN *The men of Versailles should have taken a lesson from Joseph's story. Rather than recriminations against his brutal brothers, Joseph chose to forgive and restore relationships. This was hard for the guilt-ridden brothers to understand but spoke volumes about the great character of Joseph. Anyone can hold a grudge and refuse to forgive. It takes a truly great person to put the past behind him and move forward in love and understanding. While we cannot change the past, we can change how we feel about it. Joseph chose to see the fingerprints of God all over his life rather than blame his brutal brothers for the years of hardship he suffered.*

LOOKING OUT

1. **A life watered by the tears of tragedy often becomes the most fertile soil for great growth. Joseph could identify with the suffering because he had suffered so much.**
2. **God never wastes energy or events in His children's lives; all things work together for good. Joseph knew how to deal with the poor and powerless since he had been there.**
3. **We can see the sorrow or seek the solution; the choice is ours. Joseph chose to see the fingerprints of God all over his life rather than complain about what had happened to him.**
4. **For those who are faithful, God will always feed them through the famine. Jacob's family was preserved because of the patriarch's trust in God's protection and provision.**
5. **In spite of the bumps and heartbreaks of life, God will bring His own to "an expected end." Joseph's life turned out as God had planned. The devil could not destroy him.**

LOOKING UP *May I, O Lord, understand that even the hard time I am now going through is preparation for tomorrow.*

FUTILITY

JANUARY 19

Genesis 48-50

LOOKING BACK Possibly the most highly regarded White female blues singer of all times, and one of music's most tragic figures, was born on this day in 1943. Janis Joplin appeared with Big Brother and the Holding Company at the Monterey International Pop Festival in 1967, launching her to superstar status. Among her recordings were "Piece of My Heart" and "Ball and Chain." Born in Port Arthur, Texas, Joplin wanted to kick away the restraints of her conservative community and upbringing. She drank heavily and became addicted to heroin. The drug, along with her wild lifestyle, destroyed her. She died at age 27 of an overdose, in Hollywood, California..

LOOKING IN *Some of the 12 sons of Jacob had lived on the wild side. Reuben had committed adultery with his father's concubine. Simeon and Levi annihilated a whole village, while Judah impregnated his daughter-in-law. Lying on his deathbed, Jacob recalls the sins and the successes of his boys. Only one, Joseph, comes through as pure of heart and character, wisely spending his life. Martyred missionary Jim Elliot wrote, "He is no fool who gives up what he cannot keep to gain what he cannot lose." Jacob's words about his sons serve to remind us that one day we will give an account for all we have done. May that be a time of joy rather than regret.*

LOOKING OUT

1. **Sin produces instability and ineffectiveness. Reuben forfeited his place of pre-eminence in Jacob's family because he would not control his lust. He was as unstable as water.**
2. **Unchecked anger brings death. Simeon and Levi gave vent to their anger, which resulted in the slaying of the Shechemites. Jacob was appalled by their behavior.**
3. **Accepting correction restores us to God and His plan for our lives. When Judah repented of his lustful act with Tamar, he was forgiven. The Messiah descended from him.**
4. **We are to be havens for those tossed about on the rough seas of life. Zebulun was called to dwell by the sea so he could help those who had become shipwrecked.**
5. **Laziness brings us to poverty. Issachar was strong and able but docile and lazy, resulting in his becoming a servant rather than a ruler. Success always requires hard work.**

LOOKING UP *Help me, Lord, to learn from history rather than having to reinvent the wheel. Apply Your Word to my life.*

REVELATION

Exodus 1-2

LOOKING BACK Fifty years after his death, it was revealed that King George V of England did not die of natural causes but was murdered by his physician. He died on this day in 1936, at age 71, ill and restless. The court physician, Lord Dawson, gave him a lethal injection consisting of 3/4 gram of morphine and one gram of cocaine. Historians now say that the king's last words were not "How is the Empire?" but a bitter oath directed at the doctor, as he lost consciousness. Lord Dawson's notes indicate that the fatal injections were given to assure death in time for the announcement "in the morning papers rather than the less appropriate evening journals."

LOOKING IN *Time usually reveals what has happened and why. That is certainly true with Moses. When Moses, through his own effort, attempted to right the wrongs done to his people, disaster resulted. He was forced to flee for his life. No doubt he wondered, during those 40 years, why all this had happened. Then, in the bleak desert, he began to see the sense in what God had permitted him to endure. God's call was a frightening challenge. Moses knew the awesome power of the pharaoh and his own helplessness to change things. He was reluctant to accept the assignment, arguing at every point he was not the one to do it. However, God had uniquely prepared him for the task.*

LOOKING OUT

1. We must not accept the world as it is, but challenge and change it. Moses was not willing to let abuse and prejudice rule. He struck the Egyptian in an honest effort to stop it.
2. Challenge and change must be accomplished in God's way and in God's time. Moses learned a bitter lesson. When he tried to do the job on his own, he only made matters worse.
3. Even when we botch the job, God does not give up on us or on His plan for our lives. While fleeing for his life, Moses didn't know that God's purpose for him was still in effect.
4. Mundane tasks are teaching tools God uses to prepare us for greater works. In the desert, Moses learned where the water holes were so the Israelites could survive there.
5. God hears our cries and never forgets His promises. The Israelites had been praying a long time, but God never ignored even one of their prayers. Deliverance did come.

LOOKING UP *Help me, Lord, to see my desert experience today as preparation for the work You have called me to do. I will not question the way You lead.*

LEARNING

JANUARY 21

Exodus 3-4

LOOKING BACK Seventy-five years ago today, Vladimir Ilyich Ulyanov, better known as Lenin, died. The revolutionary leader's embalmed body still resides in a glass coffin at the Lenin Mausoleum in Moscow's Red Square. Lenin led the Great October Socialist Revolution of 1917 that plunged Russia into communism. He was so dedicated to his cause that Lenin had little time for social graces or the feelings of others. When his wife's mother was ill, his wife tended her and one night collapsed exhausted into bed, saying, "Wake me if she needs me." She awoke to find her mother dead and Lenin still working. He said, "She didn't need you; she died."

LOOKING IN *Dedication is necessary for success. However, dedication without compassion can be horrendous. Moses became one of the most dedicated leaders ever, but he never lost his compassion. No doubt his desert years taught him this. He had learned that he could do nothing in his own power. The desert years had been a wonderful education for Moses. If he had not had this experience, he could never have led God's people through the burning wilderness. He had learned how to survive in that hostile environment where death awaited at every turn. Moses was thoroughly dedicated to God but also had great love and compassion for His enslaved people.*

LOOKING OUT

1. **Even deserts can be holy ground. Moses detested the desert experience, but it was there God made him compassionate and taught him things he would soon need.**
2. **God's resounding, "I Am," drowns out our weak, "I can't." God knew Moses better than Moses knew himself. Therefore, God called and had already equipped him.**
3. **Our eyes must be refocused from the problems to the promises. As long as Moses dwelled on what couldn't be done, he was helpless. Now God refocused his vision.**
4. **We already have the tools in our hands to do what God asks of us. Moses only had a staff, but when it was empowered by God, it became a rod of divine authority.**
5. **Total dedication to God's way must be made, or we will lose the deadly battle. Moses had delayed circumcising his son. God now insisted on obedience in every detail.**

LOOKING UP *May my dedication, O Lord, be mixed with loving compassion so that others might see You in me. May I remember You have uniquely prepared me for where I am right now.*

EMPTY HEADS

Exodus 5-7

LOOKING BACK Statesman, philosopher, and essayist, Francis Bacon was born on this day in 1561. He earned a reputation as one of the most brilliant men of his time. Bacon was not only a philosopher but is also credited with the idea of refrigeration for preservation of food. One of Bacon's wisest sayings is, "Read not to contradict or believe, but to weigh and consider." Bacon was born in London, England, and held several government positions. One may guess that he was of short stature because he wrote, "Wise nature did never put her precious jewels into a garret four stories high." He went on to add, "therefore...exceeding tall men had very empty heads."

LOOKING IN *The Pharaoh of Egypt during Moses' time must have been very tall because, according to Bacon's assessment, he certainly had an empty head. God had given him every chance of letting Israel go without pain. However, the pagan ruler kept thumbing his nose at God. Ten plagues would be visited upon Egypt. Hebrews believed numbers symbolized ideas. The number ten stood for completeness. God in total fairness had completely dealt with the stubborn Pharaoh. Foolishly, the powerful ruler thought he could win a contest with the Hebrew God. Not only did he lose his firstborn son, but he also brought great sorrow on the whole nation of Egypt.*

LOOKING OUT

1. Sometimes things get worse before they get better. When Moses insisted Pharaoh let God's people go, the stubborn ruler responded by making the labor harder for Israel.
2. Harder problems give God opportunity to do greater miracles. Pharaoh's stubbornness did not surprise God. He already had plans in progress to bring full and final victory.
3. When times turn tough, God reassures His people. Pharaoh's response precipitated a renewal of God's covenant with Israel. God would indeed bring them out.
4. God clearly shows us how to accomplish His task. God outlined details to Moses on what he was to do in response to Pharaoh's repeated denial. There would be no surprises.
5. Pressures increase when we decide to disobey. God forced the Pharaoh to a decision. Every decision the ruler made was wrong. Thus, in Bible shorthand, God had hardened his heart.

LOOKING UP *Help me, Lord, not to be intimidated when the enemy tries to block my ministry. Give me strength to win. May I not complain about hard times, knowing they offer greater miracles.*

FOLLY

JANUARY 23

Exodus 8-10

LOOKING BACK On January 23, 1968, North Korea seized the U.S.S. Pueblo in the Sea of Japan, claiming the ship was on a spy mission. The crew was held for 11 tense and difficult months. The vessel was confiscated and one crew member killed in the capture. When the crew was finally released on December 22, 1968, the body of Seaman Duane D. Hodges was returned to his family. Kim Il Sung became the leader of North Korea when the government was established in 1948. After that, North Korea emphasized the development of heavy industry and built up its military power. It has always had an uneasy relationship with the United States.

LOOKING IN *Reason finally won out in the U.S.S. Pueblo affair, preventing the United States and North Korea from going to war. It would have been far better for Pharoah if he would have exercised a bit of reason rather than plunging headlong into disaster. That lack of wisdom would eventually end in the death of the stubborn ruler. Only fools go against God, thinking they can win. He has all the best weapons. Each time Pharaoh hardened his heart against God's will, the heat was turned up. Rather than melting his stubbornness, the heat only hardened the ruler. Tragically, many others would suffer because of that bad decision–innocent victims of Pharaoh's folly.*

LOOKING OUT

1. **When we ignore God, He turns up the heat. Each plague increases in intensity, causing more pain to the rebellious.**
2. **God always takes care of His own in judgment. The Israelites did not suffer the same fate as the Egyptians.**
3. **Satan always seeks to cut a deal with us. Pharaoh wanted to hold the Israelites by keeping their cattle.**
4. **We must never settle for anything less than total victory. Moses firmly rejected Pharaoh's diabolical proposal.**
5. **Banishing the messenger does not negate the message. Pharaoh threatened Moses, but he could not box with God.**

LOOKING UP *Lord, help me always to be wise enough to accept Your will rather than rebel against it, not simply to avoid pain but because I love you.*

SURRENDER

JANUARY 24

Exodus 11-13

LOOKING BACK At the end of the Casablanca Conference, on January 24, 1943, President Franklin D. Roosevelt of the United States and Prime Minister Winston Churchill of England demanded nothing less than "unconditional surrender" of Germany and Japan, in order to end World War II. They issued a joint statement saying, "Peace can come to the world only by total elimination of German and Japanese war power. That means the unconditional surrender of Germany, Italy, and Japan." Some historians say that position resulted in prolonging the war. Others disagree, saying there was no other reasonable position for the Allied leaders to take.

LOOKING IN *There can be no disagreement that Moses demanded the total surrender of Pharaoh to the will of God. God had given the wicked ruler many opportunities to let the people go, but stubborn Pharaoh thought he could "out-box" God. He was wrong. That foolish decision would cost his life and the lives of the soldiers who foolishly followed his madness. Too often, some try to negotiate with the devil–thinking this is the better part of valor. They are wrong. The evil one is never content until he totally destroys. That is why we must never surrender, no matter how hard the battle is or what advice is given to us by well-meaning people.*

LOOKING OUT

1. **When we don't accept God's way when it's "on sale," we will have to pay dearly. Pharaoh could have avoided pain and sorrow if he had responded differently.**
2. **God gives us favor with our enemies when our ways please him. Although the leader of Egypt hated the Israelites, the common people gave them precious jewels.**
3. **Our loving Heavenly Father always warns of impending pain, that we might avoid it by repentance and restoration. The blood on the doorpost was offered to save all the first- born.**
4. **There is always a display of difference between those who disobey and those who follow hard after God. God always wants to show the world that it pays to serve Him.**
5. **Celebrations are set to remind us that God is faithful in keeping His promises. The Passover is still celebrated to remind us that God did exactly what He had promised.**

LOOKING UP *Lord, help me to respond to Your convicting Spirit, that I might avoid the pain and shame of judgment.*

DEATH DAY

JANUARY 25

Exodus 14-15

LOOKING BACK On January 25, 1947, "Scarface" Al Capone died at age 48 in Miami, Florida, from syphilis. He had controlled the Chicago underworld in the 1920's, running most of the illegal operations in that city. Capone's gang killed many rival gangsters and was blamed for the famous St. Valentine's Day Massacre of seven men in 1929. In 1931, a federal jury convicted Capone of income tax evasion. He served almost eight years in prison then retired to his home in Miami, where he died. Born in Naples, Italy, Capone grew up in New York City and was called "Scarface" after being stabbed in a teen-age gang fight. His crime career, though bloody, was surprisingly short.

LOOKING IN *Egypt's Pharaoh was little more than a gangster himself. Like Capone, he thought he was above God's law. Pharaoh had intimidated, harassed, and brutalized God's people for a long time. Now his death-day had come. Again, like Capone, Pharaoh did not go out in a blaze of glory but was defeated in shame. His chariots were no match for God's mud. In the long view of history, evil doesn't really last very long. Because we mortals are bound by time and space, it seems as though the gangsters of our world get away with their evil. However, God does deal with them, though human justice might fail to do so. Pharaoh learned this too late.*

LOOKING OUT

1. **The devil never gives up his territory easily. Even after the awful deaths of the Egyptians' firstborn, stubborn Pharaoh pursues Israel, bent on bringing them back into bitter bondage.**
2. **It is easier to get Israel out of Egypt than Egypt out of Israel. The people start to complain at the first point of pain. They had already forgotten their miraculous deliverance.**
3. **There is a time to pray and a time to act; we must know which to do and when. God told Moses to stop praying and get moving. Prayer is a filling station, not a terminal point.**
4. **Praise should always follow victory to underline God's faithfulness to us. Moses composed a song of remembrance so Israel would always keep the miracle fresh in their minds.**
5. **Life is filled with bitter waters, but they can be sweetened by God's tree of life. Disappointment soon followed victory, but God proved Himself faithful to His people.**

LOOKING UP *Lord, I am so quick to complain. Please help me to become a "praiser" rather than one who always carps. Also, help me remember that evil is short-lived.*

POMES

JANUARY 26

Exodus 16-18

January

LOOKING BACK They were often called POMES–Prisoners Of Mother England. On January 26, 1788, a shipload of convicts arrived in Australia to establish a prison colony to relieve crowding of British prisons. Since the Revolutionary War in America had been lost by the British, that government had to find a new place to send its prisoners other than the colonies. Captain Arthur Phillip landed his 11 ships, with their cargo of convicts, at what is now Sydney. Many of those unfortunate travelers were not desperate criminals but just political prisoners, petty law-breakers, and poor people who had been imprisoned because they could not pay their debts. They carved out a new nation.

LOOKING IN *The Israelites had long been POBES–Prisoners of Brutal Egypt. Now they had been miraculously set free from their bondage and were on their way to build a new nation. However, before they would arrive in the Promised Land, there would be many years of privation and sorrow–all because of their disobedience. God had delivered them by mighty miracles that should have prepared them for the task of taking Canaan. Rather than seeing the miracles as preparation for the task ahead, the Israelites had dismissed them and begun to complain about their present circumstances. They were out of Egypt, but Egypt was not out of them.*

LOOKING OUT

1. **Memory is highly selective, causing us to forget the grinding pain and pushing us to fantasies. Israel looked back to Egypt, saying there were better times then.**
2. **When supplies decrease, our complaints often increase. Israel didn't understand that things were tight because God didn't want them to comfortably settle in the wilderness.**
3. **Complaints against ordained leadership are really complaints against God. Moses reminded Israel that God had delivered them. They were to be careful what they said.**
4. **We cannot outsmart God or amend His orders. When the Israelites insisted on storing up the manna, they found it full of maggots. God had been explicit in His instructions.**
5. **We need memory-joggers so we will not forget God's goodness. Moses instructed Aaron to save a jar of manna so future generations would know God had amply provided.**

LOOKING UP *Help me, O Lord, to see that sometimes hard times are given so we will move forward rather than stay put. Help me never to lightly dismiss Your miracles.*

LIGHT

JANUARY 27

Exodus 19-21

LOOKING BACK Although it had been worked on for 50 years, it wasn't until this day, in 1880, that a patent was issued for the first electric light bulb. Thomas Alva Edison had finally broken through the difficulties to invent electric lights. That invention changed the world. Two years later, on September 4, at precisely 3 p.m., the 35-year-old inventor turned on the power to New York's first central generating station on Pearl Street—and 85 houses, shops, and offices suddenly blazed with the light from 400 incandescent bulbs. It was the start of a new era. For the first time, man was not confined to working during the daylight hours.

LOOKING IN *When Moses delivered the Ten Commandments from Mount Sinai, it was also the start of a new era. The light of truth and justice was snapped on. The world would never be the same. We were no longer in the dark as to what God expected of us. No longer could man claim ignorance to cover his misdeeds. God's law was clearly spelled out. The Ten Commandments have stood the test of time, for they clearly outline what God expects of us and the principles needed for a safe society. God's Word says these laws are not only written down but are also indelibly stamped on the human heart. All of nature speaks of the wisdom of these sacred laws.*

LOOKING OUT

1. Our relationship with God must come before our relationship with man. The first four commandments deal with man's obligations and attitudes toward God.
2. Honoring God means that we also respect man's life and rights. The last six commandments deal with how we treat others. We are to respect their lives and their possessions.
3. A healthy respect and fear of the Lord holds us in check. The people witnessed thunder and lightning, heard a blasting trumpet, and saw the smoking mountain of God.
4. Our response to the awesome presence of God is to make an altar in our hearts. Moses was told to make an altar so the people would understand they were to revere their God.
5. Worship must be sacred, not sensual. God instructed His people to worship Him with dignity and integrity, not in the sensual fashion by which the other nations perverted their worship.

LOOKING UP *Help me, Lord, to see that Your commandments are like stoplights: they keep me from being destroyed. Help me to love Your law and always live by it.*

EXPLOSION

JANUARY 28

Exodus 22-24

LOOKING BACK January 28, 1986, at 11:39 a.m., EST, the Space Shuttle Challenger STS-51L exploded 74 seconds into its flight and about 10 miles above the earth. Hundreds of millions around the world watched television replays of the horrifying event that killed seven people, destroyed the billion-dollar craft, and suspended all manned shuttle flights for some time. Vast amounts of money and time were spent to determine the cause of the disastrous crash. Sometime after the tragedy, the somewhat shocking report was issued to the public. The cause of the explosion was faulty seals—a small problem that only later proved to be deadly serious.

LOOKING IN *Too often we neglect the small things, thinking they will not hurt us. Yet the Bible says it is the little foxes that spoil the vine. It is a tragic mistake to overlook minor details that have the potential of destroying. For that reason, God details His expectations of us in His Word. Although these minor details are time-consuming and sometimes boring to read, they are vitally important. If we heed God's instructions, we live; ignore them and we die. Moses left nothing to chance when he gave Israel God's laws. He wanted them to understand that all of them were important. God loves us so much that He carefully outlined His expectations.*

LOOKING OUT

1. **Faithfully following God's laws protects us from the evil one and assures success. Moses is given fair and just laws for God's people. There is great blessing in keeping them.**
2. **Those who follow Christ have a great advantage. God told Moses that He would send an angel to go before them to bring them to the place He had prepared.**
3. **We are to influence the world, not let the world influence us. Israel was not to bow down before the gods of the conquered nations, no matter how appealing that might be.**
4. **Our enemies are not defeated in one fell swoop but in our daily struggles. God told Israel that He would not drive out their enemies at once, lest they become proud and boastful.**
5. **God has already allocated territory for us. We only need to take it. God had already given Israel the land from the Red Sea to the Sea of the Philistines, the desert to the river.**

LOOKING UP *Lord, help me understand that there is a purpose for everything in Scripture. Help me to seek that purpose and begin to better understand Your will.*

JANUARY 29

FREETHINKERS

Exodus 25-28

LOOKING BACK This is Freethinker's Day, celebrated each year on the anniversary of Thomas Paine's birth. Paine, an American Revolutionary leader, was the author of many influential works. "These are the times that try men's souls. The summer soldier and the sunshine patriot will in this crisis shrink from the service of their country...Tyranny, like hell, is not easily conquered," are the well-known opening words of his inspirational tract, *The Crisis.* George Washington had Paine's works read to his army to spur them on. While in a French prison for his political views, Paine wrote, "I believe in one God, and no more; and I hope for happiness beyond this life."

LOOKING IN *Freethinking is all right to a point. However it must be tempered with divine revelation, or we get into trouble. That is why God gave us His Word and why Moses carefully recorded all God's laws. The fact is the Bible came to us by revelation, not evolution. Some modern critics would like to say God's Word evolved in our thinking about the Divine. However we must remember, "Above all, you must understand that no prophecy of Scripture came about by the prophet's own interpretation. For prophecy never had its origin in the will of man, but men spoke from God as they were carried along by the Holy Spirit"* (2 Peter 1:20-21).

LOOKING OUT

1. Our offerings are to be love gifts to God, not trying taxes. The Hebrew root for the word "offering" means "to draw near." It is a good means by which we draw near to our Lord.
2. God wants us always to be aware of His presence. The tabernacle was to be set in the midst of Israel to remind them of God's presence in all aspects of their family life.
3. God's Word must have prominence in our lives. The words of Moses were put in the Ark of the Covenant to show the importance that God places on His Word.
4. God always meets us with mercy and speaks to us of His great love. The mercy seat on the Ark of the Covenant reminded Israel of the wonderful character of their God.
5. Reverence for God is doing things His way. God told Moses to make sure he constructed the Tabernacle, the Ark, and all other things, according to the specific instructions.

LOOKING UP *Help me, Lord, to understand that if I really reverence You, I will do exactly what You ask of me.*

DIGNITY

JANUARY 30

Exodus 29-31

January

LOOKING BACK Congress is supposed to be a place of great dignity. However there are times when decorum goes by the wayside. In fact, the first brawl in that august body occurred in the U.S. House of Representatives on this day in 1798 in Philadelphia. Matthew Lyon of Vermont and Roger Griswold of Connecticut got into a fist-throwing fracas. The fight escalated when Lyon spat in Griswold's face. Members of the House were appalled at the bad behavior of these two representatives who failed to control their tempers. Although a resolution to expel Vermont's Lyon was introduced, the measure failed and Lyon maintained his seat.

LOOKING IN *Dignity is demanded when we come before God. Moses went into great detail about what was expected of those who approached God. The priests had to go through certain complicated rites that were intended to underline the holiness of God. The tabernacle was set up to emphasize respect for the Creator. There is a certain "otherness" about God. While we are created in His image, we are obviously not His equal. Therefore we must approach God with the respect and reverence due Him. When Aaron's sons, and later, Eli's sons, ignored these restrictions, they lost their lives. It was vitally important for the spiritual leaders to set the pace for worship.*

LOOKING OUT

1. **We must recognize the "otherness" of God. Every aspect of these ceremonies speaks of the holiness of God.**
2. **God is with us, but there can be no familiarity. He is God, not our "big buddy in the sky." We must revere Him.**
3. **Sin keeps us from God's presence. The priests had to be made holy before they could enter into God's presence.**
4. **We must prepare ourselves for worship. The priests made elaborate preparations before approaching God.**
5. **God cannot be worshiped on our terms, only His. He is not some helpless pagan deity, but a living Creator.**

LOOKING UP *Help me, Lord, to always reverence You and remember that I serve You, rather than You serving me. Prepare my heart for worship.*

TURNING POINT

Exodus 32-34

LOOKING BACK The psychological turning point of World War II occurred on this day in 1943, when the Germans surrendered at Stalingrad. Only two pockets of starving German soldiers remained in Stalingrad. They had received no supplies since the Soviet soldiers had encircled the city the previous November. Marshall Friedrich von Paulus was forced to seek surrender terms, thereby being the first in the Nazi army to do so. Hitler was furious with von Paulus, believing he should have preferred suicide to surrender. Two days later, the last German resistance in Stalingrad ended. Some 160,000 Germans had died, and 90,000 others were captured and imprisoned in Siberia.

LOOKING IN *For Moses, the psychological turning point of his dealing with the Israelites came with the incident of the golden calf. He now knew the people would need strong laws and careful discipline if they were to remain the "chosen" of God. Moses also learned that Aaron could not be trusted to keep things under control. God's Word shows that our base nature is revealed when pressures come. Israel, left alone by Moses, succumbed to the pressures of their hard lot and demanded a massive party. It soon turned into a wild, sex orgy. Moses charged down the mountain to this sickening scene. He smashed the commandments just as they had.*

LOOKING OUT

1. **Pressure doesn't create problems—it reveals them. We can keep our bad inclinations hidden until pressures mount. Then, like the children of Israel, what we are comes out.**
2. **Weak leadership caves in to the crowd rather than standing up for what is right. Aaron revealed his weakness when he responded to the mob and made the golden calf.**
3. **Rebellion reeks with rottenness and erodes our morals. We become like the gods we worship. Israel reverted to sexual disgrace because they had adopted the pagan god.**
4. **Intercessory prayer will make a difference and bring deliverance. God was so angry He wanted to destroy Israel. Moses pleaded for the people and they were spared.**
5. **Repentance is being so sorry for our sins that we quit sinning. A plague struck the people to underline the fact that God would not permit this type of behavior again.**

LOOKING UP *Lord, when someone bumps my cup, may I be so full of You that they will see Your love and mercy. Help me to be filled with kindness and love.*

FEBRUARY............

A Fascinating Month that Holds a Difficult Assignment

February has been ignored, robbed, and moved from its place, making it a month with a fascinating history. According to legend, Romulus, who, with his twin brother Remus, founded Rome, did not include February when he made the first Roman calendar, which contained only 10 months. Numa Pompilius, who followed Romulus, added two months making February the last month of the year. Its name, Februaris, came from a Latin word meaning "to purify." The Romans purified themselves in February to prepare for festivals at the start of a new year. But Julius Caesar moved the beginning of the year from March to January, bumping February to the second month.

February originally had 30 days until the time of Julius Caesar, who took one day off February to add to July, a month named after himself because he was born at that time. The emperor Augustus took another day off February and added it to August, because he did not want July to have more days than the month named after him. Thus, February ended up with 28 days except for every leap year, when a day is added to correct the calendar. If all this sounds confusing or irrelevant, it is wise to remember that decisions and policies made long ago still affect us today.

During February, we will be reading through the last of Exodus, the books of Leviticus and Numbers, and the first four chapters of Deuteronomy. At times, we are tempted to think that these detailed laws and instructions are confusing, irrelevant, and make difficult reading. However, as we study them closer, we see they affect all of us who live on this side of the cross. It is important to study the details of these chapters because, in them, we see the great wisdom of God and His loving, caring character.

GIVING

Exodus 35-37

LOOKING BACK Travelers Insurance Company issued the first car insurance policy on this day in 1898. Interestingly, it was issued against accidents with horses. Today, automobile insurance is the most widely purchased property and liability insurance. It is one of the most important kinds of insurance because of the serious injuries and extensive property damage that can result from accidents. Drivers are legally responsible for any costs arising from accidents they cause. Although a policyholder may never receive benefits from an insurance company, the premiums have not been wasted. Insurance gives policyholders a feeling of security.

LOOKING IN *Man has always tried to insure himself against loss, whether it be life or property. However, it is evident that there is no insurance that can protect us from all that can happen. God's Word offers a wiser and better plan of insurance. Moses gave God's laws to the Israelites so they could minimize their risks and maximize their well-being. For example, the laws on giving are designed to assure God's blessings on His people even during hard times. Giving helps us move beyond innate selfishness to seek the good of others through God's work. Moses learned and taught that there would always be enough when people gave willingly.*

LOOKING OUT

1. Faith is more than what we say, think, and feel; it is what we do. Moses told the people of God's expectations in how they daily lived out the faith they possessed.
2. Giving is not a tax; it is a precious privilege. God only wanted offerings from those who willingly gave. The offerings were designed so that all could participate.
3. God speaks to us about how much we should give. Moses spoke of those "whose hearts were moved;" that is, God had urged them to give and they responded unselfishly.
4. When all joyfully give, there is always more than enough to get the job done. Moses had to instruct the people to stop giving because their generosity had met the need.
5. Giving involves far more than money. Bezelel, Oholiab, and others gave their time and talents willingly to complete the needed work on the wilderness tabernacle.

LOOKING UP *Help me, Lord, to be a giver. May I offer what I have and what I am to accomplish Your work in my world.*

GUIDANCE

Exodus 38-40

LOOKING BACK Thomas Jefferson is best remembered as a great president and as author of the Declaration of Independence. He also won lasting fame as a diplomat, political thinker, and founder of the Democratic party. He was the foremost architect of his time and a scientific farmer who cultivated the finest gardens in America. Jefferson's many inventions included the swivel chair and the dumb-waiter. On this day in 1800, Thomas Jefferson warned, "Beware of too much confidence in a man." That was good advice, especially when it relates to guidance. Jeremiah noted, "I know, O LORD, that a man's life is not his own; it is not for man to direct his steps."

LOOKING IN *Moses was a great leader and well-acquainted with the wilderness. Yet he wanted the people to trust in God, not him. As Exodus comes to a close, Moses reports that God daily gave them guidance through the cloud above the tabernacle. At night, there was fire in the cloud. Israel never moved until the cloud moved. They trusted God alone. The history of Israel makes it very clear that all went well when they trusted God. However, when they relied on their own wisdom apart from their Creator, things turned out badly. Moses wanted to burn this principle deeply into the hearts and minds of God's people so they would always turn to Him.*

LOOKING OUT

1. Revival is nothing more than doing what God asks of us. When we do, God blesses us for it. Israel completed the tabernacle as God directed and were well-compensated.
2. We must do God's work, God's way, without modifying His directions. Repeatedly, the book of Exodus emphasizes that Moses did exactly "as the Lord commanded him."
3. When we comply with God's commandments, He lets us know how pleased He is with us. When the tabernacle was completed as God instructed, the glory of God filled it.
4. When God fills our lives, there is room for nothing else. God so filled the tabernacle that the priests could not even enter. God is all-consuming in us and all-fulfilling to us.
5. Obedience brings a lifetime of God's leadership in our lives. The cloud and the fire led Israel daily. As they followed, they were kept safe, and their needs were supplied.

LOOKING UP *Help me, Lord, to follow completely Your commands. May I never veer from Your Holy Word. Help me to remember things only turn out right as I follow Your instructions.*

PRIORITY

FEBRUARY 3

Leviticus 1-3

LOOKING BACK Abraham Lincoln and his Secretary of State, William Seward, met on this day in 1865 to discuss peace with Confederate Vice-President Alexander Stevens and others at Hampton Road, Virginia. The meeting, which took place on board the ship River Queen, lasted four hours and produced no positive results. The Confederates sought an armistice first and discussion of reunion later, while Lincoln was insistent that recognition of federal authority must be the first step toward peace. Because of this difference in priorities, the bloody Civil War continued, and many more soldiers from both sides lost their lives.

LOOKING IN *President Lincoln was right in insisting on submission to authority if the Union was to survive. Likewise, we must understand that peace only comes as we submit to authority—the authority of our loving Heavenly Father. Leviticus may seem tedious to read, but it is important because it tells us we cannot have our own way in life or worship. We must follow the directions of our Creator. Those who have rebelled against this principle have broken themselves on God's unchanging laws. Only when we totally submit to our Lord and recognize Him as our full and final authority, can we have peace and joy. The sooner we learn that, the better.*

LOOKING OUT

1. How we are to worship is a revelation from God, not what we choose. Exodus ended with where Israel was to worship; Leviticus starts with how to worship.
2. God clearly outlines His expectations of us because He is always exceedingly fair. Like a good parent, God makes plain what He expects and the consequences of our choices.
3. God wants all of us. The first of the offerings in Leviticus is called the burnt offering since it is totally consumed. This symbolizes we are to offer ourselves to God completely.
4. All that we have comes from God. The grain offering was given in recognition that everything we possess comes from God, and we owe part of what we have to Him.
5. We are to be at peace with God and our fellow man. The peace offering pointed to Christ, "Who is our peace." He reconciles us with God and brings us back to each other.

LOOKING UP *Help me, Lord, to understand that offerings are far more than giving; they teach me responsibility. Help me to submit joyfully to You and Your ways.*

CONFESSION

FEBRUARY 4

Leviticus 4-6

LOOKING BACK Man's inhumanity to man has been well-documented through the years. In an effort to stop atrocities, twenty countries signed a special United Nations' document on this day in 1985. Entitled *Convention Against Torture and Other Cruel, Inhuman or Degrading Treatment or Punishment*, it had been adopted on December 10, 1984, by the U.N. General Assembly. The document defines torture as an act "by which severe pain or suffering, whether physical or mental, is intentionally inflicted to obtain information or a confession." While the U.S. did sign the document, its ratification by the U.S. Congress has never taken place.

LOOKING IN *In spite of the adoption of this well-meaning U.N. document, atrocities continue. Tragically, some cruel regimes and authorities still resort to torture to elicit confessions. There is another type of torture that the Bible clearly warns about—not a torture of physical beatings like the U.N. describes, but the loss of relationship with God and an eternity of unspeakable agony, separated from Him. However the Bible also tells us that all can avoid this pain by accepting God's plan of salvation offered through Jesus Christ. Hell was never planned for humanity; it was created for the devil and his angels. We merely share eternity with the one we serve.*

LOOKING OUT

1. Sin is serious and demands repentance. God insisted that sin be recognized for what it is and stopped. Sin is not entertainment; rather, it is that which will destroy us.
2. Covering a crime is as wrong as committing it. God's law says that when we see evil, we must expose it. If we do not, we share in the guilt. Sin, like a weed, grows and spreads.
3. God's laws give life even though we might not understand their purpose. Many regulations in Leviticus were not understood by the Israelites until much later.
4. No one is ever too poor or too weak to participate in God's Kingdom. God's law makes it possible for all to give to God. He wants our equal sacrifice, not equal gifts.
5. Restitution is required as part of repentance and restoration. God's law required those who had stolen or cheated to pay back what was taken and add more to it.

LOOKING UP *Help me, Lord, to recognize that You take sin seriously. I must be very careful how I act and react. Forgive me of my sins and cleanse me from all evil.*

SPECIAL

Leviticus 7-9

LOOKING BACK He left a job as a clerk in a Boston shoe store to become a shoe salesman in Chicago in 1856. There, D.L. Moody worked for the next four years, teaching Sunday school on the side and witnessing of his faith. Finally, in 1860, the soon-to-be-famous evangelist left the shoe business forever to spend all his time teaching, preaching, and working with the YMCA. Born on this day in 1837, Moody became one of the most beloved and dynamic preachers of all times, and his influence is still felt. He was especially anointed by God in establishing the famed Moody Memorial Church, the Moody Bible Institute, and Moody Press.

LOOKING IN *Incredible things can be done for God by those who are especially anointed of the Lord. Aaron was anointed for the priesthood. This anointing set him apart as one representing man to God and God to man. When God calls us to a certain task, He anoints us for that purpose. Not all receive the same calling, but those who are called do receive the same Holy Spirit anointing. God's Word says, "It was he who gave some to be apostles, some to be prophets, some to be evangelists, and some to be pastors and teachers, to prepare God's people for works of service, so that the body of Christ may be built up" (Ephesians 4:11-12).*

LOOKING OUT

1. **God requires individual praise, not just corporate worship. Moses instructed the people to bring their peace offerings individually as an act of praise to God.**
2. **Leaders are to be "set apart" for God's special work. The elaborate ordination service for Aaron indicates that spiritual leaders are called, anointed, and appointed by God.**
3. **God is pleased when we do not "edit" His orders but simply carry them out. Moses was careful to do as the Lord commanded. We too must take God at His Word.**
4. **God shows His glory when we do as He directs. Moses had obeyed God in ordaining Aaron to the priesthood. Now God manifested His glory to His obedient servants.**
5. **While God's glory is thrilling, we must not forget His demand for purity. The fire came out from the Lord to remind the Israelites of God's awesome power.**

LOOKING UP *Help me, O Lord, to remember to reverence Your holiness, giving deep respect to my Heavenly Father. Help me to remember I am anointed for the task You have called me to do.*

DEDICATION

FEBRUARY 6

Leviticus 10-12

LOOKING BACK Princess Elizabeth Alexandra Mary ascended to Britain's throne on this day in 1952. She suddenly became Elizabeth II, Queen of the United Kingdom of Great Britain and Northern Ireland and Head of the Commonwealth. Elizabeth succeeded her father, King George VI, who had died on the same day. Elizabeth's father had become king in 1936 after his older brother, King Edward VIII, gave up the throne to marry a divorced American woman. This event greatly changed the course of 10-year-old Elizabeth's life. It made her heir to the throne, since George VI had no sons and she was the older of his two daughters.

LOOKING IN *Privilege implies responsibility, as Queen Elizabeth soon found out. She could never again have any sort of "normal" life because of the status that had been given her. Now she had to be totally dedicated to her position. The priests of ancient Israel were also given positions of tremendous privilege. They, too, had to assume a lifestyle that others in the nation did not know. They were to represent men to God and God to men. This high and holy calling demanded they be totally dedicated to the Lord. The anointing they received set them apart. When Aaron's two "anointed" sons violated their sacred positions, disaster resulted.*

LOOKING OUT

1. **We must not modify or corrupt God's commands. Aaron's sons decided to do things their own way. It was a tragic mistake that cost their lives.**
2. **There is a responsibility beyond personal pain. Aaron and his family were not permitted to grieve over the loss of Aaron's sons and couldn't leave their area of service.**
3. **God is interested in our physical well-being as well as our spiritual health. Laws in Leviticus not only deal with spiritual matters but also those things that keep us healthy.**
4. **Being God's people demands a unique lifestyle. The Israelites were not to act and react like other nations. They were to be leaders of righteousness, just as we are to be.**
5. **Childbirth is bittersweet—joy for a new life and sadness for man's sinful condition. The unique purification ceremony reminds us of the sacredness of a new life.**

LOOKING UP *Help me, Lord, to remember that Your calling on my life is wonderful, but it does demand a dedication that goes beyond my own convenience or pain.*

SCRUPLES

Leviticus 13-14

LOOKING BACK Sir Thomas More was a man who placed conscience above convenience. Born on February 7, 1477, More was a lawyer, scholar, author, and Lord Chancellor of England. He also was known for high principles. He became a martyr because he vehemently opposed Henry VIII's divorce from Queen Catherine so the frivolous king could marry Anne Boleyn, Catherine's maid of honor. The angry king charged More with treason and had him beheaded. Later Henry VIII tired of Boleyn and had her beheaded also. In 1935, Sir Thomas More was canonized as a saint by the Catholic Church because of his stand.

LOOKING IN *In Leviticus, Moses calls on God's people to be men and women of conscience and conviction. They also are to recognize that their faith affects all of life. Tedious health laws were set down by Moses, not only to produce a healthy nation, but also to let the people know that God was involved in all of their life, not just the spiritual things. The long involved laws about leprosy helped protect the people from the highly infectious condition. However leprosy was also a word picture that explained the devastating and disfiguring effect sin has on a person. As leprosy kills the nerves, desensitizing one, so sin blunts the conscience and ultimately destroys.*

LOOKING OUT

1. Sin is deadly. The leper had to tear his clothes just as those mourning the dead. This action spoke of sin's deadly effect on the sinner and those around him.
2. Sin is infectious. Lepers had to cover the lower part of their faces for fear of spreading the disease by coughing or sneezing. Sin, too, is highly contagious.
3. Sin isolates. Lepers had to live apart from the rest of the community. This speaks of how sin tears us away from those we love and long for.
4. Sin, like leprosy, numbs us to reality. The symbolism of leprosy reminds us how sin desensitizes us, just as leprosy deadens the nerves that protect us from hurting ourselves.
5. Sin need not be terminal since there is a cure for even the most awful offense. Even the despicable illnesses in the wilderness could be treated and cured by our Lord.

LOOKING UP *Thank You, Lord, because You have provided salvation from my sins even though I don't deserve it. Forgive me of my sins and make me white as snow.*

SEXUALITY

FEBRUARY 8

Leviticus 15-18

LOOKING BACK The Boy Scouts of America was founded in Washington D.C. by William Boyce on this day in 1910. Sir Robert Baden-Powell had started the Boy Scout movement in England in 1907, when he organized a camp for 20 boys. It spread to the United States as the result of a good turn performed for Boyce. A British Boy Scout helped Boyce find his way in a London fog. Boyce then founded the Boy Scouts of America. The Boy Scout oath is: "On my honor, I will do my best: to do my duty to God and my country, and to obey the Scout Law. To help other people at all times. To keep myself physically strong, mentally awake, and morally straight."

LOOKING IN *Keeping morally straight was a priority for God's people. Each year the Israelites set aside a time for introspection–a time to review their behavior. It was in the seventh month and was when they prayed, fasted, and afflicted their souls. The purpose was to purge those things that kept them from a right relationship with their God. Moses had given the people detailed laws about God's expectations of human sexuality. Obeying these laws would assure health and happiness. Disobeying these laws would short-circuit God's design and expose mankind to disease and death. God's prohibitions were not to prevent pleasure but to enhance it.*

LOOKING OUT

1. **Immorality is not wrong because it's in the Bible; it's in the Bible because it's wrong. Leviticus deals much with human sexuality. Relationships are to be holy and pure.**
2. **Immorality is dangerous and deadly, both physically and spiritually. The admonition for purity in Scripture is so God's children will remain happy and healthy.**
3. **Time must be set aside for self-examination and humility. God's law scheduled certain times for the Israelites to look at their own lives to see if they were pleasing God.**
4. **Morality must not be derived from community consensus but from "thus saith the Lord." Just as you can't set your own watch by what you feel, there must be a standard.**
5. **Sexual purity is a vital part of our testimony and lifestyle. Leviticus prohibits adultery, homosexuality, and bestiality. These aberrations can destroy us forever.**

LOOKING UP *Lord, help me to stay morally pure so that I may be a good witness for You in my love and my life. Bring all my lustful thoughts under Your control.*

TOOLS

FEBRUARY 9

Leviticus 19-21

LOOKING BACK Fifty-four years ago today, Winston Churchill begged, "Give us the tools and we will finish the job." He was referring to the task of containing the evil intentions of Adolf Hitler who was determined to dominate the world. America was reluctant to enter the European conflict, preferring to remain aloof from the hatred and hell Hitler was spewing out, even though millions were being sent to death camps by the Nazi madman. It took the tragedy of Pearl Harbor, months later, to awaken the United States to the awful threat greedy despots pose to humanity. If proper tools had been given in the early hours of the war, many lives might have been saved.

LOOKING IN *At Mount Sinai, God gave Israel the tools needed to build a society that would curb evil and contain those who wanted to light the fires of hell on this earth. The law clearly defined what is and is not acceptable to a holy God. It also outlined the consequences when His laws are violated. Throughout history, it has been proven time and again that those who have disobeyed God's laws have spilled out a little of hell on the earth. However, when we obey God's ways, we bring peace to ourselves, our families, and our communities. We must remember that we already have the tools necessary to build a better world if we will only use them.*

LOOKING OUT

1. **God is to be our role model. Moses instructs God's people to be holy as God is holy. We are not to emulate the world but be set apart as followers of our Lord.**
2. **True faith turns us into caring and compassionate people. God's law instructed the Israelites to consistently provide for the power and powerless who lived among them.**
3. **Faith is tied closely to behavior, causing us to act and react morally. The admonition here to "love your neighbor as yourself" is quoted nine times in the New Testament.**
4. **A "higher" calling demands a higher level of responsibility. It was a privilege to be a priest, but more was demanded of them than of others in Israel.**
5. **A "higher" calling demands a higher devotion to duty. The priest had to be careful how he lived so he would not defile the holiness of God. Those who did were destroyed.**

LOOKING UP *To be a Christian means to be "Christ-like." Help me, Lord, to not just wear the label but to live the life.*

HELPING

FEBRUARY 10

Leviticus 22-24

LOOKING BACK Commenting on the growing welfare system in the United States, Hubert Humphrey said on this day in 1965, "The impersonal hand of government can never replace the helping hand of a neighbor." While the Minnesota politician acknowledged government's need to be responsible for its people, he was quick to emphasize the need for every individual to take his share of responsibility in assisting the needy. That is a good biblical principle that we all need to remember in our materialistic and narcissistic age. We are to be our brother's keeper. We must not leave caring to "professionals" or to the government.

LOOKING IN *Leviticus reminds God's people of their responsibility to God and to their fellow man. The offerings given to God were not merely for the priest's benefit but also for the welfare of the needy. In addition, each Israelite was to be compassionate, expressing care in a practical way to those "have nots" among them. God's people were to deliberately leave gleanings in their fields for the poor and provide for the needy. The Bible says, "He who is kind to the poor lends to the LORD, and he will reward him for what he has done" (Proverbs 19:17). God always takes care of those who take care of those God cares for.*

LOOKING OUT

1. **Religious leaders must hold sacred the sacrificial gifts offered by God's people. Moses instructed Aaron to treat the Israelites' offerings to God with great respect.**
2. **Gifts given for God's work must not be used for other things. Moses instructed the priest to carefully handle offerings. Misuse and abuse demanded restitution.**
3. **God expects and only accepts our very best. Moses warned the people they must not cut corners when it came to giving their offerings. They were also to cheerfully give.**
4. **While God is compassionate, we must never take Him casually. Israel was warned they must never profane the name of God but must acknowledge Him as holy.**
5. **Holidays and celebrations are set to remind us to rejoice in–and rekindle–our love for the Lord. Sabbaths and six other special times marked Israel's yearly calendar.**

LOOKING UP *Help me, Lord, to always give my very best to You and compassionately care for those You love. Help me to move out in love and mercy to the needy.*

WHITE SHIRT DAY

FEBRUARY 11

Leviticus 25-27

LOOKING BACK Symbols are important. For this reason, for many years auto workers in Michigan have worn white shirts each February 11. This unusual action marks the anniversary of the United Auto Workers and General Motors agreement, following a bitter 44-day sit-down strike at the GM Flint, Michigan factories in 1937. "Blue-collar" workers traditionally wear white shirts on this day to symbolize the workingman's dignity won through that agreement. Workers felt they were being taken advantage of because of their status. In reaction, they instituted the angry strike. The city's government has officially proclaimed the annual event as "White Shirt Day."

LOOKING IN *Regardless of one's status in life, there is a desperate need for recognition of worth and to be treated with dignity. This is one of the reasons God's Word is so important. It not only reveals the character of God but also emphasizes the dignity of man–God's special creation. This is especially evident when it comes to welfare. The book of Leviticus outlines specific guidelines on how God's people are to deal with the poor and powerless. The poor are to be treated with respect and dignity. The "haves" in society are to assist the "have-nots." These laws in Leviticus do much to let us know the attitude we must have toward the less fortunate.*

LOOKING OUT

1. **We must always remember we are tenants on this earth. God's laws are structured to make us understand this is the Lord's world and we are just stewards of His property.**
2. **Fairness to our fellow man is a cardinal rule of right worship. Leviticus says we cannot take advantage of each other but fear the Lord, Who always holds us accountable.**
3. **We must help the homeless and heal the hurting. Because of pervasive evil on earth, there will always be poverty. Believers are to reach out to help the poor and powerless.**
4. **Our world becomes brighter when we obey the Heavenly Father. Blessings reinforce behavior. Therefore, when we obey God's Word, He pours out His great blessings on us.**
5. **We cannot really break God's law; we are only broken on them. God says that if we are hostile to Him, He will be hostile to us. Opposing Him is a battle we cannot win.**

LOOKING UP *Help me, Lord, to reach out today in love to someone needy who You have intended me to help. May I always remember to respect the dignity of others regardless of their status.*

NUMBERING

FEBRUARY 12

Numbers 1-2

LOOKING BACK In addition to this being President Abraham Lincoln's birthday, February 12 is also called "Lost Penny Day." This designation sets today aside to put all those pennies stashed in candy dishes, bowls, and jars back in circulation. "Lost Penny Day" is always held on February 12 because President Lincoln is the man depicted on the lowly coin. The organizers of this annual emphasis encourage us to take those pennies and give them to a charity, shelter, or an agency that assists the homeless. They also suggest contributing them to the local Humane Society. The idea is that even a little can make a lot as we all work together.

LOOKING IN *Pennies seem so insignificant that they are often tossed aside. Many people feel the same way about themselves, especially with the world's exploding population. Some wonder how God could possibly care for them when there are so many other people in the world. God's Word emphasizes the fact that God cares much about every individual. In fact, the numbering of Israel lets us know that, no matter how insignificant we might feel, each person is dear to God. He knows us by name and is intimately involved in our lives. Our Lord says that He even knows the number of hairs on our head. The psalmist says that God knows our very thoughts.*

LOOKING OUT

1. **God wants to prove the accomplishment of His promises to us. The numbering of Israel in the wilderness was to show God had kept His Word in taking Israel out of Egypt.**
2. **God wants to show us His particular care. Like a shepherd who knows the exact number of His sheep, God wanted Israel to know He was aware of each one of them.**
3. **God wants us to be different from the world. Only the true Israelites were numbered, indicating a difference between them and the mixed-multitude among them.**
4. **God wants order and justice. The numbering of Israel made the administration of justice easier and more fair. The people could be served in a better and more expedient way.**
5. **God wants to make things easier for us. The numbering and organization of Israel made the long march toward the Promised Land safer and more comfortable.**

LOOKING UP *Help me to remember, Lord, that Your commands are given to make my life better and easier. May I ever remember that You know me intimately and love me dearly.*

KNOWLEDGE

FEBRUARY 13

Numbers 3-4

LOOKING BACK Grant Wood, American painter and printmaker known for his images of the rural Midwest, was born on this day in 1892. With Thomas Hart Benton and John Steuart Curry, Wood was a founder and leading figure in the regionalism movement that was prominent in American art during the 1930's. Wood's most famous painting is *American Gothic*, which portrays a Midwestern farmer and his daughter in front of their home. The artist primarily portrayed the people and landscape of Iowa where he lived and taught most of his life. Wood believed that artists should remain in their home communities and paint from personal experience.

LOOKING IN *Just as Wood painted from intimate knowledge of his subject, we are to pray in the same vein. We must know God intimately if we are to pray effectively. Moses, himself from the tribe of Levi, spent much time talking to the priests about God's expectations of them as representatives of God to the people. These specific instructions about prayer are not to be overlooked or merely relegated to the Old Testament. Rather, we must remember the Bible says that we are a kingdom of priests unto God. Therefore it would be wise to study the prayer life of the ancient priests and apply those principles of prayer to our own lives.*

LOOKING OUT

1. We are to be people of prayer. As priests unto our God, we have the obligation to pray for the blessings of God on others just as Israel's priest daily blessed the people.
2. We are to pray specifically for God to give others what they need. The first of the three blessings deals with a petition that God grant what is best for another's welfare.
3. We are to pray for others' renewal, enlightenment, and comfort. God's face shining on us is what the sun does for the earth in warming and sustaining it.
4. We are to pray for others to have an intimate relationship with God. The phrase about God's countenance refers to the picture of a loving father looking at his beloved child.
5. We are to pray for peace for others. The priests' blessing invoked God to grant peace to those He called His own. When we have Christ, we have the "Prince of Peace."

LOOKING UP *Help me, Lord, to daily bless others with my prayers and petitions. May I learn to pray unselfishly. As the disciples asked You, Lord, "Teach us to pray."*

SPECIAL LOVE

FEBRUARY 14

Numbers 5-6

LOOKING BACK This is Valentine's Day, one of the most widely observed unofficial holidays. Today lovers express their feelings to the objects of their affection with cards, candy, and other gifts. The origin of Valentine's Day is somewhat obscure. Some say it was selected for the celebration of Christian martyrs as a diversion from the ancient pagan observance of Lupercalia. The Romans celebrated their feast of Lupercalia as a lovers' festival for young people. Young men and women chose partners for the festival by drawing names from a box. After the spread of Christianity, churchmen tried to give meaning to the pagan festival, calling it Valentine's Day.

LOOKING IN *Regardless of the origin of Valentine's Day, it does celebrate love. God's Word talks much about love being much more than our modern definition of "feeling." Love is giving of oneself to another in a very special way! That is why God instituted the Nazarite vow of the Old Testament. Those who wanted to show their love for God in a special way could take this unique vow that required sacrifice. The vow could be for a lifetime or just a specific period of separation. Each of the stipulations of the vow spoke a powerful and specific message to the community. Samuel, Samson, and John the Baptist were all Nazarites.*

LOOKING OUT

1. **We choose whether to respond to God's calling into ministry. It was up to the individual to take, and keep, the Nazarite vow.**
2. **We are to be controlled only by God's Spirit. Nazarites had to avoid strong drink and things associated with it, because alcohol is a controlling spirit.**
3. **We are to be different from the world. Nazarites could not cut their hair. This made them stand out in the community, for they always looked different.**
4. **We must carefully avoid sin. Death has always been a symbol of sin. That is why the Nazarite was not to touch anything dead.**
5. **We must be faithful in fulfilling our calling. The Nazarite had to fulfill his vow and calling despite any personal inconvenience.**

LOOKING UP *Help me, Lord, to show You my special love for You by the way I live. May I always be an example of one who passionately loves the Lord.*

GIVING

FEBRUARY 15

Numbers 7-8

LOOKING BACK Italian astronomer and physicist Galileo Galilei was born on this day in 1564. He has been called the founder of modern experimental science. Galileo made the first effective use of the refracting telescope to discover important new facts about astronomy. He also discovered the law of falling bodies as well as the law of the pendulum, proving the theory that all bodies, large and small, descend at equal speed. Galileo designed a variety of scientific instruments. He also developed and improved the refracting telescope, though he did not invent it. This brilliant man challenged and helped overthrow the prevailing concepts of the world in his time.

LOOKING IN *It is easy to believe in what is not true, and we need people like Galileo to shake us out of our assumptions. One assumption often made is that the church only wants our money. The fact is: "giving" benefits us far more than it does the church. Those who resent giving to God are foolish. They only hurt themselves. By refusing to give to God, they not only violate His commands but also hold back abundant blessings reserved for those who are generous. "Giving" Christians have learned they cannot outgive God. The Bible says: "One man gives freely, yet gains even more; another withholds unduly, but comes to poverty" (Proverbs 11:24).*

LOOKING OUT

1. **Giving speaks of our cheerful submission to God's commands. The tribes gave because they were glad to be part of the family of God. Giving indicates membership.**
2. **Giving speaks of our equal status before God. Although some tribes were richer than others, all gave equally. God's system of tithing puts us all on the same level before Him.**
3. **Giving should start with the leaders. The heads of the tribes brought their offerings to the Lord. This speaks of the need for spiritual leaders to set the pace in giving.**
4. **Gifts are of equal importance. Moses carefully repeats the amount of the offerings the tribes give, even though all are the same. This indicates all gifts were important to God.**
5. **Giving is especially pleasing to God. Because God's nature is to give, He shows His great pleasure to Israel when the tribes make their special freewill offerings to Him.**

LOOKING UP *Help me, Lord, to understand how pleased You are when I sacrificially and willingly give to You. May I always be generous with the resources You have given me.*

NEW LIFE

FEBRUARY 16

Numbers 9-10

February

LOOKING BACK A new life started for Ulysses S. Grant on this day in 1862. That was the time he earned the nickname""Unconditional Surrender Grant" because he demanded those terms at Fort Donelson, Tennessee. This uncompromising stand grabbed the imagination of those in power and would eventually catapult Grant into the White House for two terms. During his military career, Grant led his troops with energy and determination. He developed great confidence in his own judgment and ability to learn from experience. These traits also characterized Grant's political career and endeared him to the American public.

LOOKING IN *Our reading today marks the start of a new life for Israel. They had been at Mount Sinai for 11 months and 20 days. Now God let them know it was time to move forward. Their time at the mountain had not been wasted. God had delivered His law to Moses, and he had communicated that to the people. Their "constitution" was now set. The people were ready to push on toward the Promised Land. The time at the mountain had been important, but it was not to be forever. God had great plans for His people, and He wanted them to push on to fulfill that purpose. Tragically, it would be 40 long years before they would finally reach the Promised Land.*

LOOKING OUT

1. There is a time to wait on God and a time to go. The Israelites had been at Mt. Sinai for about a year. Now God instructed them to move toward the Promised Land.
2. Praise should precede all our prayers and progress. Judah led the way on the march toward the Promised Land. The name "Judah" means, "Praise Yahweh."
3. Prayer should always precede any step we take. Whenever the ark set out to lead the Israelites, Moses prayed, "Rise up, O Lord! May your enemies be scattered."
4. We should invite others to go with us to the Promised Land. Moses invited Hobab to accompany Israel and also promised blessings to him if he chose to go along.
5. Prayer and praise should close all our activities. Whenever the ark came to rest, Moses prayed, "Return, O Lord, to the countless thousands of Israel."

LOOKING UP *Help me, Lord, to know Your timing. May I wait when You ask and move forward at Your command. Let me not lag behind You or move before You.*

LAKE WOBEGON

FEBRUARY 17

Numbers 11-13

LOOKING BACK Garrison Keillor started his popular Saturday night radio show, *A Prairie Home Companion*, 20 years ago today. The live variety program was begun as part of the National Public Radio's Folk Festival USA. It became a regular Saturday night feature in 1980 on NPR. Keillor's monologues about the mythical Lake Wobegon and his humorous ads for local businesses such as Bertha's Kitty Boutique, Powdermilk Biscuits, and the Chatterbox Cafe are accompanied by various musical groups. The show has received high critical acclaim for its creativity. The "News from Lake Wobegon" remains the show's finest feature.

LOOKING IN *"Woebegone" means "overwhelmed with woe." That is exactly the state of the complainers in Israel when times turned tough in the wilderness. In their self-pity, the Israelites soon forgot about the Red Sea crossing, plus the myriad of other miracles God had performed for them. God becomes angry with them because of their ingratitude. It's amazing how quickly we forget the great blessings of God when we find ourselves in pain or difficulty. We become so focused on the present discomfort that we forget God is still in control. We can forget that God is perfecting us and often lets these problems arise so He can work His will in our lives.*

LOOKING OUT

1. **Complaining only compounds our problems, bringing more grief on ourselves. God became angry with Israel when the people began to complain about their hardships.**
2. **Self-pity breeds discontent, blinding us to the provisions of our Lord. The rabble-rousers among the Israelites started to complain bitterly about the blandness of the manna.**
3. **God will give us help in hard times if we but ask. Moses grew weary leading the complaining people. He went to God Who told him to appoint 70 elders as helpers.**
4. **We flounder in faith when we take our eyes off God and put them on our problems. Moses was discouraged when he saw the impossibility of providing meat for so many.**
5. **Great problems give God opportunity to prove His promises. God told Moses in his discouragement, "You will now see whether or not what I say will come true for you."**

LOOKING UP *Help me, Lord, to focus continually on Your power and provision rather than on my problems and needs. May I always praise You rather than complain about my lot.*

PILGRIM'S PROGRESS

FEBRUARY 18

Numbers 14-15

LOOKING BACK John Bunyan's *Pilgrim's Progress* was published on this day in 1678. This book by the English preacher is a classic in literature and read throughout the world. It has been translated into more than 100 languages. *Pilgrim's Progress* is a religious allegory in which people and places represent vices and virtues. It has helped many believers better understand the spiritual conflicts facing them. Christian (the hero) sets out from the City of Destruction to go to the Celestial City (heaven). On the way, he meets some people who try to harm him and others who try to help him. After many adventures, Christian finally makes it to that great city.

LOOKING IN *Like Christian in Pilgrim's Progress, the Israelites were on their way to the Promised Land. They too met many who tried to hurt and others who wanted to help. Tragically, they suffered much unnecessary pain because they refused to believe God would do what He promised. God never let things get too easy for the Israelites in the wilderness because He had no intention of letting them stay there. If they had been pain–free in that environment, they never would have wanted to move on to fulfill their destiny. Their pain served as motivation for them to finally take the Promised Land. They made it at last–but not for forty long, weary years.*

LOOKING OUT

1. Faith falls to fear once we start listening to man rather than hearing God. The Israelites believed the 10 spies' reports rather than God's promise.
2. Grief will turn to bitterness and rebellion unless we turn to God in our troubles. The Israelites began to blame God for their troubles, and that led them to rebellion.
3. Intercessory prayer can turn the tide of trouble. Moses and Aaron fell on their faces in prayer for the rebellious people. God heard His servants and spared the nation.
4. There is an awful price to pay for unbelief. The disbelieving people were condemned to wilderness wandering for 40 long years. Sin always carries a high price tag.
5. God's will also involves God's timing. When it became obvious that God was angry, some of the people vowed to go on into the Promised Land; but it was too late.

LOOKING UP *Help me, Lord, to look to You in trouble rather than complain because of my circumstances. Keep moving me forward to fulfill my destiny.*

REBELLION

FEBRUARY 19

Numbers 16-18

LOOKING BACK Ezra Pound was a rebel. Fifty years ago today Pound received the prestigious Bollingen Prize for poetry for his collection *The Pisan Cantos*. This first award was steeped in controversy because the poet had been charged with treason after making pro-Fascist broadcasts in Italy during World War II. Pound's poem dealt with the corruption he saw developing in American life since the time of Thomas Jefferson and Martin Van Buren. After the war, the United States arrested Pound. He was judged insane and spent 12 years in a Washington D.C. mental hospital. He was released in 1958 and returned to Italy.

LOOKING IN *The world has known its share of rebels; even Moses had to deal with them. The insolence of Dathan and Abiram, along with Korah, resulted in tragedy for the nation. In the end, 14,700 people were dead because they had been swayed by these leaders who wanted to overthrow Moses. We must learn that we are not to touch God's anointed. If we don't agree with them or their methods, we must take them to the Lord rather than try to foment a spiritual revolution with the intent to oust them. David wisely let God take care of stubborn and sinful Saul, even though he had many opportunities to stop the violence Saul perpetrated against him.*

LOOKING OUT

1. **When people turn against us, we must turn to God. Moses, faced with the determined rebellion of the Levites, took his problems to God rather than resorting to politics.**
2. **We must stop defending ourselves and let God take up our case. Moses willingly put his future into the hands of God, knowing the Creator would judge him fairly.**
3. **You can't reason with rebellion. Moses attempted to reason with the rebel leaders but they would not listen. If they had, they would not have lost their lives.**
4. **We often accuse others of what we ourselves are guilty of doing. The rebels accused Moses of taking too much authority upon himself. However, they were the guilty ones.**
5. **It is a dangerous thing to rebel against God's chosen leadership. When reason didn't work, God stepped in and swiftly executed those who would defy His leadership.**

LOOKING UP *Help me, Lord, to be careful lest I rebel against the spiritual leadership You have ordained. May I always let You handle Your called ones.*

LEADERS

Numbers 19-21

LOOKING BACK Frederick Douglass died on this day in 1895. He was the leading spokesman of African Americans in the 1800's. Born a slave, Douglass became a noted reformer, author, and orator. He devoted his life to the abolition of slavery and the fight for black rights. In 1838, as a young man, Douglass fled from his master and went to New Bedford, Massachusetts. To avoid capture, he dropped his two middle names and changed his last name to Douglass. He got a job as a caulker, but the other men refused to work with him because he was black. Douglass then held unskilled jobs, among them collecting rubbish and digging cellars.

LOOKING IN *Douglass became a great and respected leader to his downtrodden people. Like Moses, he lived to see his people delivered from slavery but did not survive to witness the fulfillment of their dreams. Moses died before his dream of the Promised Land was fulfilled. However, his disappointment was because of disobedience in striking the rock rather than speaking to it as God has directed. This may seem a harsh punishment for such a little infraction, but it was not. Moses had been given great privilege and performed many mighty miracles. He made the awful mistake of letting his anger get the best of him, forcing him to make a disastrous decision.*

LOOKING OUT

1. **There is a right way and a wrong way to do the right thing. Moses, angry with the Israelites for their constant complaining, strikes the rock rather than speaking to it.**
2. **We must always do God's work God's way or disaster results. Moses clearly disobeyed the specific command of the Lord in striking the rock. God could not permit this rebellion.**
3. **Even though we are forgiven, we still must face the consequences of our disobedience. God forgave Moses for his behavior, but he was banned from the Promised Land.**
4. **Even when reaping sin's consequences, our faithful Father hears and heeds our prayers. The Israelites complained constantly, but God delivered them from Arad.**
5. **Victory is assured although the battle may not yet be engaged. When Og marched against Israel, God assured them before the battle started that they would win.**

LOOKING UP *Help me, Lord, to trust You more. You will give me the victory even though the battle is hard. Help me always to remember to do Your work Your way.*

MISTAKES

FEBRUARY 21

Numbers 22-23

LOOKING BACK Former White House aides, H.R. Haldeman and John D. Ehrlichman, and former Attorney General, John Mitchell, were sentenced to 30 months in prison on this day in 1975. The penalty was for their active involvement with the infamous Watergate cover-up. Watergate was the biggest political scandal in United States history. It included various illegal activities designed to help President Richard M. Nixon win reelection in 1972 and resulted in Nixon's resignation from the presidency in 1974. Haldeman, Ehrlichman, and Mitchell made huge mistakes by caving in to pressures to hide the illegal burglary at the Washington D.C. apartments.

LOOKING IN *Balaam also made a huge mistake when he agreed to prophecy against Israel for money. He obviously wanted the favor of the pagan king and fully intended to do as asked. However God intervened in a dramatic and unusual way. Balaam tried his best to curse Israel but each time ended up blessing God's people. Even the "miracle" of the talking donkey failed to dissuade him from going against God's will. Eventually, Balaam would pay the ultimate price for his disobedience. He would be killed because he advised the enemies of God to corrupt the young men of Israel by providing them with wild and appealing pagan women.*

LOOKING OUT

1. **When God says, "No!" we must not say, "Yes!" Obviously, Balaam wanted to help Balak even though God had told him not to.**
2. **God is angry with those who preach for profit. Balaam was more interested in making money than in delivering the message.**
3. **Even dumb animals are smarter than the disobedient. The donkey saw the angel blocking the path even when Balaam couldn't.**
4. **Obeying only when we are backed into a corner is not obedience. Balaam offered to turn back, but God said, "No!" Balaam had gone too far and done too much.**
5. **If God lights the candle, none can blow it out. Balak did all he could to get Balaam to prophesy against Israel, but God stepped in each time and prevented it from happening.**

LOOKING UP *Help me, Lord, to never go against Your will. May my heart always be so attuned to You that I can see what You want me to do when You want me to do it.*

WOMAN HATER

FEBRUARY 22

Numbers 24-25

LOOKING BACK A classic misanthrope (one who hates mankind) was born on this day in 1788. German philosopher Arthur Schopenhauer became widely known for fine prose and pessimism. Strongly influenced by the German philosopher Immanuel Kant, he insisted that the world we experience through our senses is mere representation. He meant that we experience the world not as it really is, but only as we represent it to ourselves. Schopenhauer never married, saying, "To marry is to halve your rights and double your duties." Among his essays is one especially angry discussion entitled *On Women.* He died alone and in his bitterness at age 72.

LOOKING IN *We don't know why the pessimistic German philosopher was so bitter toward women. However we do know the tremendous power women have over men. Men have been given the power of authority while woman have influence. The power of influence is always greater than authority. The Moabite women used their influence to destroy God's people. They lured the Israelite men to sacrifice to their gods, and before long the nation was plunged into pagan worship. This drift downward threatened the whole of God's plan of redemption. Therefore swift and sure judgment came. A plague underlined the danger of dallying with the devil.*

LOOKING OUT

1. What outsiders could not do to destroy, Israel did to herself. God protected His people from their enemies, but they, by their own lustful decisions, brought destruction.
2. You can't play with fire without getting burned. The Israelite men were drawn into idolatrous worship through their illicit relationships with pagan Canaanite women.
3. Sin always brings sickness of soul and body. God sent a plague among the people because they had blatantly disobeyed. Some 24,000 Israelites died in that judgment.
4. Sin's roots must be destroyed or they will quickly grow again. Phinehas, by his quick and decisive action, turned God's anger away and helped restore health to the people.
5. We must be careful of friendships lest they turn us away from God. God warned His people to stay away from the Midianites because they were determined to destroy Israel.

LOOKING UP *Help me, Lord, to be careful in choosing my friendships. May I always understand and remember how greatly I am influenced by those close to me.*

JOURNALIST

FEBRUARY 23

Numbers 26-27

LOOKING BACK William Shirer was born on this day in 1904. The famous journalist-author is best known for his remarkable book, *The Rise and Fall of the Third Reich,* which traced the horrific years of Adolf Hitler. Shirer used his experiences in Europe as a news correspondent to write this acclaimed history. The famed journalist always seemed to be at the forefront of history-making events and personalities. He had also become friends with the Hindu saint, Mohandas K. Gandhi, leader of India's independence movement. Gandhi was later assassinated by a dissident Hindu. Shirer, who died in 1993, also wrote a book about Gandhi.

LOOKING IN *Like Shirer, Moses was a remarkable journalist and historian. He was also at the forefront of dramatic events that would shape the entire future of the world. Moses traced the travels of God's people through the wilderness, not only as their leader but also as the recorder of events surrounding them. Unlike Shirer, Moses didn't just write history; he made it. After a long and fruitful life, Moses was about to die. He asked God to give the nation a new leader. He did not want to leave the people without someone who would finish the great vision God had given him so many years before. He found that God had already been preparing Joshua.*

LOOKING OUT

1. Generational sins need not plague us. The daughters of Zelophehad received an inheritance in spite of the fact that their father had, "died for his own sin and left no sons."
2. God is ever fair and moves to meet special needs. The case of Zelophehad's daughters was special. Moses sought God's answer in the matter. He answered compassionately.
3. God prepares us for our future. Moses had faithfully served God and now God prepares him for his death. He permits Moses to view the Promised Land.
4. Even before we pray God has prepared the answer. God had been preparing Joshua for leadership long before Moses prayed that God would send Israel a good and godly leader.
5. Leaders should be filled with God's Spirit. It was not enough that Joshua was a good military man. God's Word speaks specifically of his being filled with the Spirit of God.

LOOKING UP *Help me, Lord, like Moses, to always seek Your answer when faced with decisions beyond my wisdom. May I always remember that I must not lean on my own understanding.*

HADASSAH

Numbers 28-30

LOOKING BACK With 1,500 active chapters, it is the largest women's volunteer organization in the United States. Hadassah was begun on this day in 1912 when 12 members of the Daughters of Zion Study Circle met in New York City under the leadership of Henrietta Szold. A constitution was drafted to expand the study group into a national organization called Hadassah, Hebrew for "myrtle," and the Biblical name of Queen Esther. The new group was designed to foster Jewish education in America and to create public health nursing and nurses training in Palestine. Hadassah now has about 385,000 members, with headquarters in New York City.

LOOKING IN *The organization, Hadassah, has had tremendous impact on our world as Jewish women unite to make a difference. Women have always made a great difference in affecting society. This is especially true when they are dedicated to God and good. In a world that did not necessarily respect women, God's law gave women the respect and dignity they deserved. Also, the law insisted that men be protective of the "weaker sex." The law was a revolutionary document when it was delivered by Moses. It noted that both men and women have unique roles to fulfill on God's agenda, and there should be equal respect between the sexes.*

LOOKING OUT

1. **God always lets His loved ones know what brings pleasure to Him. The Lord tells Moses about the daily offerings, saying the aroma of these sacrifices pleases Him.**
2. **God always deals fairly. Like a good parent, God outlines His total expectations of the Israelites. Worship was to involve a sacredness to give them proper perspective.**
3. **God always keeps His promises and expects us to do the same. The binding nature of vows and pledges lets us know that God places high value on us keeping our promises.**
4. **Authority is given for protection, not frustration. The careful laws relating to a man's responsibility to women let us know that we must also help and protect the vulnerable.**
5. **Men are to be strong and loving in their relationships with wives and daughters. God holds men accountable if they use and abuse the ladies God gives them.**

LOOKING UP *Help me to remember, O Lord, that Your laws are not to keep me from happiness but are to protect me. May I respect and obey Your will for my life.*

ASSAULT

FEBRUARY 25

Numbers 31-32

LOOKING BACK The tragic Hebron Massacre occurred on this day in 1994. An American-born Jewish settler in Hebron, Israel, opened fire with an assault rifle in a crowded mosque, killing 29 people. The shooter, Baruch Goldstein, was crushed to death in the ensuing panic to flee the complex, which is sacred to both Jews and Muslims, because it is believed to contain the tomb of Abraham and his wife, Sarah. More than 400 Muslims had gathered for early morning prayers during Ramadan. In addition to those killed, 150 others were wounded. Riots broke out after the shooting, as tensions ran high between the angry Muslims and Jews.

LOOKING IN *Tragically, murder and mayhem have been part of our culture since Eden. In today's reading, the Midianites were determined to do away with God's people. That drew Israel into a brutal battle with much bloodshed. The Midianites were then thoroughly routed and punished for their earlier sin of inducing Israel to worship false gods. The victorious Israelite army and the nation divided the great spoil fifty-fifty. A special offering to God was given in appreciation for the victory. All of us are weary of war and wish that it were not part of our world. However, evil has been in the ascendance ever since Adam and Eve. One day that will change.*

LOOKING OUT

1. **Sin adds to our troubles, subtracts from our energy, and multiplies our difficulties. Dalliance with the Midianites had greatly harmed God's people. Now it had to be dealt with.**
2. **Sin has to be stomped out or it will rise up and overwhelm. The insistence on total annihilation of the Midianites seemed harsh unless we know the evil involved.**
3. **Tithes and offerings are to be given first, showing we recognize God's leadership and Lordship. Following battle, the war spoils were to be divided and God's part given first.**
4. **We must not permit fragmentation or division in the church. Israel's tribes were to stay together, lest they be divided and become vulnerable to their fierce enemies.**
5. **We are to be deeply concerned that all receive the same blessing as we do. Moses let the two-and-a-half tribes settle where they wanted, but they had to help the others fight.**

LOOKING UP *Help me, Lord, not to be so selfish that I only care about my well-being. Bless others as I am blessed. May I always give You special praise when I win my spiritual battles.*

JUSTICE

FEBRUARY 26

Numbers 33-36

LOOKING BACK President Woodrow Wilson said on this day in 1916, "Justice has nothing to do with expediency." He was absolutely right even though justice is not always realized in this world. But it would be better served if we all heeded God's Word. There is an interesting hanging in Switzerland's Supreme Court building. Entitled, "Justice Instructing the Judges," various litigants are pictured—a wife against a husband, an architect against a builder—while above these stands a group of judges. Justice (usually shown blindfolded with her sword vertical) is blindfolded with her sword pointing down to a book on which is written, "The Word of God."

LOOKING IN *True justice only comes from God. Even though the law Moses delivered from Mount Sinai was imperfect, it was still the best offered until Jesus appeared. Unlike other law codes of the ancient world, God's law was fair to all. It clearly spelled out what God expected of man and how man could best live in community. Our Lord clearly said that He did not come to do away with the law but to fulfill it or make it complete. It is a wise society that takes God's Word as the basis for justice; a foolish country ignores it. Modern society is now witnessing the tragic consequences when men throw out God's Word or simply ignore it.*

LOOKING OUT

1. **God gives us all we could ever want and need; by faith, we take it. God gave Israel the Promised Land, but they had to conquer it. We are to be locked in partnership with God.**
2. **Faith divides the land even before we enter it. Moses spends much time allotting the land to the tribes, even though, at that time, they had not entered its borders.**
3. **God calls men and women to specific tasks and uniquely prepares them for their assigned work. Moses gives the names of men who were to divide the land to the tribes.**
4. **God takes care of His servants and remembers their labors. The Levites were assigned a special place in the Promised Land. They had faithfully fulfilled their duty.**
5. **Justice does not protect the guilty but is designed to sustain the innocent. The cities of refuge assured that justice would be done, rather than mob lynching by the vengeful.**

LOOKING UP *Help me, Lord, to remember that I am to be in partnership with You in completing my assigned task. May I always obey Your law and live according to Your will.*

REMEMBERING

FEBRUARY 27

Deuteronomy 1-2

LOOKING BACK During the difficult Civil War in the United States, someone asked President Abraham Lincoln, "Is God on your side?" To this the wise leader answered, "I'm not so concerned whether God is on my side as I am whether I'm on God's side." Lincoln is well-respected for his wit and wisdom as well as being a great leader during that awful war that turned brother against brother. On February 27, 1860, Lincoln said, "Let us have faith that right makes might, and in that faith let us to the end dare to do our duty as we understand it." Lincoln must have picked his message up from Moses, who makes a similar passionate plea to God's people.

LOOKING IN *Moses, perhaps the greatest leader of a nation the world has ever known, wants Israel to always remember their lessons from history. He encourages them to have faith and do what is right. God had given them the rules for living at Mt. Sinai, so they knew what they were to do. Now, on the plains of Moab just before entering the Promised Land, Moses reminds them of that great duty. Moses would not be permitted to go into the Promised Land, but he could influence the direction God's people would take as they moved to possess what God had given them forty years before. These final sermons were like the last will and testament of Moses.*

LOOKING OUT

1. **We must declare the whole counsel of God. Moses spoke all of God's words to Israel, not just the ones they wanted to hear.**
2. **We must never become too comfortable where we are. God reminded Israel that they were to move forward, not just stay put.**
3. **God has done His part; now we must do ours. God gave the land and provision. Now it was up to the Israelites to take what God had given.**
4. **Reviewing our past prepares us for the future. On the plains of Moab, Moses reminds Israel how God had brought them from Egypt to the very border of the Promised Land.**
5. **Reminding ourselves of the rules helps keep us in line. Moses carefully reminds God's people of His expectations of them so they will keep the faith and fulfill their purpose.**

LOOKING UP *Help me, Lord, to never become so content where I am that I refuse to move where You want me to be. May I always be in the exact center of Your will.*

REARVIEW MIRROR

FEBRUARY 28

Deuteronomy 3-4

LOOKING BACK Two of President John Tyler's cabinet members were killed on this day in 1844, when a gun exploded aboard a ship in the Potomac, a tragic event that is mostly forgotten in American history. In fact, the whole presidency of Tyler seems only a footnote. For more than 75 years after the courteous, soft-spoken Tyler left office, historians dealt harshly with him. President Theodore Roosevelt said: "Tyler has been called a mediocre man, but this is unwarranted flattery. He was a politician of monumental littleness." Many historians today take a different view. They regard Tyler as a president of exceptional courage and imagination.

LOOKING IN *It is so easy to forget the past and misjudge those who lived it. For this reason, Moses carefully prepares and presents a series of sermons on the plains of Moab just before he dies. God's people must not forget how they were delivered from Egypt, preserved in the wilderness, and forgiven for their sins over and over again. They must remember that God had a great destiny for them that could only be realized as they lived by faith and obeyed God's Word. Moses reviews the nation's history in detail so it would be burned into their hearts and into the hearts of the generations that followed. They never were to forget those urgent life lessons.*

LOOKING OUT

1. God's laws are blessings, not burdens. Moses reminded Israel that God had given His law to give them joy, not to add more difficulty to their lives.
2. Obedience to God is our best witness. Moses said that other nations would see the wisdom of obeying God's laws as they watched Israel's behavior.
3. Deliverance is usually a process. When Sihon, king of Heshbon, threatened Israel, God told Moses, "See, I have begun to deliver Sihon and his country over to you."
4. We must never attempt to rewrite God's Word or emend it. God said, "Do not add to what I command you and do not subtract from it, but keep the commands of the Lord..."
5. We must never be careless with our faith. God said, "Be careful, and watch yourselves closely so that you do not forget the things your eyes have seen or let them slip..."

LOOKING UP *Lord, help me remember the wonderful victories of the past so that I might be fully prepared for my future. Forgive me when I forget the wonders You have done.*

March

A Month that is Rife with Many Superstitions

March may be the month Solomon sang about so long ago: "For, lo, the winter is past, the rain is over and gone; The flowers appear on the earth; the time of the singing of birds is come, and the voice of the turtle is heard in our land..." (Song of Solomon 2:11-12). However, the famous "lover-king" may also have been thinking of the next month (April) because March can also be a bit testy at times. The month brings in spring and ends the winter. Spring, in the northern half of the world, always begins with the vernal equinox, which occurs on March 19, 20, or 21. On this day, the center of the sun is directly over the equator.

March is the third month of the year according to the Gregorian calendar. It was the first month on the early Roman calendar and was called Martius. Later, the ancient Romans made January 1 the beginning of the year, and March became the third month. March has always had 31 days. Its name honors Mars, the Roman god of war. During this month, we will finish reading the Pentateuch (Genesis, Exodus, Leviticus, Numbers, and Deuteronomy) and begin the historical books of the Bible. These books will cover the entire period of the theocracy (Joshua, Judges, and Ruth) and reach briefly into the monarchy (1 Samuel).

There are many superstitions about March. We often hear that "March comes in like a lion and goes out like a lamb." This means that the first day of March is often stormy, and the last day is mild and warm. Another saying is, "April borrowed from March three days, and they were ill." This refers to the first three days of April, which are generally rough and blustery like March. A third saying calls the first three days of March "blind days," because they are said to be unlucky. Superstition states that if rain falls on these days, farmers supposedly will have poor harvests. Thankfully, our world does not run on human superstition but on the sure laws of nature that our loving Creator gave us.

CONSTITUTION

Deuteronomy 5-7

LOOKING BACK For over eight years the Articles of Confederation provided the legal foundation for the United States government. They were adopted by the 13 colonies on March 1, 1781. These Articles served as the basic laws for the new nation until the present Constitution went into effect in 1789. George Washington, Alexander Hamilton, and other national leaders were dissatisfied with the Articles of Confederation since amendments to it were difficult to make. A demand grew for a convention to revise them. However, at the convention the Articles were quickly abandoned and the United States Constitution written.

LOOKING IN *Today's reading contains the spiritual constitution of God's chosen people. These laws would make Israel unique among the nations of the world. Appropriately, the constitution contained a wonderful confession of faith. It is known as the "Shema," from the Hebrew word "hear," and sets out the basic concept of God's character. It emphasizes God's uniqueness. To this day, Israel has not abandoned this confession of faith. In addition to the confession, there were other laws of worship given to God's people. These worship laws reminded the people that they did not create God in their image but were created by Him. He dictated how they would worship.*

LOOKING OUT

1. **Faith starts with recognizing the character of God. Judaism's basic confession of faith (the Shema) begins with an insistence that we understand God is unique.**
2. **Worship involves everything that we are and all that we have. We are to worship God with all our heart, soul, and strength. This encompasses our body, soul, and spirit.**
3. **We must internalize God's Word. The Israelites were told that God's commandments should be written on their hearts, not just on the scrolls containing the Law.**
4. **Religious training is far more than a Sunday experience. Moses told the people they should use all opportunities to teach their children the words, wonders, and works of God.**
5. **We are to establish reminders of our responsibility to God. The Israelites were told to keep symbols of God's Word near them at all times to remind them to trust and serve Him.**

LOOKING UP *Help me, Lord, to remember my responsibility to You. May I know You more and serve You better. I will worship You as You desire, not according to my dictates.*

MIRACULOUS

MARCH 2

Deuteronomy 8-11

LOOKING BACK Rutherford B. Hayes was elected president by a margin of only one electoral vote on this day in 1877. His victory over Samuel J. Tilden in 1876 climaxed the most disputed presidential election in United States history. Hayes wasn't supposed to be elected and wasn't expected to serve, but God intervened. He and his wife quickly gained great respect for their moral leadership. A typical day in the Hayes' White House began with morning prayers. Evenings were often spent with the family singing hymns together. Concerned about the problem of alcoholism, the Hayes stopped serving alcoholic drinks at the White House, even at formal dinners and receptions.

LOOKING IN *Perhaps no other election win in American history was so obviously miraculous as that of Rutherford B. Hayes. God does intervene in the affairs of nations. Israel's history is replete with stories of the miraculous. There are astounding deliverances, marvelous victories, and dynamic individuals raised to leadership by God. Moses instructs the nation what their attitude should be when God grants miracles and gives His people victory. Moses reminds the nation that God always asks them, and us, to do the impossible so that we will learn to lean heavily on Him. God wants to work with us to accomplish His will on this earth.*

LOOKING OUT

1. God always calls us to do something we can't do. The Israelites are told they will dispossess nations stronger and greater than they. When we go with God, we can do wonderful things.
2. We must be careful whom we hear. People claimed the Anakites could not be defeated. God said they could. The Israelites had to choose which voice they would believe.
3. We are to be locked in divine partnership with our Heavenly Father. God told Israel that He would subdue the Anakites and Israel would drive them out of the land.
4. When victory comes, we must never think it is because we deserve it. God said He had given Israel victory because of the wickedness of the enemy, not for Israel's righteousness.
5. In spite of our faults, God uses us. Israel was often a stiffnecked people but God used them anyway. The spiritual petitions of a godly leader had touched the heart of God.

LOOKING UP *Lord, may I always remember that You use me, not because I am good, but because You are good and merciful.*

COMMUNICATION

MARCH 3

Deuteronomy 12-16

LOOKING BACK Alexander Graham Bell, inventor of the telephone, was born on this day in 1847. Bell acquired his interest in the transmission of sound from his father, Melville Bell, a teacher of the deaf. On March 10, 1876, Bell spoke the first electrically transmitted sentence to his assistant in the next room. Bell's other accomplishments include a refinement of Edison's phonograph, the first successful phonograph record, audiometer, and discoveries about the causes and nature of deafness. Bell's inventions ushered the world into a whole new era of mass communication, making it possible for people to speak to each other even from long distances.

LOOKING IN *Communication is necessary for relationships to develop and to be maintained. For that reason, God instructs His people on how to communicate with Him. They must first understand His "otherness" and never casually approach the Creator. God gives Moses instructions on worship as well as the way they are to live before Him. God assures His people they will be protected by Him and their needs provided as they faithfully follow the instructions given in His Word. He assures the Israelites that they will find rest and peace as they obey His Word and maintain their communication with their Creator. God wants an intimate relationship with His people.*

LOOKING OUT

1. We must tear down all points of temptation. The Israelites were told to destroy all the pagan worship sites so they would not be tempted to commit the same evil.
2. God has an assigned place for all of us. Just as the Israelites were told they had to worship where God chose, we must find the specific place where He wants us.
3. God will feed us where He has placed us. God told His people that when they got to the place He wanted them to be, He would carefully provide for all their needs.
4. We are not autonomous beings. God told Israel they were not to do as everyone saw fit but were to obey carefully the commandments He had given.
5. There is only rest and safety in the perfect will of God. When we are out of God's will, we find no peace, because only in His presence is joy and protection forevermore.

LOOKING UP *Lord, help me always to be in the center of Your will. Happiness is only found in Your presence. Help me to keep my communication with You fresh and meaningful.*

QUALIFICATIONS

Deuteronomy 17-20

LOOKING BACK On this day in 1986, Austrian President Kurt Waldheim was charged with hiding his Nazi background. He had served as secretary-general of the United Nations for 10 years before becoming the Austrian leader. Waldheim's campaign for the presidency was marked by controversy when records surfaced concerning his possible involvement in Nazi atrocities during World War II. Documents showed that Waldheim had been a German army officer in units that killed thousands of Yugoslav patriots and assisted in the deportation of many Greek Jews to concentration camps during the 1940's. Waldheim denied involvement in these actions.

LOOKING IN *Integrity in leadership is vital. Those who desire to lead a nation should have the morality to do so. That's why God gave specific instructions for the qualifications of the future kings of Israel. Hundreds of years before the nation wanted a king, God instructed Moses how those kings should behave. At first glance, the instructions seem strange. However, as they are carefully considered, it soon becomes obvious why God gave certain prohibitions and specific directions. If Israel's kings would have obeyed these directions, things would have turned out differently. We would be wise to apply these principles to our lives as "kings and priests unto God."*

LOOKING OUT

1. **We must learn to wait until God gives us what we want. Israel insisted on a king before God wanted them to have one. God had said they would have a king one day.**
2. **We are to be people of peace, not of conflict. Israelite kings were not to breed horses because they were war animals. Jesus rode on a donkey—an animal of peace.**
3. **We must be careful whom we let into our life. Israelite kings were not to have multiple wives because these women might influence them to worship other gods.**
4. **We are not to be preoccupied with getting wealth. Israelite kings were not to greatly multiply silver and gold, because riches tempt us to trust in them rather than God.**
5. **We are to internalize God's Word. Israelite kings were to keep the Word beside them, read from it every day, and write it out. In doing so, they would internalize God's laws.**

LOOKING UP *Help me, Lord, to realize that I am a king and priest to God. Help me daily to act worthy of my calling. Let me not forget that with privilege comes responsibility.*

SAFEGUARDS

MARCH 5

Deuteronomy 21-23

LOOKING BACK The U.S. Senate convened as a court on this day in 1868 to decide the fate of President Andrew Johnson. He was the first president to be impeached. Johnson became chief executive when Abraham Lincoln was assassinated. The Civil War had just ended. Johnson, a Tennessee Democrat, inherited the wartime dispute between Lincoln and Congress over how to treat the South after the war. Republicans opposed Johnson's views. Congress enacted its policies in spite of his repeated vetoes. The division was so wide that the House of Representatives voted to impeach. But, thankfully, the Senate failed by just one vote to remove Johnson from office.

LOOKING IN *Laws are enacted to prevent destructive actions such as what would have happened to the presidency if Johnson were ousted strictly on political grounds. In the heat of emotions, actions can be taken that could have a dangerous effect. Therefore, laws are designed to lift the highly charged emotions from the issues and deal justly with the matter at hand. God's laws are designed to keep us from things that will destroy us. They are exceedingly fair and wise, based not on emotion but on righteousness. The fact is that we couldn't exist as a society without God's wise safeguards. Rather than resent His laws, we should embrace them.*

LOOKING OUT

1. We are to respect other people's property. God insisted that His people take care of stray animals belonging to neighbors. It is not "finders keepers, losers weepers."
2. We are to help those in need. If an Israelite saw a neighbor struggling to get his animal out of the ditch, he couldn't just pass him by but had to stop to help.
3. We are to respect and appreciate our gender. Israelites were forbidden to cross-dress so they would respect the gender God gave them. Sex was to be a holy expression.
4. We are to be kind to animals. The commandment concerning finding a bird's nest goes to the heart of God's desire that we care for and preserve His great creation.
5. We are to assume responsibility for the safety of others. When building houses, the Israelites were to be careful so others would not hurt themselves on the construction.

LOOKING UP *Help me Lord, to realize my responsibility to others just as I recognize my responsibility to You. May I always embrace Your laws, knowing they are given to me as safeguards.*

RIGHT

MARCH 6

Deuteronomy 24-26

LOOKING BACK The Alamo fell on this day in 1836 after 13 days of fierce fighting. The siege, led by Mexican general Santa Ana, began on February 23 and reached its climax when the last defenders were slain. Some 4,000 Mexican soldiers had attacked the fort, eventually killing the 189 soldiers there. The brave Texans had refused to give up te Alamo because they believed they were defending right and resisting wrong. Texans, under General Sam Houston, soon rallied with the war cry, "Remember the Alamo" and at the battle of San Jacinto, on April 21, defeated and captured Santa Ana, who signed a peace treaty recognizing Texas's independence.

LOOKING IN *It is urgent that we defend right, or wrong will prevail. However, right must be defined by God's Word, not just the opinion of man. The many details of God's law let Israel know what God considers right and wrong. Right is not only how we react and respond to God, but also how we deal with each other. This is clearly defined, especially in the Ten Commandments. The first four of these commandments deal with our relationship with God while the last six outline our relationship with each other. The laws of God always have sound sense behind them, promoting an ordered society in which men can function and thrive.*

LOOKING OUT

1. We must protect human dignity. God's wise rules on punishment and defense are designed to prevent the dehumanizing of the human race.
2. Honesty adds to the quality and quantity of life. This quality makes our life better and assures a longer existence. The Bible says "Righteousness tendeth to life."
3. God hates dirty deals. Moses emphatically reminds the Israelites that God wants honesty in business and fair dealings with our fellow man.
4. We must always be on guard because the evil one seeks to destroy the vulnerable. Amalek was a type of Satan. Moses reminds Israel how he destroyed the vulnerable.
5. We should always remember that evil does not last forever; justice will come. Moses reminds the Israelites that one day they would destroy evil Amalek and his seed.

LOOKING UP *Help me, Lord, to be fair and honest in all my dealings. Let me always honor You by the way I handle my finances and responsibilities.*

MONOPOLY

Deuteronomy 27-28

LOOKING BACK Monopoly, the popular board game produced by Parker Brothers, was introduced on this day in 1935. The concept of Monopoly is that the winner is the one who amasses more monies and property than all other players, thereby eliminating them from the game. The element of chance does play an important part in the game, but also ruthlessness is involved. While Monopoly is only a game, it does tell us much about the condition of the human heart. Perhaps its popularity comes because it plays into man's acquisitive nature. One bumper sticker and T-shirt slogan underlines this flaw in humanity by saying, "The one who dies with the most toys wins."

LOOKING IN *Having possessions and power is not wrong, unless that becomes the driving force of our life. God's Word makes it clear that God desires to bless His obedient children. However, blessings don't come by accident. Rather, they are given by God as a reward for those who follow God passionately. And, blessings do not necessarily mean our having more possessions. Moses told Israel that if the people would just obey God's laws, they would become benefactors of more blessings than they could imagine. With those blessings comes great responsibility. We, who have received so much from God, need to give to others as our appreciation to the Lord.*

LOOKING OUT

1. **The way to the top is down—down on our knees. Moses told Israel that careful obedience to God's laws would result in His exalting them to a high position of influence.**
2. **Blessings do not depend on circumstance but on obedience. God promised Israel that no matter where they found themselves, they would be blessed if they obeyed.**
3. **Our obedience deeply affects our children. God promised that obedient ones would see their children blessed abundantly, because the parent followed God closely.**
4. **Obedience is our best witness. Moses tells the nation that all the peoples of the earth will see that it pays to serve God when we are obedient to His Word and ways.**
5. **We can stay on top if we stay obedient. God promised that as we obey we will always be at the top and not at the bottom. He takes care of us if we are careful to follow Him.**

LOOKING UP *Help me, Lord, to see that obedience makes the most sense of all. Forgive me for my rebellious attitude. Help me to reach out to the needy, because You have blessed me so much.*

DECISIONS

Deuteronomy 29-30

LOOKING BACK Riots in St. Petersburg, Russia, erupted on this day in 1917. They were over shortages of bread and coal in that country. The riots grew more violent until troops were called in to halt the uprising, but they joined it instead. The citizens turned to the Duma for leadership. The Czar, Nicholas II, ordered the Duma to dissolve itself. The parliament ignored his command and established a provisional government. Nicholas had lost all political support. He gave up the throne on March 15, an act that made the Communist Revolution of October possible. Nicholas and his family were imprisoned until Bolshevik revolutionaries murdered them in July of 1918.

LOOKING IN *Decisions have great impact. The Czar's decision to quell riots with bloodshed paved the way for Lenin and his henchmen. God's Word tells us we must be careful about decisions because the paths of life and death loom before us. Our decisions are only as good as the information we have. That is why God carefully gives all the information the Israelites need to make the decisions of their lives. Like a good parent, our Heavenly Father also outlines the consequences of decisions so His children can avoid pain. He then leaves the choices up to us whether we heed His Word or ignore it. We then become responsible for the results.*

LOOKING OUT

1. It's not that we "can't" but because we "won't." The commandments of God are not so difficult that we can't do them. God makes it easy for us to obey Him.
2. God writes His Word all over our world. God put His Word in our hearts, nature, and His book so we can know His desires. Our problem is rebellion, not ignorance.
3. God does not invade our will. Moses notes that God sets before us life and death, and then gives us the choice. He lovingly tells the consequences of choice before we make it.
4. God makes the consequences of our choice so great and grave that we can't possibly miss the point. Our decision whether we serve Him can't be casual or thoughtless.
5. God wants all humanity to be saved. The Creator's heart is bound with His creation. He pleads with the Israelites to make the right decision so they can fellowship with Him.

LOOKING UP *Lord, thank You for giving me the power of choice. May I always make the choices that please You. Teach me Your wisdom so I can make those right decisions.*

CREATIVE

Deuteronomy 31-32

LOOKING BACK Inventor Richard C. Adams died on this day in 1988. Challenged by the shortage of paint brushes during World War II, Adams invented the paint roller in 1940, while working in his basement. The United States had rationed a wide variety of products, including automobiles, gasoline, coffee, sugar, and tires. During a war, people usually earn more money and want to buy more products than they did before. But the armed forces need many of these products. Thus, manufacturers cannot produce enough of the products to satisfy demands. Rather than just complaining about the lack of paint brushes, Adams gave us the now popular paint roller.

LOOKING IN *Creativity was certainly needed as Moses was about to turn over the leadership of Israel to another and pass from the scene. Rather than complain about the situation, Moses goes to God asking for a man who would take the "chosen" ones into the Promised Land. God had already selected Joshua to be that man. Now Moses is instructed to prepare Joshua and the people for the next step in God's great plan for the nation. It would take great courage and strength for the nation to become what God intended. Moses writes a last will and testament in the form of a remarkable song reminding the Israelites of their special place in history.*

LOOKING OUT

1. Leadership should be at God's direction, not our whim. God told Moses that Joshua and he were to appear before Him for Joshua to be commissioned as the new leader.
2. Music teaches. God instructed Moses to compose a song for the Israelites to sing consistently so they would not forget the great lessons of faith they had learned.
3. More have been killed by prosperity than by persecution. God warned that when the Israelites finally arrived in the Promised Land, they would forget God's goodness to them.
4. God knows us thoroughly yet loves us anyway. God knew Israel would fall away from their commitment once inside Canaan, yet He still gave them the Promised Land.
5. Leadership demands strength and courage. God told Joshua that even though He promised the land, still there would be a struggle to wrestle it from His enemies.

LOOKING UP *Help me, Lord, to have strength and courage for the battle I fight for You. Help me to understand that I, too, have a special place in God's plan for history.*

CALLED

MARCH 10

Deuteronomy 33-34

LOOKING BACK Jan Masaryk died mysteriously on this day in 1948. From a window in Prague, Masaryk, the vocal anti-communist Czechoslovakian foreign minister, fell (or was pushed) to his death. He had been fighting a losing battle against the increasing level of communist domination of Czechoslovakia. Masaryk's body was found in a courtyard, three stories under his apartment window in Prague. It has never been determined whether he was murdered or killed himself in protest against the communist seizure of the government in February, 1948. The documented brutality of the communists proves they were capable of orchestrating Massaryk's murder.

LOOKING IN *Evil men of all nations and political persuasions often stop at nothing to grab power, even resorting to murder or assassination. The transfer of power from Moses to Joshua was much different than that in Czechoslovakia and other nations dominated by evil leaders. Moses, about to go to his eternal reward, lovingly anointed Joshua to succeed him. Joshua was probably very reluctant to assume the role of leader, since he had witnessed the great struggles of Moses. Nevertheless, God had called, and he could do nothing but answer that call. Joshua's long preparation under Moses proved to be exactly what was needed for success.*

LOOKING OUT

1. **No matter how good we are, there are still consequences to our misbehavior. Moses was banned from the Promised Land because he had sinned by striking the rock.**
2. **God shares His glory with no man. When Moses died, God buried him in a secret place so the people would not make him a minor deity. They were to worship God only.**
3. **God gives us strength until we complete the task He has assigned. Moses died at age 120, but even at that old age his eyes had not dimmed nor his strength waned.**
4. **God makes His anointing obvious. The people recognized the authority of Joshua because Moses had anointed him to be their leader, and God had put it in their hearts.**
5. **We can have a special relationship with our Lord. Moses spoke face to face with God. Each of us can have a personal relationship with Christ if we sincerely seek it.**

LOOKING UP *Help me, Lord, to have a very personal and special relationship with You. Help me to learn well in the place You have me so that I can fulfill Your plan for my life.*

PANDEMIC

MARCH 11

Joshua 1-2

LOOKING BACK One of the worst global epidemics of influenza occurred in 1918-1919. About 20 million people, including more than 500,000 Americans, died in this epidemic. On this day in 1918, the first cases of "Spanish Influenza" were reported in the U.S. when 107 soldiers became sick at Fort Riley, Kansas. By the end of 1920, nearly 25 percent of the U.S. population had suffered from this deadly flu. World-wide, more than one percent of the population had died in the relentless pandemic. The origin of the flu was never determined, though it started somewhere in Asia. The name "Spanish Influenza" came about because Spain had such a high number of cases.

LOOKING IN *Jericho was to experience something far worse than a pandemic. God was about to strike the city in judgment as His people moved to take over the Promised Land. When Joshua sent spies into the city, he realized that victory could only be achieved by God's help. When the spies returned from Rahab's house, it was more than apparent that God had already been at work to accomplish the dream of the Promised Land. Rahab told the spies that 40 years before, the inhabitants of Jericho knew they would be defeated because they had heard how God had brought Israel through the Red Sea. She wondered what had taken them so long to come.*

LOOKING OUT

1. **God often uses the unlikely and unlovely in His work. Who could have guessed that God would use a prostitute to play a major role in conquering Canaan's first city?**
2. **God always goes before us in battle. Long before the Israelite spies had arrived at Rahab's house, God had been dealing with her concerning the Israelites' destiny.**
3. **We suffer much for our unbelief. The Israelites had spent 40 needless years in the wilderness, not realizing that ever since the Red Sea, the enemy knew he was defeated.**
4. **God always takes care of those who take care of His servants. Rahab and her family would be spared the destruction, because she had reached out to help.**
5. **Faith sees what can be, not what is. The spies returned full of hope saying, "The Lord has surely given the whole land into our hands; all the people are melting in fear..."**

LOOKING UP *Help me to remember, O Lord, that You have already won the victory at Calvary. Satan is now a defeated foe! May I move forth in faith and confidence.*

HERO

Joshua 3-5

LOOKING BACK The Carnegie Hero Fund Commission was established on this day in 1904 with a five-million dollar gift from philanthropist Andrew Carnegie. The Pennsylvania resident was a leading steel manufacturer and one of the wealthiest individuals of his time. He used his huge fortune to establish many cultural, educational, and scientific institutions. The Carnegie Hero Fund Commission gives rewards for bravery. After Carnegie retired, he devoted his time largely to writing and promoting worthy causes. Carnegie donated about $350 million to various causes. He established over 2,500 public libraries throughout the world and the famed Carnegie Hall.

LOOKING IN *If Carnegie's Hero Fund had been functioning during the time of Joshua, Israel's brave leader certainly would have won the prize. Joshua succeeded in taking the Promised Land because he walked with God. He clearly recognized that all his accomplishments were because of Jehovah's goodness. Even though his faith was strong, Joshua still had his anxious moments. One of those times was just before the battle of Jericho. Pacing restlessly, Joshua encountered a heavenly being who assured him that God was with him and would help complete the assigned task. God had already gone before His people preparing the way for their conquest.*

LOOKING OUT

1. **God can strike fear in our enemies' hearts so they will not attack. All the Amorite kings' hearts melted in fear. They no longer had the courage to face the Israelites.**
2. **Success hinges on total dedication to God. Before the battle of Jericho, God commanded Joshua to circumcise the Israelites as a sign of their complete dedication to God.**
3. **God's provisions are always enough. For 40 years, the Israelites had feasted on heaven-sent manna. Now that they were entering the Promised Land, the manna stopped.**
4. **God doesn't come to take sides but to take over. The angel of the Lord told Joshua that He had come to take charge in the battle facing God's people.**
5. **Hard times are often the best times. Joshua learned he was standing on holy ground. This was the most difficult time in his life because of the battle he was to soon face.**

LOOKING UP *Help me, Lord, to remember Your provision is enough. When you close one door, You open another. Make me strong in my determination to do the task You have assigned to me.*

DIRECTION

MARCH 13

Joshua 6-8

LOOKING BACK The first Bible ever printed was completed on this day in 1462. The first books printed in Europe by movable type appeared in Mainz, Germany, between 1453 and 1456. There, Johannes Gutenberg and his associates worked to develop the printing process. One of the first books printed was a Bible in Latin, which appeared on March 13, 1462. It became known as the Gutenberg Bible, though Johann Fust and Peter Schoffer probably printed it. They printed about 150 copies, of which 21 complete copies still exist. That first Bible required six men to set the type and several months to produce. It would have an enormous impact on the world.

LOOKING IN *We are at a tremendous advantage because we have the Bible and are able to read it whenever we want. Joshua and the leaders of ancient Israel didn't have the advantage we know. When important decisions had to be made, Joshua was forced to carefully seek the face of God, lest disaster follow. For the most part he succeeded in this effort and led the nation well. It was especially critical for Joshua to know how to conquer Jericho because the walled city seemed impregnable. When God did give Joshua the instructions, they probably seemed strange and unproductive. However, Joshua knew he had to follow them explicitly if he was to gain victory.*

LOOKING OUT

1. **God gives us counsel when we ask. Joshua is given specific details on how he and Israel can conquer the walled city of Jericho.**
2. **God never asks us to do more than we can. Jericho covered 8.5 acres. That meant that the Israelites could walk around it just as God instructed.**
3. **God can confuse our enemies when we pray. The military brilliance of Israel's enemies was lost completely whenever God intervened.**
4. **God fights for us when we fight for Him. In one battle, the hailstones that God sent killed more of the enemy than Israel's warriors.**
5. **We can expect miracles when we go with God. When Joshua prayed, the sun stood still, contrary to all the laws of nature. Israel gained a great victory.**

LOOKING UP *Help me, Lord, to seek your face in the battles I fight. May I always remember that spiritual battles can only be won by using spiritual weapons.*

DECEIVED

MARCH 14

Joshua 9-10

LOOKING BACK Albert Einstein, one of the greatest scientists of all time, was born on this day in 1879. He is best known for his theory of relativity, which he first advanced when he was only 26 years old. He also made many other contributions to science. Einstein's relativity theory revolutionized scientific thought with new conceptions of time, space, mass, motion, and gravitation. He treated matter and energy as exchangeable, not distinct. In so doing, he laid the basis for controlling the release of energy from the atom. Many believe Einstein to be the most brilliant man of this, and the last, century. He died at Princeton, New Jersey, on April 18, 1955.

LOOKING IN *Brilliance doesn't necessarily equate with wisdom. Joshua, too, was brilliant. However, he wasn't always wise. This became obvious when the devious Gibeonites showed up asking for a peace treaty with the invading Israelites. The people of Gibeon concocted a deceptive strategy to protect themselves from the Israelites. Pretending to be foreigners also, the Gibeonites made a treaty with Joshua. When Joshua later discovered the truth, he forced the Gibeonites to become water carriers and woodcutters for the Israelites. Nevertheless, Joshua had to honor the covenant and was forced to lead Israel against the armies of five kings who had attacked Gibeon.*

LOOKING OUT

1. Opposition intensifies as we press closer to the promise. When the kings west of Jordan heard of Israel's great victories, they made an alliance to destroy God's people.
2. We must stay alert lest we be tricked by the enemy. The Gibeonites slyly circumvented God's directions to Israel by fooling the leaders who relied on their own discernment.
3. Prayerlessness is dangerous. Israel's leaders were fooled because they "did not inquire of the Lord." When we pray, God gives wisdom so we won't be fooled by the enemy.
4. We must keep our word even if it's painful. Israel's leaders had given their word, so they couldn't back out on the promise they had given to protect the Gibeonites.
5. God helps us make the best of a bad situation. The Gibeonites were made servants to Israel—not an ideal situation but the best solution to the problem.

LOOKING UP *Help me remember, Lord, to pray about all decisions I face lest I be deceived by the enemy of my soul. May I never become spiritually lethargic.*

BATTLES

Joshua 11-14

LOOKING BACK Today is the famed "Ides of March" Julius Caesar was warned about. Caesar, one of ancient Rome's greatest generals and statesmen, helped make Rome the center of an empire that stretched across Europe. His victories in civil war made him dictator of the Roman people, but his power frightened many of his political opponents. Even though Caesar refused the crown, many Romans suspected he intended to make himself king one day. Marcus Junius Brutus and Gaius Cassius, both pardoned by Caesar after the battle of Pharsalus, led aristocrats in an assassination plot. On March 15 (the Ides of March), 44 B.C., they stabbed Caesar to death.

LOOKING IN *Joshua was one of Israel's greatest leaders, but his fate was far different than Caesar's. The Israelites had no fear of Joshua because of his great devotion to God. The great leader would die peacefully after having conquered Canaan. He had done all God assigned him to do, and the land rested. Joshua was one of the greatest leaders Israel ever had. Jesus was named after this "captain of salvation" who led the ragtag nation into the Promised Land. Perhaps the greatest mistake Joshua made was in failing to appoint a successor, as Moses had done before. This void in leadership ushered the nation into the tragic period of the judges.*

LOOKING OUT

1. **We must not fear overwhelming odds. The more victories Joshua won, the more opposition appeared. God told him not to be afraid of those who joined others to oppose Israel.**
2. **While we fight, it's God who gives the victory. The Israelites had to engage in battle, but the Lord gave them victory. God always works miracles, not magic!**
3. **We are to completely defeat the foe. Joshua's job was not done until all enemies were subjected. We must never make peace with those things that would destroy our souls.**
4. **Many battles are long and hard, but we must faithfully fight on. Joshua waged wars against the enemies of God for a long time. We must not give up when we become weary.**
5. **Rest comes only after we have completely done God's will. After Joshua had completed his assignment, rest from war came on the land. Our rest is still to come.**

LOOKING UP *Lord, help me stand firm in determination to conquer in battles I face. Help me to be strong and brave. May I follow Your direction and will in every detail of my life.*

SPIRIT

MARCH 16

Joshua 15-17

LOOKING BACK James Madison, fourth President of the United States, was born on this day in 1751. Often called the Father of the Constitution, he helped design the checks and balances that operate among Congress, the President, and the Supreme Court. He also helped create the U.S. federal system, which divides power between the central government and the states. In his younger years Madison had spent six months studying Hebrew, philosophy, and other subjects to enter the ministry, but a weak speaking voice prevented him from doing so. He turned to politics and was active to the end of a long life. In old age Madison was president of the University of Virginia.

LOOKING IN *Like Madison, Caleb didn't believe in retirement. Even in old age Caleb remained vitally active in the affairs of Israel. He went to, and won, a battle long after his 80th birthday. Caleb's faith in God gave him strength to the very end. God's Word promises that old age will not deter those who serve Him. The Bible says, "The righteous will flourish like a palm tree, they will grow like a cedar of Lebanon; planted in the house of the LORD, they will flourish in the courts of our God. They will still bear fruit in old age, they will stay fresh and green..." (Psalm 92:12-14). The remarkable life of Caleb reminds us that God will fulfill this wonderful promise.*

LOOKING OUT

1. God is faithful to fulfill His promises. Many years had passed, but Caleb was not forgotten. He was given an inheritance because he had believed God some 40 years before.
2. Faith earns us a special position. Caleb was not of Judah's tribe but was given land in their assignment because he had stood with Joshua against the 10 doubting spies.
3. We are never too old to do great exploits for God. Caleb drove out the hostile Anakites to take his land even though he was well into his 80's. Faith gave him special strength.
4. Good leaders challenge others to great deeds. Caleb challenged Othniel to capture Kiriath Sepher by offering his daughter as a prize. Othniel rose to the challenge.
5. Good people are giving people. Caleb showed his gracious spirt by giving the upper and lower springs to his daughter. If we love, we give, and in giving we are godly.

LOOKING UP *Help me, Lord, to have the same spirit Caleb had. May I be full of faith and courage despite my age. Help me never to grow old in spirit even as I age in body.*

ALLOCATION

Joshua 18-21

LOOKING BACK Jim Bridger—hunter, trapper, fur trader, guide, and one of the greatest American frontiersmen—was born on this day in 1804. While searching for furs in the Rocky Mountains in 1824, Bridger became probably the first white person ever to see the Great Salt Lake. He and a friend rediscovered the South Pass of the Rocky Mountains, and he was one of the first white people to see the wonders of the area that became Yellowstone National Park. Bridger's vast geographical knowledge proved invaluable when the overland stage routes were planned. He climaxed a useful career by scouting for explorers and the U.S. army. Bridger died on July 17, 1881.

LOOKING IN *Like Bridger, Joshua was a great scout, exploring places his people had never been. During his long life, Israel's leader brought them into the Promised Land and allocated sections of the new country to the 12 tribes. The purpose of the careful allocation was to prevent conflict among the tribes and to assign responsibility for the welfare of the land. They were to be satisfied with what God had given them, rather than trying to expand their borders to gain more wealth and resources. By respecting these borders, each tribe would become a good neighbor and would maximize the use of its own land. Joshua carefully and prayerfully made these decisions.*

LOOKING OUT

1. **Our work is not done until total victory is ours. Joshua and Israel had conquered much of the land. However, seven Israelite tribes still had not received what God had promised.**
2. **There is a time to wait and a time to move. Joshua asked, "How long will you wait before you begin to take possession of the land?" It was now time for them to move.**
3. **Victory demands a good plan. Joshua not only told the Israelites to move on to possess the land but also laid out a careful plan to help them accomplish the task.**
4. **All our decisions should be made "in the presence of the Lord." Joshua was careful to record that the allocation to the tribes was decided while in the presence of God.**
5. **Spiritual leaders are to exercise powerful influence. The Levites were given land and supported by the people to assure continued strong spiritual emphasis for the nation.**

LOOKING UP *Lord, teach me when it is right to wait and right to move on in faith. Always help me follow You carefully. May I remember that You have allocated a place for me to do Your will.*

"NO!"

MARCH 18

Joshua 22-24

LOOKING BACK Grover Cleveland was born on this day in 1837. He was the only President who served two terms that did not directly follow each other. Cleveland won the presidency in 1884 but lost it four years later to Benjamin Harrison. He ran against Harrison again in 1892 and won a second term. As President, Cleveland had the courage to say "No!" He said it often—to farmers who sought easy money to pay their debts, to manufacturers who wanted high protective tariffs, and to veterans who wanted bigger pensions. While these "Nos" made Cleveland very unpopular in his time, they have added to the respect in which history holds him.

LOOKING IN *Saying "No!" is not always easy and many times means that we stand against the crowd. Mobs often form and perpetuate violence because there is no one with the courage to stand up against popular opinion. That happened in Israel when two-and-a-half tribes constructed a shrine on the wrong side of the Jordan. Popular opinion was that they were building the altar to compete with the shrine God had instructed them to make for the entire nation. In anger, the offended mob determined to go to war over the issue. However, wisdom prevailed. Someone said, "No! Let's get more information before we raid our brothers." That decision spared Israel a civil war.*

LOOKING OUT

1. **Affirmation develops faith and faithfulness. Joshua was careful to affirm the faithfulness of the two-and-a-half tribes, saying they had done all that Moses had requested.**
2. **Our good can be misunderstood. The two-and-a-half tribes built an altar near the Jordan. Their motivation was misunderstood and raised the ire of other tribes.**
3. **Decisions made before all the facts are known endanger us. The angry tribes pushed for war against the two-and-a-half tribes before they knew the reasons for building the altar.**
4. **Wisdom demands we get more information. Rather than react rashly, the Israelites responded rightly by sending a delegation to find out why the altar was built.**
5. **Communication builds bridges of understanding rather than walls of opposition. The Israelites learned the two-and-a-half tribes had constructed the altar for a good purpose.**

LOOKING UP *Help me, Lord, to remember that jumping to conclusions isn't good exercise. Help me to really hear all the issues before acting. My decisions are only as good as the information I have.*

LAWLESSNESS

MARCH 19

Judges 1-2

LOOKING BACK Wyatt Earp was born on this day in 1848. The famed gunslinger is best known for the gunfight at the O.K. Corral in Tombstone, Arizona. Earp was a deputy United States marshal in 1881, when a feud developed between Ike Clanton's criminal gang and three of the Earp brothers—Wyatt, Virgil, and Morgan. Virgil was Tombstone's marshal. The feud peaked in October, when the Earps and their friend Doc Holliday shot to death three of Clanton's gang at the O.K. Corral. The Earps said they were trying to make an arrest. Others said it was murder. The fact is that Tombstone was a lawless town where murder and mayhem reigned.

LOOKING IN *Lawlessness is the keynote of the whole book of Judges. From the first to last chapter there are criminals, along with rather dubious heros. Joshua had failed to appoint a spiritual leader for the nation as Moses had done. When Joshua died, the nation drifted into sin and bondage. This void in leadership fomented rebellion and divisiveness, making the nation vulnerable to attack from their enemies. Soon oppression and bloodshed filled the land. However, when the people repented and sought God, He raised up judges or "deliverers" to bring them out of bondage and bring them back to God. This cycle of sin-sorrow-salvation continues throughout the book.*

LOOKING OUT

1. **Left leaderless, we have a tendency to stray. Judges starts with the acknowledgment that Joshua did not leave Israel with a strong leader as Moses had done years before.**
2. **Praise should precede all petition and spiritual warfare. When Israel asked who should go first in war, the answer was Judah. This tribe was the "praiser" of the nation.**
3. **We are to help our brothers in their conflict. The tribe of Judah asked the Simeonites to help them. God expects us to reach out with assistance to others in their bitter battles.**
4. **When we go with God, we always win. Judah and Simeon went to battle against the Canaanites and Perizzites. They won that conflict because God gave them victory.**
5. **We reap what we sow. When Adoni-Bezek was captured and mutilated, he admitted he had done the same to 70 others. He had done to him what he had done to others.**

LOOKING UP *Help me, Lord, to be a "praiser." I know there is power in relying on You to help me win all my battles. Help me to always be obedient to You and avoid "lawlessness."*

MASTERING

MARCH 20

Judges 3-5

LOOKING BACK He wanted to be remembered as a great president but history will probably deny him that title. Lyndon Baines Johnson, like three other vice-presidents in United States history, became chief executive upon the assassination of the nation's leader. He rose to the presidency on Nov. 22, 1963, following the fatal shooting of President John F. Kennedy on a street in Dallas, Texas. A stunned nation rallied behind the energetic and ambitious new president, a product of the Texas hill country. Reflecting on the tragic events surrounding the assassination, Johnson said on this day in 1965, "A nation is molded by the tests that its people meet and master."

LOOKING IN *Many times tests come because God orchestrates them. The book of Judges says, "These are the nations the LORD left to test all those Israelites who had not experienced any of the wars in Canaan..." The writer of Judges then goes on to explain the reason for these tests, "He did this only to teach warfare to the descendants of the Israelites who had not had previous battle experience." Tests are seldom welcomed and always hard. Yet, through these testing times, we learn more than we could in any other situation. Testing times are also growing times as we learn the extent of our own commitment, weakness, and utter dependence on God.*

LOOKING OUT

1. **There is always a test. Even though the Israelites were finally in the Promised Land, God still had prepared tests for them.**
2. **Tests always have a reason. Israel's new generation had not learned to depend on God when the chips were down. It was a critical lesson they had to internalize.**
3. **Tests always have a purpose. God used the conflicts the Israelites faced to teach his children how to fight the enemies of God.**
4. **Tests reveal the depth of our faith. Stress revealed whether the Israelites would follow the commandments of God fully or lean on their own understanding.**
5. **Failing God's tests brings sorrow to ourselves and others. The Israelites married foreigners who corrupted their faith and drew them away from God. Pain always followed.**

LOOKING UP *Help me, Lord, to remember that the trial or temptation that I am facing right now is only a test. Give me strength to endure it and the wisdom to learn from it.*

VIEWPOINT

MARCH 21

Judges 6-8

March

LOOKING BACK German composer Johann Sebastian Bach was born on this day in 1685. He is considered one of the greatest musical geniuses of all time. Bach's career is one of the wonders of music. In addition to supporting a large family and fulfilling his many duties as a musician and conductor, he wrote hundreds of compositions, including nearly 300 religious and nonreligious choral works called cantatas. Bach was born in Eisenach, Germany, and his parents died before he was 10. In 1707, he married his cousin, Maria Barbara. They had seven children before she died. A year later, he married again and had 13 children with this wife. Bach developed serious eye trouble, and in his last years he was nearly blind. He died of a stroke in 1750 at age 65.

LOOKING IN *Looking at Bach's upbringing and circumstances, one would not think he could rise to the towering peak that he did. There was nothing remarkable about him, but God had gifted Bach with unusual talent. Gideon, too, came from a very ordinary family. Until that fateful day he was visited by an angel who addressed him as a "mighty man of valor," Gideon thought of himself as a helpless slave to a oppressive and angry people. However, God's viewpoint of Gideon was quite different. God saw Gideon not for what he was but for what he could become when he gave himself to God. It took some persuading but finally the genius in Gideon came out.*

LOOKING OUT

1. There is seldom change without pain—the greater the pain, the greater the change. Midian brutally oppressed Israel until the nation cried out to God. He sent Gideon to them.
2. God sees us as we can be, not as we are. Gideon saw himself as a helpless victim but God saw him as a valiant warrior. We seldom know our potential but God does.
3. The "why?" question is seldom answered because the "what now?" question is far more important. God ignores Gideon's "why?"question and tells him to get busy.
4. Self-correction must occur before we move to correct others. Gideon had to destroy the idol in his own house before bringing the nation to deliverance and revival.
5. Fleeces do not necessarily indicate lack of faith but can be a sincere desire to be certain of God's calling. Gideon wanted to know absolutely what God wanted of him.

LOOKING UP *Help me, Lord, to view myself as You view me rather than being preoccupied with my "I can'ts."Help me to remember that with You I am a majority.*

ANIMOSITY

MARCH 22

Judges 9-11

LOOKING BACK The first Indian massacre in America almost wiped out the settlements near Jamestown, Virginia, 378 years ago today. Colonists and Indians got along well at first, as the English treated the various Indian tribes as independent powers and bought land from them by treaties. But mistrust gradually developed between the colonists and Indians, and minor incidents flared into wars. On March 22, 1622, Chief Opechancanough led a furious assault along a 140-mile front, killing 347 colonists. The survivors retreated to Jamestown and laid plans to massacre the Indians. Twelve horrible and brutal years of warfare followed.

LOOKING IN *Much as the Indians must have felt, the Ammonites resented the Israelites in their land. After all, the Ammonites had been there for decades and now the Israelites were invading their territory. Tempers flared and brutal, bloody incidents occurred. The Ammonites were determined to destroy God's people. The only leader Israel could find to deliver them was Jephthah, a despised exile whom they had to ask to come back to help them. Jephthah was a burning shame to his proud family. However, when threatened with extinction, the clan members swallowed their pride and begged for help. Jephthah fought, and won, a great victory.*

LOOKING OUT

1. **Our background doesn't doom us to defeat. Jephthah was the illegitimate son of his father with a prostitute and was hated by his half–brothers, who drove him away from home.**
2. **We must be careful whom we step on going up the ladder of success because we will meet them coming down. Jephthah's half brothers had to beg for Jephthah's help.**
3. **When we are anointed by God for a task, no one can stop us. Jephthah was obviously selected by God to lead Israel. Even though he was at first rejected, he rose to leadership.**
4. **Negotiations should be the first step in trying to settle problems. Jephthah tried to persuade the Ammonites to settle their dispute peacefully but they refused to do so.**
5. **When we try to make deals with God, we always lose. Foolishly, Jephthah tried to bribe God to attain victory. He paid a dear price—the loss of his daughter's future.**

LOOKING UP *Help me, Lord, to be careful how I treat those with whom I disagree. It just might be that I may need their help one day.*

DECISIONS

MARCH 23

Judges 12-15

LOOKING BACK Decision can have a devastating impact on our future. On this day in 1933, the German Reichstag voted to give dictatorial powers to the Nazi regime under the leadership of Adolf Hitler. At the time it didn't seem like such a great decision. However, history reveals that it turned out to be horrendous. Discontented Germans had turned to Nazism in increasing numbers because the party promised economic help, political power, and national glory. Hitler's fiery personality and talents as an orator also had a strong influence. That decision, made on this day decades ago, plunged the world into a bloody war, resulting in the deaths of millions.

LOOKING IN *It wasn't just one decision but a series of decisions that ruined Samson. This gifted God-ordained man had it all but wasted it all because he could not control his passions. Because he was so strong and virile, Samson thought he could get away with what he wanted. For 20 years he lived as he wished and cared little about consequences. But it all caught up with him. His continuing selfish decisions had a devastating effect. He took what he wanted and went where he wished, relying on his physical strength and magnetic personality. However, his lustful decisions finally brought him down. We don't break God's laws—we are broken on them.*

LOOKING OUT

1. God raises up special people for special times in history. Even before Samson was born, God began preparing him for the unique task of delivering Israel from the Philistines.
2. It is easier to see God in retrospect than in the raw reality of the present. Only after the angel did not reappear, did Manoah and his wife realize who had visited them.
3. We are internally programmed for our destiny as God's Spirit stirs us. As Samson grew into maturity, God's Spirit began to prod him toward God's plans for his life.
4. The rough road of rebellion starts with the smooth path of selfishness. Tragically, Samson had a fatal flaw—self indulgence. This would be his downfall in years to come.
5. When we are ruled by emotions rather than by God's Word, sorrow results. Samson knew God's law but chose to ignore it. This decision would eventually destroy him.

LOOKING UP *Help me, Lord, to keep my emotions and passions in check, lest I follow my lustful desires and lose my whole future and family.*

HANGING ON

MARCH 24

Judges 16-18

LOOKING BACK John Wesley Powell was born on this day in 1834. In 1869, this American geologist led the first expedition down the canyons of the Green and Colorado rivers. Powell and his men nearly drowned in the raging waters. After one of his crew died while shooting the rapids, three others abandoned the group. They determined to walk out, saying Powell could never make it through the canyon. However, Powell's crew discovered the rapids they had just traversed were the last in the canyon. The three who left the Powell party were never seen or heard from again. Powell became the first white person to go through the vast canyon, which he named the Grand Canyon.

LOOKING IN *We must never give up too soon. Perhaps that is what Samson did. For 20 years, he had strutted across the pages of Israel's history, leading the nation as he wished. Then Delilah brought him down. It wasn't actually that haircut in the lap of his mistress that did Samson in. Rather, it was his own unchecked lust and selfishness through the years. God's Spirit had left His disobedient servant and Samson became like any other man. Now, blind, depressed, and enslaved, Samson killed himself. If he would have just thrown himself on God's great mercy, he still might have had a good future because God is always restoring what the devil destroys.*

LOOKING OUT

1. **Immorality weakens us even if its effects are not immediately felt. Samson spent the night with a prostitute, another step in his rapidly increasing downward slide.**
2. **Our choice of intimates shapes our destiny. Samson fell in love with Delilah, a woman without loyalty or morals. She would soon prove to be the death of him.**
3. **Lust blinds us to good judgment. Samson should have seen Delilah's obvious intent. However, he was so caught up in his raging passion that his good sense was blunted.**
4. **Sin so desensitizes us that we can't even know when God's Spirit departs from us. Years of rebellious living had seared Samson's conscience, blunting spiritual sensitivity.**
5. **The end of sin is always death. For 20 years, Samson had gotten away with his lustful living. However, payday always comes. He was blinded, brutalized, and a suicide victim.**

LOOKING UP *Help me to remember, Lord, that immorality is not entertainment; it is death. Keep me pure before You! Help me not to give up too soon but always to hold onto You.*

CRUELTIES

Judges 19-21

LOOKING BACK On this day in 1944, Nazis occupying Rome executed 300 Italian priests, Jews, and women, and two 14-year-old boys. This senseless brutality was in retaliation for the deaths of 33 German soldiers killed by Italian partisans. Adolf Hitler had demanded 50 Italian lives for each German life, but German officials in Italy lowered the number. While his empire lasted, Hitler murdered about six million Jews—over two-thirds of the Jews of Europe. More than three million Soviet prisoners of war were starved and worked to death. Hitler's victims also included large numbers of gypsies, Poles, Slavs, Christians, mental patients, and Communists.

LOOKING IN *Brutality and mayhem result when strong spiritual leadership is missing. Israel learned this during the tragic time of the judges. As long as good and godly persons ruled the land, peace and safety existed. However, devoid of spiritual influence, the nation turned to unspeakable cruelties. The book of Judges must be read and understood in the light of what happens to a people when they forget God and fail to respond to His discipline. God's laws are given so that we can know Him and also learn to live together in society. When we disregard these instructions, we open ourselves and our loved ones to horrendous evils.*

LOOKING OUT

1. **Sin may start as a small spark, but it sets the world on fire. The Benjamites' sin erupted into a massive civil war. There are always grave consequences to our bad behavior.**
2. **Sin affects more than the sinner. The tragic rape of the Levite's concubine affected the whole nation. Our sin doesn't just hurt us, but all those we love and who love us.**
3. **Correction comes only if we go to God. The Israelites built an altar and presented burnt offerings and sacrifices in their sorrow. This was the first step in returning to God.**
4. **Death and destruction reign when we try to do things our way. The Israelites brutally massacred the people of Jabesh-Gilead, sparing only 400 virgins for Benjamin's tribe.**
5. **Without strong spiritual leadership the nation goes to pot. The sad epitaph of the Book of Judges is, "In those days Israel had no king; everyone did as he saw fit."**

LOOKING UP *Help me understand, Lord, that my sin doesn't simply affect me but many other innocent people. Help me to communicate how important it is to hear and heed God's Word.*

NEW LIFE

MARCH 26

Ruth 1-4

LOOKING BACK Soviet Cosmonaut Serge Krikalev returned to a new country on this day in 1992. After spending 313 days in space in the Soviet Mir space station, Krikalev returned to earth to find the Soviet Union no longer existed and in its place was the Commonwealth of Independent States. Originally scheduled in October, 1991, the cosmonaut's return was delayed by five months due to his country's disintegration and the ensuing monetary problems. For 74 years, the people had suffered under the oppressive Soviet empire. Now, suddenly, that was all changed as a new breath of freedom swept the land.

LOOKING IN *Just as the oppression and pain of the Russian people under the Soviets didn't last forever, so Naomi's and Ruth's great sorrows had their end. Naomi, Orpah, and Ruth had suffered devastating losses when their husbands died. While Orpah decided to return to her parent's home, Ruth chose to accompany Naomi back to Bethlehem. It was a good decision because the Lord would use the new land to give her a new life. These shattered widows entered Bethlehem filled with woe and bemoaning their fate. However, God had good things planned for them in spite of their feelings. They would soon find that pain doesn't last forever.*

LOOKING OUT

1. There is still tenderness in the times of trial and sorrow. Even though the Book of Judges depicts the awful sin in the land, still there were people around like Ruth and Boaz.
2. Sorrow can blind us to God's goodness. Even though Naomi had suffered immeasurable loss, God had good plans for her, even if she felt there was no use going on.
3. God is always watchful over us and provides what is best for us. It was not by accident that Ruth began to reap in the fields of Boaz. God had especially directed her there.
4. Selflessness is richly rewarded by our watching God. Ruth had given up her homeland and probably her family to go with the grieving Naomi. Now God gave her Boaz.
5. God gives us joy in proportion to our sorrow. Both Ruth and Naomi were blessed when baby Obed was born. The great sorrows of the past fade in the joys of the present.

LOOKING UP *Help me to know, Lord, that today's sorrow will not last forever. The resurrection comes! May I continue to trust You even though my feelings are raw and my tears great.*

BIRTHDAY

1 Samuel 1-3

LOOKING BACK Happy birthday today to the woman who wrote "Happy Birthday." Patty Smith Hill was born in 1868. She, a schoolteacher and author, wrote the lyrics of the song, "Good Morning To All," which later became known as "Happy Birthday To You." Her older sister, Mildred J. Hill, composed the melody for the song, which was first published in 1893 as a classroom greeting in the book, *Song Stories for Sunday School*. Eleven years after writing the song, Hill added a stanza beginning with "Happy Birthday to You." It wasn't long before that simple song became the most frequently sung song in the world. Patty Smith Hill died in 1946 at age 78.

LOOKING IN *It was certainly a happy birthday for Hannah who, after long years of praying, gave birth to little Samuel. Hannah's life had been hard. Her husband loved her dearly and she loved her husband. However, her deepest desire to become a mother had not been realized. Hannah went before God in passionate prayer, and the loving Heavenly Father heard her pleas. She promised God that she would give her boy back to Him if He healed her of barrenness. God faithfully kept His promise to her and the last judge of Israel was born. Hannah was careful to keep her oath to God. To her surprise and delight, God honored her with more children.*

LOOKING OUT

1. **Faithful worship reaps rich rewards. Samuel's parents went faithfully to Shiloh each year to worship God. It was there that God made a beautiful promise to them.**
2. **No matter how much we are loved, if our life's dream is unfulfilled there is an awful void. Elkanah loved Hannah totally, but it was not enough. She wanted a son.**
3. **At times, even our spiritual leaders misunderstand the burden of our hearts. Eli mistook Hannah's desperate prayers as drunkenness. He was dead wrong.**
4. **God always keeps His promises. Just as God promised, Hannah gave birth to a son, whom she was determined to give back to God as an offering of thanksgiving.**
5. **God always rewards us when we keep our word. Hannah gave Samuel to the Lord as she had promised. God graciously gave her three more sons and two daughters.**

LOOKING UP *Help me to be faithful in my worship, Lord, because I know that this greatly pleases You. May I always remember that as I submit to Your perfect will, things turn out well for me.*

REVIVAL

MARCH 28

1 Samuel 4-7

LOOKING BACK A series of accidents beginning at 4 am, EST, at Three Mile Island on the Susquehanna River in Pennsylvania, occurred on this day in 1979. Located 10 miles southeast of Harrisburg, the nuclear facility seemed safe enough. The accident occurred with overheating, caused by an interruption in the reactor's cooling system, resulting in severe damage to a reactor core. However, a protective building that contained the reactor largely prevented the radioactive debris from being released into the environment. The accident was responsible for extensive reevaluation of the safety of existing nuclear power generating operations.

LOOKING IN *Tragedies often make us reevaluate existing circumstances and the way we live. That happened with Israel long ago. For 20 frustrating years, the precious Ark of the Covenant had been kept from them. This was a great tragedy because the Ark symbolized God's presence among His people. For these two decades, the people prayed for the Ark to be restored. In answer to those prayers, God raised up Samuel to lead the repentant nation in a revival that would rectify many old wrongs and get the nation started out on the right foot again. Israel found that God is always willing to restore His people to fellowship when they humbly come back to Him.*

LOOKING OUT

1. **Prayers are not always answered immediately. Israel prayed for 20 years that the Ark of the Covenant be restored to them before it came back.**
2. **Halfhearted repentance never works. Samuel wanted to make sure the Israelites turned to God with all their hearts.**
3. **God wants exclusive place in our hearts. Samuel said that not only must Israel turn from idols, but they had to serve God exclusively.**
4. **Public confession underlines our intent. Samuel poured water on the ground to indicate to the nation that there was no turning back on their commitment.**
5. **Revival is always challenged by the evil one. Satan stirred up the Philistines to attack Israel. The evil one can't stand to see revival among the saints.**

LOOKING UP *Help me, Lord, to persevere in my prayers, knowing that You forget none of them. May I give You my whole heart, holding back nothing from You.*

PERCEPTION

1 Samuel 8-10

LOOKING BACK Perception sometimes is more endearing than reality. English astrologer John Partridge so offended readers by his foolish predictions that he became the target of parodies and jokes. The most serious was that of satirist Jonathan Swift. Under the pseudonym Isaac Bickerstaff, Swift published his own almanac for the year 1708, in which he predicted that Partridge would die at 11 p.m., March 29, 1708, of a "raging fever." Poor Partridge made the mistake of trying to prove he was still alive, only to find that writers, citizens, and even the court were more amused by continuing the fiction of his death. Fiction was more appealing to them than fact.

LOOKING IN *Israel was in love with the perception that a king would be good for their country. When Samuel's evil sons gave them excuse to demand a king, the elders of Israel rose to the occasion. Samuel tried to inject a dose of reality but they refused to listen. He told them a king would levy heavy taxes against them, draft their sons into army service, causing many of them to be killed, and would enlist their daughters in demeaning services. However, the stubborn elders were sure that Samuel was merely trying to protect his turf. They preferred their own fantasy to the facts laid out by God's servant. Later, they would see how wrong they were.*

LOOKING OUT

1. **Nepotism is bad if the relatives are corrupt. Samuel appointed his two sons as judges of Israel, but both of them were evil rebels. God's people rejected their appointment.**
2. **We must not grab too quickly what God has for us. God planned to give Israel a king (Deuteronomy 17) but the people wanted it instantly. In doing so, they rejected God.**
3. **God will give us what we want but sometimes we may not want what we get. God told Samuel to warn Israel of the difficulties they would face if they got a king.**
4. **Rebellion never listens to reason. Even though Samuel faithfully relayed God's message to Israel, they stubbornly insisted they wanted a king immediately, if not sooner.**
5. **What looks good on the outside may not be good for us. Saul had all the physical characteristics of a king but would prove to be a disaster for Israel. They should have waited.**

LOOKING UP *Lord, help me learn to wait for your gifts at Your time rather than insisting on them in my time. Make me listen to Your Word no matter how it goes against what I want.*

MISTAKES

MARCH 30

1 Samuel 11-13

LOOKING BACK The lead pencil with attached eraser was patented on this day in 1858. It is the most widely used writing and drawing instrument in the world. Some pencils write underwater, and others are used by physicians to mark their patients' skin before surgery. Astronauts take pencils into space because they are unaffected by gravity, pressure, or conditions in the atmosphere. More than 10 billion pencils are produced annually throughout the world. The United States alone manufactures almost 2 billion pencils yearly—more than any other country. One of the best things to ever happen to pencils was when the simple eraser was added to it.

LOOKING IN *Mistakes are part of the human experience, making erasers necessary. Thankfully, God has a big eraser for our sins if we honestly face them rather than trying to excuse our behavior. Saul's problem was that he always tried to justify his sins rather than deal honestly with them. That stubborn trait eventually cost him the kingdom and his life. If only he would have turned to God and stopped trying to excuse his behavior, Saul would have been saved and the history of Israel would have been quite different. Tragically, Saul could not admit his mistakes, much less his sins. That fatal fault would forever eliminate him from God's hall of heros.*

LOOKING OUT

1. **When we trust in ourselves rather than God, we fade in fear when overwhelmed. Saul's men looked to their own resources and when the Philistines amassed, some ran away.**
2. **God makes His instructions very clear so we know what to do. Samuel clearly told Saul that he would come to make the sacrifice demanded before battle. Saul was to wait.**
3. **When we look to circumstances rather than to God, we often panic. When Saul saw his army melting away he stepped in to make the sacrifice—an act clearly forbidden.**
4. **Real repentance is refusing to give excuses but facing what we have done wrong. Saul tried to excuse his behavior by blaming the circumstances. It wouldn't wash with God.**
5. **God wants His leaders to seek His heart, not their own advantage. Saul lost the throne because he was more interested in his agenda than in what God wanted.**

LOOKING UP *Help me, Lord, to look to You and carefully obey all of Your clear instructions for my life. Help me to be wise enough to admit my mistakes and ask forgiveness for my sins.*

IMPOSSIBLE

1 Samuel 14-15

LOOKING BACK In 1903, on this day, Richard Pearse did what many people thought was impossible. Pearse was a farmer and inventor who flew a monoplane of his own design several hundred yards along a road near Temuka, New Zealand, and then landed it on top of a 12-foot 1–1 high hedge. Pearse had built the craft, which consisted of a steerable tricycle undercarriage and an internal combustion engine. He, arguably, made the first powered airplane flight. It wasn't until December 17, 1903, that Orville and Wilbur Wright—two American bicycle makers—made what most believe to be the first successful powered airplane flights in history near Kitty Hawk, North Carolina.

LOOKING IN *Man's genius helps him do many wonderful things. Sometimes man can accomplish what most think is impossible just as Pearse did. However, there is a limit over which he cannot go. Yet, with God, all things are possible. Jonathan and his armor bearer learned they could do the impossible with God. While the Israelite army quaked in fear of the enemy, Jonathan and his armor bearer proved that with God they were in the majority. God honors the faith of those who trust Him. The whole Hebrews' Hall of Faith (chapter 11) is filled with men and women who dared to try the impossible because they believed God would help them.*

LOOKING OUT

1. **When our faith is focused, mountains are moved. Jonathan had great faith in God saying, "Nothing can hinder the Lord from saving, whether by many or by few."**
2. **God gives us assurance as we do His will. Jonathan looked for a sign along the way to be assured that God was in the battle. God faithfully gave him that needed sign.**
3. **We can do the impossible when God is with us. Jonathan and his armor bearer were able to do more than a whole raiding party because their trust was in the God of Israel.**
4. **God puts fear in our enemies' hearts when we trust and follow Him. Two men were able to strike terror in the enemy because God caused the Philistines to panic.**
5. **When we do our part, God always does His. We are locked in divine partnership with our Lord. Jonathan and his armor bearer gained victory because God was with them.**

LOOKING UP *Help me, Lord, to remember that with You we are a majority. You help me accomplish great things. May I never fall to fear but rise to Your command.*

APRIL

An Interesting Month of Dramatic Change

April is the time of dramatic change in our part of the world. All through the Temperate Zone of the Northern Hemisphere, the appearance of the outdoor world usually changes more this month than in any other period of the year. Ice and snow disappear, grass grows green, and leaves appear on bushes and trees. Small animals that hibernate are usually out of their burrows. Birds fly northward or settle down to raise families. Butterflies and bees gather nectar from the first flowers. April is mainly a sowing time on many northern farms. In some parts of the world, April is harvest time for grain. In the Southern Hemisphere, people enjoy mild autumn days, a nice respite before the onset of winter.

April is the fourth month of the year, according to the Gregorian calendar, which is used in almost all the world. The Romans called the month *Aprilis*, a name that may come from a word meaning "to open," or it may come from Aphrodite, the Greek name for the goddess of love. April was the second month in an early Roman calendar, but it became the fourth when the ancient Romans started using January as the first month. During April, the professional baseball season begins in the United States. Amateurs in many other sports are lured out of doors with the first warm days. Householders begin their spring cleaning and start work on their gardens and lawns.

April is an active month. On April 1, children and grown-ups play jokes on one another. Easter nearly always falls in April, bringing with it other Christian celebrations such as Palm Sunday, Maundy Thursday, and Good Friday. The Jewish festival of Pesah (Passover) often comes early in April. The Chinese celebrate the Pure and Bright Festival in early April. People in England and Canada celebrate St. George's Day to honor the patron saint of England.

During this month, we read 1 Samuel 16 through 2 Kings 10. This portion of Scripture, like the month of April, is filled with sound and fury. It notes dramatic changes in the life of God's people. The old theocracy gives way to a monarchy, with all of its intrigues and tragedies.

FOOLED

APRIL 1

1 Samuel 16-17

LOOKING BACK This is April Fools' Day, when people play tricks on each other. A favorite joke is to send someone on a fool's errand, a search for something that doesn't exist. No one knows where the this custom began. Some believe it may have started in France, where the old New Year's festival was observed from March 25 to April 1, ending with an exchange of gifts. In the mid-1560's, King Charles IX changed the New Year to January 1. People who still celebrated the New Year in April were called "April fish" and were sent mock presents. Others say that April Fools' Day may be related to the ancient Roman spring festival Hilaria.

LOOKING IN *All of Israel was "fooled" by Goliath, whose bravado made them believe he was invulnerable and the nation could do nothing but submit to the brutality of the Philistines. Every day when he came out to challenge Saul's army, the soldiers quaked in fear. Then one day David showed up. He immediately saw through Goliath's charade. David knew that God was bigger than the bragging giant. He gave Goliath the ultimate insult by showing up to fight the giant without armor or sword. Goliath was so insulted that he lost control. David immediately moved to take advantage of the situation. God gave great victory and the Philistines fled in terror.*

LOOKING OUT

1. Our problems always seem overwhelming. The Israelites were terrified of Goliath because he appeared invulnerable. However, God knew there was a weak spot in his armor.
2. Satan always tries to intimidate. Goliath verbally assaulted Israel to strike terror in their hearts. Satan is "like a roaring lion," but his threatening words are hollow.
3. We must be careful what we hear; it shapes our reactions. Defeat kept the Israelites down because they listened to Goliath's words rather than to God's promises.
4. God always seems to pick the unlikely to do the impossible. Of all Jesse's sons and the other warriors, David was the most unlikely to come against Goliath.
5. When we do our part, God always does His part. David moved out in faith against Goliath. He fired the fatal stone, but it was God Who guided the unlikely missile.

LOOKING UP *Help me, Lord, to listen to the right voice. I must hear Your promises, not the doubts of man. May I always remember that the giants in my life are no match for Your power.*

IRRECONCILABLE

1 Samuel 18-19

LOOKING BACK Popular advice columnist Ann Landers has tried for years to make today "Reconciliation Day," a time when differences between people are resolved and we all learn to get along with each other. Landers, whose real name is Esther Pauline "Eppie" Friedman Lederer, is considered one of the most influential people in the United States. Her daily column is published in about 1,000 newspapers in the United States and other countries. She writes, "Since 1989, I have suggested that April 2 be set aside to write that letter or make that phone call and mend a broken relationship. Life is too short to hold grudges. To forgive can be enormously life-enhancing."

LOOKING IN *While Landers' intent is good, the fact is there are some relationships that cannot be restored because one or both parties refuse to correct bad behavior. That was the case between Saul and David. The more popular David became, the more belligerent Saul grew. Israel's first king deeply resented David. As Saul's jealousy grew, he became more and more irrational. Soon Saul was totally out of control and determined to destroy the object of his hatred. There were many attempts to reconcile Saul and David, but all failed because Saul refused to change his evil ways. Finally, David had to flee for his life, lest the insane king destroy him and his family.*

LOOKING OUT

1. Best friends are those who share common beliefs. Jonathan and David became the best of friends because both their hearts were pure and clean before the Lord.
2. Unchecked jealousy and anger open us to evil spirits. Saul's jealousy led him to anger over David's success. Soon an evil spirit began to dominate Saul.
3. God keeps us safe when we are in His will. Saul was bent on killing David. Twice, Saul hurled a spear at the young shepherd boy, but each time David escaped harm.
4. Success depends on God's presence. The reason David went from one victory to another is best explained by the notation, "because the Lord was with him."
5. The diabolical plots of the enemy are thwarted when we walk with God. Saul schemed to have David murdered by offering his daughter in marriage as a reward, but it didn't happen.

LOOKING UP *Lord, help me to stay in the center of Your perfect will, for there, You protect and provide. Please help me to do my part to mend broken relationships.*

FRIENDSHIP

1 Samuel 20-21

LOOKING BACK American naturalist John Burroughs was born on this day in 1837. Widely recognized as a writer on outdoor life, Burroughs made the beauties of the outdoors seem real to both children and adults. His description of birds, flowers, and a variety of natural settings in North America became increasingly poetic and philosophical over the course of his career. He was born in Roxbury, New York, and spent his youth on his father's farm, working, reading, and studying. Burroughs' view of nature put him in the tradition of Henry David Thoreau and Ralph Waldo Emerson. In 1877, he wrote, "Time does not become sacred to us until we have lived it."

LOOKING IN *Only in looking back do we fully appreciate the value of the times we have spent with friends and loved ones. David and Jonathan had spent some wonderful times together but now they had to part because Saul was intent on murder. Time had become sacred to them, for they never again would be together. Jonathan was David's best friend who always remained loyal. Jonathan is one of the most admirable men in Scripture. He knew God had chosen David to be king rather than himself. He never let jealousy, resentment, or bitterness drive a wedge between himself and David. Jonathan gave up what he couldn't keep and gained what he couldn't lose.*

LOOKING OUT

1. God often lets us go through tough times because these times toughen us. God could have prevented Saul's pursuit of David. He didn't so David could identify with sufferers.
2. You can't hide sin forever. Saul's fury bubbled to the surface, revealing his diabolical plans to Jonathan. Until this moment, Jonathan believed his father would not hurt David.
3. When we stop lying to ourselves, the truth may be painful, but we can face reality. Jonathan had long denied Saul's awful intentions. Now he knows how to deal with this evil.
4. Good men do right regardless of the personal cost. Jonathan could have inherited the throne but desired to please God more than he wanted power and prestige.
5. Real friendship puts oneself on the line. Jonathan risked his life by being a friend of David. God can give us special friends who will stick by us regardless of the sacrifice.

LOOKING UP *Help me, Lord, to recognize the great friends You have given me, and may I be a faithful friend. Help me to appreciate the time You have given me with those I love.*

VIOLENCE

APRIL 4

1 Samuel 22-23

LOOKING BACK Civil rights leader Martin Luther King, Jr., was murdered on this day in 1968, in Memphis, Tennessee. While organizing the "Poor People's Campaign," King went to Memphis to support a strike of Black garbage workers. There, James Earl Ray, a White drifter and escaped convict, shot and killed King. Ray pleaded guilty to the crime in March, 1969, and was sentenced to 99 years in prison. In spite of King's stress on nonviolence, the civil rights leader often became the target of violence. White racists threw rocks at him in Chicago and bombed his home in Montgomery, Alabama. Finally, violence ended King's life at the age of 39.

LOOKING IN *Evil men always resort to violence in pursuit of their wicked ends. That is what Saul did when he determined to destroy David. Even though David was innocent of any charges, Saul relentlessly pursued him. Not only did David have to flee for his own life, but his whole family was also put in extreme jeopardy. They were forced to leave their homes and live on the run. No amount of persuasion could convince Saul to spare David's life. David would have suffered the same fate of assassination if Saul would have had his way. Thankfully, God protected the life of Israel's greatest king. In spite of his great army, Saul could not track down David and his men.*

LOOKING OUT

1. **Sometimes our trials deeply affect others. David's family members are unfairly caught up in the pain he suffers at the hand of Saul.**
2. **God gives us those who can identify with our suffering. Some 400 people of similar sorrow gather around David as he flees from the mad king.**
3. **Problems do not excuse our responsibilities. Although David is fleeing for his life, he must take care of his parents and their needs.**
4. **During trials, we are often confused. David did not know what awaited him, although God had promised success to the future king.**
5. **God gives clear direction when we are confused. Gad, a prophet of God, is sent to tell David what to do.**

LOOKING UP *Lord, when I am confused in the midst of my trials, help me to continue to trust You. May I always remember that You will send direction to me.*

JUSTICE

APRIL 5

1 Samuel 24-25

LOOKING BACK A bomb exploded on this day in 1986 at a discotheque in West Berlin, Germany, killing two American soldiers and a Turkish woman. American intelligence attributed responsibility to Libyan head-of-state Muammar el-Qaddafi, and ordered a retaliatory air strike on Libya. The April 14, 1986, bombing attack resulted in 37 dead, including Qaddafi's daughter. Nearly two years later, West German authorities arrested 27-year-old Christine Gabriele Endrigkeit, charging her with the discotheque bombing. It is now thought the bombing was ordered by Syrian agents, and grave questions about justice being done have been raised.

LOOKING IN *In spite of the best intelligence, it is not always possible to get the facts straight. That is one of the reasons God's Word insists that we leave vengeance and getting even in His hands. All hell usually breaks loose when we insist on vengeance and retaliation. David wisely resisted the temptation to end his problems with Saul by killing the vulnerable leader. Rather, David chose to put his case in God's hands and not soil his own with the blood of God's anointed. Many years of suffering remained for David, but he stood steadfast in righteousness. The cold facts of history reveal that David made the better and wiser choice.*

LOOKING OUT

1. We must never take the law into our own hands, but let God settle matters. David had ample opportunity to end his difficulty with Saul but would not touch God's anointed.
2. We cannot ignore evil but must confront it with a determination to do things God's way. David confronted Saul with truth, although the mad king would ignore it.
3. Sin makes emotional wrecks of us, destroying our common sense and reasoning ability. Saul was obviously out of touch with reality. He continued to plunge downward.
4. Even good people can act badly at times. David had acted nobly with Saul but furiously determined to kill Nabal when the greedy rancher refused to honor his commitments.
5. God will send someone to help keep us from evil if our hearts are turned toward Him. Abigail is used by the Lord to stop David from a sin that would have disgraced him.

LOOKING UP *Help me, Lord, always to wait on You for justice rather than rushing in to grab it for myself. May I never be bent on getting even but trust You to make things right.*

TEFLON

APRIL 6

1 Samuel 26-27

LOOKING BACK Teflon was invented on this day in 1938. Teflon is a trade name for the synthetic material used in cookware, insulation, and many other products. Roy J. Plunkett, an American chemist, invented this substance, which is inert; that is, it does not react with most other chemicals. It also resists moisture and remains stable in extreme heat and cold. Teflon feels slippery to the touch, and adhesive materials will not stick to it. The invention has dramatically changed the way many people now cook their food. Because of its unique nature, the word "teflon" has entered political jargon to describe a person to whom scandal won't stick.

LOOKING IN *In many ways, David was the teflon king. Even though scandal finally did stick to him, Saul's diabolical plots to destroy David did not. The reason Saul couldn't destroy David had nothing to do with his personality but with the fact God protected David wherever he went. Knowing Saul's madness, David escaped to Gath and was protected by Achish. Even though Saul had the entire Israelite army at his disposal, he could not run down David and his ragtag group of men. In fact, twice David had a perfect opportunity to kill the mad king and stop the craziness. Each time, he resisted, saying he would not touch the Lord's anointed.*

LOOKING OUT

1. Sometimes time and distance are needed to solve a problem. David understood he could not reason with Saul but had to leave the country lest the mad king kill him.
2. Often putting time and distance between the problem and ourselves brings respite. Saul stopped pursuing David when he learned that the shepherd boy had fled to Gath.
3. We must never get chummy with the world. Although David settled in Gath, he refused to dwell in the royal city which would compromise his convictions and calling.
4. God makes our enemies be at peace with us when our ways please Him. Achish was not a friend of Israel, but he protected David. God blinded his eyes for that season.
5. We can continue to do God's work even when we are kept from the place God has called us. David carried out his campaigns while an exile in enemy territory.

LOOKING UP *Help me, Lord, to know that You will protect me from harm and danger as I put my trust in You. May I always remember that no harm can come to me with You as my Protector.*

TALENT

1 Samuel 28-29

LOOKING BACK Billie Holiday, the most moving jazz singer of her time, was born on this day in 1915. She was admired for the uniquely bittersweet quality of her voice and for perfect phrasing. Although Holiday was often described as a blues singer, she was principally an interpreter of popular songs. Billie Holiday was born in Baltimore and raised by her mother in a Black ghetto. She made her first recordings with Benny Goodman in 1933. Her most distinctive work was recorded between 1936 and 1944. Tragically, after 1950, drug addiction increasingly affected her health and her career. She died, hopelessly addicted, at age 44.

LOOKING IN *Talent alone does not assure success. Saul stood head and shoulders above all others in his day but died a hopeless suicide. Saul had it all. He was handsome, intelligent, and charismatic. In addition to these appealing qualities, Saul possessed great humility. However, when he was thrust into power, Saul began to believe all those wonderful things people said about him and threw humility aside. That was the first step downward for this very capable king. Tragically, in the last years of Saul's tumultuous life, Israel's first king went mad. God's Spirit had departed from Saul, and, in desperation, he consulted the fraudulent Witch of Endor.*

LOOKING OUT

1. **It's wise to withhold our words until God works things out. David would have been forced to fight his own people, but God stepped in to deliver him from this dilemma.**
2. **We can't withdraw from heaven's bank if there are no deposits there. Saul was spiritually bankrupt. When he needed God's direction, it wasn't available to him.**
3. **When we leave God out, we seek desperate and foolish ways to get divine direction. Saul violates his own laws by seeking a medium to try to raise the spirit of Samuel.**
4. **Psychics are frauds. The witch of Endor was shocked when Samuel's spirit actually appeared. This revealed she was a fraud preying on people's vulnerability.**
5. **Our reaction to rebuke should be repentance, rather than rushing on in our bad behavior. Saul should have fallen on his face in repentance, rather than merely caving in to fear.**

LOOKING UP *Help me, Lord, to make regular deposits in heaven's bank by my prayers, obedience, and service. Please keep me humble at all times so that I won't fail and fall.*

TRAGEDY

APRIL 8

1 Samuel 30-31

LOOKING BACK A simple tragedy captured the attention of the world on this day in 1949. Three-year-old Kathy Fiscus of San Marino, California, fell into an abandoned well-pipe while playing. The pipe was only 14 inches wide and 120 feet deep. Rescue workers toiled for two days while national attention was focused on the tragedy. Newspaper and media reports kept a concerned nation aware of the workers' progress. It was all in vain as little Kathy's body was recovered on April 10, 1949. An alarmed nation suddenly became attentive to other abandoned wells and similar hazards, and "Kathy Fiscus Laws"were enacted, requiring new safety measures.

LOOKING IN *David and his men experienced a great tragedy at Ziklag, their home base. While they had been away, the Amalekites had raided David's camp, kidnaped the wives and children, and taken all that he and his men possessed. This crisis revealed the depth of David's faith and trust in God. While David's men fell apart and spoke of stoning their leader, David encouraged himself in the Lord and did something about the tragedy they had suffered. That moment clearly defined the great faith David had in his Lord to restore all the enemy had taken from them. God helped David to not only get back what had been taken but to also get spoil from the defeated enemy.*

LOOKING OUT

1. **Just because we are doing God's work doesn't keep us from abuses by Satan. David was obeying God completely, but the Amalekites still kidnaped his family.**
2. **The first step in dealing with sorrow is to grieve. David and his men wept until they could weep no more, when they discovered the camp raided and all of their families gone.**
3. **The second step in dealing with sorrow is to look up rather than out for someone to blame. David's men vented anger on David, but the future king looked up to the Lord.**
4. **The third step in overcoming trouble is prayer. David inquired of God before rushing out in pursuit of the Amalekites. He knew the real battle was spiritual.**
5. **The final step in conquering trouble is to regain all that was lost. God told David to "pursue, overtake, and recover all." David got back more than he had lost.**

LOOKING UP *Lord, help me to remember the spiritual principles of overcoming trouble when faced with crises. Help me to remember that You can restore all that the evil one has taken.*

FALLEN

APRIL 9

2 Samuel 1-2

LOOKING BACK At 1:30 p.m., on April 9, 1865, the Civil War ended in the United States. General Robert E. Lee surrendered to General Ulysses S. Grant, ending four years of horrific war that cost more than 500,000 lives. The historic meeting took place at Appomattox Courthouse, Virginia. Lee and his men did not expect the kindness they received in that bitter surrender. General Grant was very gracious to the southern general and his soldiers. The Confederates were permitted to keep their horses and go free to their homes, while Confederate officers were allowed to retain their swords and side arms as well. Grant had written the terms of surrender.

LOOKING IN *Graciousness is a marvelous quality in a leader. Grant forever earned the love of his country for the way he treated Lee. David had the same quality of graciousness. Even though Saul was a bitter enemy, when the mad king fell, David refused to gloat that his enemy was finally dead. Rather, David graciously insisted that the nation give proper honor to Saul in spite of his madness and evil. A beautiful song was written by David for the occasion, admonishing Israel not to denigrate the fallen king, but to remember the good things Saul and Jonathan had done for their country. This was not to be a time of further animosity but a period of healing for the nation.*

LOOKING OUT

1. **Evil men never understand the mindset of the righteous. The Amalekite reporting to David thought the future king would reward him. His words condemned him to death.**
2. **Good men never gloat when their enemies are defeated. David refused to glory in the death of Saul but insisted that the Israelites sing a song of praise for the tragic king.**
3. **We must look for the good in others rather than emphasizing their bad points. David taught the Israelites to sing of Saul's victories, not his agonizing weaknesses.**
4. **Putting down spiritual leaders opens the church up for ridicule and criticism. David knew the Philistines would delight in Saul's death, shaming Israel and disgracing God.**
5. **Fallen church leaders are to be mourned, not ridiculed. David taught the Israelites to sing, "How the mighty have fallen in battle." Failure is never to be deified.**

LOOKING UP *Help me today, Lord, to affirm my brothers and sisters rather than finding ways of criticizing them. May I never gloat over the troubles of my enemies but love them as my Lord commanded.*

VICTORY

APRIL 10

2 Samuel 3-5

LOOKING BACK On the morning of April 10, 1942, American and Filipino prisoners were herded together by Japanese soldiers on Mariveles Airfield in the Philippines for what became known as the "Bataan Death March." The day before, 75,000 exhausted troops had surrendered to the Japanese. Most were forced to march about 65 miles to prison camps. Many of the weary perished from disease and mistreatment. During the brutal six-day march, they were given only one bowl of rice per person. Some 5,200 Americans and many more Filipinos died in the march. This horrendous death march forever entered history as one of the war's greatest atrocities.

LOOKING IN *War is always brutal and deadly. As General Sherman said so eloquently, "War is hell!" David knew his share of war even though he didn't relish its fruits. God had given him great victories over all the enemies that threatened to destroy Israel. The nation's fight was one for survival, with David being chosen to lead the battle. David would be forced to fight God's enemies for years because the evil one was so determined to destroy God's people. It was a brutal and bloody time for the nation. They were often outnumbered and ill-equipped. Yet, through it all, they were victorious. David rightly attributed all victories to the Lord.*

LOOKING OUT

1. Victory over our enemies doesn't come in one fell swoop but over a period of time. David defeated the Philistines, although it took nearly a lifetime to accomplish.
2. No foe is too strong for the Lord to defeat. Though the enemies of Israel were formidable, God gave David victory wherever he went. We need never be intimidated.
3. The wealth of the wicked is reserved for the righteous. Because David loved God and did His will, he took gold from Israel's enemies and brought it to God's people.
4. All the resources we have gleaned should be dedicated to God. David carefully dedicated all spoils of war. He knew that all things belong to God.
5. God gives recognition to those who faithfully follow Him. David was given acclaim after he had faithfully accomplished God's will and way.

LOOKING UP *Help me, Lord, to fight my battles with determination so that I might always please You. May I always remember that You alone give me the victory.*

JOY

APRIL 11

2 Samuel 6-8

April

LOOKING BACK American statesman Edward Everett was born on this day in 1794. He was one of the greatest orators of his day and the chief speaker at Gettysburg, Pennsylvania, November 19, 1863, the day that Abraham Lincoln delivered his famous Gettysburg Address. Everett's speech was long and colorful, while Lincoln's was exceedingly brief and simple. Antagonistic newspapers regaled the president's speech as being an embarrassment to the nation while praising Everett's oration. Yet, Everett knew the real truth. He wrote to Lincoln, "I should be glad if I could flatter myself that I came as near to the central idea of the occasion in two hours as you did in two minutes."

LOOKING IN *Many historians believe the Gettysburg Address was a defining point in American history. They say it reshaped the nation by reminding them that they were one people dedicated to one principle–that of equality. It was also a defining moment in Israel's history when David brought the Ark of the Covenant to Jerusalem. He was emphatically saying to the country that just as Jerusalem was to be the political heart of the kingdom, so God was to be the heart of the nation. The Ark of the Covenant's residence in Jerusalem was highly symbolic and meaningful because it represented the presence of God. It is no wonder David danced joyfully when bringing the Ark there.*

LOOKING OUT

1. Careless worship displeases God. David tried to move the Ark of the Covenant without regard to the specific instructions God had given to Israel.
2. God always blesses us when we do things right. David learned from his mistake and brought the Ark to Jerusalem as instructed in Scripture.
3. We can get our way but not like what we get. David had insisted on having Michal in marriage. However, Saul's daughter became an angry and bitter woman.
4. We cannot cave in to pressure. David refused to buckle down under the harsh criticism of his angry and embittered wife.
5. We must never desecrate holy things. Michal made the tragic mistake of denigrating the holy worship of David. She would pay a harsh penalty for her action.

LOOKING UP *Help me, Lord, to approach You with reverence, knowing that You demand and deserve that respect. Teach me how to worship You in the beauty of holiness.*

SPARK

APRIL 12

2 Samuel 9-12

LOOKING BACK The first shots of the Civil War were fired on this day in 1861. Confederate shore batteries commanded by General P.G.T. Beauregard opened fire on the federal garrison at Fort Sumter in Charleston Harbor. Just three years later, on this day, Confederate troops, commanded by Major Nathan Bedford Forrest, massacred Black Union troops after capturing Fort Pillow, Tennessee. The hellish fire, sparked by that first angry shot in 1861, wasn't quenched until more blood was spilled by Americans than in all other wars combined. The Civil War not only divided the nation but also separated families. In some ways, the nation's wounds have never healed.

LOOKING IN *The opening shots of the Civil War seemed small but flared into hellish fury. What often starts as a spark can erupt into a raging, destroying fire. David learned this when he gave in to his passion and took Bathsheba. The consequences of that lustful act would forever stain his reputation and bring him untold pain. Not only was David affected, but also the lives of many others were shattered by his awful sin. David's own family was torn apart by his evil behavior. It would be hard for him to discipline his disobedient boys when he himself had failed so miserably. What started out as a small private affair ended up a horrible public shame.*

LOOKING OUT

1. God always rebukes His disobedient children. God sent Nathan to confront David because God loved His servant so much He didn't want David's sin to break their relationship.
2. It's always easier to see someone else's deplorable sin rather than acknowledge our own. David was quick to condemn the miscreant in Nathan's fictional story.
3. Forgiveness doesn't cancel all consequences. While David was forgiven, there were serious repercussions to what he had done. He would suffer their effects for years.
4. Our sin always brings disgrace on God's work. Nathan told David the enemies of God would mock God because of the terrible thing that David did with Bathsheba and to Uriah.
5. God lovingly helps us even when we are suffering the consequences of our own bad choices. God still blesses David with a son after the tragic loss of their firstborn.

LOOKING UP *Lord, help me to keep my passions in check so I will please You and avoid the terrible pain sin brings. Forgive me for the things that I have done to displease You.*

FRIENDSHIP

APRIL 13

2 Samuel 13-14

April

LOOKING BACK This is "Holocaust Day," established by Israel's Knesset as a memorial to the Jewish dead of World War II. It was on this day in 1945 that British and American troops liberated the German extermination camps of Belsen and Buchenwald. The first camp freed was Buchenwald, north of Weimar, Germany, where about 56,000 prisoners, many of them Jewish, perished. The world was shocked and saddened when it became fully aware of the horror Hitler and his minions perpetrated on the innocent. Tragically, it took far too long for friends of the oppressed Jews to step forward and end the hell that had been unleashed on them.

LOOKING IN *Too often, we fail to see the hurts and hunger of those about us and permit violence to continue far too long. Joab saw the hurt in David's eyes because the king and his son were alienated. It was true that Absalom had committed a horrible evil in revenging the rape of Tamar, his beloved sister. Absalom had brutally killed his own brother, Amnon, the perpetrator of the rape. Absalom fled to escape punishment for his evil and lived in exile. Joab, on seeing the pain of the separation, attempted to bring reconciliation to David and his son. Joab proved a real friend to David in this matter. He truly wanted to bring the two together.*

LOOKING OUT

1. **Real friends try to heal the hurt of those near to them. Joab could see the pain David suffered because his son was alienated from him. Joab moved to reconcile the two.**
2. **God can give us creativity to reach those whose hearts are hard. David was set against his son, but Joab discovered how not only to get David's attention but make him hear.**
3. **Anger often blinds us to injustice. David's anger at Absalom kept the two separated. The wise woman of Tekoa helped bring the matter into clear focus for David.**
4. **God is always seeking ways to reconcile his wayward children. The woman of Tekoa captured the very heart of God by her statement to the angry but grief-stricken king.**
5. **Comfort and prosperity mean nothing if we have no relationship with God. Absalom said, "What's the use of dwelling in Jerusalem if I can't see the face of the king?"**

LOOKING UP *Lord, help me to be a real friend by knowing the hurts of others and reaching out to help them. May I not be so caught up in my own world that I fail to care for others.*

BETRAYED

APRIL 14

2 Samuel 15-17

LOOKING BACK John Wilkes Booth assassinated President Abraham Lincoln on this day in 1865, because he believed Lincoln had betrayed America in standing against slavery and the South. Booth entered Lincoln's private box at Washington's Ford Theater a few minutes after 10 p.m. and shot the president through the head. Booth then leaped to the stage below, shouting in Latin, "Thus always to tyrants." Booth broke his leg in the fall but escaped through a back door. He was hunted down and shot a few days later in Virginia. Betrayal, or even the perception of it, always raises great emotion, often leading to disastrous events.

LOOKING IN *David was betrayed by Absalom, his own son. Absalom fomented revolution and drove his father from Jerusalem. The rebel son also sexually assaulted David's concubines as the ultimate insult to his father. At first, it appeared that those aiding Absalom would succeed in unseating David and taking the kingdom for themselves. David's previous shameful behavior with Bathsheba had eroded his base of support. In addition, there were always willing enemies lurking nearby. In that tense time, real friends stood by David while others joined Absalom. Through it all, David rested his future with the Lord. It proved to be a wise choice.*

LOOKING OUT

1. Real friends stick with us through thick and thin. Things had turned bad for David but Ittai refused to abandon his friend. Loyalty is a wonderful and godly trait.
2. We are not to use religion to achieve our own ends. David refused to let the Ark of the Covenant come with him because it was sacred, not a good luck charm.
3. We must always put our fate in God's hands. Wisely, David rested his case with God saying, "...I am ready; let him do with me whatever seems good to him."
4. Even when the enemy has the upper hand, we possess a powerful weapon unavailable to him. Although Ahithophel's betrayal was devastating, David's prayer prevailed.
5. God puts people in strategic positions to help in times of crisis. Hushai was uniquely qualified to be used of God to confound the advice given to David's enemies.

LOOKING UP *Help me rest in You, Lord, for I know that regardless of circumstances, You will bring me out. Like David, I rest my future with You.*

FLATTERY

APRIL 15

2 Samuel 18-20

LOOKING BACK Famed American painter Thomas Hart Benton was born on this day in 1889. He wanted American art to be democratic, portraying scenes from the daily life of ordinary people in a direct and easily understood style. Benton took most of his subjects from the Midwest where he lived. He painted both the difficulties and pleasures of being a farmer, railroad worker, miner, saloonkeeper, or politician. He also created scenes of family life. Benton became nationally known and painted works in and about Hollywood and New York City. In his quest for realism, Benton was not always flattering to the subjects he painted.

LOOKING IN *One of the things that makes the Bible so believable is its realism. It does not flatter the personalities who people its pages but tells it as it is. This is especially true when it comes to the life of David. Scripture portrays David as an extremely talented but flawed man. David could write beautiful love songs to God pledging his loyalty but then fall into sexual sin with Bathsheba. He could be loving and forgiving but also remain angrily alienated from his son for many months. He could bring his boy back from exile and then refuse to see him until finally forced to do so. David was a great man, but like us, he was only a man.*

LOOKING OUT

1. **Sin's payday is always hard and hurtful. David reaps a tragic harvest because of his complicity with Bathsheba. Sin is never worth the awful cost it exacts from the sinner.**
2. **Leadership demands strength in sorrow. David crumbles in grief because of Absalom's death. Joab shocks David back to his responsibility by reminding the king of his duty.**
3. **Greatness is forgiving those who have hurt us deeply. Shimei had blatantly brutalized King David. Now that the tables are turned, David graciously forgives Shimei.**
4. **Trust must be re-earned once it is doubted. David doesn't know the truth about Mephibosheth's loyalty but gives him opportunity to reestablish trust and friendship.**
5. **God greatly rewards those who stand with His servants. Barzillai had been faithful to David even when things looked bad. Now the old man is greatly rewarded by the king.**

LOOKING UP *Help me, Lord, to stand strong in stress, not caving in to the great pressures around me. Thank You for forgiving my sins and restoring me to Yourself.*

INJUSTICE

APRIL 16

2 Samuel 21-22

LOOKING BACK On this day in 1995, twelve-year-old Iqbal Masib was shot to death in Pakistan because he spoke out against child labor laws. Prior to his murder, Masib had received numerous death threats when he blasted Pakistan's policy concerning working children, but many did not take the threats seriously. Masib, who had been sold into labor as a carpet weaver at the age of four, spent the next six years shackled to a loom. He began speaking out against child labor after escaping servitude at the age of ten. In November of 1994, he spoke at the international labor conference in Sweden. Five months later he was gunned down by—some say—the "carpet mafia."

LOOKING IN *Terrible injustice is not a new problem in our world. The Gibeonites experienced it at the brutal hands of Saul. Israel had entered a sacred pact to protect the Gibeonites, but Saul blatantly ignored it and brutalized them. Years passed without justice being given to the hurting Gibeonites. God finally got the attention of Israel by sending a devastating drought. David sought the reason for the problem and learned that God was angry because of the broken vow. David moved quickly to correct wrongs done to innocent people. The Gibeonites were given justice and the drought stopped. God's blessings returned to the chosen nation.*

LOOKING OUT

1. **The shadow of sin falls far into the future. Israel suffered three years of drought because of Saul's sin against the Gibeonites. The pain drove David to make things right.**
2. **Zeal without obedience brings sorrow. Saul had slain the Gibeonites in "his zeal for the Lord." However, Israel was supposed to protect the Gibeonites, not destroy them.**
3. **Those who hurt others will one day be hurt themselves. Saul and his family had decimated the Gibeonites. Even though many years passed, those who sinned had to pay.**
4. **Great love inspires us to correct wrongs. David saw the sacrificial and undying love of Rizpah. He was quickly moved to give a proper burial to the sons of Saul.**
5. **When justice is done, health returns to a nation. Once the Gibeonites received justice, God began again to answer the nation's prayers, bringing them blessings.**

LOOKING UP *Help me remember, Lord, that even though judgment tarries, it will come to those who disobey. Help me to always keep my promises and be just.*

BATTLES

2 Samuel 23-24

LOOKING BACK On April 17, 1961, the United States launched the infamous Bay of Pigs fiasco in Cuba in an attempt to overthrow Fidel Castro. The mission failed, resulting in great embarrassment to the American government. Not only did Castro remain in power, but he seemed to gain more strength because of this aborted attempt. Some 1,500 Cuban exiles had been encouraged to invade Cuba at the Bay of Pigs on the south coast. They had been promised direct U.S. military action, including air cover, to insure the success of the invasion. President John F. Kennedy had approved the plan but refused to send military aid. Castro's forces then crushed the invasion.

LOOKING IN *Before launching a revolution, one should be sure of its success. David won all his battles because he was always careful to ask God's direction and help before entering them. Thus, he was assured victory even before the first battle cry was given. In addition to this assurance, God had also given David a group of extremely talented warriors who had been toughened by long years of wilderness training. Their fantastic exploits could be the grist of many books and movies. Called "The Mighty Men," these fighting men were indeed remarkable. Their exploits are recorded as examples to us in our faith-walk and fight.*

LOOKING OUT

1. **God gives us victory over great odds. Although Josheb-Basshebeth was one against 800, he won the victory because God was with him.**
2. **God helps us stand when others fall. Eleazar stayed in the battle and won though others retreated.**
3. **God gives us faith when others flee in fear. Shammah took a determined stand in the middle of a bean field and won.**
4. **God encourages us with loyal friends. David was deeply moved by the selfless sacrifice of his loyal followers.**
5. **God helps us win in impossible circumstances. Benaiah, though faced with several impossible situations, won his battles.**

LOOKING UP *Lord, may I always remember that You will help me win the battles You have ordained for me no matter what the odds.*

WARNINGS

APRIL 18

1 Kings 1-2

LOOKING BACK Paul Revere's famous ride took place on this day in 1775. The well-known Boston silversmith carried the news to Lexington of the approach of the British. He warned the patriot leaders Samuel Adams and John Hancock of their danger and called the citizens of the countryside to arms. His exploit inspired Henry Wadsworth Longfellow's *Paul Revere's Ride,* one of the most popular poems in American literature. Revere also served as a special messenger for the Boston patriots. Two days before the ride that placed him in all the history books, Revere had galloped to Concord to warn patriots there to move their military supplies.

LOOKING IN *Paul Revere's timely warnings were critical to the success of the American Revolution. A similar timely warning was given to David by Bathsheba and the prophet Nathan. Even though the ailing king wanted Solomon to succeed him on the throne, Adonijah, David's spoiled son, determined that he was to be king instead. David's reluctance to name a successor had opened the door for Adonijah's rebellion. Hearing of the planned coup, Nathan informed Bathsheba, who told David. The brash pretender to the throne was thwarted in his attempt, and Solomon was appointed. Adonijah's foolishness would later cost him his life.*

LOOKING OUT

1. Greed sets us up for destruction. David, now old, had not yet named a successor to the throne. Adonijah made a greedy grab for power rather than let God's will be done.
2. An undisciplined child is dangerous to himself and others. David had spoiled Adonijah. The Bible says he never asked the young rebel, "Why do you behave as you do?"
3. Procrastination can breed rebellion. Because David had not declared a successor, Adonijah thought he could grab the throne in spite of the fact God had selected Solomon.
4. God thwarts the diabolical plans of the evil one. Adonijah's rebellion stopped short because Nathan and Bathsheba convinced David he must name a successor.
5. Our future really is in our hands. Solomon forgave the rebellion of Adonijah but warned him he must not grab for power, or he would die. Tragically, Adonijah didn't listen.

LOOKING UP *Help me, Lord, to be content to wait on Your will rather than grabbing for possessions or power. I only want what You want me to have.*

IMP

1 Kings 3-6

LOOKING BACK The Branch Davidian complex in Waco, Texas, went up in flames on this day in 1993 with 86 of its members inside. A tense 51-day confrontation between the cult and federal forces ended with the apparent mass suicide of cult members, including the leader, David Koresh. The end came as federal agents began battering the compound with armored vehicles. Nine people escaped, but the 86 who perished included 17 children. This awful event gave birth to an even greater tragedy. Timothy McVey, who, along with Terry L. Nicholls, bombed the federal building in Oklahoma City, said he did so in retaliation for the Branch Davidian fiasco.

LOOKING IN *David Koresh, leader of the Branch Davidians, started out well but ended up tragically. It's not the start that wins a race but the finish. Solomon started his race in fine fashion but never finished what God had planned for him. In fact, he very well may have lost his eternal soul. From the beginning, we can see why Solomon failed. At the start, he sought God about decisions, but before long he began to think himself so smart and capable that he could make it on his own. Not only did he make bad alliances with women who did not know God, but he also sacrificed on the high places. Sadly, Solomon wasn't totally sold out to God.*

LOOKING OUT

1. We must be careful who we bring into our lives, for they will greatly influence us. Solomon made an alliance with Pharaoh and married his daughter. It was a mistake.
2. A double-minded person will eventually fall. Solomon showed his love for God by walking according to God's statutes. However, he was not fully dedicated to God.
3. Wanting what God wants brings us better blessings. When God asked Solomon what he wanted, the king asked for wisdom. The request greatly pleased God.
4. God's blessings are always conditional. God gave Solomon wisdom and wealth and told him those blessings would continue if Solomon carefully walked in His ways.
5. Our special gifts from God will be tested and proven. God gave Solomon great wisdom which was quickly tested. Soon, all could see that Solomon had been gifted by God.

LOOKING UP *Lord, please help me to be totally sold out to you. Make me want what You want, because I know that will please You and bring better blessings.*

JOY

APRIL 20

1 Kings 7-8

LOOKING BACK This day in 1986 was a joyful and emotional time for Vladimir Horowitz. After 61 years in the West, the famed pianist returned to the Soviet Union to give his first recital there in six decades. Horowitz was born in Kiev, Russia, and at the age of six began to study piano with his mother. When he was 17, he graduated from Kiev Conservatory and immediately began to make a name for himself. Horowitz became one of the world's greatest musicians. He left his homeland because of the oppressive political climate and stayed away for 61 long years. When the Soviet Union's relationship with the West began to thaw, Horowitz was able to return to Russia.

LOOKING IN *Horowitz's day of joy was unduplicated in his long and productive life. Solomon had a similar day of utter joy and high emotion when God's Temple was finally dedicated. This had been a great dream God had put in David's heart and then transferred to Solomon. It had taken years of hard and exacting labor to build the magnificent structure, but now it was done. Some scholars say Solomon's Temple cost more than two billion dollars to construct. Making dedication day even more wonderful, God's presence filled the Temple in such a way that the priests couldn't move about. This was the greatest day in the long life of King Solomon.*

LOOKING OUT

1. When we obey, God makes His presence known. The Ark was brought to the Temple. In response, God filled His house with a cloud so awesome the priests couldn't minister.
2. Public prayers teach people and touch God's heart. Solomon prayed publicly to remind the people of the faithfulness of God. There are to be both closet prayers and public prayers.
3. Praise should start with the recognition that God keeps all of His promises. Solomon began his blessing by reminding all that God had done what He said He would do.
4. Faith is a daily walk, not just a one-time experience. Solomon reminded the people that God's blessings depended on their continued faithfulness to God's Word.
5. Joy comes when we have done what God has asked, regardless of the cost. The people went home happy after the dedication, because they had done what God wanted.

LOOKING UP *Help me, Lord, always to recognize that You are the God Who keeps every promise. I rest in You! Thank You for the days of great joy You have placed in my life.*

SHOT DOWN

APRIL 21

1 Kings 9-11

April

LOOKING BACK The famed Red Baron of Germany was shot down on this day in 1918. Baron Manfred von Richtofen was one of the Allies' most formidable enemies during World War I. He singlehandedly downed 80 planes in two years, flying his Fokker triplane which he had painted a flaming red. This unique feature earned him the title, "The Red Baron." The daring flying ace died in a crash, and his body was recovered by Royal Flying Corps pilots who buried him with full military honors. He once admitted, "I am a hunter. My brother Lothar is a butcher. When I have shot down an Englishman, my hunting passion is satisfied for a quarter of an hour."

LOOKING IN *Germany's "Red Baron" was such a formidable enemy to the Allies that his name is still spoken with awe and respect by those in the military. In fact, Charles Schultz often features the Red Baron's name in his "Peanuts" comic strip when Snoopy fantasizes on top of his dog house. Solomon had some formidable enemies also. As long as Solomon served God, his enemies couldn't touch him. However, when the old king strayed away from his Creator, God permitted the enemies to pile up on him. Rather than seeing this as a loving rebuke from a God Who desired reconciliation, Solomon continued his disobedient ways and died in disgrace.*

LOOKING OUT

1. The path of sin starts small but soon broadens to a busy highway of destruction. Solomon thought little about marrying foreign wives, but he soon found sin had trapped him.
2. Our problem is not ignorance but rebellion. God's Word had made it perfectly clear that the kings of Israel were not to have multiple wives. Solomon knew but did it anyway.
3. Age doesn't bring wisdom; God gives it. Solomon grew older but not wiser. In his old age, his heart turned to the advice of his foreign wives rather than God's Word.
4. God's love turns to anger when we continue to deliberately disobey. God first called Solomon "Jedidiah" because He loved him so. Now, God was extremely angry.
5. When God lifts His hand of protection from us, all hell breaks loose. Solomon found himself surrounded by hostile enemies who threatened his life and his throne.

LOOKING UP *Help me, Lord, not only to start the race but finish it well. Keep me close to the cross. Help me see that some troubles come to me as Your loving warnings.*

MOTTO

APRIL 22

1 Kings 12-13

LOOKING BACK It was on this day during the last months of the Civil War that the United States Congress passed a bill putting "In God We Trust" on U.S. coins. That was in 1864, but not all coins minted since then have carried the motto. There have been attempts by some to eliminate the saying, although they have never succeeded in this effort. In 1955, Congress passed a law requiring that all U.S. coins and paper money carry the motto. The first paper money to have "In God We Trust" were $1 bills issued in 1955. The law provided that the motto be added to all U.S. paper money when printing plates were made for the new high-speed presses.

LOOKING IN *While most are grateful that we acknowledge God on our money, it takes more than a motto for a nation to be righteous. Israel was God's chosen people in name but often failed that responsibility in practice. Solomon had strayed from the path clearly marked by his godly father. Now, the nation's slide continued. Rehoboam stepped into leadership after Solomon's long and prosperous reign. It seemed that at the start things might be different. Rehoboam wisely asked advice from Israel's elders. Driven by his own selfishness and greed, however, he ignored that good advice and turned to the whims of his younger friends. It split the kingdom.*

LOOKING OUT

1. **Continued sin makes a nation vulnerable. Solomon's disobedience so weakened Israel that when his son took over, the enemies started banging at the door.**
2. **Without a moral compass, we cave in to the advice that seems most appealing. Rehoboam received good advice from the elders, but his weakness drew him the other way.**
3. **Wisdom from the world spells disaster; we must learn to listen to God. Rehoboam's bad decision split the kingdom, creating chaos and confusion for generations to come.**
4. **When good leaders fail, bad leaders take over. Jeroboam portrays himself as the savior of the nation, but, in actuality, he turns the people away from God toward destruction.**
5. **Too often, we seek advice from those who agree with us. Jeroboam had already decided to alienate the people from God before he took the advice to set up the golden calves.**

LOOKING UP *Help me, Lord, to be finely tuned to You rather than cave in to the applause and opinions of the crowd. Help me to hear and accept good advice from those who love You.*

RETURN

APRIL 23

1 Kings 14-15

LOOKING BACK In 1985, on this day, the Coca Cola company made a dramatic and foolish decision: they changed the formula of their 99-year-old recipe for their soft drink. Leaders of the company sincerely believed that the younger generation wanted a new taste and the change would greatly enhance their business. In fact, they had researched the issue and felt this was the wise route to go if they were to keep ahead of competition. It soon became abundantly clear that the executives were wrong. The public clamored for the old Coke. The rather embarrassed executives were forced to retreat. They brought out the old "Classic Coke."

LOOKING IN *New is not always better. Israel had experimented with "new" ways of operating their divided countries. Many of their kings had disdained the old ways of serving God. Enamored by their own wisdom, they turned away from God, only to see chaos and pain follow. This was the situation when God raised up Asa. This godly king longed for the old days when David led the people in righteousness. He encouraged the people to seek God, knowing God's blessings on them would return. Asa's message took root. Soon Judah, too, longed for that time, and revival came. When God's people return to Him, they are protected from the evil one.*

LOOKING OUT

1. In the midst of darkness, God can give us light. Sin had brought Judah low. Asa came on the scene to bring revival. He did what was right in the eyes of the Lord, as David had done.
2. We must deal with sin, even when it is extremely hard to do so. Asa loved God so much that he deposed his own grandmother because of her continued evil.
3. God blesses us when we are fully committed to Him. Even though Asa was not able to bring down the high places, his heart was completely given over to God.
4. The battle against evil never stops. Asa warred with Baasha, the evil king of the northern nation, all the days of his rule. Satan never stops trying to crush God's kingdom.
5. God will give us wisdom to conquer our enemies. Asa successfully stopped Baasha's diabolical plans in a creative way. God can give us wisdom to outmaneuver the enemy.

LOOKING UP *Help me, Lord, to be fully committed to You. Give me wisdom to win my spiritual battles, realizing that Satan will never stop his insidious attacks.*

SEARCH

APRIL 24

1 Kings 16-18

LOOKING BACK George N. Bascom, the West Point graduate appointed to track down the famed Indian chief, Cochise, was born on this day in 1836. Bascom was given the assignment to search out the Apache chief who was believed to be responsible for an 1861 raid on an Arizona ranch. Bascom arrested Cochise at Apache Pass, but the wily chief escaped and declared war, launching a reign of terror known as the "Apache Wars." The bloody battle raged until finally, in 1869, frontiersman Thomas J. Jeffords led General Oliver O. Howard to Cochise to discuss peace. Cochise agreed to stop fighting and moved his band to a reservation in Arizona.

LOOKING IN *Elijah was as wily in hiding from Ahab as Cochise was in escaping the U.S. Army. The prophet became very unpopular with Israel's evil king and his wicked wife. The king and Jezebel so hated Elijah that he had to spend much of his time on the run. Everywhere Elijah went, God provided for him, sometimes in most surprising ways. One of the best examples of God's unusual provision was when God instructed the prophet to go the brook to be fed by ravens. After the brook dried up, God told Elijah to go to a widow who would feed him. This too was surprising since that widow and her son were dying of starvation.*

LOOKING OUT

1. We must never be turned off by God's surprises. Elijah was probably shocked to learn that God would feed him by ravens. God often surprises us with His answers.
2. We are fed where we are led. God told Elijah to go to the brook in Kerith Ravine because God would feed him there. We must be in God's will if we are to receive His provision.
3. When one door closes, God opens another. When the brook dried up, God told Elijah to go the widow of Zarephath for provision. God always takes care of His own.
4. God always works on both ends of a problem. Before Elijah showed up at the widow's house, God had already told her she would be used to provide what he needed.
5. Responding in faith puts deposits in our heavenly bank account. The widow obeyed the prophet even when it seemed foolish to do so. Later, she was richly rewarded.

LOOKING UP *Help me, Lord, not to be turned off by Your surprising provision for me. Let me always be grateful. May I see Your provision even in the strangest circumstances.*

HIGHWAYS

APRIL 25

1 Kings 19-20

April

LOOKING BACK On this day in 1901, the first automobile license plate was required in the United States. New York led the way in demanding that vehicles have plates. Officials there felt it would be a creative way to finance the growing need for new roads. Soon other states followed suit. Today, much of the roadway system across America is financed by plates and various taxes on fuels needed for trucks and cars. The first fully paved trans-American highway, connecting New York to San Francisco, was the famous Lincoln Highway, begun in 1913 and completed in 1927. Travel became an American pastime, changing the face of this country.

LOOKING IN *Elijah didn't have the fancy highways he needed to escape the wrathful pursuit of Ahab and Jezebel. His escape route was treacherous and extremely difficult, wearing the already weary prophet to the bone. In his exhaustion, Elijah falls into deep depression. Nothing he can do or think can pull the prophet out of this deep funk. God carefully watches over His weary servant, sending an angel to feed him and lift him up. There is still much work for Elijah to do. God gets his attention with sound and fury but does not yell at the discouraged prophet. Rather, He speaks to Elijah in the still, small voice, encouraging him and putting him back on his feet.*

LOOKING OUT

1. Spiritual victories stir up the hordes of hell. Jezebel was furious with Elijah because the prophets of her god had been debunked and destroyed.
2. Even the strongest can become weak at times. Elijah had faced down 850 hostile pagan priests but now cowered in fear before one woman.
3. At times, we must have God's touch to relieve depression. Elijah could not shake the feeling of doom that swept over him until God sent the angel to touch him.
4. We often have to quiet down if we are to hear from God. God was not in all the wind and noise Elijah experienced. Rather, He was in the still, small voice.
5. Self-pity distorts our perception of reality. Elijah thought he was the only one who hadn't caved in to evil. He was so wrong. Thousands still stood firm in their faith.

LOOKING UP *Help me, Lord, in my times of weakness. Thank You that You do not abandon me when my faith fails but lovingly restore me to my full strength.*

ASSOCIATIONS

1 Kings 21-22

LOOKING BACK One of history's most bizarre characters was born on this day in 1894. Rudolf Hess served as deputy leader of the Nazi Party in Germany and was Adolf Hitler's private secretary. In 1941, Hess flew a plane to Scotland to persuade Britain to get out of the war, saying that Hitler had no knowledge of the plan. Hess was imprisoned in Britain until after the war when he was sentenced to life imprisonment for war crimes. Hess committed suicide in Spandau Prison at age 93. Historians trace many of the atrocities of Hitler's era to the fact many men with deeply flawed characters became friends of Hitler, and together they unleashed hell on this earth.

LOOKING IN *Whom we select as friends influences the direction of our lives. Historians believe Hitler could never have done the dastardly things he did if he had not had those wicked men around him who pushed him on and applauded his actions. Jehoshaphat unwisely became pals with Ahab, a determined enemy of God. That foolish union between the righteous king of Judah and the evil king of Israel was an unmitigated disaster. Jehoshaphat was soon drawn into a battle he could, and should, have avoided. Later, Jehoshaphat's son would marry the daughter of Ahab. That association would introduce a reign of terror on Judah such as they had never known.*

LOOKING OUT

1. **Consorting with unbelievers draws us into compromising positions. Jehoshaphat should never have formed a close association with Ahab, the evil king of the northern nation.**
2. **Seeking only preachers who agree with us can be dangerous. Ahab didn't want spiritual advice. When it was demanded, he turned to prophets who spoke to please him.**
3. **Prophets who preach only to please are not really our friends. A spiritual leader must deliver the message God wants, regardless of the receiver or the reception of it.**
4. **You can run, but you can't hide. Ahab tried to circumvent the prophecy of Micaiah by disguising himself in battle. His effort was futile, for he was downed by a stray arrow.**
5. **Righteous people learn from their mistakes and refuse to repeat bad behavior. Jehoshaphat learned that evil association breeds disaster and refused to join Ahaziah.**

LOOKING UP *Help me, Lord, to choose my friends carefully, for they will deeply affect my decisions. May I always be a friend who brings out the best in others.*

SULLIED

APRIL 27

2 Kings 1-3

LOOKING BACK President Ulysses S. Grant was born on this day in 1822. Grant was a great general who led the Union armies to victory over the Confederates in the bloody Civil War. On April 9, 1865, Grant received General Robert E. Lee's surrender at Appomattox Courthouse, Virginia. Later, Grant, extremely popular because of his actions in the Civil War, became the 18th president of the United States. He was a good man, but scandal plagued his tenure as president. Sadly, Grant's appointees to various offices sullied his fine reputation during the eight years of his presidency. His administration was scandalized because he could not pick the right kind of friends.

LOOKING IN *Jehoshaphat also was a good man and even a good king. However, he too had problems in picking the right kind of friends. Jehoshaphat formed political and personal alliances with those who sullied his reputation. He made an alliance with Ahab, king of Israel. At first, this seemed like a brilliant move for little Judah. The immediate result was beneficial to both kingdoms. Years of conflict between the two nations came to an end, and both kingdoms were strengthened. But, the alliance proved disastrous because it introduced much evil into Judah. Sin is infectious. Before long, Judah suffered from the same illness that affected Israel.*

LOOKING OUT

1. Half-hearted commitment is never enough. Joram was not nearly as bad as Ahab, his father, but Israel's new king failed to follow God fully. God always wants all of us.
2. Mixed marriages draw us into conflict. The marriage between Jehoshaphat's son and Ahab's daughter obligated Judah's king to fight battles he could have avoided.
3. A godly reputation helps us in times of trouble. Elisha refused to assist Israel's king because of the nation's evil. Because of Jehoshaphat, the great prophet agreed to help.
4. Music prepares us to hear from God. Elisha called for a harpist to play so his troubled spirit could be calmed enough to hear from heaven. Such is the power of spiritual music.
5. God can give us victory in unusual ways. God instructed Elisha what to do to defeat the Moabites. It was unexpected and strange advice, but it worked perfectly.

LOOKING UP *Help me, Lord, to be fully committed to You. I know You want all of my heart, not just part of it. Again, today I pray that You guide me in selecting my friends.*

REWARDS

APRIL 28

2 Kings 4-5

LOOKING BACK The "biological clock gene" was discovered on this day in 1994. Northwestern University announced on April 28 that the gene governing the daily cycle of waking and sleeping, called the circadian rhythm, had been found in mice. Never before pinpointed in a mammal, the biological clock gene was found on mouse chromosome #5. Biological clocks in people work on schedules essential to life and health. The term "biological clock" also refers to a woman's child-bearing years. People who want to be parents often talk about how their "biological clock is ticking." They are anxious to produce offspring before it runs out.

LOOKING IN *The Shunammite woman's biological clock was ticking, and no one was more aware of that than she. The woman and her husband had graciously provided lodging for God's prophet without any expectation of reward. However, one cannot bless God's servants without being blessed in return. When Elisha learned that the woman's deepest desire for a child had been denied, he prayed and God gave the kind woman a son. The childless couple was thrilled with this unexpected blessing. They probably thought it a small sacrifice to give the prophet a room. However, God saw their unselfish love and gave them more than they could ever dream.*

LOOKING OUT

1. God takes care of those who take care of His work. The widow of a prophet receives a miracle from God because her late husband had been faithful to the Lord.
2. God provides as we obey. Elisha told the woman what to do to receive God's provision for her household. The oil multiplied as she obeyed the prophet's instructions.
3. God takes care of those who take care of His servants. The Shunammite woman provided a place to stay for Elisha. Soon God blessed her and her husband with a son.
4. Miracles provide faith for greater miracles. The Shunammite woman's faith was strengthened by the first miracle. Now, she needed an even greater one from God.
5. Sometimes we need to persist in prayer until the answer comes. The dead son was not restored right away. Life returned as Elisha prayed and held on to God.

LOOKING UP *Help me, Lord, not to give up too soon. Teach me to be persistent in my prayers for Your will. Help me also always to take care of Your anointed servants.*

LARGER

APRIL 29

2 Kings 6-8

LOOKING BACK William Randolph Hearst seemed larger than life. The famous American publisher of newspapers and magazines was born on this day in 1863. Hearst developed a sensational journalistic style and spent millions of dollars to interest and attract readers. Critics described his style as yellow journalism. Born in San Francisco, he attended Harvard University but was expelled in 1885 because of a practical joke he played on professors. Hearst's father, a mining magnate and U.S. Senator, then gave him the San Francisco Examiner. Hearst made this newspaper a remarkable financial success and made himself famous.

LOOKING IN *Like Hearst, the prophet Elisha seemed larger than life. However, Elisha was a godly man whose life was filled with mighty miracles. One of the greatest happened when Samaria was gripped with devastating famine. Ben-Hadad, the brutal king of Aram, had besieged the city so long that people were dying by the score. It appeared there was no hope. Just when it seemed there was absolutely no way to survive the siege, Elisha appeared on the scene with an astounding prophecy. His words were so fantastic they could hardly be believed. Even the king's aide called the prophet's words fantasy. However, God performed the miracle Elisha prophesied.*

LOOKING OUT

1. **Even the most desperate situation can turn around quickly when God is with us. Elisha assured the nation that the famine would end quickly and people would be fed.**
2. **Doubting can make us miss the miracles. The king's unbelieving aide scoffed at Elisha's prophecy. Sadly, he would never see the great miracle God was about to perform.**
3. **Sometimes action is required for us to see a miracle. In desperation, the lepers decided to visit the enemy camp. They found God had given victory and the camp was deserted.**
4. **God does fight our battles when we are in His will. The Arameans had deserted their camp because God had caused them to hear the sound of a mighty charging army.**
5. **Blessings of God are to be shared with the needy. The lepers knew it was not right for them to hoard what they had been given by God. They shared their bounty.**

LOOKING UP *Help me, Lord, to be generous and share with others what You have graciously given to me. Help me always to remember that nothing is impossible with You.*

FINAL JUSTICE

APRIL 30

2 Kings 9-10

LOOKING BACK Adolf Hitler died by his own hand on this day in 1945. The evil Nazi leader had spread death as no person has done in modern history. "Have no pity! Act brutally!" he told his soldiers. Hitler's forces killed about six million European Jews as well as about five million other people that Hitler regarded as racially inferior or politically dangerous. But by April 1945, Hitler had become a broken man. He shook so badly that aides questioned his survival. The war he had forced was lost. Hitler's head, hands, and feet trembled constantly. He was tortured by stomach cramps. Deep in his bunker, Hitler and his mistress killed themselves.

LOOKING IN *During those horrific days when Hitler stomped across the stage of history, many feared that justice would never come. It does seem at times that evil will never end and good will fail. That is only an illusion. God will make things right just as He did when Ahab's family brutalized God's people for so long. God raised up fanatical Jehu who unleashed a war of harsh retaliation on Ahab's household. He killed Jezebel and all the sons of wicked Ahab, sparing no one who had perpetrated violence. The land was finally cleansed of this evil. For many years, Ahab and Jezabel had their wicked way, but evil did not last forever.*

LOOKING OUT

1. God anoints us for a purpose, with power to accomplish His divine will. Jehu was specifically chosen to bring judgment on Ahab's house for their horrible sins.
2. We cannot know peace without purity. When those of Ahab's house asked if Jehu came in peace, he replied, "How can there be peace when such sin abounds in the land?"
3. God never forgets or forgives unrepentant injustice. Ahab's son was killed on the very ground his father had stolen from Naboth many years before. Justice will be served!
4. All sin must be stamped out or it will grow again. The guilty sons of Ahab were finally brought to justice during the sweeping purge of Jehu. Evil must be eliminated.
5. Evil will one day be conquered, and those who perpetrate it will be brought to awful shame. The temple of Baal, once proud and sensuous, became a public bathroom.

LOOKING UP *Lord, help me to remember that You will bring justice even though it seems long in coming. May I trust You enough to rest in Your promises and wait for Your justice.*

May

A Month of Great Beauty with Many Celebrations

May is one of the most beautiful months of the year in the North Temperate Zone. It was the third month according to the early Roman calendar—March, being the first. Later, the ancient Romans used January 1 for the beginning of their year, and May became the fifth month. May has always had 31 days. There are several fascinating stories about how the month of May was named. The most widely accepted explanation is that it was named for Maia, the Roman goddess of spring and growth. Her name seems to be related to a Latin word that means increase or growth. During this month, we will do some spiritual growing by reading the remainder of 2 Kings, 1 and 2 Chronicles, and the first six chapters of Ezra.

During May, the snow and ice have melted, and summer's intense heat has not yet begun. The first garden crops begin to sprout. Trees and grass are green, and wild plants are in bloom. Wild flowers that blossom in different parts of North America include the jack-in-the-pulpit, anemone, hepatica, forsythia, dogwood, and blue, yellow, and white violets. Many birds have built their nests, and mother birds are sitting on the eggs, which will soon hatch. The sheer beauty of this time encourages joyful celebrations.

Celebrations have abounded in May from early times. Ancient Romans held ceremonies in honor of their goddess, Maia, on May 1 and again on May 15. This was also a time sacred to Flora, the Roman goddess of flowers, prompting the Romans to celebrate May 1 with flower-decked parades. Long ago, the English started observing many May Day customs. Maypoles were erected in village parks. On the morning of May 1, the village youths went to the woods and gathered "mayflowers," or hawthorn blossoms, to decorate the Maypole. Girls wore their prettiest dresses, each hoping that she would be elected May queen. The queen then danced around the Maypole with her "subjects."

POWER WOMEN

2 Kings 11-12

LOOKING BACK Mary Harris "Mother" Jones was born on this day in 1830. She was a well-known figure in the United States labor movement in the late 1800's and early 1900's, helping organize unions, largely among coal miners. She also helped found the Industrial Workers of the World. After the death of her husband and four children in the Yellow Fever epidemic of 1867 and loss of her belongings in the Chicago fire of 1871, Jones devoted her energies and life to organizing and advancing the cause of labor. Jones was arrested many times. The jailing of a woman who was more than 70 years old aroused great sympathy for the labor movement.

LOOKING IN *Women can make a difference in areas one would not expect. "Mother" Jones made a great difference in the labor cause, improving the lot of those who could not speak for themselves. Athaliah, the queen mother of Israel, also made a great difference but in a negative way. Rather than improving the quality of life among her people, she perpetrated violence and evil. She even killed her own grandchildren so she could grab the throne of Judah. Athaliah reigned in Judah for over six bloody years. However, evil never lasts. Her day of judgment and death finally arrived. She reaped what she had sown.*

LOOKING OUT

1. **The evil one seeks to destroy, but God protects those doing His will. Joash is saved from death by his aunt, in spite of Athaliah's drive to destroy all heirs of the throne.**
2. **Evil lasts for a while but will be put down. Athaliah ranted and raved for over six horrible years. Her bloody reign was cut short by Jehoiada's righteous rebellion.**
3. **The righteous rise up when given the right leadership. Jehoiada provided the spark needed to throw off the yoke of bitter oppression Athaliah had put on the nation.**
4. **When we determine to be the Lord's people, the influence of evil is destroyed. Israel made a covenant with God and then rose up to destroy the despicable idols of Baal.**
5. **Joy returns when we return to God. After Athaliah's death, all the people of the land rejoiced, and the city was quiet. Righteousness sets the stage for peace and prosperity.**

LOOKING UP *Help me, Lord, to provide the spiritual leadership that will inspire others to right living. Give me the strength to stand against evil and speak up for good.*

INFLUENCE

2 Kings 13-15

LOOKING BACK Italian artist, scientist, and inventor Leonardo da Vinci died on this day in 1519. He is known as one of the greatest painters and most versatile geniuses in history. His portrait, "Mona Lisa," and his religious scene, "The Last Supper," rank among the most famous pictures ever painted. In addition to da Vinci's great works of art, he also invented the first parachute and drew plans for the helicopter. Like many Renaissance artists, Leonardo sometimes worked as an engineer or military architect. He produced designs for a variety of war machines, among them tanks, machine guns, and movable bridges. His influence is still felt centuries after his death.

LOOKING IN *Great men live through their influence long after their lifetime. Elisha was such a man. This remarkable prophet had been used by God in such dramatic ways that kings sought him out for advice and help. Although weak and feeble in old age, Elisha was consulted when crisis came. Powerful enough to perform miracles and appoint kings, yet sensitive enough to weep over the fate of Israel, Elisha, disciple and successor to Elijah, proved to be both prophet and statesman. Chosen by God and handpicked by Elijah in the latter half of the ninth century B.C., Elisha directed the historical drama of Israel. His influence is still felt today.*

LOOKING OUT

1. **Good men sometimes suffer. Just because Elisha was a great prophet did not mean he was immune from the human condition. He also felt pain.**
2. **We never retire from God's calling on our lives. Elisha, though old and feeble, prophesied powerfully to the timid king.**
3. **We are the tools, but God is the power behind us. Elisha places his hands over the king's symbolizing God's power to be used through those hands.**
4. **We must always be bold when doing God's work. Jehoash timidly obeys the prophet's words and is sharply rebuked by Elisha.**
5. **Our effectiveness and influence can go far beyond this earthly life. Elisha touched others long after his death.**

LOOKING UP *Help me, Lord, not to be half-hearted in doing Your work. Rather, let me approach my assignment with boldness and enthusiasm.*

MACHIAVELLIAN

2 Kings 16-17

LOOKING BACK Niccolo Machiavelli was born on this day in 1469. Many scholars consider Machiavelli to be the father of modern political science. This Italian statesman and writer viewed the state as an organism, with its ruler as the head and its people as the body. He said a healthy state is unified, orderly, and in balance; but an unhealthy state is disorderly, unbalanced, and may require strong measures to restore it to normalcy. Machiavelli called for a leader to use any means necessary to preserve the state, resorting to cruelty, deception, and force if nothing else worked. As a result, the word "Machiavellian" came to mean cunning and unscrupulous.

LOOKING IN *Many scholars say Machiavelli was misunderstood and, thus, has gotten a bum rap. While that may be true, another ruler of long ago used Machiavellian principles and is not misunderstood. Ahaz was the son and successor of Jotham, king of Judah. He was the father of Hezekiah. The Bible characterizes Ahaz as an evil man who participated in the most monstrous of idolatrous practices. Ahaz's name means "he has grasped," and he became known as one of Judah's most despicable leaders. His actions were blasphemous. His horrible and disobedient 16-year reign was contemporary with the prophets Isaiah and Micah.*

LOOKING OUT

1. **Decency disappears when we give ourselves to evil. Ahaz turned from God and copied the behavior of God's enemies. He soon sacrificed his own children to idols.**
2. **When we stand for nothing, we fall for everything. Without a personal relationship with God, Ahaz started sacrificing to idols on every hill and under every tree.**
3. **If we reject God, we won't have His help when the crunch comes. Ahaz had to turn to the king of Assyria when his enemies threatened, because he had rejected God.**
4. **Unholy alliances distort faith and make us captives. Ahaz's alliance with Tiglath-Pileser caused him to copy a pagan altar and give deference to the king of Assyria.**
5. **Sin destroys us and our reputation. During his 16–year reign, Ahaz was known as an evil man who participated in the most monstrous of idolatrous practices.**

LOOKING UP *Help me, Lord, to follow You totally and not make evil alliances with those who do not serve You. Help me to boldly stand up for truth and be uncompromising in my convictions.*

ENDED

MAY 4

2 Kings 18-20

LOOKING BACK Mobster Al Capone entered federal prison on this day in 1932, ending his bloody reign of crime. During the 1920's, Capone built a brutal criminal empire in Chicago that created murder and mayhem. Capone had come to Chicago to work for a racketeer. A series of gangland shootings soon left the violent and clever Capone in control. His gang dominated liquor, gambling, and prostitution rackets. They fought off rival gangs with submachine guns and corrupted police and politicians with bribes. Finally, Capone was convicted of income tax evasion. After eight years in prison, he retired to his mansion in Florida where he died in 1947 from syphilis.

LOOKING IN *Few, if any, mourned the passing of Al Capone. Most give a sigh of relief when brutal and bloody men come to the end of their lives. That certainly was the case when Ahaz finally expired. Ahaz had led Judah down the path to destruction, in spite of warnings from the prophets Micah and Isaiah. He had placed an altar made from a Syrian model in God's Temple. Now the wicked king was dead, and Judah rejoiced. The final humiliation came when he was not buried in the royal tombs. A new wind of reform started sweeping through the land. Hezekiah, unlike his evil father, took the throne and began to make things right.*

LOOKING OUT

1. **We don't have to be victimized by generational sins. Hezekiah's father was an evil king, but Hezekiah didn't follow in his footsteps. He was a good and godly man.**
2. **We must be careful to worship the Lord, not an experience. Israel turned the brazen snake pole into an idol. Once it had been a means of healing for the nation.**
3. **Trust in God puts us in a higher class. Because Hezekiah followed the Lord fully, the Bible says there was no one like Hezekiah-either before or after.**
4. **Righteousness means that we hold fast to God despite the shifting sands of life. Hezekiah remained steadfast, never turning away from the Lord.**
5. **When we please the Lord, He causes us to prosper. The Bible records that Hezekiah was successful in everything he did because of his great trust in the Lord.**

LOOKING UP *Help me, Lord, to always be steadfast in my life for You, turning neither to the right nor to the left. Help me always to please You by the way I think and act.*

CINCO DE MAYO

2 Kings 21-23

LOOKING BACK Today is Cinco de Mayo, a holiday celebrated by Mexicans and Mexican Americans. The name is Spanish for Fifth of May and commemorates the victory of a Mexican army over a French army at the Battle of Puebla on May 5, 1862. The Mexican army, led by General Ignacio Zaragoza, won the battle even though the French force was better armed and three times as large. The battle occurred after Emperor Napoleon III of France sent troops to Mexico to conquer the country. Cinco de Mayo is celebrated in Mexico with parades, festivals, music, and dancing. In the U.S., celebrations include parades, folk dancing, speeches, carnival rides, and music.

LOOKING IN *Relief from oppression is always a cause for celebration. Judah had suffered much oppression because of their sin. When the Book of the Law was discovered and repentance made, the nation's joy was restored. Josiah's reign brought back a respect for God and ushered the nation into a time of magnificent joy and peace. Josiah's name appropriately means, "Yahweh heals." He succeeded his father Amon, an idolatrous king, who ruled for only two years before being murdered by his servants. At eight, Josiah became king due to wishes of "the people of the land" who had put his father's assassins to death. He reigned for 31 years.*

LOOKING OUT

1. **When we search for God, we find His Word. When Josiah began to repair the Temple, his workers found a copy of God's Word. This find sparked a revival in the land.**
2. **God's Word clearly lets us know God's expectations of us. Josiah tore his robes when he learned from the Word that the whole nation had been living in disobedience.**
3. **God never points out a problem without offering the solution. Hilkiah and his assistants went to talk with the prophetess Huldah to see what the nation should do.**
4. **God always forgives those whose hearts are sincere. Huldah announced God's response to Josiah. The nation would be forgiven when they repented of their sins.**
5. **God delays judgment when we seek His face in true repentance. Josiah was promised that he would not see the destruction of the nation because of their continued sin.**

LOOKING UP *Help me, Lord, to love Your mercy and quickly correct all those things You show me that I do wrong. Thank You for the conviction of the Holy Spirit that keeps me on track.*

CONSCIENCE

2 Kings 24-25

LOOKING BACK President Woodrow Wilson led the United States through World War I and gained lasting fame as a champion of world peace and democracy. He was one of the most remarkable men in American history. Before reaching the heights of popularity as a world statesman, he had achieved success in two other careers. As a scholar, teacher, and university president, he greatly influenced education. As a political leader, he brought reforms to state and national government. On this day in 1911 Wilson said, "The man with power but without conscience, could, with an eloquent tongue, if he cared for nothing but his own power, put the whole country into a flame."

LOOKING IN *Wilson's wise words have been proven time and again throughout history. The Bible reports that many of Judah's kings were responsible for setting their nation on fire. Jehoiakim is an example. This son of Josiah, by his blatant disregard for God's Word, brought the wrath of Babylon down on the nation. Jehoiakim was a throne name given to him by Pharaoh Neco of Egypt, who deposed his brother Jehoahaz. His original name had been Eliakim. Jehoiakim reigned for 11 years. At first Judah was subject to Egypt, and then when Babylon defeated Egypt, Jehoiakim transferred his allegiance to Babylon but rebelled after three years.*

LOOKING OUT

1. **We get into trouble when we lean on our own understanding rather than God's Word. Jehoiakim had been told not to oppose Nebuchadnezzar. He didn't listen.**
2. **When we disobey God, the hordes of hell come against us. God sent hostile forces against Jehoiakim because he had blatantly disobeyed His specific instructions.**
3. **God's holiness will not tolerate sin. Judah fell because of the awful sins committed by the nation and its leaders. They had been warned to repent but continued to rebel.**
4. **God's judgment is always right, because He looks on the heart, not just outward acts. Though Jehoiachin reigned only three months, God saw that he was wicked.**
5. **We lose it all when we continue to plunge headlong in our sinful ways. Judah lost the Temple treasures they had long cherished because they repeatedly refused to repent.**

LOOKING UP *Help me, Lord, to turn from any rebellion so I may be forgiven and rest in joy with You. May I never lean on my own understanding but always seek You for wisdom.*

UNHEARING

MAY 7

1 Chronicles 1-2

LOOKING BACK Ludwig van Beethoven was one of the greatest composers in history. His most famous works include the third (Eroica), fifth, sixth (Pastorale), and ninth symphonies. His famous "Symphony No. 9 in D Minor" was performed for the first time at Vienna, Austria, on this day in 1824. Known as the "Choral" because of his use of voices in symphonic form for the first time, the ninth was his musical interpretation of Schiller's "Ode to Joy." Beethoven was completely deaf when he composed it. It was said a soloist had to tug on his sleeve, when the performance was over, to get him to turn around and see the enthusiastic response he couldn't hear.

LOOKING IN *Often, when we read these chapters of 1 Chronicles, we are "unhearing" because the detail is tedious and the names unfamiliar. Like Beethoven, we need to be "tugged on the sleeve" to remind us there is something very important to learn in these difficult chapters. The attention to detail, that we see here, lets us know God cares about the little things in our lives and worship. Often we think God too big or busy to be bothered with small things. This passage shows us He is not. This section also reminds us that God never forgets anyone, anywhere, at any time. He is intimately involved in all of His creation and deeply loves those He creates.*

LOOKING OUT

1. God never forgets any of us. Even though the Israelites were His chosen people, Chronicles carefully lists others who are just as important to Him.
2. God is more than a tribal god. Israel was "chosen" as God's messenger to the world, but this does not mean He is theirs, alone. He is God of all peoples everywhere.
3. God cares for the displaced and disgraced. Hagar represents those who are uprooted and put down. God carefully lists her descendants because He loves them.
4. God has no second-class citizens. Even though the sons of Keturah and Abraham were not "chosen," God records their lives because He cares for all alike.
5. God cares for the disobedient. Esau rejected his birthright, but his descendants are faithfully recorded in Scripture. God still cares about those who disobey him.

LOOKING UP *Lord, help me to better understand and appreciate Your great love—a love that will not let me go. Help me to express this love to those You have placed in my life.*

UNEXPECTED

1 Chronicles 3-5

LOOKING BACK Harry S. Truman was born on this day in 1884. He became president at one of the most critical moments in American history. Truman had been vice-president for only 83 days when President Franklin D. Roosevelt died on April 12, 1945. World War II still had to be won. Plans to establish the United Nations organization had just been started. Not many people thought that Truman would rise to the task before him. Before this time, he was known mainly for his work as chairman of a wartime Senate investigating committee. However, Truman met the challenges with courage, determination, and imagination, becoming a great president.

LOOKING IN *Often those of whom we expect the least surprise us the most. Truman was thought to be only a political hack, not the great statesman he proved to be. Among all the names listed in Chronicles is one that surprises. Jabez is the abused child of the Bible. His name sounds like the Hebrew word for pain. Jabez's mother bore him in pain. The Bible doesn't say what that pain was, but every time she called him, Jabez was reminded that he brought pain to her. He was probably unwanted and unloved. Yet, in spite of all that, he became more honorable than all his brothers. How Jabez succeeded, when he was doomed to fail, is outlined in this reading.*

LOOKING OUT

1. We need not be destroyed by our predispositions. Jabez was at a distinct disadvantage because his mother didn't want him. However, he rose above all the others.
2. The first step to healing is to seek the right solution. Jabez knew he needed help so he called on God. The answer to our hurts is found only in our Savior.
3. Specific prayer should be made for specific problems. Jabez didn't just pray a general prayer but was specific in his request to the Lord. He knew the help he needed.
4. We must daily pray for God to keep us from temptation. Jabez knew he was vulnerable to certain weaknesses, and specifically asked the Lord to keep him from this harm.
5. God hears and heals the hurting heart. Jabez became more honorable than all his brothers because he had called on the God of Israel. God is able to heal our deepest hurts.

LOOKING UP *Help me, Lord to always turn to You when I need healing for my hurts. You, alone, can make me well. Help me to understand my predispositions and turn to You in times of hurt.*

EXAMPLES

1 Chronicles 6-7

LOOKING BACK Radical abolitionist John Brown was born on this day in 1800. His attempt to free the slaves cost a number of lives and helped, indirectly, to bring about the American Civil War. From his youth, Brown hated slavery and aided fugitive slaves escaping to Canada. He organized a league among Blacks for their protection against slave-catchers. His efforts became more bloody as time passed. In Kansas, Brown led an expedition of men who brutally murdered five pro-slavery settlers. He was captured at Harpers Ferry, West Virginia, and hanged for his crimes. Brown's mission was right but his methods wrong, doing more harm than good.

LOOKING IN *Just like Brown's actions, both good and bad, the list of those in Chronicles is a mixed bag. There are heros of faith listed here but also some scoundrels. For example, Levi's tribe is counted. Levi himself had brought shame to Jacob by joining with Simeon in a brutal murder scheme. Yet his descendants became those who represented God to man and man to God. Issachar, the ninth son of Jacob, is listed. Even though the tribe was not prominent in Israel's history, they were important to God. Benjamin and his descendants are mentioned. Among the scoundrels of this small tribe was Israel's first king, disobedient Saul.*

LOOKING OUT

1. **Bad backgrounds do not condemn us to failure. Levi was condemned for his great evil, yet Moses and the priests come from that tribe.**
2. **Redemption is always possible. The Levites were given special status because they stood up for God and against evil at Mt. Sinai.**
3. **Courage is required in God's service. Azariah confronted King Uzziah when he stepped over the boundary separating kings and priests.**
4. **God's Word can change a nation. Hilkiah found the Book of the Law, which brought great revival to the backslidden people.**
5. **Pain doesn't last forever. Jehozadak was the high priest who returned from exile in Babylon with Zerubbabel. The captivity was over and restoration begun.**

LOOKING UP *Thank you, Lord, because You forget no one. May I draw lessons from the lives of those good people named in the Chronicles and duplicate their dedication.*

TRAGIC FIGURES

MAY 10

1 Chronicles 8-10

LOOKING BACK One of the South's most able Civil War generals died on this day in 1863. General "Stonewall" Jackson fought his greatest battle in May of 1863. Jackson took his Second Corps around Union forces near Chancellorsville, Virginia. Jackson's men struck from behind and drove the enemy back in wild disorder. At nightfall, Jackson went ahead of the line to scout. In the darkness, some of his own men mistook him for the enemy and shot him. As Jackson lay wounded, doctors amputated his left arm. Lee remarked, "He has lost his left arm, but I have lost my right arm." Jackson died of pneumonia eight days after he was shot.

LOOKING IN *Saul, Israel's first king, was also a great general. He proved himself by delivering the city of Jabesh-gilead and was acclaimed king at Gilgal. From Gibeah ("Saul's Hill"), he drove the Philistines from the hill country and fought other enemies of Israel. However, this great general was a tragic figure with a flawed character. In his final wretched condition, he consults the witch at Endor. The following day, Saul and three sons are killed at the hands of the Philistines on Mount Gilboa. Saul's body is beheaded and hung on the walls of Beth-shan, from where it is later rescued and buried by the grateful inhabitants of Jabesh-gilead.*

LOOKING OUT

1. **God sees success differently than we do. Many would call Saul successful because he forged Israel's first kingdom, but God called him a failure because he was unfaithful.**
2. **God's Word is to be heeded, not just heard. Saul crumbled because he did not keep the Word of the Lord. He heard it often but refused to let it guide his life.**
3. **Evil spirits are not to be tampered with. Saul consulted a medium to get direction when God refused to speak to him, leading to his eventual downfall.**
4. **Failure to pray begets failure. Saul did not enquire of the Lord. He only sought God when he was pushed into a corner. God wants an active relationship with His children.**
5. **Continued rebellion finally cuts us loose from a loving God. Saul was given many years to correct his bad behavior. He refused to do so and finally was cut off.**

LOOKING UP *Help me, Lord, always to be faithful to You, for that is what You deem as real success. May I not just seek You when I am in trouble, but have a daily relationship with You.*

TIMING

MAY 11

1 Chronicles 11-12

LOOKING BACK Timing is vital. Charles Warren Fairbanks was born on this day in 1852. He served as Vice-President of the United States under Theodore Roosevelt. Fairbanks had desperately wanted to be president, and would have, had he timed it better. Fairbanks rejected an offer to be William McKinley's running mate in 1900. If he had accepted, Fairbanks would have become president, rather than Roosevelt, when President McKinley was assassinated in 1901. Fairbanks hoped to be the presidential candidate in 1908. But he didn't get along well with Roosevelt, and the President helped William Howard Taft win the nomination.

LOOKING IN *David knew all about timing. Samuel had anointed him as king of Israel, but it would be many years before he actually took the throne. David refused to rise up against Saul, Israel's first king, opting to wait for God's perfect timing. This obedient attitude paid off handsomely for David. Hearing of the deaths of Saul and Jonathan, David avenged the murder of Saul and sang a lament over the fallen. He then moved to Hebron where he was crowned king. This led to war with Israel under Saul's son Ishbosheth. Then, Ishbosheth was suddenly assassinated. At that point, the northern tribes crowned David king at Hebron, uniting all Israel under him.*

LOOKING OUT

1. God's great blessings are worth the wait. David had waited a long time to become king, and now his time had come. He had wisely refused to move before God's time.
2. God builds our reputation during the hard times. The years of difficulty David suffered proved to be a blessing. The people clearly saw the character of this great man.
3. We can do the "impossible" when God is with us. No one had been able to conquer Jerusalem, but David succeeded because it was God's will and time. He was God's man.
4. When we go with God, we become more and more effective. David's power and reputation grew daily because he faithfully loved and served God.
5. Good men are God's gift to godly leaders. God raised up many "mighty men" around David to help him lead. God always gives us helpers to accomplish our assigned tasks.

LOOKING UP *Help me, Lord, to learn to wait on Your blessings even though the days seem long before they come. May I always remember that Your will must be done in Your time.*

SYMBOLS

1 Chronicles 13-16

LOOKING BACK Florence Nightingale was born on this day in 1820. More than any other, she symbolizes the nursing profession. Wounded British soldiers in the Crimean War called her "The Lady with the Lamp" when she walked their hospital halls at night. At 16, Florence thought she heard God's voice telling her she had a special mission in life. Her family opposed her decision to become a nurse, but that didn't stop her. When Britain and France went to war with Russia in the Crimea, the secretary of war asked Nightingale to take charge of nursing. She sailed for the Crimea with 38 nurses and became a legend by her tender and loving care.

LOOKING IN *Just as Nightingale has become a symbol of nursing, the Ark of the Covenant was Israel's symbol of God's presence. A very ancient poem, the "Song of the Ark" in Numbers, sheds light on the Ark's function in the wilderness wanderings. The Ark was the symbol that guided the pilgrims and led them in battle. If they acted in faithlessness, failing to follow this guidance, the consequences could be drastic. The Ark was also regarded as the throne of the invisible deity or His footstool. All were excited when David wanted to bring it to his new capital. However, when the king failed to read God's instructions for transport, tragedy resulted.*

LOOKING OUT

1. **Reading God's Word helps us prevent pain. If David had read God's Word and then transported the Ark in the right manner, tragedy would have been avoided.**
2. **Doing things right assures success. After David had consulted God's Word, he assigned the proper people to transport the Ark. Things turned out well.**
3. **God makes our errors plain so we can see and correct our mistakes. David, having understood what he did wrong, instructed the priests and Levites regarding God's expectations.**
4. **Great joy comes when we have fully obeyed God's Word. The Ark of the Covenant was brought to Jerusalem with singing, dancing, and rejoicing.**
5. **The enemy always seeks to rob us of our joy. David's wife was furious at the sight of David dancing before the Lord. She began to despise him in her heart.**

LOOKING UP *Help me, Lord, to always consult Your Word so that I might do Your will, Your way. Thank You for Your correction, even though at times it is painful.*

"STOPS"

1 Chronicles 17-20

LOOKING BACK American evangelist D.L. Moody started noonday prayer meetings in London on this day in 1867. The 30-year-old preacher had created a great stir through his soul-winning efforts in both the United States and Britain. He went on to found Moody Memorial Church, the Moody Bible Institute, and the Moody Press in Chicago. Passionate for the Lord, Moody left his job as a shoe salesman in Chicago to devote his time to Sunday school ministry and YMCA activities. The soon-to-be-famous evangelist was conducting great revival campaigns with singer and hymn writer Ira D. Sankey. Moody became the world's most acclaimed evangelist of his day.

LOOKING IN *Just as Moody was passionate for the Lord, David also wanted to do something to prove his great love for God. He dreamed of building a beautiful home for God in Jerusalem. The Temple would be a place for the national worship of Yahweh. One Hebrew expression for temple is hekal, meaning "palace or great house." It described a home for God or for an earthly king. After David had built himself a cedar palace, he thought it only proper he should build one for Yahweh, too. It seemed like such a grand idea that even the prophet Nathan wholeheartedly agreed. However, God was not as enthusiastic and stopped the project.*

LOOKING OUT

1. **Good ideas are not always God's ideas. David loved God and wanted to build a house for Him. It sounded like a good idea, but that was not what God wanted David to do.**
2. **Even good and godly men can be swept up with an idea that is not pleasing to God. Nathan initially endorsed David's building plans but later learned he was wrong.**
3. **The "stops" of a good man are also ordered by the Lord. God told Nathan to have David stop the Temple-building project. God had other plans for Israel's king.**
4. **God never takes something away from us without giving us something better. David was forbidden to build a Temple but received an eternal heritage for his family.**
5. **We are often overwhelmed by the sheer goodness of our God. David is staggered by God's promise to forever establish his family as heirs to the throne.**

LOOKING UP *Lord, help me to want everything You want me to have and to reject all You don't want me to have. Thank You for stopping me when I'm going the wrong direction.*

CENSUS

1 Chronicles 21-23

LOOKING BACK On May 14, 1948, the modern nation of Israel officially came into being. The surrounding Arab nations immediately attacked the new state in the first of several Arab-Israeli wars. Also on this day, the United States became the first country to officially recognize Israel as a nation. Israel was founded as a homeland for Jews from all parts of the world. More than four out of five of its people are Jews. Even Jews who live elsewhere consider Israel their spiritual home. Almost all the non-Jews in Israel are Arabs. Since the beginning of the reformed nation, the hostile and overpowering enemies of Israel have tried to crush it but have not succeeded.

LOOKING IN *Today, nearly 70 percent of Israel's population is composed of "secular" Jews rather than "orthodox" Jews. Ancient Israel was much different. Leaders like David led the nation in strict obedience to God. When leaders were disobedient, they were brought to task just as David was when he ordered an unauthorized census. While the Bible does not explain why taking the census was wrong, some scholars have speculated that David had shifted his focus of trust from God to his large and powerful army. God sharply slapped his hands to remind David that no matter the size of his nation, God was still Israel's Protector-Provider.*

LOOKING OUT

1. **Success can blind our eyes to Satan's devices. David had arrived and achieved incredible success. At that moment, the evil one blind-sided him with the idea of a census.**
2. **God warns us when we are about to do wrong. God sent Joab to warn David not to take a census. Joab was probably the only one who could have gotten David's attention.**
3. **Pain always gets our attention. It wasn't long after the census that David experienced great pain. He wisely determined that the discomfort came because of his disobedience.**
4. **Knowing the character of God helps us make good choices. David was given a choice as to the discipline he was to receive. He knew God was more merciful than man.**
5. **Our offerings must be true sacrifices. David refused to accept the threshing floor of Araunah as a gift, saying he would not sacrifice anything that had cost him nothing.**

LOOKING UP *Help me, Lord, to know Your character and to always give You gifts that are true sacrifices. Help me to quickly correct my wrongs when I have gone astray.*

MINISTERS

1 Chronicles 24-25

LOOKING BACK Captain Bartholomew Gosnold became the first Englishman to land on the New England coast on this day in 1602. Later, he helped secure grants of American charters and belonged to the first governing council of the Jamestown, Virginia colony. Jamestown was America's first permanent English settlement. The 104 original settlers were all men and boys. Survival of the Jamestown settlement was doubtful for the first 20 years. Swampy land, bad water, and inadequate food and shelter contributed to high death rates. Disorganized leadership also added to their problems. About two-thirds of the original group died of disease and starvation.

LOOKING IN *One of the main reasons Jamestown survived was because they finally got organized. Organization is vital for any successful endeavor. That is why David carefully organized those who would minister in God's Temple. Each group was divinely called and appreciated for its contribution. The priests' functions primarily involved sacrifices at the altar and worship in the shrine. Other activities were blessing the people, determining the will of God, and instructing the people in the law of God. This instruction included the application of the laws of cleanness. Some of these functions, like blessing and teaching, would not be reserved for priests alone.*

LOOKING OUT

1. **Ministers and ministries are to be in cooperation, not competition. Israel's priests were chosen impartially and worked in cooperation to accomplish God's will.**
2. **All those who minister should be shown equal respect. Although some of the Levites were not priests, they were given the same respect as those who did serve.**
3. **Music can be a powerful preacher. Musicians were chosen "for the ministry of prophesying." Lilt and rhythm in presentation make truths easier to remember.**
4. **There is no "lesser service" in the Kingdom of God. The Temple gatekeepers were like our modern day church ushers. They were given great respect and appreciation.**
5. **Those called to govern should be under the government of God. Commanders for the tribes who served the king and their country were established. They were called of God.**

LOOKING UP *Help me, Lord, to love and respect all of those who serve You by being spiritual leaders. May I be placed in service where You feel I can be my best for You.*

FRIENDS

MAY 16

1 Chronicles 26-27

May

LOOKING BACK President Woodrow Wilson was known not only for his wisdom but also for his wit. Historians consider Wilson one of the three or four most successful presidents of the United States. They agree that, as a spokesman for humanity in a world crisis, he stood for integrity, purity of purpose, and responsibility. Not even Wilson's enemies suggested he was weak or stupid. They knew he was honest and that not even friendship could turn him aside from what he thought was right. He also had a sharp tongue that could cut to the quick of a matter. On this day in 1914, he said, "Some Americans need hyphens in their names because only part of them has come over."

LOOKING IN *Wilson's witty and caustic comment was intended to point out the divided loyalties many Americans exhibited when the war in Europe exploded. That first bloody World War forced those who straddled the fence to get off on one side or the other. Crisis always makes us choose sides. That happened when Absalom tried to rip the kingdom from David's hands. Now there could be no more divided loyalties. Each person around the king and his rebellious son had to choose where his loyalties lay. Those who opted to stay with David made the wise choice, since God was not through with His obedient servant.*

LOOKING OUT

1. **Wise leaders put wise people around them. David appointed his uncle as an adviser, not because Jonathan was a relative, but because he was a wise man.**
2. **Fathers must not abandon their parental responsibility. Tragically, David left the raising of his sons to Jehiel, which proved to be a disastrous decision.**
3. **Betrayal brings bitter pain. Ahithophel abandoned David during Absalom's rebellion, breaking the king's heart. Later, Ahithophel would commit suicide.**
4. **Real friends are forever. Hushai, David's good friend, gave counsel to Absalom, buying time for David to establish new headquarters and gather forces for a new strategy.**
5. **Ruthless ambition breeds tragedy. Power-hungry Joab tries to push Adonijah to the throne over Solomon. After David's death, Solomon ordered Benaiah to kill Joab.**

LOOKING UP *Thank You, Lord, for giving me friends who help me accomplish the task You have assigned to me. May I always appreciate them and their unselfish work.*

FINANCES

MAY 17

1 Chronicles 28-29

LOOKING BACK On this day in 1792, the New York Stock Exchange was established. Some two dozen merchants and brokers joined to create the organization. In fair weather they operated under a buttonwood tree on Wall Street. In bad weather they moved to the shelter of a coffeehouse to conduct their business. Today, the NYSE is in the Financial District. Wall Street is a short, narrow street in New York City. With Broad and New Streets, it forms a triangle where the New York Stock Exchange and many great commercial houses and banks are located. The district is the heart of United States' banking and business and a worldwide symbol of finance.

LOOKING IN *Great institutions almost always have small starts. That was true of Solomon's magnificent Temple. David was not permitted to build God's house, but he was allowed to raise funds for the building. David now makes a last lavish, personal gift for the Temple building fund. His example and appeal precipitate a willing, joyful response from the people, and the gifts pour in. Deeply moved, David thanks God from his heart that such giving is possible from men, who apart from God's goodness have nothing. His prayer is one of the greatest in the Old Testament and shows just why this man could be described as "a man after God's own heart."*

LOOKING OUT

1. **Structured times of praise should be made when victories are won. David called for a public praise meeting after the people had responded in faithful giving to God's work.**
2. **All that we have to give to God, He has first given to us. David was overwhelmed with the thought that he would be able to give generously to a God Who has everything.**
3. **Testing reveals our character and is part of God's plan for our lives. David understood why God permitted certain trials and stated that God was pleased with integrity.**
4. **When we give, our hearts follow. David was thrilled with the willing offerings of the people for the Temple. He knew that where their treasure was, their hearts would be also.**
5. **We pray passionately for our children, but it's their decision whether they faithfully follow the Lord. David did all he could for Solomon, but his son made the final choice.**

LOOKING UP *Help me, Lord, to always be a willing and generous giver to You and Your work. I boldly ask for greater financial blessings so that I might give more to Your work.*

BLESSINGS

MAY 18

2 Chronicles 1-5

LOOKING BACK Napoleon Bonaparte proclaimed himself emperor of France on this day in 1804. Napoleon is both a historical figure and a legend. His life has fired the imaginations of great writers, film makers, and playwrights. Their works have done much to create the Napoleonic legend. He was one of the greatest military commanders in history, but was also a power-hungry conqueror. Standing 5 feet 2 inches tall, Napoleon was an inspirational and dramatic leader. He could also be cynical and demanding. He was overly ambitious. Napoleon's insatiable ambition ultimately drove him to overextend his power, leading to his downfall.

LOOKING IN *Solomon, like Napoleon, was a legend in his time. He too was powerful and overly ambitious. At first Solomon relied on God for wisdom. However, as his power and prestige grew, so did his pride. Solomon was born to David and Bathsheba after the death of their first son. Although not the oldest living son of David, he was crowned king, after his mother and Nathan the prophet intervened and secured David's decision to have Solomon succeed him. Solomon is remembered most for his wisdom, his building program, and his wealth generated through trade and administrative reorganization. He also wrote 3,000 proverbs and 1,005 songs.*

LOOKING OUT

1. **Security comes from God alone. Solomon was firmly established in the kingdom because "the Lord his God was with him and made him exceedingly great."**
2. **God takes note of those who seek His counsel first. Solomon began his prosperous reign by first going to God. In response, God told him to ask whatever he wanted.**
3. **Unselfish prayers bring great benefit. Solomon asked for wisdom and knowledge to guide the people rather than for riches, long life, or unbridled power. God gave it all to him.**
4. **God cares for those who care for those He loves. Because Solomon wanted to rule God's people wisely, God gave him great wealth–far more than he could imagine.**
5. **Blessings are not always what we think. While there was nothing wrong with the gifts God gave Solomon, the new king wasn't mature enough to handle prosperity.**

LOOKING UP *Help me, Lord, to have the character to handle the many blessings You will bring my way. Teach me to pray unselfish prayers, for I know that pleases you.*

UNFORGETTABLE

MAY 19

2 Chronicles 6-7

LOOKING BACK In 1780, on this day, near-total darkness descended on New England for no apparent reason. Many frightened people believed doomsday had arrived. At New Haven, Connecticut, Colonel Abraham Davenport opposed adjournment of the town council by saying, "I am against adjournment. The day of judgment is either approaching or it is not. If it is not, there is no need for adjournment. If it is, I choose to be found doing my duty. I wish therefore that candles may be brought." To this day, no scientific, verifiable cause for this widespread phenomenon has been discovered. That unusual day was one never to be forgotten.

LOOKING IN *The day Solomon dedicated the Temple was also unforgettable. Darkness didn't descend, but God clearly made Himself known to the people. His glory so filled the new Temple that the priests couldn't enter to minister. The prophet Isaiah made it clear that this earthly Temple was viewed as a microcosm of the heavenly Temple, where the King of the universe really dwells. The quaking and smoke of the Lord's presence at Sinai were manifested at the Temple dedication. Israel understood that it was only by God's grace that He consented to dwell with His people. On that special day, God's people were given a glorious memory, never to be erased.*

LOOKING OUT

1. God is equally at home in the hard times as well as in the good. God had told Solomon He would dwell in a dark cloud and now in the magnificent Temple made for Him.
2. Public testimony to God's faithfulness increases faith. Solomon reminded the people that God had accomplished exactly what He had promised to David.
3. God is big enough to create the whole universe but small enough to live within our hearts. Solomon acknowledged God's greatness and asked that He hear His servant's prayer.
4. When trouble comes, our first response should be to go to God. Through his prayer, Solomon admonished the people that they should seek God in times of great distress.
5. God wants all the world to know Him. Solomon publicly proclaimed in his prayer that all the peoples of the earth should know God's name and learn to love Him.

LOOKING UP *Help me, Lord, to publicly proclaim the goodness and greatness of my Lord to the lost. May my life and words always be an example of one who loves You passionately.*

MYSTERY

2 Chronicles 8-10

LOOKING BACK On this day in 1932, Amelia Earhart became the first woman to fly solo across the Atlantic. Just five years later, on July 2, she and her navigator, Fred Noonan, disappeared without a trace while trying to fly around the equator. They had left New Guinea the day before to begin the longest leg of the journey, a 2,600-mile flight to Howland Island in the central Pacific Ocean. The next day, a U.S. Navy vessel picked up radio messages from Earhart in which she reported empty fuel tanks. But efforts to make radio contact failed. A massive search found no trace of plane or crew. The disappearance remains a mystery that has never been solved.

LOOKING IN *Another mystery never solved is why Rehoboam turned down the advice of the wise elders and accepted the "insane" direction of the young rebels. It is clear he took three days to think about his decision, but we are never told why he made this very bad choice. In reaction to Rehoboam's decision, the northern tribes revolted and made the rebel Jeroboam their king. Rehoboam was left with only the tribes of Judah and Benjamin. Even then he didn't learn his lesson because he continued the pagan ways which Solomon had allowed. Before long he was threatened from all sides. He was forced to fight against Jeroboam and Pharaoh Shishak of Egypt.*

LOOKING OUT

1. We must be wise because sin is always crouching at the door. The moment Solomon was no longer alive, Jeroboam, the rebel, jumped in to foment revolution.
2. It's always best not to make a decision with a gun to your head. Rehoboam wisely asked for three days to consider the demands made by Jeroboam and his rebels.
3. It is unwise to listen to the advice of men over the counsel of God. Rehoboam did ask advice from various men but failed to seek clear direction from the Lord.
4. A pampered lifestyle keeps us from identifying with the suffering. Rehoboam and his young cohorts didn't care about the people's needs, but only their own happiness.
5. We have hell to pay when we continually disregard the poor, powerless, and suffering. Rehoboam almost lost his life because of his callous attitude toward the needy.

LOOKING UP *Help me, Lord, to always be aware of the desperate needs of others, and help me minister to them. May I always seek and accept wise counsel from godly people.*

RIGHT

MAY 21

2 Chronicles 11-14

LOOKING BACK Although not the founder of the Red Cross, Clara Barton brought it to the United States on this day in 1881. She had begun her career as a teacher, but soon her humanitarian interests led her into nursing. During the Civil War, Barton became a legend for her love and tender care. Her work during that war left her exhausted and weak. In 1869, she went to Switzerland for a rest. It was there that she learned of the International Committee of the Red Cross, an organization based in Geneva. She was deeply impressed with their work. After finishing nursing duties in the Franco-Prussian War, Barton went home and established the Red Cross in America.

LOOKING IN *Amazing things can be done when the one hoping to accomplish those things has right on his side. When threatened, King Abijah of Judah knew he was in the right, because God had made a covenant that David's heirs would always rule Judah. Because this was the will of God, Jeroboam's efforts to destroy the tiny nation came to nothing. Even though Abijah followed the sins of Rehoboam, he still maintained proper worship in Jerusalem. He did not fully serve the Lord, but God still protected Abijah and preserved Judah. God never forgets a promise. Abijah was remembered for his large family and is listed in the ancestors of Jesus in Matthew.*

LOOKING OUT

1. Satan's forces always seem overwhelming. When the hostile Northern Kingdom under Jeroboam threatened Judah, they outnumbered the little nation two to one.
2. It is futile to fight the will of God. Abijah reminded the attacking forces of the Northern Kingdom that God had given the kingship to David and his heirs, not Jeroboam.
3. Immaturity and indecisiveness make us vulnerable to the enemy's tactics. Abijah noted that Rehoboam failed because he was inexperienced and couldn't make good decisions.
4. We are never overwhelmed when we are in God's will. Jeroboam surrounded Abijah's troops but could not win the battle in spite of the great advantage Jeroboam held.
5. Victory depends on God's help, not our own power. Abijah recognized he had won the war because he and his people relied on the Lord, the God of their fathers.

LOOKING UP *Help me, Lord, not to be intimidated by the overwhelming odds I face. Rather, let me trust You. May I always remember that You are with me no matter what I have to face.*

THE WORD

2 Chronicles 15-18

LOOKING BACK On this day in 1967, "Mister Rogers Neighborhood" premiered on public television out of Pittsburgh, Pennsylvania. Fred Rogers, a Presbyterian minister who feels this program is his "divine calling," hosts the long-running PBS children's show. "Mister Roger's Neighborhood" has affected several generations of children. Puppets and human characters interact in the neighborhood of make-believe. Rogers plays the voices of many of the puppets and has educated young viewers on a variety of important subjects. His gentle manner and friendly presentation make him an important and subtle influence on modern American society.

LOOKING IN *Often we underestimate the great impact subtle influence and education have on a society. This can be clearly seen by the remarkable results of an unusual approach Jehoshaphat made three years after becoming king of Judah. He was the son and successor of Asa, occupying the throne for 25 years as king of Judah. Jehoshaphat was an able ruler and a faithful worshiper of Yahweh. No doubt many questioned the wisdom of Jehoshaphat's command to emphasize Bible-study groups throughout Judah. Yet, not long after this religious education started, the military threat toward the nation abated, and new monies poured into Judah's coffers.*

LOOKING OUT

1. God stays with us as long as we stay with Him. Jehoshaphat became very prosperous because in his early years he sought God with all of his heart.
2. God gives us highly creative ideas when we stay close to Him. Although Jehoshaphat increased his military, the threat to the nation remained until God gave him an unusual idea.
3. Integrating God's Word into our national life brings the Creator into our defense system. As Judah began studying God's Word, God put fear in the hearts of their enemies.
4. Bringing God's Word into our national life opens the windows of heaven. The enemies of God began to pay tribute when the nation became a people of the Word.
5. Our nation becomes more powerful when we make the Bible part of our national expression. Jehoshaphat grew in power and influence because Judah lived in God's Word.

LOOKING UP *Help me, Lord, to be a person of the Word. I want to read it and heed it every day of my life. Help me to get God's Word to my community and to my nation.*

FINISHED

2 Chronicles 19-20

LOOKING BACK The leaders of Israel announced the capture of Nazi Adolf Eichmann on this day in 1960. Eichmann, a lieutenant colonel in the Nazi secret police, was convicted and executed for his part in the killing of about six million Jews during World War II. He had directed the deportation of Jews, from Germany and the occupied countries, to concentration camps. After the war, Eichmann escaped to Argentina and lived under an assumed name. Israeli agents seized the fugitive in May 1960 and took him to Israel for trial on charges of crimes against the Jewish people, crimes against humanity, and war crimes. He was convicted and hanged in 1962.

LOOKING IN *The world breathes a sigh of relief when wicked men are brought down and their evils finished. Jehoshaphat's two-and-a-half decade rule was filled with success. However, there were times of great difficulty. Ammon, Moab, and Edom joined forces to destroy Judah, but this evil alliance was defeated and their wrongs finished. Judah's trust in God was amply vindicated. The invaders quarreled among themselves and left the spoil to Judah. The one thing Jehoshaphat did that ultimately proved disastrous was his alliance with Ahab, king of Israel. The immediate result was beneficial, but it proved to be horrific.*

LOOKING OUT

1. **When we find ourselves in trouble, our first line of defense is prayer. Jehoshaphat confronted his crisis by going to God in passionate prayer.**
2. **Prayer and praise clear the deck of our lives so we can see more clearly. After prayer and praise, Jehoshaphat moved from the problem to the possibility.**
3. **Praise should always precede a change in circumstances. Jehoshaphat led Judah in a praise meeting even before the battle was engaged.**
4. **Praise moves us from panic to peace. As the people of Judah lifted their voices in praise, peace came. They knew God was with them, and He would give them victory.**
5. **God always gives us far more than we ask. The victory was so great for Judah that it took three days for the people to gather the spoils of war.**

LOOKING UP *Father, help me to be a "pray-er" and a "praiser." Teach me to praise You even before the battle is won, because I know You are always with me.*

VIOLENCE

2 Chronicles 21-23

LOOKING BACK Abolitionist John Brown killed five pro slavery Kansans on this day in 1856. Brown was a radical whose attempt to free the slaves cost a number of lives and helped, indirectly, to bring on the American Civil War. In 1855, he followed five of his sons to Kansas. They settled in Osawatomie and worked to keep Kansas from becoming a slave state. In May 1856, proslavery men attacked and burned the nearby town of Lawrence. Two days later, Brown led an expedition to Pottawatomie Creek, where he and his men brutally murdered five pro slavery settlers. Three years later, Brown was captured and hanged.

LOOKING IN *Violence never settles things and simply breeds more violence. Athaliah brutally murdered her own grandchildren to gain the throne but only enjoyed her power for a few years. The wife of Jehoram and mother of Ahaziah, she was either the daughter of Ahab and Jezebel or of Omri, king of Israel. She brought the northern court's devotion to Baal to the court of Judah and exercised great political influence during her son's one–year reign. When Ahaziah died from battle wounds, she tried to gain power for herself by having all male heirs killed. She ruled for six years. Finally, Jehoiada, the priest, led a revolt, bringing about Athaliah's death.*

LOOKING OUT

1. **Sin desensitizes and destroys. Evil Athaliah was so power-hungry she ordered the deaths of her own grandchildren. Sin takes over our senses when we give in to it.**
2. **God protects from the enemy's destruction. Athaliah thought she had killed all potential heirs to the kingdom, but God had prompted Jehosheba to hide little Joash.**
3. **God has an appointed time for evil to end. Wicked Athaliah reigned for six bloody years, but then Jehoiada moved to oust her from her pinnacle of power.**
4. **God has a plan for evil to end. God gave Jehoiada a detailed and successful plan for the ousting of Athaliah. In God's time, it all came down just as planned.**
5. **God executes vengeance on those who oppose Him in their bloody rebellion. While trying to flee for her life, Athaliah was put to death at the Horse Gate.**

LOOKING UP *Help me, Lord, to stay far away from sin, because I know it will take over one's life and destroy. May I always remember that You will right the wrongs done to humanity.*

PRIDE AND POWER

2 Chronicles 24-25

LOOKING BACK Evangelist and claimant of the title "Elijah the Restorer" was born on this day in 1847 at Edinburgh, Scotland. John Alexander Dowie came to Chicago in 1890 where he started a sect that stressed divine healing. He also founded Zion City, Illinois, in 1901, as a home for his church. With 5,000 followers, Dowie created a unique community without pharmacies, physicians, theaters, or dance halls, and where smoking, drinking, and eating pork were prohibited. Dowie's ostentatiously expensive, personal lifestyle and unwise use of funds got him expelled from the church in 1907. He died a year later on March 9.

LOOKING IN *Pride and power are twin perils to the successful. These sins toppled Dowie just as they had toppled King Amaziah, the ninth king of Judah. Amaziah was the son of Joash and father of Uzziah. He was 25 years old when he ascended the throne, becoming very successful. Encouraged by his victory in Edom, Amaziah challenged Israel's King Joash to battle. Though Joash tried to avoid a conflict, Amaziah persisted and was defeated. The Temple and royal palace were plundered, the wall of Jerusalem was pierced, and Amaziah was taken prisoner. After his release, Amaziah fled to Lachish, where he was murdered.*

LOOKING OUT

1. **Being half right is never right. Amaziah did what was right in the sight of the Lord, but not wholeheartedly. God demands full commitment from those who follow Him.**
2. **We are not to be unequally yoked with unbelievers. The prophet warned Amaziah that he must not use the 100,000 soldiers he had hired from the Northern Kingdom.**
3. **We must fight our battles God's way; He is the Lord of the war. The prophet reminded Amaziah that God has the power to help or overthrow.**
4. **When we have done wrong, it is wise to cut our losses and make things right. Amaziah worried about the money he had paid to the Israelites, but the prophet said to forget it.**
5. **If we don't hear, we have to feel. Flushed with pride after his astounding victory, Amaziah threatened the Northern Kingdom in spite of being warned not to. He died.**

LOOKING UP *Help me, Lord, to follow You with all of my heart because I know that You demand all of me. May I always fight my spiritual battles as You direct, and then I will always win.*

COURAGE

MAY 26

2 Chronicles 26-28

May

LOOKING BACK On February 24, 1868, the House of Representatives voted 126 to 47 to impeach President Andrew Johnson. Then, the Senate organized itself as a court to see if Johnson needed to be removed from office. On this day in 1868, the impeachment trial ended when the Senate failed to convict. Senator James Grimes of Iowa, stricken with paralysis, came in on a stretcher and voted "not guilty." The roll call vote lasted over an hour, and the outcome was in doubt until the very end. The final tally of 35 "guilty" and 19 "not guilty" acquitted Johnson by one vote and spared the nation the shame of removing a president for mere political reasons.

LOOKING IN *Johnson was so hated that it took great courage for the senators to vote "not guilty." Fortunately, enough of them had deep convictions and the courage to do the right thing. Deep convictions always take courage. The priests who opposed Uzziah's evil had convictions and the courage to stand. Tragically, Uzziah is not so much remembered as the leader who brought Judah to a golden age rivaling David's and Solomon's empires, but as the "leper king." His prideful attempt to usurp the priestly prerogative of offering incense in the Temple made him a leper. Uzziah was denied burial in the royal tombs at Jerusalem; he was buried in a field.*

LOOKING OUT

1. **We must never underestimate the power of influence. Uzziah made the right decisions and opted for the right choices, as long as he was under Zechariah's influence.**
2. **God's blessings only extend to the end of our obedience. As long as Uzziah sought the Lord, God made him prosper. Blessings are tied to our relationship with God.**
3. **Power can distort reality and discourage others from working with us. Uzziah was greatly helped by God and by others, "until he became powerful."**
4. **When we lift ourselves up, we fall down. Pride brought Uzziah low. In his arrogance, he chose to take the role of priest as well as king, something strictly forbidden by God.**
5. **Courage puts conviction before convenience. Azariah and 80 other brave priests, in spite of personal danger, confronted the arrogant king about his wrong.**

LOOKING UP *Help me, Lord, to have the courage of conviction so that I may stand for what is right. Keep me from pride lest I displease You and lose Your wonderful blessings.*

CHANGE

2 Chronicles 29-30

LOOKING BACK Thomas Jefferson made an interesting observation on this day in 1788. He said, "The natural progress of things is for liberty to yield and government to gain ground." Jefferson is best remembered as a great president and as the author of the Declaration of Independence. He also won lasting fame as a diplomat, political thinker, and a founder of the Democratic Party. His comment about liberty and government was intended to alert all to the tendency for good things to deteriorate if we don't carefully attend to them. The law of our world is not evolution but deterioration. We must keep careful watch, or things will always get worse.

LOOKING IN *Jefferson's belief that good things deteriorate was certainly true when it came to Judah's religious life. Judah had drifted away from the Lord. Hezekiah changed all of that. When he was 25 years old, he began his reign by reopening the Temple and removing the idols. Temple vessels that had been desecrated during Ahaz's reign were sanctified for use. Sacrifices were initiated with singing and the sounds of musical instruments. Hezekiah even destroyed the bronze serpent Moses had erected in the wilderness, so people would not view it as an object of worship. Hezekiah organized the priests and Levites for worship and reinstituted the tithes.*

LOOKING OUT

1. **Revival starts when we want to please God. Hezekiah, although young, had a passion for God and His house. He ordered that the Temple be opened and repaired.**
2. **Revival starts with self. Hezekiah brought all the priests together and instructed them to consecrate themselves, for they would help lead the revival.**
3. **Revival comes when the whole church gets involved. After the priests consecrated themselves, they were to consecrate the Temple, removing all the defiling items.**
4. **Revival preserves life. Hezekiah knew the reason for the nation's trouble was its turning away from God. He also understood that revival would revitalize the country.**
5. **Revival brings great joy. When revival started sweeping through the land, all of Judah sensed a joy the people had not known for many years. There is joy in God's presence.**

LOOKING UP *Lord, send a revival to our land and let that revival start in me. I consecrate myself to You today. May I never cave in to the world spirit about me but keep my focus on You.*

TROUBLE

MAY 28

2 Chronicles 31-33

May

LOOKING BACK Amnesty International was founded on this day in 1961. The Nobel Prize-winning human rights organization was founded by London lawyer Peter Berenson, when he read about the arrest of a group of students in Portugal. He launched a one-year campaign called "Appeal for Amnesty" which grew into the famed organization. Today, Amnesty International has a million members, in 150 countries, who work to free all prisoners of conscience, abolish the use of torture and the death penalty, and guarantee human rights for women. While some may question all of its agenda, there is no doubt this organization has had a positive impact in our world.

LOOKING IN *In ancient Judah, there was no organization such as Amnesty International pleading for victims when King Manasseh ruled in evil madness for 55 long years. His antics not only angered God but brought untold pain to the nation. Manasseh was a son of good King Hezekiah. However, goodness is not hereditary. Manasseh, who reigned longer than any Judean king, is known for his unfaithfulness to God. Second Kings blames him for Judah's ultimate destruction and exile. Judah's most wicked king was finally brought to his knees by the king of Assyria, who put a ring in Manasseh's nose and took him to Babylon. In his later years, Manasseh turned to God.*

LOOKING OUT

1. **Too much, too soon is as bad as too little, too late. Manasseh achieved unlimited power at age twelve, but was not mature enough to accept the responsibility. He became evil.**
2. **God has no grandchildren. Each person and generation must make the decision about following God. Manasseh had a good father but chose to go the other path.**
3. **God lets evil go on for awhile, but there is always a reckoning day. Manasseh had a hook put in his nose and was carried away captive by the king of Assyria.**
4. **Pain gets our attention, and if we turn to God, He will forgive. Even though Manasseh had been so evil, God lovingly forgave him when the hurting king repented.**
5. **You can't "unring" a bell. Manasseh had been forgiven and then tried to undo all the evil he had fostered. Tragically, that which he had unleashed couldn't be stopped.**

LOOKING UP *Help me, Lord, to remember the terrible consequences of sin, and help me avoid it every day. Give me those things, only, that help me grow closer to You.*

RESTORED

2 Chronicles 34-36

LOOKING BACK Charles II was restored to the throne of England on his birthday, this day in 1660. He had lived in exile after the execution of his father, King Charles I, in 1649. That year, the Scots proclaimed Charles "King of Scotland." Puritan leader Oliver Cromwell defeated his army in 1651, and Charles fled to France. After Cromwell died in 1658, the English people became increasingly dissatisfied with the government that Cromwell had established. In 1660, Parliament invited Charles to return and declared him king. He reigned for the next 25 years, surviving two wars, the Great Plague, the Great Fire of London, and an assassination attempt.

LOOKING IN *Just as England wanted to restore rulership to the king, God wanted to be restored as leader of His people. Israel had deliberately walked away from God. The people flirted with other gods while the nation spiraled downward. They refused to listen to God's prophets whom He had sent to warn them of coming disaster if they didn't repent. Even after the Northern Kingdom had gone into captivity, Judah refused to repent. More than 100 years before the Babylonian Exile, Isaiah predicted Judah's fall. In addition, Micah, Zephaniah, Jeremiah, Habakkuk, and Ezekiel agreed that Judah would fall. Now the exile had come; God's leadership would be restored.*

LOOKING OUT

1. God always fulfills His promises. Both Isaiah and Jeremiah had said that a king named Cyrus would let God's people go home. It happened just as they prophesied.
2. What we see as a sad conclusion may simply be a bright beginning. The book of Chronicles ends and Ezra's book begins with the same notes. God has not forgotten His people.
3. We may be cast down, but we are not cast out. God does permit us to go through hard times but He is always with us and will restore what Satan has stolen.
4. We are corrected but never abandoned. Israel would learn that the purpose of the exile was to redirect them and purge the nation of its flirtation with foreign gods.
5. The fire is only to burn out the dross. The 70 years of captivity in Babylon forever eliminated the propensity for pagan worship in Israel.

LOOKING UP *Help me, Lord, to realize that Your discipline is always directive rather than punitive. You permit pain so I will come back to the proper path.*

COURAGE

Ezra 1-3

LOOKING BACK Joan of Arc was burned at the stake on this day in 1431. She was a simple but courageous peasant girl who rescued France from defeat in one of the darkest periods of the Hundred Years' War with England. Her first great triumph was leading a French army against the English, who had laid siege to the city of Orleans. She is often called the "Maid of Orleans" in honor of that victory. In 1430, the Burgundians captured her at Compiegne. Although important prisoners could bring high ransoms, the English wouldn't give her up to the French. They acquired her for a large sum and had her burned at the stake, claiming she was an agent of the devil.

LOOKING IN *Joan's courageous death led many to fear they had witnessed the martyrdom of a saint. Spiritual courage is common among those who love God. The book of Ezra speaks of that courage. It begins with the story of the first Jews who returned to Jerusalem from captivity and faced great antagonism and opposition. Their main objective was to rebuild the Temple. Its foundation was laid but the building delayed. Haggai and Zechariah encouraged the people to finish the project, which they did in 515 B.C. Then they "celebrated the dedication of this house of God with joy." The priests of Israel courageously offered sacrifices to God in spite of threats and intimidation.*

LOOKING OUT

1. **The first step to a nation's renewal is to rebuild the altars. Seven months after the Israelites returned from captivity in Babylon, the priests began to rebuild an altar to God.**
2. **All hell hates us when we determine to rebuild a moral society. Those who hated God and His people tried their best to stop the sacrifices, but they couldn't do so.**
3. **When we start to draw near to God, He moves us to mission. The Israelites sacrificed at the rebuilt altar and soon were stirred by the Spirit to rebuild their torn-down Temple.**
4. **Praise and thanksgiving should accompany all our work for the Lord. As the foundations of the Temple were being laid, the Levites led the people in great praises to God.**
5. **You can't work for God without being greatly blessed. When the Temple foundations were laid, the people broke out in shouts. Memories and joy mingled together.**

LOOKING UP *Help me, Lord, to rebuild the altars in our nation so we might become, again, what You want us to be. I rejoice as I see You work in my family and among my friends.*

DETERMINATION

MAY 31

Ezra 4-6

LOOKING BACK The Civil War "Battle of Seven Pines" was fought on this day in 1862. In a bloody campaign, Confederate General Joseph Johnston's troops defeated McClellan's Army of the Potomac at Fair Oaks, Virginia. McClellan was called "Young Napoleon" after the famous French military genius Napoleon I. Some rank McClellan as a great general, but most believe he was too cautious on the battlefield. Although the Confederates scored a major battlefield victory, and McClellan's forces withdrew the next day, the effect of the battle did little to ease the pressure on the besieged Confederate capital of Richmond. The Confederates won the battle but lost the war.

LOOKING IN *Just as the Confederates scored a major win, but ultimately lost, so Israel's enemies were successful for awhile but went down in defeat. The Israelites had been brutalized by the Babylonians for 70 years. When they returned home to Jerusalem to rebuild their Temple, other angry enemies oppressed them. These harsh opponents were successful in stopping the work on the Temple for 15 long years. However, God sent Haggai and Zechariah to the discouraged people to prod them back to the task. With new determination, God's people began to build again and they soon completed the task. God's enemies had scored a round but lost the fight.*

LOOKING OUT

1. **We are always tempted to compromise convictions. When Israel's enemies couldn't stop the Temple rebuilding, they sought to join them so they could thwart the work.**
2. **Sometimes we have to stand up for things even though it isn't "politically correct." Zerubbabel told their enemies, "You have no part with us in building a temple to our God."**
3. **Discouragement is one of the enemy's strongest tools. When the enemies of God couldn't thwart the work, they hired people to join them in discouraging the Israelites.**
4. **The enemy often uses rumor and innuendo to circumvent the work of God. The enemies of Israel wrote to Artaxerxes, filling him with lies about Israel's intentions.**
5. **Sometimes it seems the enemy has succeeded in stopping God's work. It would be 15 long years before work on rebuilding God's Temple could be resumed.**

LOOKING UP *Help me, Lord, to remain strong in the teeth of hard opposition. Keep me true to my assigned task. May I never be intimidated by the enemy or compromise my convictions.*

JUNE

A Month of Weddings and Flowers

Trees and shrubs are most often at their freshest during the month of June, and there are more flowers than at any other time of the year. June especially is the month of roses. In fact, June's special flower is the rose. The rose, one of the most beautiful of all flowers, is a symbol of fragrance and loveliness. Both the United States and Iran have chosen it as their national flower. Several states and a Canadian province have also selected the rose as their official flower. Washington D.C. has the American Beauty rose; Georgia chose the Cherokee rose. The wild rose is the official flower of Iowa, North Dakota, and Alberta.

Weddings also dominate the month of June. Some authorities believe the Romans named the month for Juno, the patron goddess of marriage. Others trace the name to a family name, Junius. The Junius family was powerful and important throughout the early history of ancient Rome. Regardless, from early Roman times, June was believed to be the best time for marriages. It is the sixth month of the year according to the Gregorian calendar, but was the fourth month in the early Roman calendar. The Romans later moved the beginning of the year to January 1, making June the sixth month. June once had 29 days, but when the Roman statesman Julius Caesar reformed the calendar in 46 B.C., he gave June thirty days.

Spring ends and summer begins on June 20, 21, or 22 in the Northern Hemisphere. In the Southern Hemisphere, fall ends and winter begins during this month. The start of winter brings cold, rainy weather to that part of the world. In some regions of our part of the world, green fruit is just beginning to appear. Bees move from flower to flower gathering nectar. Baby birds of some species have hatched, and their parents are kept busy bringing them food. It is a month of new life.

During June, we finish reading the book of Ezra, study Nehemiah and Esther, and then take on the oldest book in the Bible, Job.

INSPIRED

JUNE 1

Ezra 7-8

LOOKING BACK A single heroic act can capture the imagination and greatly affect people and history. That was certainly true with Captain James Lawrence, who died on this day in 1813. Lawrence was a United States naval officer who commanded the Chesapeake in an attack on the British ship Shannon during the War of 1812. The Shannon easily captured the Chesapeake, and Lawrence was fatally wounded. After he was wounded, he gave the command, "Don't give up the ship." This determined and heroic statement by the dying captain became a watchword of the U.S. Navy and has inspired tenacity in the face of hostility ever since.

LOOKING IN *When Haman planned the first holocaust, Esther's heroic act of total devotion to God saved her people. Not only did Esther affect her generation but, no doubt, had much to do with the fact that her husband's son, Artaxerxes, was favorably disposed toward God's people. Ezra found his task a lot easier because the pagan king was benevolent. Ezra's greatest contribution was his teaching, establishing, and implementing "the book of the law of the Lord" among the returned Jews. Tradition says he authored Chronicles and Ezra-Nehemiah. Ancient rabbis said if Moses had not received the law from God, Ezra would have. He is often called "the father of Judaism."*

LOOKING OUT

1. **The shadow of a life falls far into the future. Esther married Artaxerxes' father and probably greatly influenced the king, making him favorable toward the Jews.**
2. **Those well versed in God's Word can make a significant difference in our world. Ezra had given himself to God's Word and was now prepared to lead Israel in revival.**
3. **God gives us favor so we can accomplish His tasks. Ezra had found great favor in the eyes of Artaxerxes, for God had moved on the heart of the pagan king.**
4. **Praise should always follow answered prayer. Ezra led the people in a formal statement of praise to God for the miracles He had done in turning the heart of the king.**
5. **When we go with God, we will be bold as lions. Ezra was unafraid to ask the pagan king for assistance because, as Ezra explained, "the hand of the Lord was on me."**

LOOKING UP *Help me, Lord, to remember You have called me to a special and important task. Teach me more about Your Word so I will be properly prepared for the work You have for me.*

PURITY

JUNE 2

Ezra 9-10

LOOKING BACK French novelist and essayist Marquis de Sade was born on this day in 1740. His works were considered so obscene that many of them remained unpublished until the mid-1900's. Sade wrote that criminal acts and sexual abnormalities are natural to human behavior. Sadism (the enjoyment of cruelty) comes from his name. While still in his 20's, de Sade began to show signs of being mentally disturbed. He was involved in many scandals over acts of cruelty and sexual behavior. He spent a lot of years in prison for these actions. Finally, de Sade was placed in an insane asylum in 1803, where he died nine years later.

LOOKING IN *Standing totally opposite to de Sade's hedonistic philosophy, Ezra insisted on righteousness. He declared that evil must not be part of behavior for God's people. Israel's long moral slide downward had brought bitter pain and 70 long years of captivity. Ezra led the nation in genuine repentance, bringing them back to their faith. He taught faithfulness to God, Who had brought home the exiles. Ezra so believed in the sacredness and practicality of the Scriptures that he had them read to the people and insisted that their teachings be carried out. Ezra also was a person of prayer, as can be seen in his long confessional prayers.*

LOOKING OUT

1. Real conviction brings shame and heartbreak. Ezra said he was too ashamed and disgraced to lift up his face to God. He tore his robe and beard as an outward sign of sorrow.
2. There is a reason for our pain. Ezra wisely noted in his prayer that the reason hard times had come to the nation was because they had blatantly disobeyed God's Word.
3. We never get what we deserve. Ezra acknowledged that their punishment was not nearly as bad as they deserved. Such is the mercy of our loving Heavenly Father.
4. We do get less than we deserve. Although we don't get what we deserve, punishment does come when we disobey God. Without pain, there would never be change.
5. Passionate prayer produces results. God not only heard Ezra's prayer, but that prayer also inspired conviction in the hearts of the Israelites until they, too, wept and began to repent.

LOOKING UP *Help me, Lord, to grieve and pray for the sins of our nation. Forgive us for totally disregarding Your Word. Keep me from those sins that so easily trip me up.*

ABDICATION

Nehemiah 1-3

LOOKING BACK The Duke of Windsor and Mrs. Wallis Warfield Simpson were married on this day in 1937. The Duke, as King Edward VIII, had abdicated the throne so he could marry the American divorcee. Edward had become king of Britain on January 20, 1936, and gave up the throne on December 11 that same year. He fell in love with Simpson, but his government and many of his subjects were opposed to accepting her as queen, causing him to abdicate and leave England in self-imposed exile. His brother, George VI, who succeeded him, gave him the title, Duke of Windsor. Many feel that Edward selfishly turned his back on his God-ordained duty.

LOOKING IN *Nehemiah certainly did not abdicate his role when God called him to do something about the Jerusalem problem. Nehemiah held the distinguished position of cupbearer to the king of the Persian empire. This was an office of trust; tasting the king's wine and food, the cupbearer stood between the king and death. That Nehemiah, a Jew and a captive, served this Gentile king in such a strategic capacity was an unusual credit and honor to this man of strong character. When visitors to Susa informed Nehemiah that Jerusalem's walls were in ruin, he was so upset he cried and mourned for days. He prayed, and King Artaxerxes permitted him to go to Jerusalem.*

LOOKING OUT

1. **Bad news is not always bad. Nehemiah received the bad news from Jerusalem. However, that prompted him to start praying so something could be done about the problems.**
2. **Going to God must be our first reaction to hard situations. Nehemiah talked to God before he dared talk with the king. He knew that God alone could help.**
3. **Praise reinforces God's promises, paving the way for our faith. As Nehemiah praised God for His goodness, faith was built in his heart for his people and their nation.**
4. **No matter what our job, God has strategically placed us. Nehemiah was a cupbearer to the king. As such, he did not expect to have the power to influence—but he did.**
5. **God answers prayer at unexpected times in unexpected ways. While Nehemiah was serving the king, the answer to his prayer suddenly arrived in stunning fulfillment.**

LOOKING UP *Help me, Lord, to never forget the power of prayer. You do hear, and You will answer my pleas. Thank You for speaking to my heart and letting me work for You.*

ONE MAN

JUNE 4

Nehemiah 4-6

June

LOOKING BACK Americans drive more than 2 1/4 trillion miles a year. Henry Ford, more than any other man, is responsible for the popularization of the automobile. It was on this day in 1896 that the first Ford car was completed in a brick workshed in Detroit, Michigan. Today, 90 percent of all U.S. households own a car, and more than 55 percent own two or more. In 1903, Ford organized his company, at first producing only expensive cars. Ford soon began working to make a simple, sturdy car that large numbers of people could afford. He achieved one of the first such cars with the Model T, which appeared in 1908. Sales of these "cheap" cars changed the face of America.

LOOKING IN *One man can make a deep impact regardless of detractors and opposition. Nehemiah was such a man. He would let nothing stop him from completing his God-given vision. Nehemiah's first act on arriving in Jerusalem was to inspect the walls at night. He then called an assembly, convincing the people of the need for rebuilding the walls. Nehemiah was an excellent leader who demonstrated engineering knowledge and brilliant organizing ability. The work began, but trouble soon arose from without and within. Sanballat and his friends tried to stop the work. Economic issues caused trouble within. Nehemiah effectively dealt with both matters.*

LOOKING OUT

1. **We draw the lightning when we start to do a work for God. Sanballat and Tobiah were furious when Nehemiah started rebuilding the walls of an unprotected Jerusalem.**
2. **Ridicule is one of the devil's most effective weapons. Sanballat and Tobiah started a concert of catcalls and sneers in an orchestrated effort to stop the walls' reconstruction.**
3. **The proper response to ridicule is to talk to God about it and keep on working. Nehemiah prayed that God would take care of his enemies while he continued the rebuilding.**
4. **Prayer and preparation are twin pillars of safety. Nehemiah not only prayed but also posted guards to watch for those who would disrupt the work.**
5. **Opposition not only comes from the outside but, many times, from those within the ranks. Many Jews began to discourage the workers by spreading negative words.**

LOOKING UP *Help me, Lord, always to be positive in my words so that I might encourage rather than discourage. May I always remember that opposition will come when I do Your work.*

WORDS

Nehemiah 7-8

LOOKING BACK Words have dramatic effect. On June 5, 1851, Harriet Beecher Stowe's *Uncle Tom's Cabin* appeared as a serial in an antislavery Washington D.C. newspaper. Stowe wrote the book to criticize slavery, which she considered a national sin. She hoped that her novel would help bring slavery to an early and peaceful end. However, the book increased the hostility of many Northerners toward the South. Southerners, on the other hand, considered Stowe's description of slavery inaccurate. They called the book an insult and an injustice. Historians believe the bitter feelings aroused by *Uncle Tom's Cabin* helped ignite the bloody Civil War.

LOOKING IN *The words at the Water Gate in Nehemiah's day also had a nation-shaking effect. Nehemiah gathered all Israel to hear words—not just any words but God's Word. Ezra read from the book of the law of Moses. This was probably the Pentateuch (Torah) or some part of it. While Ezra read, others helped by giving "the sense, so that the people understood the reading." This probably included translating the Hebrew scripture into Aramaic, the commonly spoken language. As the people listened to God's Word, they began to weep and repent. This resulted in a wonderful revival that swept throughout the land.*

LOOKING OUT

1. We all need help in better understanding God's Word. Ezra read the Word of God to the people and appointed godly teachers to help explain its meaning to them.
2. God's Word gives light, showing us how to walk so we will not stumble and fall. The people wept as they heard the Word. Nehemiah reminded them it was for correction.
3. God's Word brings joy—not sorrow. Nehemiah told the people not to weep but rejoice, for God's Word would keep them from those things that kept them from God.
4. The more we know God, the happier we are. The Israelites celebrated with great joy because they now understood the plans God had for them.
5. God's Word helps us know the kind of worship our Lord desires. The Israelites learned about the Feast of Weeks through reading God's Word and rushed to observe it.

LOOKING UP *Help me, Lord, always to love Your Word, for it will keep me from what displeases You. Not only let me read Your Word, but help me to share it with others.*

DEDICATION

Nehemiah 9-11

LOOKING BACK American patriot Nathan Hale was born on this day in 1755. He was hanged by the British as an American spy when he was only 21 years old. His conduct and courage have made him one of America's most remembered heroes. General George Washington had asked for a man to pass through the British lines to obtain information on their position. Hale volunteered, obtained the information, but was captured by the enemy. Hale was condemned to hang and, with remarkable calmness of mind and spirit, prepared for his execution. Before the hanging he made a speech, reportedly saying, "I only regret that I have but one life to lose for my country."

LOOKING IN *Dedication such as Hale's is not only remarkable but also highly commended. Israel had such dedication when they stepped forward to make a sacred covenant with God at Water Gate. In making this covenant, they moved beyond words to actions in their repentance. A covenant was a pact, treaty, alliance, or agreement between two parties of equal or unequal authority. The covenant or testament is a central, unifying theme in Scripture. God made covenants with individuals and the nation Israel. Here Israel made a sacred covenant with God. It was far more than a contract; it was a sacred agreement with the eternal Creator.*

LOOKING OUT

1. **We must be careful in our associations because they affect us deeply. The Israelites promise they won't dilute their faith with mixed marriages.**
2. **We must set aside time for worship. The Israelites make a sacred pledge to God that they will keep the Sabbath day holy and observe all other sacred days.**
3. **We have a divine responsibility to protect our environment. The Israelites promise to let the land lie fallow once every seven years to restore its vitality.**
4. **We must always support God's work willingly. The people pledge that they will carefully and faithfully take care of the needs of God's house and His priests.**
5. **We must not neglect God's house. The Israelites make a sacred covenant to never again forsake God's house as they had done for so many years.**

LOOKING UP *Lord, today, I make a sacred covenant with You to do those things that please You. Thank you that You have given me the joy of supporting Your work with prayers and finances.*

TOUGH LOVE

JUNE 7

Nehemiah 12-13

LOOKING BACK "Man stands to revere, he kneels to pray," Henry David Thoreau said on this day in 1841. Thoreau was an American writer who is remembered for his attacks on the social institutions he considered immoral and for his faith in the religious significance of nature. A southern gentleman once asked how he could recognize George Washington at a meeting of the Continental Congress. He was told, "George Washington is the man who kneels when the Continental Congress stops for prayer." Both Thoreau and Washington recognized the importance of humility before God and the need to show Him reverence.

LOOKING IN *A far different attitude was held by Tobiah who had moved into the Temple during Nehemiah's absence from Jerusalem. Tobiah arrogantly strutted, but his power was cut short when Nehemiah returned and, in a display of tough love, threw him out of God's house. Tobiah had been one of the major adversaries of Nehemiah's rebuilding efforts at Jerusalem. He is called an "Ammonite," probably because his family fled there at the destruction of Jerusalem. Tobiah enjoyed aristocratic favor, with the title "servant" bestowed on him by the Persian ruler. He opposed the rebuilding of Jerusalem because it would weaken his political authority in the area.*

LOOKING OUT

1. When we become aware, we become responsible. When the Word of God was read, the Israelites learned that no Ammonite or Moabite was to be admitted to the assembly.
2. God faithfully explains the "why" of His prohibitions. The Ammonites and Moabites were forbidden to join the assembly because they had maliciously opposed God's will.
3. Ignorance of God's Word sets us up for sorrow. Eliashib should have known God's Word but didn't, even though he was a priest. Tobiah, the enemy, had moved into the Temple.
4. Decisive action must be taken, although at times it is not "politically correct." Nehemiah returned to Jerusalem to find Tobiah in the Temple and proceeded to throw him out.
5. Tough love must be used when blatant evil is involved. The religious leaders had knowingly disobeyed God. Nehemiah now had to bring hard correction to them.

LOOKING UP *Help me, Lord, to hide Your Word in my heart that I might not sin against You. Give me the courage to practice "tough love" when it is necessary.*

HEROINES

JUNE 8

Esther 1-2

LOOKING BACK The first public award to a woman in America was given on this day in 1697. It was awarded to the husband of Hannah Duston, on her behalf, for a brutal and bloody retaliation. Two months earlier, on March 16, hostile Indians attacked Haverhill, Maine, capturing Hannah, killing her baby, and slaying or capturing 39 others. She was taken to an Indian camp from which she escaped on April 29. In her escape, Hannah killed 10 Indians with a tomahawk and scalped them as proof of her deed. She was awarded 25 pounds from angry citizens for her "heroic deed." In that day of hostility between the Indians and Whites, Duston was considered a genuine heroine.

LOOKING IN *Esther also lived in a time of brutality and bloodshed. Haman determined to do away with all the Jews in history's first "holocaust." His dastardly crime was prevented, however, because God had raised up a bold young woman who risked her own life to save the Jews. The holocaust was averted, and God's people were spared extinction. Esther's Jewish name was Hadassah. The Persians renamed her Esther. The name Esther was the Persian personal name meaning "Ishtar," who was the Mesopotamian goddess of fertility and war. Esther is the story of a Jewish orphan girl raised by her uncle, Mordecai, in Persia. She became a heroine by saving her people.*

LOOKING OUT

1. **Personal pain often follows impulsive behavior. When King Xerxes calmed down after ousting Queen Vashti, he began to miss her and regret his angry decision.**
2. **The intricate webs of our lives are woven by an all-wise God who brings us to the place we are to be. Esther ended up in Mordecai's house, the exact place where God could use her.**
3. **Even though the competition might be tough, when God destines us, we will come out on top. Many beautiful young girls competed for the king's attention, but Esther won out.**
4. **God gives us favor with the right people to get his job done. Esther quickly won the affection of the king's eunuch, who had tremendous influence on who would be chosen.**
5. **Good seed will bring a wonderful harvest in God's time. Mordecai's heroic deed saved the king's life but was not rewarded until the exact time God chose it to be recognized.**

LOOKING UP *Help me, Lord, to remember that all the events of my life have been ordered by You for Your purpose. May I boldly step forward to fulfill what You intend for my life.*

RIGHTS

JUNE 9

Esther 3-5

LOOKING BACK Human rights attorney Luis Kutner was born on this day in 1908. Kutner, who died in 1993, was responsible for the release of many unjustly confined prisoners. He became known as "the Springman" because he had helped free famous prisoners such as Hungarian Cardinal Joseph Mindszenty and former Congo President Moise Tshombe. One of his best known successes was the release of controversial poet Ezra Pound. During World War II, the poet had broadcast Fascist propaganda to the United States. He was arrested for treason and imprisoned. In 1946, Pound was judged insane and spent twelve years in a mental hospital. He was later released.

LOOKING IN *Unfortunately, there were no human rights' attorneys available when wicked Haman hatched his diabolical plot to murder all the Jews. Haman was an Agagite. Apparently, the term "Agagite" means a descendant of Agag. It is probably a synonym for Amalekite, since "Agag" is a common title used for the Amalekite kings. In the Bible, only Haman is called an Agagite. He became prime minister under the Persian king Ahasuerus and was a fierce enemy of the Jews. Haman devised a massive plot to exterminate them. In particular, he had a gallows erected on which he hoped to hang Mordecai because Mordecai would not bow to him.*

LOOKING OUT

1. **When the laws of God conflict with the laws of man, we must obey God's higher laws. Mordecai refused to bow to Haman because he had determined only to bow down to God.**
2. **Anger and hatred are infectious, blinding us to reason and breeding prejudice. Haman was infuriated with Mordecai and hated him. That spread to prejudice against all Jews.**
3. **Feeding prejudice drives us to destroy the object of our hatred. Haman was determined to kill all Jews because his hatred had multiplied so rapidly and relentlessly.**
4. **Evil is subtle and will trap us if we are not careful. The king was taken in by the ruse Haman prepared. The careless and clueless king gave the orders to exterminate.**
5. **Confusion reigns when evil succeeds. After the horrific edict was issued and the king's couriers gave the news, all of the capital city staggered in confusion over the orders.**

LOOKING UP *Help me, Lord, to carefully destroy any prejudice lest I let hate grow and it destroy me. Help me to remember that sin is ever crouching at the door, and I must always be on guard against it.*

SLEEPLESS

JUNE 10

Esther 6-8

LOOKING BACK Some days are life-changing. On June 10, 1935, in Akron, Ohio, Dr. Robert Smith completed his first day of permanent sobriety. "Doctor Bob" and William G. Wilson founded Alcoholics Anonymous on that day. A.A. is now a worldwide organization of men and women who help each other solve their common problem of alcoholism. They also offer to share their recovery experiences with others who have a drinking problem and want to do something about it. There are about 85,000 local groups in the United States, Canada, and 130 other countries, concerned only with the personal recovery and continued sobriety of individual alcoholics.

LOOKING IN *Xerxes had a day that changed his life also. Xerxes was the Persian king who reigned from 486-464 B.C., known in the book of Esther as Ahasuerus. He was the son of Darius the Great and grandson of Cyrus the Great. He campaigned militarily against the Greeks, avenging the loss at Marathon in 490. However, his armada suffered a crippling defeat in the Bay of Salamis in 480, and he soon lost interest in attempting to defeat the Greeks. The day that changed his life was really a night when he couldn't sleep. He had the court records read to him and, in them, learned of Mordecai's loyalty. That knowledge would forever change his thinking.*

LOOKING OUT

1. Sometimes sleepless nights are divinely orchestrated. King Xerxes had a bad case of insomnia. In an effort to sleep, he had the boring records read and found a surprise.
2. God brings our good deeds to light at just the right time. Some time before, Mordecai had saved the life of the king but had received no compensation. Now it was God's time.
3. Coincidences are not always coincidences. Haman just happened to appear before the king when Xerxes was pondering how he would reward Mordecai's faithfulness.
4. Pride blinds us to reality. Haman was so caught up with himself that he thought, "Who is there that the king would rather honor than me?" It was a foolish thought.
5. In love, God tries to reach even the most despicable and hard-hearted sinner. Haman was filled with hate, but God staged this great humiliation to bring him to his senses.

LOOKING UP *Help me, Lord, to take advantage of any sleepless nights by asking You to communicate with me. Help me to remember that perhaps some of my sleepless nights are God-ordained.*

STRONG-MINDED

Esther 9-10

LOOKING BACK The first woman to be elected to the United States Congress was born on this day in 1880. Jeannette Rankin was a Republican who served from 1917 to 1919 as congresswoman at large from Montana. Years later, in 1940, she was elected to the U.S. House of Representatives for one term. Rankin created much controversy when she voted against the United States' participation in World War I and was the only member of the House to vote against entering World War II in 1941. This strong-minded woman also publicly opposed U.S. involvement in the Korean War and the Vietnam War. She never wavered in her convictions.

LOOKING IN *Esther was also a strong-minded woman, far more than a mere beautiful face. She never wavered in her convictions, either. Esther's strength and determination were clearly seen in the aftermath of Haman's defeat when her influence brought about the destruction of all the Jews' enemies in the land. The action was indeed harsh, but necessary, because so many had determined to kill the Jews. In commemoration of the nation's deliverance, the 14th and 15th of Adar became annual feast days, preceded by a fast on the 13th. Jews still celebrate Purim by reading the book of Esther aloud and remembering many more miracles of deliverance.*

LOOKING OUT

1. **Though evil seems overwhelming, the tables can turn quickly. Haman had plotted his holocaust, but the very day it was planned, something far different took place.**
2. **God can strike fear into the hearts of our enemies so they help us rather than stop us. The nobles, satraps, governors, and king's administrators helped the Jews because of fear.**
3. **When we have the advantage, we must not take advantage. The Jews had the upper hand but refused to take plunder from the enemies who had tried to destroy them.**
4. **We must mark victories with times of celebration that give glory to God. The Jews instituted the Feast of Purim as a time to especially praise God for their deliverance.**
5. **We must never forget the attempts of evil to destroy all that is good. The Feast of Purim also served as a reminder of how diabolical evil is in its intent to annihilate.**

LOOKING UP *Help me, Lord, to remember that You can quickly turn my sorrow into song. I trust You. Also, may I always remember to set aside time to thank You for Your great deliverance.*

ACCUSED

JUNE 12

Job 1-2

LOOKING BACK They are, "A vile race of quislings—to use the new word—which will carry the scorn of mankind down the centuries." That accusation was made about the Nazis by Winston Churchill on June 12, 1941. History has proven Churchill right, because the Nazis were responsible for murdering millions of innocent victims. Nazism developed in Germany during the 1920's. Led by the dictator Adolf Hitler, the Nazis controlled that European nation from 1933 to 1945. Nazism promised to build a harmonious, orderly, and prosperous society for all Germans. Instead, it brought terrorism, war, mass murder, disgrace, and a little bit of hell.

LOOKING IN *While Churchill's accusation against the Nazis was correct, the devil's accusations against Job were not. Satan tried to paint Job as a "quisling" who only served God for selfish reasons. History proved the evil one was wrong. Job apparently lived in the patriarchal or pre-patriarchal days, for not only does he not mention the Law or the Exodus, but he is pictured as a wealthy nomad who was still offering sacrifices himself. Undoubtedly, Job was a most respected man, for not only did the prophet Ezekiel refer to him as one of the greatest of Israel's ancestors, but James used him as an excellent example of patient and persistent faith.*

LOOKING OUT

1. **Satan can't stand to see the righteous prosper. Job was blameless and upright; he feared God and shunned evil. This is exactly the kind of person the enemy seeks to destroy.**
2. **Parental responsibility doesn't stop when children are grown. Every day Job offered sacrifices and prayers for his ten adult children.**
3. **The very nature of Satan is to accuse and question the followers of God. The book of Job lets us know that the devil has rightly earned his title of "accuser of the brethren."**
4. **We are in a test tube being held up to the principalities of the universe. Job was unaware that he was being put on display to show angels and demons God's power.**
5. **We must move beyond loving God to trusting Him, even in dark and difficult times. Job had to look beyond his circumstances to the character and promises of God.**

LOOKING UP *Help me, Lord, to remember in my test that I am on display to show the power of God's love. May I be faithful to You no matter how difficult my trial.*

MISSILES

JUNE 13

Job 3-7

LOOKING BACK The modern missile age dawned on this day in 1944 when German flying bombs struck England in World War II. The Chinese had used unguided rockets as fireworks, perhaps as early as the 1200's, and by the 1300's such rockets were used widely in Asia and Europe. During the early 1800's, Britain developed unguided, rocket-powered missiles that could carry explosives, using them widely in wars fought in Asia, Europe, and North and South America. The military use of rocket missiles dropped off during the late 1800's because artillery weapons had become so accurate that they were more effective. Then, Germany developed the first guided missiles.

LOOKING IN *Job's three friends launched some pretty powerful and destructive verbal missiles at the suffering saint. The first to attack was Eliphaz. He was a Temanite and may have been a descendant of Eliphaz, the son of Esau. Teman was fifty miles south of the Dead Sea, just east of Petra. Some understand Teman to designate southern Edom in general. Eliphaz did have some good things to say, but they were irrelevant to the situation Job faced. Job's sin had not brought on his problems, so the advice Eliphaz offered missed the point. Eliphaz's recorded speeches to Job are marked by a simplistic, theological traditionalism and a tone of moral superiority.*

LOOKING OUT

1. **No one is blameless before God. Eliphaz said that all have sinned and come short of the glory of God. While this is true, it missed the point of Job's suffering.**
2. **Trouble comes to all; it is an inevitable part of life. Eliphaz wisely observed that man's life on this earth is filled with difficulty.**
3. **The best course in times of trouble is to turn to God. Eliphaz spoke the truth, but again, this particular advice did not help Job in his predicament.**
4. **We should accept the reproof of our Lord. Eliphaz noted that when we are being disciplined, we must submit, not rebel. This is true, but Eliphaz's diagnosis of Job's problem was wrong.**
5. **There are times when we can do nothing but wait for God's deliverance. Eliphaz told Job that God would eventually help if Job would repent.**

LOOKING UP *Father, forgive me for all those foolish times I have offered my advice, not really knowing the circumstances. Let me not give advice but simply share Your Word.*

QUOTES

Job 8-10

LOOKING BACK Those wishing to appear wise often throw quotes around. They should pause to thank John Bartlett, born on this day in 1820. He was an American editor and compiler of the book that bears his name. Bartlett became known chiefly for the book *Familiar Quotations*, which is still being published. A notebook he kept, for the convenience of customers at his University Book Store in Cambridge, Massachusetts, developed into the first edition of the *Quotations*. Though Bartlett had little formal education, he created one of the most widely-used reference books in the English language. No quotation of his own is among the 22,000 wise words listed.

LOOKING IN *Bildad and Job's other two friends seem to have had their own collection of quotations they threw at suffering Job. Many of those words were wise and true. However, they failed to apply to the situation in which Job found himself. When Job responded negatively to their "quotations," the three friends grew angrier and more vociferous in their attacks on Job. Bildad was a Shuhite, perhaps a member of a group of nomadic Arameans. His speeches reveal him as a defender of traditionalist theological views. He argued that a just God does not punish the innocent. Therefore, Job should admit he was suffering the just fate of the wicked.*

LOOKING OUT

1. **People often say the cruelest things when we are going through heartbreak. Bildad accused Job's dead children of having deserved what happened to them because of their sin.**
2. **Speaking for God is foolish when we don't have all the facts. Bildad insisted that if Job would only repent, God would restore his fortunes. It was a foolish statement.**
3. **Tradition is not always the best and brightest teacher—it can be wrong. Bildad insisted that Job consider history and see that his problem was because of his sin.**
4. **Even "wise" words are unwise when they don't apply to the situation. Bildad spewed out some wise words, but they failed to take into account what was happening to Job.**
5. **God's promises are true, but we must also consider His timing. Bildad spoke of Job's restoration but failed to understand God's timing differed from his own.**

LOOKING UP *Help me, Lord, to offers words of comfort and affirmation to those in pain, not words that hurt them more. Help me not to be so wise in my own conceits.*

MALIGNED

JUNE 15

Job 11-14

LOOKING BACK Rachel, wife of President Andrew Jackson, was born on this day in 1767. Sadly, she was maligned all her life because of a misunderstanding. When Jackson lived in the Nashville boardinghouse of Mrs. John Donelson, he met her daughter, Rachel, who was separated from her army officer husband. Believing that Lewis Robards had obtained a divorce, she and Jackson married in August of 1791. In 1793, they learned Robards had not been granted a divorce until September of that year. The Jacksons were remarried on January 18, 1794. The confusion surrounding their marriage and remarriage made the couple targets of vicious gossip.

LOOKING IN *Job knew what it was to be misunderstood and maligned by people who refused to understand all the circumstances. In spite of all the defenses Job offered, his tormentors continued to pound on him without mercy. Zophar, the Naamahite, was the third friend who pounced on the helpless and hurting Job. Zophar probably was the youngest of the three "comforters," since he is mentioned last. He was the sharpest critic of the three men and was more philosophical in his criticism of Job. His words were coarser and his dogmatism more emphatic. Although there was a place called Naamah in Judah, doubt remains that it was Zophar's home.*

LOOKING OUT

1. **Pain plus pretentious people drive us to the edge. Job was so frustrated with arrogant friends that he blurted out, "Doubtless you are the people, and wisdom will die with you."**
2. **Platitudes do little to ease those who are heartsick. Job's pain was great, yet his friends just threw stale cliches at him—things most people already knew.**
3. **It is dangerous to speak for God unless clearly directed to do so. Job asked, "Will you speak wickedly on God's behalf?" We must be careful what we say that God says.**
4. **Only with Christ is there a clear understanding of the afterlife. Even righteous Job didn't know for sure about immortality. He asked, "If a man dies, will he live again?"**
5. **Even the greatest of pain cannot destroy our hope if we know God's character. Job suffered greatly, but he knew his God would count his steps but forgive his sin.**

LOOKING UP *Help me, Lord, to remember that even in my greatest pain, I will stand because of Your grace. Thank You that Your faithfulness goes far beyond my ever-changing feelings.*

IDENTIFYING

JUNE 16

Job 15-17

LOOKING BACK John Howard Griffin was deeply concerned about racial problems in the United States. He was born on this day in 1920, and died September 8, 1960. Griffin was an author and photographer, intent on understanding what it meant to be an African-American in modern America. In an effort to make an accurate assessment, Griffin blackened his skin by use of chemicals and ultraviolet light. He carefully kept a journal as he traveled through the South. This unusual approach resulted in his writing his best-known book, *Black Like Me*. As a result of his action, Griffin felt he could better understand the pressures our Black brothers and sisters feel.

LOOKING IN *Job's three friends never did understand what it meant to be in pain like Job. From their "exalted" position of pride, they looked down their noses at their tormented friend and assumed he deserved all he was getting. Eliphaz, Bildad, and Zophar were not satisfied with Job's answer to their first speeches. Now, Eliphaz speaks again, reminding Job that all people (including Job) had sinned and needed to repent. Thus, if he would just repent, God would forgive him, and all the world would be right once more. Job realized that he was getting nowhere with his three friends, so he called upon the rest of creation to witness to his integrity.*

LOOKING OUT

1. **When we are down, the enemy attacks our witness. Eliphaz blistered Job by charging, "But you even undermine piety and hinder devotion to God."**
2. **When we are down, the enemy attacks our purity. Eliphaz continued to castigate Job by saying, "Your sin prompts your mouth...your own lips testify against you."**
3. **When we are down, the enemy attacks our wisdom. Eliphaz cynically asked Job, "Are you the first man ever born?...Do you listen in on God's counsel?"**
4. **When we are down, the enemy attacks our faith. Eliphaz questioned Job's sincerity, saying, "Are God's consolations not enough for you, words spoken gently to you?"**
5. **When we are down, the enemy attacks our integrity. Eliphaz insisted Job was a sinner and admonished Job to listen to him if he ever wanted to get better.**

LOOKING UP *Help me, Lord, to remember that I'm in a battle, and the devil will bring harsh charges against me. Help me to be wise enough to keep silent when others attack me.*

HOPE

JUNE 17

Job 18-21

LOOKING BACK The televised hearings on the Army dispute with Senator Joseph McCarthy ended on this day in 1954. McCarthy, a Wisconsin Republican, made numerous charges—usually with little evidence—that certain public officials and other individuals were Communists or cooperated with Communists. He first gained national attention in 1950, when he charged that Communists dominated the State Department. Accusations and investigations spread quickly and affected thousands of people. Librarians, college professors, entertainers, journalists, clergy, and others came under suspicion. McCarthy irresponsibly made accusations without any proof.

LOOKING IN *It is easy to make charges without evidence. That's what Job's friends did. When Job tried to give them evidence, they rejected all reason and insisted they were right. Bildad reminded Job of the many proverbs which spoke of the fate of the wicked. In so doing, he was implying that what had happened to Job was the result of his sin. Zophar was hurt that he and his friends were being ignored, if not totally disagreed with. Thus, he declared that the wicked would suffer great pain and anguish and that all the forces of nature would turn against them. No doubt, Zophar included Job in this group. Job emphatically rejected this line of reasoning.*

LOOKING OUT

1. **When the storm rages, sometimes all we can do is hold on and ride it through. No amount of praying on Job's part could alleviate the pain of what was happening to him.**
2. **Often God lets us stand alone so we will learn to lean on Him. Job said he was alienated from his brothers and his acquaintances were completely estranged from him.**
3. **Hope holds us to God when death has a grip on our throats. Job, at the bottom, could say, "I know my redeemer lives, and that in the end he will stand upon the earth."**
4. **God will bring us out no matter how hopeless our situation seems. Job could add confidently, "And after my skin has been destroyed, yet in my flesh I will see God."**
5. **God is a faithful friend, not some distant stranger. Job knew the character of God; he could say, "I myself will see him with mine own eyes—I, and not another."**

LOOKING UP *Help me, Lord, to learn more about Your character so I can trust You more. When I am in the storms of life, help me to hold on to You until the troubles pass.*

TENACITY

JUNE 18

Job 22-24

LOOKING BACK George Leigh Mallory believed it could be done, although he never lived to see it. The English explorer and mountain climber was born on this day in 1886. Mallory's dream was to conquer the highest mountain in the world, Mount Everest, which at that time had never been scaled. Some said it never would be. Mallory believed it could be conquered and is best remembered for his answer when asked why he wanted to climb Mount Everest: "Because it is there." He was last seen climbing through the mist toward the summit of Everest on June 8, 1924. Seventy-five years later, Mallory's body was discovered near the top of the mountain.

LOOKING IN *Job had the same kind of hope Mallory possessed. He couldn't see through the mist of his troubles. His wife had given up on him, but he held on. Job had tenacious faith and truly believed God would somehow rescue him. Though they listened to him patiently, Job's friends were also becoming increasingly frustrated. Thus, Eliphaz intensified his charge (that Job's suffering was the result of his own sinfulness) by listing the various sins of which he thought Job was guilty. Once more Eliphaz called upon Job to repent. By this time, Job was in such pain that he all but ignored Eliphaz's comments and cried out for relief.*

LOOKING OUT

1. **In times of deep trial, it seems as though God is nowhere around. Job cried out, "If only I knew where to find him; if only I could go to his dwelling..."**
2. **God is always fair even though life isn't. Job felt if he could only talk with God face to face, the Lord would understand and do something about his troubles.**
3. **Even though we might not feel God's presence, He is always there. Job didn't feel God was near. Still he said confidently, "But he knows the way I take..."**
4. **Good living gives us confidence. Job knew that after he was tested, he would come forth as gold. He had been careful to follow in the ways and the will of God.**
5. **God is sovereign! Job couldn't understand all that was happening to him, but he knew God was in control. He said, "But he stands alone, and who can oppose him?"**

LOOKING UP *Help me, Lord, to remember that You are in charge of my life. I serve You; You do not serve me. Even when I don't feel Your presence, I know You are always there.*

SENTIMENT

JUNE 19

Job 25-28

LOOKING BACK On June 19, 1855, the Statue of Liberty arrived at Bedloe's Island in New York Harbor. It was given to the United States by France as an expression of friendship and of the ideal of liberty shared by both peoples. The idea of the statue as "Mother of Exiles" is expressed in the poem written by Emma Lazarus and inscribed on a bronze plaque on the pedestal of the monument. In part, the poem says, "Give me your tired, your poor, Your huddled masses yearning to breathe free, The wretched refuse of your teeming shore. Send these, the homeless, tempest-tost to me. I lift my lamp beside the golden door!" The inscription is indeed a lovely sentiment.

LOOKING IN *Too often our offer to help those in deep pain is merely sentiment, not action. That was certainly the case with Job's friends. Bildad now speaks and he refuses to be outdone. He reminds Job again to consider the nature and character of God, for since He was not unjust, Job surely must have sinned. Job, in sarcastic tones, asks the friends where they got their wisdom. He then pleads with them to look to God for real understanding and faith. Apparently, at this point, the three friends, having exhausted their arguments, once again become silent. Job then turns to reflect both upon the true nature of wisdom and his own place in existence.*

LOOKING OUT

1. **True wisdom is always heaven-sent, not earthbound. Job eloquently says that no one and no thing on this earth is completely wise.**
2. **Wisdom is God's gift to us; it cannot be purchased by man. No amount of money can buy true wisdom, but God gives it to those who ask.**
3. **Only in knowing God can we know real wisdom. Suffering Job acknowledges that God is the source of all wisdom. We cannot know it apart from Him.**
4. **Wisdom starts in bowing before God in humble adoration. Man can accumulate certain knowledge, but wisdom is reserved for the reverent.**
5. **Wisdom is walking away from sin. Job sees that sin debilitates man and blinds his mind to truth and wisdom. Only the pure in heart can truly see.**

LOOKING UP *Help me, Lord, to bow reverently before You, asking that You give me Your wisdom as I walk through this world. Thank You for always giving good gifts to those who ask.*

SOLILOQUY

JUNE 20

Job 29-31

June

LOOKING BACK On this day in 1893, in one of the most celebrated trials of all times, Lizzy Borden was found "not guilty" of murdering her parents. She had been accused of killing her father and stepmother with an ax. The bloody corpses of Andrew and Abby Borden were found on August 4, 1892. Suspicion fell on Lizzie because she was in the house and had the best opportunity to commit the crime. Lizzie had been active in charitable and religious groups, and many wealthy townspeople, women's rights organizations, and other groups supported her. Many other people felt sure of her guilt, however, and rumors about Lizzie became widespread.

LOOKING IN *While there may be some lingering questions about Lizzy Borden's guilt, there are none about Job's. His friends had falsely accused him and forced Job to defend his righteousness. Job sought to live a righteous life. He was still hurting and did not understand why. Thus, in a beautiful soliloquy, Job cried out, reminding God of how he had lived faithfully in the past and had been respected for it. Now, when he was suffering, everyone had turned against him, and death seemed very near. Thus, Job issued a final plea for God to vindicate him. With this, Job's case was made. He paused to await an answer from God.*

LOOKING OUT

1. **Good men tell the truth. In defending himself from his friends' charges, Job says he should be punished "if I have walked in falsehood or my foot has hurried after deceit..."**
2. **Good men don't give in to lust. In defending himself from his friends' charges, Job says he should be punished "if my heart has been enticed by a woman..."**
3. **Good men are just. In defending himself from his friends' charges, Job says he should be punished "if I have denied justice...if I have denied the desires of the poor."**
4. **Good men are not greedy. In defending himself from his friends' charges, Job says he should be punished "if I have...said to pure gold. 'You are my security.'"**
5. **Good men face their sins. In defending himself from his friends' charges, Job says he should be punished "if I have concealed my sin as men do by hiding guilt in my heart."**

LOOKING UP *Help me Lord, to understand the kind of person You want me to be and to become that type of person. Forgive me for my sin, and may I always walk with You.*

PHILOSOPHERS

Job 32-34

LOOKING BACK French philosopher Jean-Paul Sartre was born on this day in 1905. He believed that each of us wants to become God, and God cannot possibly exist. He expressed those ideas in novels, plays, and short stories, as well as in theoretical works. In his book, *Being and Nothingness*, Sartre wrote, "Man can will nothing unless he has first understood that he must count on no one but himself; that he is alone, abandoned on earth in the midst of his infinite responsibilities, without help, with no other aim than the one he sets for himself, with no other destiny than the one he forges for himself on this earth." The troubled philosopher died in Paris in 1980.

LOOKING IN *Elihu was also a troubled philosopher. Although he believed in God, his understanding of the Creator was distorted. Elihu gives four speeches trying to justify God's actions. First, he contends that God speaks to all people, and thus, even though he is a young man, he has every right to speak and even has the understanding to do so. Second, he reiterates that God is just and what has happened to Job is well-deserved. Third, he seeks to show that God honors the righteous and condemns the prideful, just as He has Job. Fourth, he pleads with Job to accept what has happened to him as God's discipline and to humbly repent.*

LOOKING OUT

1. When our pet theories are challenged, we often react very badly. Elihu was incensed because Job's friends couldn't convince Job of his sin. Elihu rudely jumped in.
2. Arrogance pushes us to insane and inane statements and positions. Elihu presumed that he had an inside track on what God was thinking on this whole matter with Job.
3. Pride pushes God off the throne and puts us there. Elihu was so full of himself that he bragged, "But now Job, listen to my words; pay attention to everything I say..."
4. Arrogance is ugly, causing us to drop all pretense of manners and niceness. Elihu was brutal in his attack on the ailing Job. He screamed at him, "You are not right!"
5. If a person thinks he knows all the answers, he is only showing his ignorance. Elihu ordered Job to either speak up or "listen to me; be silent, and I will teach you wisdom."

LOOKING UP *Help me, Lord, to always have a humble spirit and a gracious attitude to all I meet. May my ministry to others not be shot through with arrogance but filled with understanding.*

THEOLOGY

JUNE 22

Job 35-37

LOOKING BACK You don't have to live long to live well. George Vancouver was only 41 years old when he died, but he had already accomplished much. The English navigator and explorer was born on this day in 1757. Vancouver Island and cities in Washington and in British Columbia, Canada, are named after him. Vancouver, reaching the American continent in 1792, made valuable charts of various coasts. His surveys of the west coast of North America from San Diego to southern Alaska were highly valuable pioneering achievements which made him famous. Vancouver died very young, but during his short life he made a great contribution to our world.

LOOKING IN *Elihu was also a young man when he took on the task of straightening out Job. However, unlike Vancouver's, Elihu's efforts were not applauded. Elihu, son of Barachel the Buzite, was arrogant, angry, and insulting to suffering Job. His theology was basically sound, but there were huge gaps in Elihu's understanding of the situation. He would have been wise to have kept quiet. Interpreters differ concerning the significance of Elihu's speeches. His words seem to be somewhat more insightful than those of the other three friends, yet they still prove unsatisfactory as an explanation of Job's suffering*

LOOKING OUT

1. **Human reasoning sounds logical but is almost always wrong. Elihu's arguments were high-sounding and convincing. However, they were wrong. Job was not a sinner.**
2. **We should be suspicious of those claiming to have a special corner on truth. Elihu bragged to Job, "Be assured my words are not false; one perfect in knowledge is with you."**
3. **Good theology is not enough to bring healing—we need the Master's touch. Much of what Elihu said was correct. However, Job needed God's healing, not theological words.**
4. **We can know all about God but not really know Him. Elihu was a good theology student in many ways but, obviously, didn't have a personal relationship with God.**
5. **When we cut through all the high-sounding words, a harsh spirit is revealed. There is nothing colder than cold theology. Elihu was bereft of all human warmth.**

LOOKING UP *Help me, Lord, to love theology, but not forget people need a touch, not cold words of correction. May I never project the idea that I have a special corner on truth.*

THUNDERSTRUCK

JUNE 23

Job 38-39

LOOKING BACK On this day in 1968, the Viet Nam War became the longest war in American history, beginning in 1957 and ending in 1975. About 58,000 American military personnel died in the war, and about 300,000 were wounded. South Vietnamese deaths topped one million. North Vietnamese losses ranged between 500,000 and one million, in addition to countless civilians killed. The United States spent over $150 billion on the war. Bombing alone cost four times more than the combined U.S.-British bombing of Germany in World War II. The war made refugees of up to 10 million South Vietnamese, or about half the country's population.

LOOKING IN *Man always seems to make things worse when he tries to correct things with his own wisdom, just as happened in Viet Nam. Job's friends didn't help the suffering saint by their caustic words; they only made matters worse. Suddenly, out of the midst of a whirlwind, God spoke. Basically, God said two things: (1) He described the marvels of creation and asked Job if he could have done any better. Job quickly responded that he could not, for he, too, was just a creature; (2) God described how He controlled the world and everything in it, and then asked Job if he could do a better job. Job said he couldn't and didn't need to, now that he had seen God.*

LOOKING OUT

1. **God often speaks during the storms of our life. Significantly, God interrupted Elihu in the midst of the young man's arrogance to talk with His servant Job.**
2. **When God speaks, all other voices are silent. Only what He says is important. The advice of Job's friends faded into meaninglessness as God began to question His servant.**
3. **Our so-called "wisdom" is most often words without knowledge. Job had said he would like to ask God questions but was stunned to learn God questioned him.**
4. **When God questions, there is no room for any excuses. Job was stunned as God began to ask him questions that amazed him. The suffering Job was shamed into silence.**
5. **We can't possibly know the reasons for things being as they are, for we only see part of the picture. God reminded Job through questions that he knew only in part.**

LOOKING UP *Help me, Lord, not to question the way You lead but to faithfully follow no matter what. May I always remember that in questioning You, I am really expressing my own arrogance.*

THE END

JUNE 24

Job 40-42

LOOKING BACK Henry Ward Beecher, the famed brother of novelist Harriet Beecher Stowe, was born on this day in 1813. He was an eloquent, dramatic, and witty Protestant preacher whose sermons were original and timely. In his sermons, and in the book *Evolution and Religion*, Beecher tried to reconcile the Bible and evolution. Beecher served as a Presbyterian pastor in Lawrenceburg and Indianapolis, Indiana, until 1847. From then until his death, he ministered as pastor of the Congregationalist Plymouth Church in Brooklyn, New York, and was perhaps the most famous preacher of his time. His dying words at age 74 were, "Now comes the mystery."

LOOKING IN *The mystery of Job's life fell behind him once his test was over. When God questioned Job, God was apparently very pleased with him and his responses. However, He rebuked the three friends and commanded that they ask Job to seek intercession for them. Then, God restored all Job's fortunes and even gave him more children. In the end, Job found meaningful life, not in intellectual pursuits or even in himself, but in experiencing God and in his faith relationship to Him. Job had not understood why God had permitted such hardship in his life, but in the end, Job knew God better and loved Him more. The pain was nothing compared to God's blessings.*

LOOKING OUT

1. Too often, we speak when we should be listening. Job was so overwhelmed by God's voice that he bowed in repentance, admitting he spoke things he didn't understand.
2. A personal encounter with God drives us to our knees. Job's meeting with God was so dramatic that he said, "Therefore I despise myself and repent in dust and ashes."
3. God despises arrogance and demands the proud bow before Him. He told Job's friends they must repent of their words and attitudes, and ask Job to pray for them.
4. Blessings come once we have obeyed God. Job was restored to health and returned to prosperity once he obeyed God's command to pray for his three friends.
5. God's stories always have good endings. God not only gave Job back what he had lost but doubled his wealth. The point was proved that Job would remain faithful.

LOOKING UP *Lord, help me to remember in my great times of trial that Your stories always have wonderful endings. Please forgive me for the times I have been impatient waiting on You.*

INCOMPLETE

JUNE 25

Psalms 1-9

LOOKING BACK Benjamin Franklin, statesman, inventor, and publisher, had a marvelous way with words. Many of his sayings preach the virtues of industry, frugality, and thrift. "Early to bed and early to rise, makes a man healthy, wealthy, and wise." "God helps them that help themselves." "Little strokes fell great oaks." Other sayings reflect a shrewd understanding of human nature. "He's a fool that makes his doctor his heir." "He that falls in love with himself will have no rivals." On June 25, 1745, Franklin wrote, "It is the man and woman united that makes the complete human being...a single man...is an incomplete animal. He resembles the odd half of a pair of scissors."

LOOKING IN *What Franklin said about man and woman may or may not be true. However, man without God is certainly incomplete. The Psalms let us know the extent of our need for our Creator. Much of the Old Testament consists of the history of Israel or God's commands to His people. The Psalms are a special part of the Old Testament because they tell about people's personal responses to God. The Psalms reveal the individual's feelings when faced with both the joys and sorrows of everyday life. The Psalms contain hymns praising and thanking God and prayers to God in times of trouble. The first psalm tells us how to be happy.*

LOOKING OUT

1. Happiness happens when we decide not to believe like, behave like, or belong to the world. Psalm 1 carefully outlines those things that will bring happiness to us.
2. We are locked in an eternal conflict, but we can have joy for our journey. Psalm 2 speaks of how the wicked always oppose the righteous, but the Lord will give us victory.
3. No matter the opposition, we can rest in peace because God is with us. Psalm 3 defines the Heavenly Father as a shield around the believer, keeping him safe from harm.
4. There is a special place of intimate fellowship we can have with our Lord. Psalm 4 speaks of trusting in the Lord, and says that He has set apart the godly for Himself.
5. God forgives us because He is good, not because we deserve it. Psalm 6 is a prayer for God's mercy with the psalmist noting God saves because of His unfailing love.

LOOKING UP *Help me, Lord, to trust You more. Help me remember that You protect me from every harm. Bring me into that very special place of intimacy with You.*

COMFORT

JUNE 26

Psalms 10-18

LOOKING BACK John Tyler became the first U.S. president to marry in office on this day in 1844. Twenty-two months earlier Tyler was grief-stricken when his beloved wife Letita died of a stroke. However, joy came again to the president when he met Julia Gardiner. Tyler was cruising on the U.S.S. Princeton to watch the firing of a new naval gun when it suddenly exploded, killing eight people, including Julia's father. The death brought Tyler and Julia close together. They were married in New York City. Julia was a popular First Lady for eight months and delighted the capital with her brilliant entertaining. President Tyler and his second wife had seven children.

LOOKING IN *Even though he was grief-stricken, President Tyler felt exceptionally blessed when Julia came into his life. Their love gave both of them a new lease on life after the tragedies they had suffered. David knew firsthand how one's grief can turn to joy because of God's goodness. He celebrates the loving Heavenly Father in psalms that resound with high praise. In Psalm 16, David says that the man who sets his heart on God and puts his life in God's hands finds joy and security for the present and need not worry about what lies ahead. Heartbreak does happen in life, but God is there to lovingly comfort the broken and restore the fallen.*

LOOKING OUT

1. **No God–no good! The psalmist notes that apart from God there is no good thing in his life. God is his "all-in-all" just as He is the fulfillment of our life.**
2. **We are meant to enjoy the Christian friends God has given us. David took delight in those who served God faithfully and called on His name.**
3. **God has ordained our lot in life. The psalmist notes that God has assigned him his portion and made his lot secure. David rested in this great knowledge.**
4. **Sleepless nights offer opportunities for communication with God and instruction from Him. David talked with God whenever he couldn't sleep.**
5. **God will let us know where and how to walk. David knew that God would reveal the choices he should make that would bring joy to the Heavenly Father.**

LOOKING UP *Help me, Lord, to please You with my choices in life. Thank You because You are always there, and You have ordained my life and destiny.*

COURAGE

JUNE 27

Psalms 19-24

LOOKING BACK Helen Keller was born on this day in 1880. A serious illness, which her doctor called "acute congestion of the stomach and brain," destroyed her sight and hearing before she was two years old. Because of this, she was unable to speak and was entirely shut off from the world. But she rose above her disabilities to become internationally famous and help disabled people live fuller lives. An enthusiastic and untiring traveler, Keller lectured in more than 25 countries on every continent except Antarctica. During World War II, she worked with soldiers who had been blinded in the war. Wherever she appeared, she brought new courage to blind people.

LOOKING IN *We need not waste our grief. Just as Helen Keller turned her sorrow into blessing for others, the psalmists used the sorrow of their lives to encourage others through these sacred worship songs. There are 150 poems or songs in the Psalms. The book is sometimes called the Psalter. These songs were probably part of the religious ceremonies of the ancient Israelites. Even today, the Psalms are used in both Jewish and Christian worship services. When David wrote Psalm 23, he never dreamed it would be the most popular psalm in the Bible. This psalm is now quoted all over the world because it faithfully depicts the great love of our Lord.*

LOOKING OUT

1. Life's greatest guide is God's Word. It never leads us astray. Psalm 19 speaks of God's laws noting, "By them your servant is warned; in keeping them there is great reward."
2. Giving to God is like putting money in the bank. Psalm 20 notes that God remembers our sacrifices and gives us the desires of our hearts when we are faithful to Him.
3. Feelings may be real, but they are not always true. Psalm 22 asks, "My God, my God, why have you forsaken me?" This expression was only a feeling, not a fact.
4. We are not alone and abandoned on this planet. Psalm 23 lets us know that our Lord is the Good Shepherd Who daily cares for us and leads us in His good paths.
5. We must come clean before the Lord or He will not hear us. Psalm 24 notes that only those whose sins are covered are permitted to come into God's presence.

LOOKING UP *Help me, Lord, to remember that feelings change. I must rely on Your Word, not on my whims. Help me learn to praise You for Your character, not just because things are going well.*

CHAINS

JUNE 28

Psalms 25-30

June

LOOKING BACK French philosopher Jean-Jacques Rousseau was born on this day in 1712. He was the most important writer of the Age of Reason, a period of European history that extended from the late 1600's to the late 1700's. Rousseau's philosophy helped shape the political events that led to the French Revolution. His works have influenced education, literature, and politics. Rousseau's last works are marked by emotional distress and guilt that reflect his attempt to overcome a deep sense of inadequacy and to find an identity in a world that seemed to have rejected him. He glumly wrote, "Man is born free, and everywhere he is in chains."

LOOKING IN *Chains that hold men imprisoned are really spiritual, though they often appear physical. We can only be truly free when we give ourselves to God. The psalmists understood this clearly. David spoke of how we can be free from fear and the uncertainty of direction when the passion of our heart is to know and serve God. Psalm 27 tells of the great strength we receive when we fully give ourselves to God. He says that the man whose priorities are right has nothing to fear. He knows where to turn in trouble and his hope is well-founded. God's Word promises to deliver us from all our fears. This promise is for all, not just a "special" few.*

LOOKING OUT

1. **Fears flee and anxieties are brought under control when we trust in God. Psalm 27 speaks of the great strength we receive from the Lord when we walk close to Him.**
2. **The passion of our lives must be focused on God if life is to make sense. The psalmist said the only thing that he desired was to dwell in the house of the Lord and seek Him.**
3. **No matter what we do or where we go, God will not forsake us. David noted that even if his mother and father would forsake him, God would never give him up.**
4. **God will give us wisdom for our ways if we but ask Him. David cried out to God to give guidance. He prayed, "Teach me your way, O Lord; lead me in a straight path..."**
5. **Things may be bad right now, but they will get better. With great confidence, David declared, "I will see the goodness of the Lord in the land of the living."**

LOOKING UP *Help me, Lord, to want what You want and to always dwell in the center of Your perfect will. Like the psalmist, I pray, "Teach me your way, O Lord; lead me in a straight path."*

JUNE 29

CELEBRATION

Psalms 31-35

LOOKING BACK Amid great rejoicing by some, Jewish and Arab Jerusalem became a single city on this day in 1967. In 1949, at the end of the first Arab-Israeli War, Jerusalem was divided between Israel and Jordan. Israel controlled the western part of the city. Jordan controlled the eastern section, including the Old City, a walled section of Jerusalem dating from biblical times. Jerusalem is the capital and largest city of Israel and one of the world's holiest cities. It is also one of the oldest continuously inhabited cities in the entire world. Nearly three-fourths of Jerusalem's population are Jews. The remainder includes Muslims and a small number of Christians.

LOOKING IN *Many thought peace would come when Jerusalem was again one. However, that didn't happen. There is much tension in this holy city with great divisions remaining between Jews, Christians, and Muslims. Peace and happiness can only come as all of us obey God. Psalm 34 is a masterful song about peace and happiness. The psalmist tells of God's faithfulness. He cannot help but share this truth. He owes his peace and happiness to God. In the psalmist's experience, the man who honors God finds life. His misfortunes may be many, but God brings him through them all. This wonderful psalm celebrates God's tender care for His people.*

LOOKING OUT

1. Happiness is a decision. Psalm 34 offers a formula for joy. The first step is to praise God no matter what happens. David said, "I will extol the Lord at all times."
2. We need to be selective in what we say. Pursued by Saul, David had much to complain about, but he determined to speak only of God's goodness rather than his problems.
3. God can take away all our fears as we trust in Him. David, fleeing for his life from the jealous king, could say of the Lord, "He delivered me from all my fears."
4. We must be careful because we create worlds with our words. David said those who wanted to have a good and long life should learn to carefully bridle their tongues.
5. God is especially near when we go through hard times. David rightly noted, "The Lord is close to the brokenhearted and saves those who are crushed in spirit."

LOOKING UP *Help me, Lord, to always praise You regardless of the difficulties I face in my life today. Thank You that You are interested in my happiness and joy.*

GREED

Psalms 36-41

LOOKING BACK Former Secretary of the Interior Albert B. Fall was indicted by a Federal grand jury on this day in 1924. He was charged with bribery in connection with his leasing of the Teapot Dome Oil Reserve in Wyoming. Fall was Secretary of the Interior under President Warren G. Harding and the first Cabinet member convicted of a felony committed while in office. An investigation revealed Fall had accepted a $100,000 "loan" and more than $300,000 in cash and bonds to finalize a deal that would bring millions to unscrupulous businessmen. He was sentenced to a year in prison and fined $100,000. He served nine months in prison but never paid the fine.

LOOKING IN *Greed drives many people. Perhaps this is why God's Word insists we give generously to help the poor. The first three verses of Psalm 41 list the great benefits to those who are generous. David says that happy is the man who helps those in need because when trouble finds him, he finds that God is at hand to help. The rest of this remarkable psalm outlines the psalmist's own case: his illness, his isolation, his reliance on God. Then, verse 13 is a formal stanza of praise to God, to mark the end of the first book of Psalms. There are five separate books in the book of Psalms. The first book starts at chapter one and continues through chapter 41.*

LOOKING OUT

1. **When we help the helpless, God helps us in our times of trouble. Psalm 41 records that God will quickly come to the aid of those who are quick to help the poor.**
2. **When we help the helpless, God gives us a longer and better life. David says of the one who helps the poor, "The Lord will protect him and preserve his life."**
3. **When we help the helpless, God will abundantly bless us. David said of the compassionate, "Blessed is he who has regard for the weak...he will bless him in the land."**
4. **When we help the helpless, God will deliver us from our enemies. David noted that benefactors to the poor will not be surrendered to "the desire of their foes."**
5. **When we help the helpless, God heals us. David noted about the person who is careful to care for the unfortunate that, "The Lord will sustain him on his sickbed."**

LOOKING UP *Help me, Lord, to care for those You care for. I will minister consistently to the poor and needy. Thank You for the wonderful promises of blessings when I care for others.*

JULY

A Hot Month Named for a Famous Leader

In most countries in the Northern Hemisphere, July is usually the hottest month of the year. July is one of the winter months in the Southern Hemisphere. Except for cold Antarctica and the cold rainy part of South America, the climate during July is mild in most countries in the Southern Hemisphere. In the northern half of the world, grass and leaves often lose their greenness if there is little rain. Some flowers thrive on the heat and are most brilliant during July. The air is full of the hum of insects, and birds dart everywhere in search of food. July is a month of abundant life.

July was the fifth month in the early calendar of the Romans. They called the month *Quintilis,* which means fifth. Later, the Romans moved the beginning of the year to January 1 but did not change the names of the months. In 46 B.C., Julius Caesar gave it 31 days. The Roman Senate renamed the month Julius in honor of Caesar, because he was born in that month, and to recognize the dynamic impact he had on the Roman empire. Julius Caesar was one of ancient Rome's greatest generals and statesmen. He became a brilliant military leader and helped make Rome the center of an empire that stretched across Europe. Caesar also won fame as an orator, politician, and writer. His victories in civil war helped him become dictator of the Roman people. But his power frightened many of his political opponents, and a group of them assassinated him on March 15 (the Ides of March), 44 B.C.

During July, we finish the Psalms, move on to the Proverbs, study Ecclesiastes, enjoy the Song of Solomon, and start the prophetic books. For much of the month, we will be studying what is known as the wisdom books of the Bible. Most of the ancient Near Eastern wisdom material is found in some type of poetic structure. Until recent years, these structures have been a mystery because they did not seem to rhyme either in meter or sound as modern languages do. However, Bishop Robert Lowth, in A.D. 1753, unlocked the key to this poetic writing when he discovered that Hebrew poetry rhymed in thought. The beautiful and intricate poetic structure of these wisdom books makes their month's study both interesting and exciting.

QUAKERS

JULY 1

Psalms 42-49

July

LOOKING BACK The first Quakers arrived in America on this day in 1656. George Fox of England founded Quakerism. His spiritual experience led him to witness what he called the "Inner Light of Christ that dwells in the hearts of ordinary people." Fox began preaching in 1647. The word "Quaker" was originally meant to insult Fox, who told an English judge to "tremble at the Word of the Lord." The judge called Fox a "quaker" and the name stuck. Early Quakers, or Friends, as they preferred to be called, developed radically fresh forms of worship and business based on a trust in the Holy Spirit and faith that ordinary lay people were able to receive the Spirit.

LOOKING IN *In Psalm 42, the psalmist struggles with difficulties but knows there is an "inner light." He can't feel God's presence but knows that the Heavenly Father has not forgotten him, and one day he will rejoice again. This chapter starts the second book of Psalms which stretches from Psalm 42 through Psalm 72. Both Psalm 42 and Psalm 43 share the same theme and the same refrain. Originally, they probably were a single poem. The psalmist is in exile in the north, surrounded by godless men who mock his faith. Deeply dispirited, he contrasts past joys with the unhappy present. He is filled with longing for God's presence.*

LOOKING OUT

1. **There is a thirst that only God can quench. The psalmist cries out that as the deer pants for the water, his soul pants for God. Nothing but God can satisfy this deepest hunger.**
2. **Sometimes sorrow is so overwhelming, it blocks out the face of God. The psalmist tells of his deepest pain as he reaches for God but doesn't feel His presence.**
3. **All things "come to pass." Even the deepest hurt doesn't last forever. The psalmist remembers his past joys and looks forward to the time the present sorrow will cease.**
4. **God remains faithful regardless of our feelings. The psalmist pauses to remind himself that, "By day the Lord directs His love, at night his song is with me."**
5. **Hope holds us even in the darkest night. The psalmist twice asks, "Why are you downcast, O my soul?" because "I will yet praise him, my savior and my God."**

LOOKING UP *Help me, Lord, to remember that You are there even when my feelings dull my sensitivity to You. Thank You that You lift me up when I am feeling down.*

HALFWAY

JULY 2

Psalms 50-57

LOOKING BACK At noon today, 182-and-a-half days of the year will have elapsed with the same number of days remaining before the new year. For many, this will be a day to review past activities and a time to reevaluate priorities for the rest of the year. For others, the day will pass as most others do without giving thought to the past or future. Some will feel the year slipping by all too quickly, while those in great pain wonder if this time of difficulty will ever cease. Both feelings are normal as we move through the various seasons of life. We must remember that life is filled with both winters and summers. The present season will pass.

LOOKING IN *David was in a very hard season of his life when he penned Psalm 57. He must have felt his years on the run from Saul would never end. He was hiding in a cave to escape a mad king who was determined to destroy him. In spite of the difficult circumstances, David believed God would fulfill the purpose for his life, and he would not die by the hand of Saul. This psalm is really a prayer from David as he is surrounded by ferocious enemies. Circumstances may be black, but David knows that the man who fills his mind with God can sing His praises, come what may. David's faith was rewarded, although deliverance was long in coming.*

LOOKING OUT

1. There is a shelter in the time of storm. The psalmist determines to take refuge in the shadow of God's wings, knowing the loving Heavenly Father will keep him safe.
2. God will finish what He has started in our lives. The psalmist is confident that God will fulfill the purpose of his life. Christ always helps us fulfill our destiny.
3. If we take care of our relationship with God, He will take care of our enemies. The psalmist notes that God sends help from heaven against those who would defeat and destroy.
4. God doesn't keep us "from" trouble but sustains us "in" trouble. The psalmist admits he is in the midst of lions and ravenous beasts, but God will deliver him from them.
5. Knowing God's character strengthens us for the stress. The psalmist could rest even when he was in great trouble, for he knew the nature of our loving God.

LOOKING UP *Help me Lord, to know You will keep me safe even when the storms of my life terrify and threaten. Help me to know Your character better so that my faith will grow.*

RESCUE

Psalms 58-66

LOOKING BACK An Israeli commando unit staged a daring raid on Entebbe Airport in Uganda on this day in 1976. Entebbe is a major city in eastern Africa and a port on the northwest shore of Lake Victoria. In 1976, Palestinian terrorists hijacked a French airplane and forced the pilot to land the plane at Entebbe. They held more than 100 of the passengers—chiefly Israeli citizens—as hostages. A week later, Israeli commandos staged a secret and daring raid at the small airport. The brave commandos freed all the hostages, except three who were killed in crossfire between the rescuers, the terrorists, and Ugandan soldiers.

LOOKING IN *David knew defeats as well as victories. He also knew what it was to be held hostage by evil forces. Mad King Saul had kept David and his family on the run for many years. However, there was something even more important that David knew. The psalmist knew His God would rescue him and preserve him for the work He had ordained. Psalm 62 captures David's optimism because of his great faith in God. He could rest in God because he knew God's strength and love. Humbly trusting, the psalmist commits his cause to God. Man is bent on destruction, but what is he? Power belongs to God, Who wields it with love and justice.*

LOOKING OUT

1. **There is no place to run but to God. The psalmist wisely recognized that in some situations there is no one on this earth who can help you. However, God is always there.**
2. **We can tell God our troubles, knowing He can do something about them. The psalmist encouraged people to trust the Lord and to spill out their sorrows to Him.**
3. **Knowing God's strength helps us trust in Him at all times. David knew God would help him because so many times before God had come to his rescue.**
4. **Knowing God's love helps us trust Him at all times. David recognized the great love of God, Who not only provided and protected but also cared deeply for him.**
5. **God rewards us for what we do, not just for what we say, think, or feel. David understood that faith is how we live out our lives in the good times and in times of great stress.**

LOOKING UP *Help me, Lord, to know both Your strength and Your love so I will trust You at all times in my life. May I always remember that defeat is never terminal when I trust in You.*

DEFEAT

JULY 4

Psalms 67-72

LOOKING BACK On this Independence Day, it would be well to remember that defeat need not be terminal. Today marks the disastrous defeat of George Washington's troops by the French in 1754. His army was routed near Fort Duquesne, leaving the Ohio Valley under French control. It was the first military action for the 22-year-old Washington, and he was soundly defeated. Washington returned to Williamsburg two weeks later. However, the colonists did not blame the young colonel for losing but praised Washington and his men for their bravery. Later, the fort was recaptured. Washington went on to become a famous soldier and America's first president.

LOOKING IN *Psalm 69 contains the words of a man facing defeat. The psalmist is in desperate trouble through no fault of his own. He says his suffering is borne for God's sake, and he prays that God, in His love, will rescue him. The guilt of his tormentors is clear. He prays that they will be punished for all they have done. He pleads that God will set him free once again to praise Him. This psalm is one of the most quoted in the New Testament because it underlines the character of God. In spite of the psalmist's state, he knows that God is all powerful and loving. God is gracious and can restore no matter what the situation. Defeat need not be terminal.*

LOOKING OUT

1. **God knows everything about us yet still loves us. The psalmist is amazed that God still cares for Him regardless of his faults.**
2. **How we react in crisis does greatly affect others. The psalmist does not want to fail in his faith, because he knows it will discourage others who are struggling.**
3. **God answers our prayers out of His good love, not because we are so good. The psalmist underlines the wonderful nature of our loving Heavenly Father.**
4. **Praise is more pleasing to God than our prayers. The psalmist notes that our praise indicates that we have a loving trust in the goodness of our God.**
5. **We are to always praise God for what will be, not just for what now is. The psalmist is not yet out of his trouble but reaches forward in faith, praising God for a rebuilt nation.**

LOOKING UP *Thank You, Father, for what You are working out in my life. I may not see the victory as yet, but I know it is coming because I understand a little of Your wonderful character.*

FULL SPEED AHEAD

Psalms 73-77

LOOKING BACK American naval officer David Farragut was born on this day in 1801. During the Civil War, Farragut won the nickname of "Old Salamander" when he ran his boats under heavy gunfire between the New Orleans forts and the Mobile Bay forts. He sailed up the Mississippi River with his heavy seagoing ships to bombard Vicksburg in 1862. That was a year before Grant captured the city by land and led a fleet that attacked Mobile in 1864. The Union sailors commanded by Farragut fought their way into Mobile Bay, captured or destroyed enemy ships, and occupied the forts. He won fame during that battle by yelling "Damn the torpedoes! Full speed ahead!"

LOOKING IN *Farragut's disregard for danger in his determination to reach his goal is echoed by many of the Bible's psalmists. In spite of vicious attacks by their enemies, they determine to move "full speed ahead" because of their faith in God. They know His protection and provision despite the circumstances. When they are discouraged, they enter God's presence. He readjusts their thinking and gives them new courage. Psalm 73 is the classic example. It starts the third book of Psalms with the note that this is an unjust world. Asaph despaired at the prosperity of the wicked, until God changed his viewpoint when he went to God's house to worship.*

LOOKING OUT

1. God favors those who are good. Asaph notes, "Surely God is good to those who are pure in heart." All can come to Him and receive this special loving treatment.
2. A crisis of faith is a common experience. Asaph admits his feet almost slip and doubts cloud his mind when he looks at the circumstances of good and evil men.
3. Worship puts things in proper perspective. Asaph believed a lie until he went into God's house and there discovered that it was not over until it was over.
4. Regardless of our emotions, God holds us close to His heart. Asaph admits he was grieved and bitter, senseless and ignorant before God, but God loved him anyway.
5. The best place to live is next door to God. Asaph remarks, "But as for me, it is good to be near God. I have made the Sovereign Lord my refuge."

LOOKING UP *Help me, Lord, not to neglect worship, for it is then that I get a proper perspective of eternity. Thank You that You correct my viewpoint when I come into Your presence.*

HEROISM

JULY 6

Psalms 78-83

LOOKING BACK John Paul Jones, often called the Father of the American Navy, was born on this day in 1747. His heroism against a larger and better-equipped fleet established a tradition that has never been forgotten. His reply to a British demand to surrender, "I have not yet begun to fight," has become a famous Navy slogan. That statement came during a brutal battle between Jones' ship, the Bonhomme Richard, and Britain's vessel, Serapis. In 1779, Jones and his squadron met a large British convoy in the North Sea and attacked the lead ship. The British demanded surrender, but Jones refused. After three hours of hand-to-hand fighting, the British surrendered.

LOOKING IN *Psalm 78 calls God's people to heroism. The psalmist explains the failure of those whose faith had failed in the past. He turns to Israel's long history to make his point. He says that for a long time Ephraim was the most powerful of the 12 tribes. Joshua was an Ephraimite, and the tribe had great prestige under the judges. But now the tribe had lost its leadership. There were specific reasons this had happened. He says God gave them the law to remind them of Him, but they disobeyed it. They forgot what had happened in Egypt and the desert–the miracles, the rebellions, the punishments. Most of all they failed to become heros of the faith and lost out.*

LOOKING OUT

1. We cheat on God when our faith fails. Asaph notes that God considered Israel's decision to believe the 10 spies' negative report as an affront to His good character.
2. There are things we must never forget. God had performed many miracles for Israel, but the people refused to remember them when they faced trials.
3. We only hurt ourselves when we want what God doesn't want us to have. The Israelites insisted on meat in the desert even though God knew it wasn't good for them.
4. Miracles don't necessarily convince. Asaph recalls that "in spite of his wonders, they did not believe." Like us, they rationalized God's miracles as natural coincidences.
5. In spite of our unfaithfulness, God remains faithful to us. Asaph reminds wayward Israel, "Yet he was merciful; he forgave their iniquities and did not destroy them."

LOOKING UP *Help me, Lord, so that my faith doesn't fail. Let me do everything You have equipped me to accomplish. May I never forget the wonderful things You have done for me in the past.*

ASSASSINS

JULY 7

Psalms 84-91

July

LOOKING BACK Four persons, convicted of complicity with John Wilkes Booth in assassinating President Abraham Lincoln, were hanged on this day in 1865. After shooting Lincoln, Booth fled to Maryland, where David E. Herold, a former druggist's clerk, joined Booth and helped him escape to Virginia. Besides Herold, the conspirators included George Atzerodt, a carriage maker, who planned to murder Vice President Andrew Johnson; Lewis Paine, a former Confederate soldier, who was to kill Secretary of State William H. Seward; and Mrs. Mary E. Surratt, the owner of a Washington D.C. boarding house where the plot was hatched.

LOOKING IN *History—and our own observation—prove that the world is a very dangerous place. There are those, who for various reasons, want to kill, maim, and destroy. Yet, in the midst of this hostility, God promises protection for those who love Him. Today, we start the fourth book of Psalms' five books. This fourth section begins with the oldest psalm in the Bible, Psalm 90, and continues through Psalm 106. It includes one of the Bible's most familiar songs—Psalm 91. This beautiful hymn of faith encourages us to completely trust and rest in the Lord. Under God's protection, nothing can touch the person of faith.*

LOOKING OUT

1. **We are safe from all harm when we rest in God's shadow. This psalm of trust portrays the careful oversight God gives to those who turn their lives over to Him.**
2. **Problems will come, but they cannot destroy the true believer. No matter whether they come early or late in life, we are more than conquerors through Christ Who loves us.**
3. **Angels are real and are sent by God to watch over us. The psalmist notes that God will command His angels concerning us to guard us in all our ways.**
4. **Whether we can see the troubles come, they strike unexpectedly, or are all in our mind, we rise above them. The lions, snakes, and dragons picture this clearly.**
5. **God promises His children quality and quantity of life. Christ has made death obsolete so that the promise of long life is very real and very available to all who accept Him.**

LOOKING UP *Help me, Lord, to stay underneath Your shadow where there is perfect protection and peace. I trust Your great promises of protection for here and eternity.*

NECESSITY

JULY 8

Psalms 92-102

LOOKING BACK English poet Percy Bysshe Shelley drowned on this day in 1822, just a month before his 30th birthday. He had struggled with faith all his short life. In 1811, Shelley was expelled from Eton College for writing a pamphlet called *"The Necessity of Atheism."* He then eloped with 16-year-old Harriet Westbrook but abandoned her three years later to run away with Mary Wollstonecraft Godwin. Although both said they did not believe in marriage, Shelley and Mary Godwin were married after Harriet killed herself. Shelley felt that spiritual truth was not based on either supernatural revelation or natural experience. His final poems are grim and sorrowful.

LOOKING IN *Unlike Shelley's sorrowful poems, Psalm 92 is a joyous celebration of God to be sung on the Sabbath. It clearly outlines the lifelong benefits of a strong and vibrant faith. The psalm could well be titled, "The Necessity of Belief." It is a joyous thanksgiving in music for all that God has done, His goodness to each individual and to all His people. Psalm 93 proclaims that the Lord reigns eternal and almighty. It reminds us that His laws and holiness are unchanging. Psalm 94 speaks of God's justice, while Psalms 95 though 100 form a group of songs written in exultant praise of the God Who reigns over all His creation. Then, Psalm 101 is the king's manifesto.*

LOOKING OUT

1. **It is healthy to have an attitude of gratitude. In this "song for the Sabbath" the psalmist notes that it is good to praise the Lord and to make music in His name.**
2. **Only those tuned in can hear. While those who love God understand that life is a journey into eternity, "the senseless man does not know, fools do not understand."**
3. **Security always comes to those who honor God. The psalmist notes that the righteous will flourish like the palm tree. He stands firm no matter how severe the storm.**
4. **You are never too old to do great things for God. His Sabbath song affirms that even in old age those who serve God will have a productive life for the Master.**
5. **God is always fair to those who serve Him. The psalmist knows that the character of God is trustworthy in all situations and that God will always do good to His own.**

LOOKING UP *Help me, Lord, to remember to praise You for Your steadfast love to me and to all those who love You. Help me to be tuned to You so I might clearly hear Your voice.*

BENEFITS

JULY 9

Psalms 103-106

LOOKING BACK Black surgeon Daniel Hale Williams' bold action has resulted in great benefits for mankind. He performed the first open heart surgery on this day in 1893 at Providence Hospital on Chicago's south side. Williams was the first surgeon to repair a tear in the pericardium (sac around the heart). This brilliant doctor also helped improve medical opportunities for Black people. In 1891, he founded Provident Hospital in Chicago, the country's first interracial hospital and training school for Black nurses and interns. Later, Williams established a nursing school for Blacks in Washington, D.C., and surgical clinics in Nashville, Tennessee.

LOOKING IN *While Dr. Williams performed the first physical open heart surgery, God has been doing that, spiritually, from the beginning of humanity. He offers salvation, which corrects the evil heart of mankind, providing him with astonishing benefits. In Psalm 103, we learn some of those benefits. Today's songs complete the fourth book of Psalms. Psalm 104 speaks of God, the Great Creator. The psalmist marvels at the grandeur and detail of all that God has made. Psalm 105 praises God for His covenant with Israel, while Psalm 106 discusses Israel's disobedience. This last song forms a confession of the nation's sins from the beginning to the present.*

LOOKING OUT

1. **The first benefit of salvation is relief from guilt. David praises the Lord because the Lord forgives us of our sins; that is, He lifts the heavy load of guilt from us.**
2. **The second benefit of salvation is healing of hurts caused by sin. David acknowledges that sin rips us apart, but our loving Lord heals all of our diseases.**
3. **The third benefit of salvation is rescue from those things that would destroy us. Each of us has a downward pull in our lives. God redeems our lives from the pit.**
4. **The fourth benefit of salvation is that it makes us loving and tender. The psalmist notes that God crowns the lives of His followers with love and compassion.**
5. **The fifth benefit of salvation is an overall improvement of the quality of our life. David notes that God satisfies our desires with good things and renews our youth.**

LOOKING UP *Help me, Lord, to understand the great benefits that come from repenting of my sins to follow You. Help me always to keep short accounts, repenting whenever I sin.*

INVOLVEMENT

JULY 10

Psalms 107-110

LOOKING BACK Reformer John Calvin was born on this day in 1509. His brilliant mind, powerful preaching, many books, large correspondence, and capacity for organization and administration made him a dominant figure of the Reformation. Calvin expanded the idea that Christianity was intended to reform all of society. He lectured and wrote on politics, social problems, and international issues as part of Christian responsibility. Many of Calvin's ideas were controversial, but no other reformer did so much to force people to think about Christian social ethics. He was the first Protestant leader in Europe to gain partial church independence from the state.

LOOKING IN *Calvin was absolutely right in insisting that God and believers can make a great and positive difference in society. The psalmists knew this. Throughout their songs, they encourage their nation to rely on God. Psalm 107 is such a psalm, whose single theme is praising God because He is the nation's Redeemer. The psalmist offers four word pictures of Israel's deliverance from captivity. God never leaves us alone to fend for ourselves. If we but turn to Him, He offers solace, deliverance, healing, and direction. The psalmist stood assured of God's assistance. Psalm 107 starts the last of the five books in Psalms, spanning this song through Psalm 150.*

LOOKING OUT

1. **Problems that we face can be solved by going to God in prayer. God's provision should be followed by praise. The psalmist gives assurance of God's help for those who ask.**
2. **There is help for those who are emotionally shattered. The word picture of the distressed traveler represents the tormented soul.**
3. **There is help for those addicted to destructive things. The prisoner represents the people who are bound by habits that will destroy them.**
4. **There is healing for the ill. The sick man here is restored to health as testimony to the fact that the God Who created the human body is certainly able to repair it.**
5. **There is a wisdom to win when we ask God for it. Sailors, brought safely to their destination, represent all of those needing guidance and getting it from God.**

LOOKING UP *Help me, Lord, to not simply enjoy my faith but to move out into my community to make a difference. I know You will give me wisdom to do what You have assigned.*

DESTINED

JULY 11

Psalms 111-118

July

LOOKING BACK Today marks the anniversary of President Abraham Lincoln appointing Major General Henry W. Halleck as Commander in Chief of the Union armies during the Civil War. Halleck, bright and talented, was an obvious choice. However, he failed to develop strategy with imagination and aggressiveness, forcing Lincoln to appoint General Ulysses S. Grant to replace Halleck in 1864. Though Grant had been a business failure, and even had a blemish on his military record, he proved to be a brilliant general who brought an end to the bloody war. Most historians agree that Ulysses S. Grant seems to have been especially destined for that task.

LOOKING IN *It's not always the best and the brightest who come out on top. In Psalm 118, the psalmist admits rejection by others but declares that God would lift him up to a position of prominence and importance. He couldn't trust men, but he could wholly rely on the God Who would never fail him. This remarkable psalm is the last in a group linked traditionally with the Jewish Feast of Tabernacles (Harvest) and Passover. In Jewish homes, Psalms 113 and 114 are sung before the Passover meal, while Psalms 115 through 118 are sung after. This was probably the song that Jesus and His disciples sang right after they had eaten the Last Supper.*

LOOKING OUT

1. When God is for us, it doesn't matter who stands against us. The psalmist declares he isn't afraid because he goes with God and, therefore, "What can man do to me?"
2. Man cannot be trusted, but God can. The psalmist notes that it is better to take refuge in the Lord than to trust in princes. Man will let us down, but God will hold us up.
3. We are assured of victory regardless of how the present looks. The psalmist declares confidently, "I will not die but live and will proclaim what the Lord has done."
4. We may not be the best and brightest, but we are destined to come out on top. The psalmist declares, "The stone the builders rejected has become the capstone."
5. Regardless of what is happening right now in our lives, this is God's day. The psalmist asserts, "This is the day the Lord has made; let us rejoice and be glad in it."

LOOKING UP *Help me, Lord, to remember that You made this day, and I will treat it as a special gift from You. May I always be grateful and rejoice in the day You have given me.*

AWARENESS

JULY 12

Psalm 119

LOOKING BACK An awareness of truth can make a dramatic difference in life and lifestyle. On this day in 1957, the Surgeon General of the United States announced that a scientific link between cigarette smoking and lung cancer had been established. Other studies soon followed that uncovered additional health risks to those who use tobacco. That truth has precipitated an avalanche of ad campaigns that encourage people to stop smoking and try to persuade youngsters from starting the filthy habit. For many, the truth about tobacco has altered their lives. Tragically, many others fail to take the warnings seriously and end up paying for their negligence with their lives.

LOOKING IN *Psalm 119 is a magnificent song of 22 stanzas praising the value of ultimate truth–God's Word. Reading and heeding God's Word dramatically alters our way of thinking and our lifestyle. It will keep us happier, healthier, and holier. Tragically, many ignore God's Word and soon learn by experience they should have paid attention to it. Psalm 119 is the longest psalm of all and the most formal and elaborate in concept. There are 22 eight-verse sections. Each section begins with a successive letter of the Hebrew alphabet, and each verse within the section begins with the same letter. The psalmist uses 10 different words to describe God's Word.*

LOOKING OUT

1. **There are wonderful things hidden in the Bible, and God will reveal them to us. The psalmist prays, "Open my eyes that I may see wonderful things in your law."**
2. **Obedience is a learned behavior. The psalmist passionately prays, "Teach me, O Lord, to follow your decrees; then I will keep them to the end."**
3. **Pain is not our enemy; it's our friend. The psalmist acknowledges that before he was afflicted, he went astray, but after pain touched him, he obeyed God's Word.**
4. **God's Word is not a rule book; it is a flashlight. The psalmist notes, "The unfolding of your words gives light; it gives understanding to the simple."**
5. **God's Word is relevant to all generations for all time. The psalmist says, "Long ago I learned from your statutes that you established them to last forever."**

LOOKING UP *Help me, Lord, to learn to love Your Word more each day so I might please You with my life. Teach me to better understand the Bible so I might be more effective for You.*

PROTECTION

JULY 13

Psalms 120-131

LOOKING BACK Confederate General Nathan Bedford Forrest was born on this day in 1821. After the war, Forrest served as the first leader of the Ku Klux Klan, a White-supremacist organization that attempted to "protect" the southern way of life by denying Blacks their civil rights. The KKK was formed as a social club in Pulaski, Tennessee. In 1871, Congress passed a law giving authority to use federal troops against the Klan. The KKK soon disappeared and didn't reappear until 1915 when William J. Simmons organized a new Klan in Atlanta, Georgia. Today, it is estimated there are about 6,000 members in this organization that has sparked so much fear.

LOOKING IN *Tragically, many unspeakable atrocities are committed in an effort to "protect" what selfish and evil men want. In Psalm 121, God is pictured as the "Protector." However, His protection is for good men who will walk in His ways and do His will. This psalm is the second in a series of what is known as the "Songs of Ascents." They were thought to have been sung by pilgrims on their way to Jerusalem to celebrate the three great annual feasts. Pilgrims traveled together for protection and companionship. In many of the "Songs of Ascents," the thought and imagery focuses on Jerusalem, the Holy City. Psalm 134 is the last in this fascinating series.*

LOOKING OUT

1. **God is the only true source of safety in the universe. The Israelites sang in their travels, "My help comes from the Lord, the Maker of heaven and earth."**
2. **God never has a "timeout" when it comes to caring for us. The singers of Israel taught the people to say, "He who watches over Israel will neither slumber nor sleep."**
3. **God not only protects but comforts us in hard times. The Israelites rang out the praise, "The Lord watches over you; the Lord is your shade at your right hand."**
4. **God makes us so secure that nothing in this world can destroy us. The psalmist proclaimed, "The sun will not harm you by day, nor the moon by night."**
5. **God has signed on as our Protector for the whole trip. The Israelites could confidently sing, "The Lord will watch over your coming and going both now and forevermore."**

LOOKING UP *Help me, Lord, to know You better so that I may trust You more as my Provider-Protector. May I always remember there is no safety in this hostile world apart from You.*

WINNING

Psalms 132-139

LOOKING BACK Civil War General John Pope hated to lose. He had brought charges against a Union soldier, resulting in a celebrated military inquiry. Fitz-John Porter served under Pope during the second Battle of Bull Run. During the battle, Porter refused to obey Pope's "questionable" order to attack Confederate forces. The Union forces eventually lost the battle, and Pope charged Porter with disobedience, disloyalty, and misconduct. Porter was court-martialed, found guilty, and dismissed from the army. Looking back over events, Pope bragged on this day in 1862, "I come from the West where we have always seen the backs of our enemies."

LOOKING IN *David almost always saw the backs of his enemies as they fled from him. There were times when victory seemed elusive, but somehow David always won. That "somehow," he says, was because of God's faithfulness. In Psalm 139, he praises the Lord, Who had led him all his life and brought him victories. This "Psalm of the Unavoidable God" tells us that we are God's great design and that we are all carefully crafted by Him. The psalm is concerned with God's all-knowingness and "everywhere-presentness," not in an abstract way but in a highly personal way. Because of this, David says he will always align himself with God's purposes.*

LOOKING OUT

1. **God can read us before we get it written. David says God knows his thoughts from afar, and before a word is on his tongue, God knows it completely.**
2. **No matter where you have to go, God has been there first. David says, "If I go up to the heavens, you are there; if I make my bed in the depths, You are there."**
3. **We are art pieces God has carefully crafted. David is amazed because we are knit together by God in our mothers' wombs. We are fearfully and wonderfully made.**
4. **We will be on the earth just as long as the Lord decides. David says, "All the days ordained for me were written in your book before one of them came to be."**
5. **Our response to "the unavoidable God" is reverence and service. David cries out for God to search him and know his heart, cleansing him from any offensive way.**

LOOKING UP *Cleanse me, Lord, from all those things that displease You. Help me to follow You completely. Thank You for Your tender loving care of Your children.*

SAINTS

Psalms 140-150

LOOKING BACK Frances Xavier Cabrinias was born on this day in 1850. Canonized in 1946, she was the first U.S. citizen to be made a saint by the Roman Catholic Church. Born in Italy, the 13th and youngest child of a farmer, Cabrinias wanted to be a missionary to China. In 1889, the nun came to the United States, where she immediately displayed the courage, hope, vision, and endurance of a pioneer. She lived in New York City and Chicago and traveled in Latin America. She opened many charitable institutions, including orphanages, schools, and free clinics and founded hospitals in New York City and Chicago, earning the love and respect of many.

LOOKING IN *Those who follow Christ passionately cannot help but reach out to the hurting and homeless, because that is the nature of their Savior. In Psalm 145, David clearly outlines the loving character of the Heavenly Father. He encourages us to praise the Lord so all may come to know this God. The book of Psalms ends with a group of songs in praise to God, probably written to be used in public worship. Psalms 145 through 150 form this special section. They are still sung by many Jews today in their daily prayers. Each psalm of 146 through 150 begins and ends with an "Alleluia" ("O praise the Lord"). These last five songs are often called, "The Hallelujah Psalms."*

LOOKING OUT

1. **God's character is that of a wise, loving Father. David reverently proclaims, "The Lord is gracious and compassionate, slow to anger, and rich in love."**
2. **The purpose of praise is that all men might find the Lord. David encourages God's people to praise Him "so that all men may know of Your mighty acts."**
3. **God's provisions always come just at the right time. David notes, "The eyes of all look to you, and you give them their food at the proper time."**
4. **God is the One Who fulfills our deepest desires. David lovingly notes that God delights in satisfying the desires of all living things and of those who fear Him.**
5. **God is never impersonal toward His creation. Despite what some say, David notes that "the Lord is righteous in all his ways and loving toward all he has made."**

LOOKING UP *Help me, Lord, to speak to others often about Your wonderful love so they might know You. May my life always be filled with praise and thanksgiving.*

INSTRUCTION

Proverbs 1-4

LOOKING BACK "Fat Boy," the experimental atomic bomb, was set off on this day in 1945, in the New Mexico desert, ushering the world into the nuclear age. The plutonium bomb vaporized the steel scaffolding holding it, as the immense fireball rose 8,000 feet in a fraction of a second, ultimately creating a mushroom cloud to the height of 41,000 feet. At ground zero, the bomb emitted heat three times the temperature of the interior of the sun. All plant and animal life for a mile around ceased to exist. When informed by President Truman at Potsdam of the successful experiment, Winston Churchill solemnly responded, "It's the Second Coming in wrath."

LOOKING IN *Contrary to the purpose of the atomic bomb, God's Word was created for instruction, not destruction. Man knows how to kill, but only God can give life. In this world of destruction, God teaches us what will bring life and joy. The book of Proverbs contains the essence of Israel's wisdom. It provides a godly world-view and offers insight for living. Proverbs 1:7 provides the perspective for understanding all the proverbs: "The fear of the Lord is the beginning of knowledge; fools despise wisdom and instruction." "Fear of the Lord" is biblical shorthand for an entire life in love, worship, and obedience to God.*

LOOKING OUT

1. **God's Word gives us wisdom. In introducing the Proverbs, Solomon says they are for attaining wisdom. God is the only real source of this quality of life.**
2. **God's Word teaches discipline. Solomon notes that by reading and heeding the proverbs, we are put in control of ourselves. Discipline is necessary for any success.**
3. **God's Word instructs us how to live on planet earth. Solomon insists that these divinely inspired proverbs help us do what is right, just, and fair.**
4. **God's Word helps us to use the resources God has given us. Solomon declares that these proverbs teach prudent living. Prudence is the ability to use our resources well.**
5. **God's Word teaches us discretion. This is the ability to say and do the right things. Solomon says he wrote the proverbs to help us learn this characteristic.**

LOOKING UP *Help me, Lord, to become a fully developed person as I love Your Word and live by its precepts. Let me hide Your Word in my heart that I might not sin against You.*

CREATIVITY

JULY 17

Proverbs 5-9

LOOKING BACK English clergyman Isaac Watts was born on this day in 1674. He wrote more than 700 hymns and psalms, along with theological treatises, volumes of sermons, and books on ethics, psychology, and teaching. Watts was considered one of the greatest preachers of his time. His best hymns are noted for simplicity of poetic structure, apt use of figures of speech, and emotional vitality. Many still appear in most English hymnals. He wrote "Joy to the World," "O God, Our Help in Ages Past," and "When I Survey the Wondrous Cross." Watts is an example of a talented person who wisely used the resources God had given him.

LOOKING IN *In Proverbs 5, Solomon warns that sin short-circuits our creativity and brings great pain. If we dissipate our energies with dissolute living, we waste our limited resources and will never accomplish all that God wants us to do. The proverbist uses the example of an adulteress to clearly make his point. If we are to live up to the potential God has given, we must stay away from all that cripples creativity. Proverbs is a product of the educational system of ancient Israel. Children were educated primarily at home. Thus, the Proverbs reflects the teachings of parents trying to raise their children to become successful and responsible adults.*

LOOKING OUT

1. **Sin is sweet at the start but bitter in the end. Solomon says the lips of an adulteress drip honey, and her speech is smoother than oil. Ultimately she is bitter as gall.**
2. **Only the very foolish sacrifice long-term goals for short-term satisfaction. Those who commit adultery give no thought to their way of life. Their action ends in great pain.**
3. **We must stay as far away from sin as possible. Solomon admonishes those tempted to sin, "Keep a path far from her, do not go near the door of her house."**
4. **If we don't hear, we will feel. Solomon notes that if a person doesn't stay away from sexual infidelity, his life will end in shambles and extreme pain.**
5. **Faithfulness is a decision. Solomon encourages us to determine to be satisfied with the mate God has given us rather than seek fulfillment in an adulterous relationship.**

LOOKING UP *Help me, Lord to remain faithful not only to You but also to my family and friends. Bring my thoughts and imaginations under Your control so I can be my best.*

JULY 18

RULING

Proverbs 10-12

LOOKING BACK Ralph Waldo Emerson ranks as a leading figure in the thought and literature of American civilization. He was an essayist, critic, poet, orator, and popular philosopher. Emerson brought together elements from the past and shaped them into literature that had an important effect on later American writing, influencing the work of Henry David Thoreau, Herman Melville, Walt Whitman, Emily Dickinson, Henry James, and Robert Frost. He has been described as belonging to the tradition of "wisdom literature." On this day in 1876, he observed, "Great men are they who see that spiritual is stronger than material force, that thoughts rule the world."

LOOKING IN *Emerson was absolutely right in his observation. That is why the book of Proverbs is so important to read and study. If we read and heed God's Word, we will rule our spirits and greatly impact our world. While some of the Proverbs are intended as instruction from parents to children, other sections may have come from a palace school for the training of government officials. The book of Proverbs has earned universal appeal because it contains material valuable to all people who hope to live a life of wisdom, honesty, responsibility, self-control, and respect for God. Many of the book's sayings have become part of everyday speech.*

LOOKING OUT

1. **Discipline hurts, but it also heals. Proverbs says that if we love discipline, we love knowledge. God's chastening is always directive, not merely punitive.**
2. **God cares how we care for the earth and the things He has created for it. Proverbs says,"A righteous man cares for the needs of his animals."**
3. **We are never to expect to get something for nothing. Proverbs encourages hard work and honesty. It says that hard work reaps rewards; financial fantasies do not.**
4. **Our tongue is either our friend or our enemy. Proverbs notes that how we talk returns to us either in great blessings or bitter cursing.**
5. **Cruel comments cut to the quick, but wise words heal. Proverbs instructs us to use our tongues as instruments of healing and help.**

LOOKING UP *Father, please help me always to remember to be careful what I say and how I say it. Teach me to speak the truth in love, bringing healing and help through what I say.*

PARTNERSHIP

JULY 19

Proverbs 13-15

LOOKING BACK The first women's rights convention in the United States opened on this day in 1848 at Seneca, New York. Elizabeth Cady Stanton, along with Lucretia Mott, organized the affair. During the 1830's, Stanton became interested in women's rights and in abolition. During the 1850's and the Civil War, she worked hard for women's rights and for the end of slavery. After slavery was abolished in 1865, Stanton broke with abolitionists because they favored voting rights for Blacks but not for women. It was at that first women's rights convention in 1848 that Stanton emphatically declared, "Man cannot fulfill his destiny alone..."

LOOKING IN *Stanton's words are wise and true. Men and women do need each other. More importantly, we need God if we are to succeed. Proverbs 15 speaks about that partnership, offering much wise and practical counsel. As we walk toward God, we find we are walking away from death and destruction. In spite of being a collection of collections, the book of Proverbs displays a unified, richly complex world-view. Proverbs 1-9 introduces this world-view and lays out its main themes. The short sayings of Proverbs 10-31 are to be understood in light of the first nine chapters. They simply say that the beginning and end of wisdom is to fear God and avoid evil.*

LOOKING OUT

1. Those who love Christ must watch their words. The writer notes, "A gentle answer turns away wrath, but a harsh word stirs up anger."
2. Real wealth is deposited with those who love God. Proverbs notes that "the house of the righteous contains great treasure" in contrast to the income of the wicked.
3. Only those who love God can expect answers to prayer. Proverbs notes, "The Lord detests the sacrifices of the wicked, but the prayer of the upright pleases him."
4. A little is a lot when God is in it. Proverbs wisely says, "Better a little with the fear of the Lord than great wealth with turmoil." Sin sucks the joy out of everything.
5. Although walking toward God is not easy, it does separate us from the pain of our lives. Proverbs says, "The road of the godly leads upward, leaving hell behind."

LOOKING UP *Help me, Lord, to walk toward You, knowing the closer I am to You, the further I am from my pain. When I fail or fall, help me to get up and start toward You again.*

RIOT ACT

JULY 20

Proverbs 16-19

LOOKING BACK Today, to "read the riot act" usually means telling children to quiet down. In old England, however, reading the riot act meant something different. The law that gave birth to this now famous saying was enacted on this day in 1715. The "Riot Act" law said that if 12 or more people were unlawfully assembled to create a disturbance, an authority was required "with a loud voice" to command silence and read the Riot Act proclamation. Once the act was read, any persons failing to comply with its restrictions within one hour were to be seized, apprehended, and carried before a justice of the peace by the order of England's King George.

LOOKING IN *English authorities felt the Riot Act was necessary because we humans have a tendency to stir up conflict. Proverbs talks a lot about conflict and how to resolve it peacefully. In Proverbs 16, many of the sayings deal with how to find personal peace in a war-torn world. Following lessons on wisdom found in the first nine chapters of Proverbs, Solomon now moves on to give practical instruction that covers every aspect of life. Proverbs 10 through 22:16 contain these sayings. In this collection, the sayings often get their punch from contrast. The second line of each saying is the antithesis of the first and reveals sound thinking.*

LOOKING OUT

1. **We need God's Spirit because we are blind to our own faults. Proverbs says, "All a man's ways seem innocent to him, but motives are weighed by the Lord."**
2. **We have a definite edge when we give it all to God. Proverbs notes, "Commit to the Lord whatever you do, and your plans will succeed."**
3. **We don't have to fight when we are right. Proverbs declares, "When a man's ways are pleasing to the Lord, he makes even his enemies live at peace with him."**
4. **We have been given an incredible power to bring healing to others. Proverbs asserts, "Pleasant words are a honeycomb, sweet to the soul and healing to the bones."**
5. **Self-control is the secret to great success. Proverbs wisely notes, "Better a patient man than a warrior, a man who controls his temper than one who takes a city."**

LOOKING UP *Help me, Lord, to consider carefully all of the wise sayings in Your Word and apply them to my life. Holy Spirit, remind me of the truths of Your Word all during the day and night.*

PRACTICAL

JULY 21

Proverbs 20-22

LOOKING BACK Marshall McLuhan was born on this day in 1911. The Canadian professor and writer proposed theories on mass communication that bred widespread debate. McLuhan argued that each major period in history takes its character from the medium of communication used most widely at the time. He said electronic communication—especially television—now dominates the lives of all Western peoples, affecting their way of thinking and their institutions, so much so, that people in all parts of the world become deeply involved in the lives of everyone else. McLuhan also stated, "Most people are alive in an earlier time, but you must be alive in our own time."

LOOKING IN *Life does change quickly and, as McLuhan noted, few keep up with the progress. We must be "alive in our time." What is most fascinating is that the Bible, although old, is so relevant. It has proved to be a book for all times because of the divine wisdom found within its pages. In our fast-changing world we now need, more than ever, the unchanging Word of God. In Proverbs 22, timeless truths are given, relevant not only back then but as fresh as this morning's sunrise. God's Word was "alive" in the long ago and is still "alive" today. The Bible is not only spiritual but practical, and only foolish people ignore it.*

LOOKING OUT

1. **A good reputation is like money in the bank. Proverbs states, "A good name is more desirable than great riches; to be esteemed is better than silver or gold."**
2. **A parent's job is to create a taste for God in the hearts of his or her children. Proverbs promises, "Train a child in the way he should go and when he is old he will not turn from it."**
3. **We cannot give without getting in return. Proverbs notes, "A generous man will himself be blessed, for he shares his food with the poor."**
4. **Discipline is a good and necessary part of life. Proverbs proclaims, "Folly is bound up in the heart of a child, but the rod of discipline will drive it far from him."**
5. **We must not take advantage of the helpless. Proverbs warns, "Do not exploit the poor...for the Lord will take up their case and will plunder those who plunder them."**

LOOKING UP *Help me, Lord, to remember You care how I treat the helpless. May I always be loving and kind. May I always protect my reputation so that I might be a good witness for You.*

EVIL

JULY 22

Proverbs 23-25

LOOKING BACK One of the most notorious criminals in U.S. history was gunned down on this day in 1934. John Dillinger was "Public Enemy #1," sought for a series of bank robberies and narrow escapes from the law. He was also wanted for the murder of a policeman. Dillinger was hiding in Chicago when he was betrayed by Anna Sage. She told federal agents she would wear a red dress when she and a girlfriend accompanied Dillinger to the Biograph theater. Dillinger was fatally shot as he left the theater, and Sage became famous as the "woman in red." Even though Dillinger got a lot of attention, he was no Robin Hood. He was an evil and diabolical criminal.

LOOKING IN *Evil ones may grab headlines for a season, but they never succeed for long. Among other things, Proverbs 24 makes this point very clear. Also, this chapter lets us know we must try to rescue those being led away to their deaths by evil ones. Once we become aware of the evil being done to them, we must not stand by and let it happen. Proverbs 22:17 through 24:34 contain two collections of sayings of wise men. It seems likely that this part of Proverbs makes creative use of material from outside of Israel in addition to material from its own elders. These proverbs focus on justice and hard work and offer a derogatory sketch of the lazy man.*

LOOKING OUT

1. Tough times come to test our character. Proverbs notes that if we falter in times of trouble, our strength is small. We are to ask God for additional strength for stress.
2. Once we become aware, we become responsible. We are to rescue those in deep trouble and not say we knew nothing about it. God sees what we know and will deal with us.
3. We may get knocked down, but we won't be knocked out. A righteous man may fall seven times, but he rises again. The wicked crumble in times of adversity.
4. God hates gloating. Proverbs warns, "Do not gloat when your enemy falls; when he stumbles do not let your heart rejoice, or the Lord will see and disapprove..."
5. God hates man's vengeance. Proverbs advises, "Do not say, 'I'll do to him as he has done to me; I'll pay that man back for what he did.'" Vengeance is God's job.

LOOKING UP *Help me, Lord, to remember that my failure is not permanent. I can rise again because of Your love. Thank You that You are the God of second chances.*

SCANDAL

Proverbs 26-29

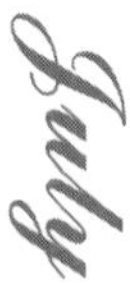

LOOKING BACK President Ulysses S. Grant died on this day in 1885 after a long bout with cancer. A quiet, unassuming man, he had an almost shy manner. Grant's presidency was clouded by disgrace and dishonesty. During the two terms Grant served as president, Congressional investigations revealed widespread corruption in both state and local governments. The president was slow to realize that some persons who pretended to be his friends couldn't be trusted. Several of his appointees became involved in these scandals, bringing disgrace on the beloved Civil War general. Grant himself was honest. Few historians think he was ever personally involved.

LOOKING IN *In Proverbs 28, we read about unscrupulous men who take advantage of others. The Bible says they will not prosper forever, and the riches they have extorted will be given to others. History often proves the truth of this assertion. Also, those who do evil always have to look back, worrying they will get caught. Sin is just not worth the emotional cost. Proverbs 25 through 29 contain more of Solomon's sayings collected by King Hezekiah. When Hezekiah repaired the temple, some of his workers found what may have been an unpublished collection of Solomon's sayings. The king published them and they became part of the book of Proverbs.*

LOOKING OUT

1. Guilt makes us paranoid, but forgiveness sets us free. Proverbs notes, "The wicked man flees though no one pursues, but the righteous are as bold as a lion."
2. When we respect the law, we make a big dent in evil. Proverbs says, "Those who forsake the law praise the wicked, but those who keep the law resist them."
3. Those who take advantage of the vulnerable will lose it all. The writer of Proverbs notes that one who increases his wealth by exorbitant interest amasses it for another.
4. God detests those who talk the talk but won't walk the walk. Proverbs cautions, "If anyone turns a deaf ear to the law, even his prayers are detestable."
5. We can't get away with sweeping sin under the rug. Proverbs says, "He who conceals his sins does not prosper, but whoever confesses and renounces them finds mercy."

LOOKING UP *Help me, Lord, to stay free by confessing my sins and renouncing them. Keep me true to You. May I never take advantage of those who are down and out but help them back up.*

WOMAN'S TOUCH

Proverbs 30-31

LOOKING BACK Martin Van Buren died on this day in 1862, after serving as the eighth president of the United States. Since Van Buren's wife died 18 years before her husband became president, White House parties were limited to simple dinners. Many visitors found the Executive Mansion atmosphere formal and austere, even with Van Buren's four sons present. Dolley Madison especially regretted the lack of a woman in the household, so she introduced the president's eldest son, Abraham, to Angelica Singleton. A romance developed and the two were married. Angelica became the White House hostess, bringing a woman's touch to the White House.

LOOKING IN *Proverbs ends with an ode to the woman's touch. Here is a remarkable picture of the power of women for good and for ill. The last chapter closes with a lovely acrostic poem about the ideal wife. She is responsible, capable, hardworking, and completely trusted. Not only do her husband, family, and household depend on her provision and foresight for their physical needs, but also they owe her their well-being on a much deeper level. Her influence extends beyond this immediate circle to society at large. She finds ample scope for all her gifts in the wider sphere of buying, selling, and business transactions. The secret of her success is the "fear of the Lord."*

LOOKING OUT

1. Women have enormous influence on a man's life. King Lemuel pleads, "O son of my vows, do not spend your strength on women, your vigor on those who ruin kings."
2. A good wife is the most priceless possession a man can have. The Proverbist says about a woman of noble character, "She is worth more than rubies."
3. A faithful woman frees a man from the awful torment of jealousy. Proverbs says, "Her husband has full confidence in her."
4. A godly woman is one who lives a life of consistency before her family. Proverbs notes, "She brings him good, not harm, all the days of her life."
5. Wise women know the only thing that lasts is a good character. Proverbs states, "Charm is deceptive, and beauty is fleeting; but a woman who fears the Lord is to be praised."

LOOKING UP *Thank You, Lord, for the gift of a good woman in my life. May I always cherish her and help her as she continues to walk faithfully before You and fulfill her many responsibilities.*

VANITY

JULY 25

Ecclesiastes 1-4

LOOKING BACK Italy's dictator Benito Mussolini was ousted from office on this day in 1943. Mussolini founded fascism and ruled Italy for almost 21 years. He had dreamed of building Italy into a great empire, but he led his nation to defeat in World War II and was finally executed by his own people. Two weeks after the Allied attack on Sicily began, the Facist Grand Council met for the first time since December of 1939 and took a confidence vote, resulting in Mussolini's being removed from office and placed under arrest. Italy's King Victor Emmanuel ordered Marshall Pietro Badoglio to form a new government. On April 27, 1945, Mussolini was shot to death.

LOOKING IN *Although dictators, kings, and potentates all strut proudly across the stage of history, they are eventually brought down. This underlines the preacher's assertion in Ecclesiastes that fame, power, and wealth are fleeting. Life is meaningless apart from God. Ecclesiastes, at first, seems like a despairing book, but it is crammed full of thoughtful contemplation. The narrator of Ecclesiastes is troubled that there is injustice in the world and that the meaning of life is hidden from all people. He urges us to enjoy the pleasures of life; but one should not make pleasure the goal of living because, in the end, life is empty, or the "vanity of vanities."*

LOOKING OUT

1. **Life apart from God is totally meaningless. The preacher cries, "Meaningless! Meaningless! Utterly meaningless! Everything is meaningless!" Only God gives perspective.**
2. **Without an eternal purpose, life is despairing. The preacher notes that what goes around comes around. Without a spiritual viewpoint, life is boring and depressing.**
3. **Too often, what we seek is impossible to keep. Fame is fleeting and wealth deceptive, for we will not be remembered long after our passing from this earth.**
4. **Experience simply verifies the truths found in God's Word. The preacher brought himself a lot of pain because he decided to see for himself rather than listen to God.**
5. **Pride pushes us to chase after the wind. The preacher thought himself wise and resourceful, so he decided to experiment rather than accept what God had told him.**

LOOKING UP *Help me, Lord, to learn from Your Word rather than life's painful experiences. May I always remember there is no meaning to this life apart from You.*

PAIN

JULY 26

Ecclesiastes 5-8

LOOKING BACK We quote it today, not knowing where it came from. Yet, it wasn't a sports figure who first said it, but a defeated politician. On this day in 1952, Adlai Stevenson remarked, "There are no gains without pains." Stevenson was the Democratic nominee for President of the United States in 1952 and 1956. Dwight D. Eisenhower defeated him both times. Stevenson served as U.S. Ambassador to the United Nations from 1961 until his death in 1965. He was a grandson of Vice-President Adlai E. Stevenson and became governor of Illinois by the largest plurality in the state's history. However, none of this helped make him a winner in the presidential race.

LOOKING IN *In Ecclesiastes 7, the preacher talks about the gain of pain. He says that God places adversity and prosperity in people's lives to help keep them on track. When they get too confident, hard times come so they will look up. In good times, they are not to forget His provision. Ecclesiastes is a book which focuses on the limits of life to teach wisdom. This point of view comes from Solomon, whose wealth, wisdom, and glory placed him at the upper limit of human success. From his royal pinnacle, he surveyed life and judged it to be vanity due to the inescapable limits God and sin place on even the most successful human being.*

LOOKING OUT

1. **Life is much more than one long party. The preacher encourages us to build a good reputation and invest our energies in things that are serious, not frivolous.**
2. **We should always look forward, not backward. It is a waste of time and energy to pine about the "good old days," because memory blurs the reality of those times.**
3. **Good times and bad times come to keep us balanced. The preacher says to rejoice in prosperity and to consider in adversity; God gives both to give us eternal perspective.**
4. **Moderation is the ideal for our lives. The preacher advises us to stay in the middle of the road and not drift to either side. Jesus also encouraged moderation.**
5. **We must watch what people do rather than listen to what they say. The preacher admonishes, "Do not pay attention to every word people say."**

LOOKING UP *Help me, Lord, to remember that both good and bad times help me keep my heart turned to You. Thank You that Your Word helps me keep a proper perspective in life.*

FUTILITY

JULY 27

Ecclesiastes 9-12

LOOKING BACK One of the world's bloodiest wars ended on this day in 1953 when the Korean War armistice was signed. The war had lasted three years and 32 days. It was the first war in which the United Nations played a military role. About a million South Korean civilians were killed, and several million were made homeless. Some 580,000 U.N. and South Korean troops and 1,600,000 Communist troops were killed, wounded, or reported missing. The United States provided about 90 percent of the troops, military equipment, and supplies. Interestingly, both sides claimed victory at the end of the two years of truce negotiations.

LOOKING IN *In spite of the deaths and destruction, many question whether the Korean War accomplished anything of lasting value. Ecclesiastes verifies that man's activities are futile apart from God. Two important points come from Ecclesiastes and are repeated several times: (1) "Fear God, and keep his commandments: for this is the whole duty of man" and (2) God's sovereign actions are beyond human ability to change. Because of this, we should enjoy life and its ordinary pleasures of work and play, food and drink, love and family; all are gifts from God. The preacher explains that God has done this "that men should fear before him."*

LOOKING OUT

1. We must work even if we feel our efforts are futile. The preacher's word picture advises, "Cast your bread upon the waters, for after many days you will find it again."
2. Generosity prepares us for the hard times. The preacher says, "Give a portion to seven, yes to eight, for you do not know what disaster may come upon the land."
3. Habits determine our destiny. The preacher observes, "Whether a tree falls to the south or to the north, in the place where it falls, there will it lie."
4. We must never let circumstances determine our work. The preacher says, "Whoever watches the wind will not plant; whoever looks at the clouds will not reap."
5. We are to throw all our anxieties on the Lord. The preacher insists, "So then, banish anxiety from your heart and cast off the troubles of your body..."

LOOKING UP *Help me, Lord, to take the wisdom of Your Word and apply it to all that I must confront today. Help me daily to remember my Creator, and all will be well with me.*

LOVE

JULY 28

Song of Solomon 1-8

LOOKING BACK World War I started 85 years ago today when Archduke Francis Ferdinand of Austria-Hungary and his wife were assassinated at Sarajevo, Bosnia, by a Serbian nationalist. This war lasted four years and took the lives of nearly 10 million troops. Also on this day in 1943, the Hamburg Firestorm exploded. More than 42,000 civilians were killed when 2,326 tons of bombs were dropped on Hamburg, Germany, by the Allies in World War II. At the center of the firestorm, the winds uprooted trees, and flames burned eight square miles in the eight hours the fire lasted. Death and destruction always result when men turn from love to greed and hatred.

LOOKING IN *The Song of Solomon is a beautiful poem that extols the virtues of love. Love gives life and builds rather than destroys. Wars would cease if we only learned to love and give more. The Song of Solomon refers explicitly to human love and sexuality, which is unusual in religious literature. For this reason, Jewish and Christian traditions have tended to view the book as allegory. It has been considered a representation of God's love for the Hebrew people or Christ's love for the church. But most scholars recognize the book's origins in the language of human love. God gives us the capacity to love and be loved by one He has created for us.*

LOOKING OUT

1. A loving relationship is life's greatest fulfillment. Solomon's bride says, "Let him kiss me with the kisses of his mouth—for your love is more delightful than wine."
2. Love requires a great investment of emotional energy and time. Friends of the loving couple comment, "We rejoice and delight in you; we will praise your love..."
3. Love overlooks flaws in the object of affection. Solomon saw beauty in his bride, although she felt her complexion was not as lovely as it should have been.
4. Love must be a two-way street. Not only did Solomon love his bride, but she returned that love. He praised her for her beauty, and she reciprocated with words of affection.
5. Love builds a strong and lasting home. Solomon lovingly responds to his bride's words by saying, "The beams of our house are cedars; our rafters are firs."

LOOKING UP *Help me, Lord, to invest the necessary energy and time into the relationship with the one You gave me. Thank You for giving me the capacity to love and be loved.*

CONSEQUENCES

JULY 29

Isaiah 1-4

LOOKING BACK Adolf Hitler became president of Germany's National Socialist (Nazi) Party on this day in 1921. The consequences would shatter the world. Hitler spread death as no person has done in modern history. "Have no pity! Act brutally!" he told his soldiers as he ordered that those who opposed him be executed and that hundreds of thousands be thrown into prison. Hitler particularly hated and persecuted Jews. He and his minions were responsible for killing about six million European Jews as well as about five million other people, whom Hitler regarded as racially inferior or politically dangerous. Among them were many believers who stood against the evil.

LOOKING IN *Isaiah emphasized there would be dire consequences to those who opposed God by taking advantage of the vulnerable. Hitler, a broken and defeated man, committed suicide only 13 years after he took power. Those brutalizing others earn God's wrath. Evil never wins, though it spills hell out on earth for a while. Isaiah said God's backslidden people worshiped with their lips but did as they pleased with their lives. The prophet spoke for God, saying judgment would soon follow, but there could be salvation if they repented. Isaiah's ministry spanned the period from his call until the last years of Hezekiah or the early years of Manasseh.*

LOOKING OUT

1. **Sin never makes sense; in sinning we only hurt ourselves. Isaiah asks, "Why should you be beaten anymore? Will you persist in your rebellion?"**
2. **Hypocritical worship only makes matters worse for us. God tells his disobedient people, "Your incense is detestable to me...I cannot bear your evil assemblies."**
3. **God refuses to listen to us when we persist in sin: "When you spread out your hands in prayer, I will hide my eyes from you; even if you offer many prayers, I will not listen."**
4. **Our faith must turn into action. God tells Israel they must seek justice, encourage the oppressed, defend the cause of the fatherless, and plead the case of the widow.**
5. **No matter how great our sin, God will forgive if we repent. God invites us to come reason with Him: "Though your sins are like scarlet, they shall be white as snow."**

LOOKING UP *Help me, Lord, to remember that You consider worship to be far more than mouthing praises to You. May my worship be pure because I have sought Your forgiveness for my sins.*

ANGELS

JULY 30

Isaiah 5-7

LOOKING BACK Labor leader "Jimmy" Hoffa disappeared "into thin air"on this day in 1975, while he was making a bid to return to power following his release from prison. Hoffa had been convicted of jury tampering and misusing union funds, which earned him the stiff prison sentence. He wrote a book defending himself in which he calls for angels to swear to his innocence. Yet, in spite of his plea for the divine beings to attest his innocence, many believe Hoffa was guilty as charged. Hoffa was last seen outside a restaurant in Bloomfield Township, near Detroit, Michigan. Police believe he was kidnaped and murdered, but his body was never found.

LOOKING IN *Angels are very real. Isaiah learned this when he had a stunning vision of God and His heavenly hosts. The prophet would never be the same after that encounter. These heavenly beings defied the prophet's description. However, for Isaiah, it was God Who was the centerpiece of heaven. Isaiah, the son of Amoz, was born in Judah, no doubt in Jerusalem, about 760 B.C. He enjoyed a significant position in the contemporary society and had a close relationship with the reigning monarchs. His education is clearly evident in his superb writing, which has gained him an eminence in Hebrew literature hardly surpassed by any other.*

LOOKING OUT

1. **Grief often focuses our attention on the eternal. Isaiah saw the Lord the year King Uzziah died. The king had been a good man gone wrong. Isaiah was grieved by this turn.**
2. **There is a spiritual dimension that supercedes all that we see with our physical eyes. Isaiah said the angelic hosts saw the glory of the Lord filling all the earth.**
3. **When we see God, we see how far we fall short of His perfection. Isaiah cringed before the awesome presence of God, crying out, "I am a man of unclean lips."**
4. **God's forgiveness makes us worthy to stand before a holy God. One of the seraphs took a coal from God's altar and touched the prophet's mouth, purifying him.**
5. **When our will is aligned with God's will, we respond readily to His call for our life. Isaiah quickly responded to God's call by crying out, "Here am I; send me!"**

LOOKING UP *Help me, Lord, to see You in Your holiness so that I might quickly step forward to do Your will. Cleanse my life of all impurities so I might represent You better.*

MALIGNED

JULY 31

Isaiah 8-12

LOOKING BACK Andrew Johnson, the much maligned 17th President of the United States, died on July 31, 1875. He was the first president to be impeached. Johnson became chief executive when Abraham Lincoln was assassinated. The Civil War had just ended, and Johnson inherited the wartime dispute between Lincoln and Congress over how to treat the South after the war. Congress enacted its harsh policies in spite of Johnson's repeated vetoes. The conflict became so great that the House of Representatives impeached Johnson. The Senate, however, failed by one vote to remove him from office. Johnson was not returned to the presidency after his term ended.

LOOKING IN *Wicked men had maligned and tried to do away with our Lord, but they, too, could not succeed. Jesus conquered all their attempts. Even death could not destroy Him. In Isaiah 9, the prophet looked ahead to the coming of our Lord. He told us the wonderful benefits to those who accept Christ. In addition to the prophecies concerning Christ, Isaiah told the Jews to have faith and to trust only in God, not in political or military actions. The prophet stressed the idea that God saves, protects the faithful, and punishes His enemies. This first section of Isaiah's remarkable book also taught that God's power is universal, not limited to the Jews.*

LOOKING OUT

1. **Jesus is the Author and Finisher of our faith. Isaiah's word picture about the government being on His shoulders illustrates the responsibility Jesus assumes over our lives.**
2. **Jesus is the Counselor with all the right answers. Not only does our Lord save us, but He also gives us wisdom in handling the difficult issues of our lives.**
3. **Jesus is our Provider-Protector. As the Mighty God and Everlasting Father, our Lord assumes the role of One Who is able to provide all we need and protect us from harm.**
4. **Jesus is the only true source of peace. He is the Prince of Peace. This simply means that whatever turmoil is in our lives, Jesus will give us grace and glory.**
5. **Jesus continues to mature us until we are totally His. Isaiah noted that the increase of His government and peace has no end, and that applies both personally and universally.**

LOOKING UP *Help me, Lord, to better understand all the wonderful benefits that are mine through knowing Jesus. I ask You, Lord, always to be the living center of my existence.*

AUGUST

A Month Named for a for Cold, Calculating Ruler

August is the eighth month of the year according to the Gregorian calendar. The Romans called the month *Sextilis*, which means sixth. They later renamed it in honor of the emperor Augustus. Because July, named after Julius Caesar, had 31 days, the Roman Senate lengthened the month to 31 days by taking a day from February. They didn't want to give the impression that Augustus' month was in any way inferior to Julius Caesar's. Augustus, meaning "the exalted," was the name given Gaius Julius Caesar Octavianus (Octavian) when he became the first Roman emperor in 27 B.C. The period of the Roman Republic ended and the era of the Roman Empire began under Augustus.

Augustus was a cold, calculating statesman, but he knew how to win popular affection. He was the ruler of Rome when Jesus was born. After his death, the people of the Roman Empire worshiped him as Divine Augustus. The remains of his tomb and many of his buildings can still be seen in Rome. Augustus' influence was so far-reaching that it lasted, and even increased, for nearly 200 years. Rome achieved great glory during Augustus' reign, and the period came to be known as the Augustan Age. This period was the golden age of Roman literature and architecture. Such famous writers as Virgil, Horace, Ovid, and Livy lived during this time, under the patronage of the emperor.

In the temperate zone of the Northern Hemisphere, August is the height of summer. The longest days of the year are past, but August is apt to be one of the hottest months. In far northern regions and high mountain areas, chilly nights and frosts warn that summer is nearly at an end. In the Southern Hemisphere, August signals that winter will soon be over. Goldenrod, wild asters, and other tall-growing flowers of late summer brighten the fields. The insects of fields and woods are noisier and more numerous than in other months. Some birds are already preparing to fly south. Vacation spots are busier during August than any other time. Travelers in other countries usually begin to turn homeward. During this month we will be reading Isaiah, Jeremiah, Lamentations, and Ezekiel.

DIARY

AUGUST 1

Isaiah 13-17

LOOKING BACK Anne Frank made her last diary entry on this day in 1944. Frank's Jewish family hid for two months in a warehouse to escape the horrendous evil of the Nazis. Thirteen-year-old Anne kept a journal during the time of their hiding, saying in her last entry, "I'll keep on trying to find a way of becoming what I would like to be, if..." Three days later the family was discovered. Anne and her sister were sent to a concentration camp, where Anne died at age 15, two months before the liberation of Holland. Her diary was found later and published in 30 languages. The words of this young girl, whose life was cut short by evil, have inspired thousands.

LOOKING IN *While Hitler bragged that his Reich would last a thousand years, it only survived a short 13. Evil doesn't last forever, no matter how horrendous it is. Isaiah saw the despairing evils of Babylon, Assyria, Philistia, Moab, and Damascus. He told his nation that one day these evils would be dealt with, and nations that had oppressed would be oppressed. Particularly, Moab would soon experience a change in fortunes. In just three short years, Moab suffered exactly what Isaiah had forewarned. Moab fell to Assyria in successive campaigns and then to Babylon. Israel was not to rejoice in this disaster but reach out to help the Moabites.*

LOOKING OUT

1. **This earth is a battlefield, not a playground. Babylon represents the forces of evil that dominate our planet. Isaiah sees God warring against this pervasive entity.**
2. **One day evil will be completely destroyed, never to rise again. Isaiah says Babylon would be so destroyed that only wild animals would inhabit where men had once been.**
3. **God has good things planned for His people. When the judgment of evil finally comes, God will take care of those who love Him and reward them according to their works.**
4. **Pride brings about the downfall of all those who take it up. Satan fell from heaven because of his unmitigated pride. His ambitions always centered around himself.**
5. **One day the evil one will be brought so low that those tormented by him will look back and say, "Is this the man who shook the earth and made kingdoms tremble?"**

LOOKING UP *Help me, Lord, always to keep things in proper perspective. Evil will fail and the right will prevail. When my enemy falls, may I be there to help him up.*

INVASION

AUGUST 2

Isaiah 18-21

LOOKING BACK On orders from President Saddam Hussein, the Iraqi army invaded Kuwait on this day in 1990. Hussein claimed that Kuwait presented a serious threat to Iraq's economic existence by overproducing oil and driving prices down on the world market. After conquering the capital, Kuwait City, Saddam Hussein installed a military government in Kuwait, prior to annexing it to Iraq. He claimed that Kuwait was historically a part of Iraq. This led to the 100-hour war against Iraq, Operation Desert Storm. The war was won quickly and Saddam put back in his cage. However, he continued to be a thorn in the side of the coalition that had challenged him.

LOOKING IN *Assyria threatened Judah's existence much as Saddam Hussein did to Kuwait's survival. God sent Isaiah to His people to let them know the invaders would be turned back on the very eve of victory. That is exactly what did happen. The prophet also foretold the disintegration of Egypt. The prophet said this would involve falling to their enemies, a ruined economy, and a breakdown of leadership. Just as Isaiah predicted, Egypt was defeated by Assyria when Sennacherib's army besieged Jerusalem. Further defeats culminated in the sack of Thebes in 663 B.C. However, Isaiah said God's judgment would be a prelude to Egypt's ultimate conversion.*

LOOKING OUT

1. God always speaks to His children whenever they face trouble. Sargon attacked Ashdod, but God gave a special message of direction to His children through Isaiah.
2. God speaks so clearly that it is impossible to misunderstand. Isaiah was told to present his message in such a way that no one could possibly miss the message.
3. God's spokesmen must point to the message, not to themselves. Isaiah went naked and barefoot, only to attract attention to the urgent message God told him to deliver.
4. No matter how appealing it might be to seek deliverance from other sources, there is only one way out of distress when the enemy attacks—God, our Protector-Provider.
5. If we look to men for help, we will always be disappointed. If we rely on God, He always brings us out. Isaiah told the nation they must not look to Egypt or Cush.

LOOKING UP *Help me, Lord, to remember that You alone can help me when the forces of evil come against me. May I always be an encouragement to God's people when they are under attack.*

TEMPORARY

Isaiah 22-24

LOOKING BACK John T. Scopes was born on this day in 1900. He was the central figure in the famous "Scope's Monkey Trial" of 1925. Scopes was an obscure twenty-four-year-old teacher who became the focus of world attention when he was charged with violating Tennessee law by teaching evolution. Scopes didn't utter a word at the trial, which was dominated by two famous lawyers: William Jennings Bryan and Clarence Darrow. Scopes was convicted and fined $100, but later the verdict was upset on a technicality. The flamboyant lawyers strutted and sputtered on the world stage for awhile, but then, like all others, faded into history.

LOOKING IN *No matter how much noise a person makes, he is eventually swallowed up by time. Isaiah told arrogant Shebna that he would be thrown like a ball from his proud office. Shebna served as the chief aide to Hezekiah, a good and godly king. However, he obviously circumvented much of the good that Hezekiah planned. Isaiah issued this scathing rebuke to Shebna, telling him God would soon throw him out. Then, the prophet reminded Shebna's replacement, Eliakim, not to be too secure, since he would be in that position only for a short season. Eliakim would find himself unable to cope with his hangers-on, and his authority would be short-lived.*

LOOKING OUT

1. We must never forget that this earth is not our final home. God instructs Isaiah to tell Shebna not to be so arrogant as to think his home here is permanent.
2. No matter how one tries to fortify himself, his ultimate destiny is decided by the Lord. Shebna was told that he would be rolled up like a ball and thrown into a foreign country.
3. God harshly judges those who harshly judge and hurt others. Shebna apparently had arrogantly persecuted the innocent, and now he would be deposed.
4. When God puts one in position, he will not be deposed until God decides. Eliakim was to be placed in Shebna's job and would be secured firmly like a nail.
5. Those whom God calls to replace faithless leaders must remember they will not be in that position forever. Eliakim was warned not to repeat the arrogance of his predecessor.

LOOKING UP *Help me remember, Lord, that one day I will give an account for the way I handled my assigned job. May I always remember that I am on a journey to my Heavenly Father.*

JUDGMENT

AUGUST 4

Isaiah 25-27

LOOKING BACK After disappearing on June 21, three civil rights workers were found murdered and buried in an earthen dam outside Philadelphia, Mississippi, on this day in 1964. The three young men were workers in the Mississippi Summer Project organized by the Student Nonviolent Coordinating Committee. They were in that southern state as part of an effort to increase Black voter registration. Prior to their disappearance, James Chaney, Andrew Goodman, and Michael Schwerner were detained by Neshoba County police on charges of speeding. When their car was found burned on June 23, President Lyndon Johnson ordered an FBI search for them.

LOOKING IN *There are many inequities and injustices in our world that seem to go unpunished. However, Isaiah tells God's people there will come a day when all wrongs will be made right, and those who have perpetrated these evils will be brought to task. God will not permit sin to go unpunished forever or the oppressor to go free. Isaiah 24 through 27 speaks of God's final judgment and victory over all the forces of evil. Isaiah has been addressing his remarks to specific nations but now becomes universal in his comments. But God's purpose is not just to condemn. Isaiah's chapter on judgment is followed by three chapters on restoration.*

LOOKING OUT

1. There is a rhyme and reason to this earth and to our lives. Isaiah exalts the Lord, Who has done marvelous things planned long ago—even before the world was created.
2. The poor and dispossessed have a friend in our Lord. Isaiah notes that God has always been a refuge for the poor and needy in their distress, a shelter in the time of storm.
3. Attacks from the enemy are relentless and seem overwhelming. Isaiah likens these attacks to a storm driving against a wall and to the unbearable desert heat.
4. One day our tears will be a thing of the past. The prophet notes that God will soon wipe away the tears from all faces and remove the disgrace of His people.
5. One day we will look back and see that even in the hardest of times, God was faithfully sustaining us. We will say, "This is our God; we trusted in him, and he saved us."

LOOKING UP *Help me, Lord, never to be so overwhelmed by difficulties that I fail to see Your faithful sustaining hand. Help me to care for the poor because they are dear to Your heart.*

LIFE-SERVICE

AUGUST 5

Isaiah 28-31

LOOKING BACK Credited with saving the lives of over 1,000,000 Jews from Nazi extermination, Raoul Wallenberg was born on this day in 1912. Adolf Eichmann, a Nazi official who directed the transport of Jews to concentration camps, ordered Wallenberg to stop interfering with German plans for the Jews. Wallenberg refused. Eichmann tried to have Wallenberg assassinated, but the attempt failed. Toward the end of the war, Wallenberg was arrested by Soviet troops at Budapest, Hungary, on January 17, 1945. According to the Soviet press agency Tass, he died in a Moscow prison on July 17, 1947. Wallenberg was a genuine international hero.

LOOKING IN *Many were deeply concerned about what Hitler was doing to the Jews, but Wallenberg did more than just fret. His brave action would cost his life but save many others. Isaiah reminds us that faith is far more than lip-service—it's life-service. Real faith drives the believer to do something for God, not just to wish to be effective. And, there is always a cost for life-service. After the chapters on universal judgment for mankind, Isaiah turns again to warnings to God's rebellious people. He says the pleasure-loving city is ripe for plucking, and Assyria's hand is outstretched to take it. The leaders of the nation have not led but misled the people.*

LOOKING OUT

1. **Faith is "life service," not mere "lip service." God says, "These people come near to me with their mouth and honor me with their lips, but their hearts are far from me."**
2. **Faith involves "revelation" from God, not the "regulations" made by men. God says, "Their worship of me is made up only of rules taught by men."**
3. **God eventually brings all false belief systems down. Isaiah says that God will perform wonder upon wonder, and the wisdom of the wise will perish.**
4. **Try as they may, evil men can never hide their thoughts and deeds from God. Isaiah notes that man may think he can manipulate God, but He is the potter and they are the clay.**
5. **The world will not always be as it is now. Hold on! Justice does seem a long time coming, but it will come. "Once more the humble will rejoice in the Lord."**

LOOKING UP *Lord, help me to remember that what I do is far more important than what I say. Even so, may the words of my mouth and meditations of my heart be acceptable to You.*

HOPE

AUGUST 6

Isaiah 32-35

LOOKING BACK On this day in 1945, at 8:15 a.m. local time, an American bomber, the "Enola Gay," dropped an atomic bomb named "Little Boy" over the center of the city of Hiroshima, Japan. The bomb exploded about 1,800 feet above the ground, killing more than 105,000 civilians and destroying the city. Another 100,000 persons were injured and died as a direct result of the bomb and the radiation it produced. After Japanese leaders failed to respond to the bombing, the United States dropped a larger bomb on Nagasaki on August 9. It killed about 40,000 people. Later, thousands more died of injuries and radiation from the two bombings.

LOOKING IN *Man has succeeded in producing mass weapons of war that can wipe out humanity on this planet. Tragically, too many weapons of war have already been used and far too many people destroyed by man's evil toward his fellow man. Isaiah lamented the violence among men. He looked forward to a time when we would reach out to others in love and protection rather than anger and destruction. Isaiah 32 through 35 speak of the glorious future God has planned for this world and the dark days preceding that time. There will be a time of lasting peace, justice, and righteousness. The Messiah-King will reign, but evil must first be swept away.*

LOOKING OUT

1. We must be refuges for those who are beaten and battered. Isaiah says that when Christ comes, each man will be like shelter from the wind and a refuge from the storm.
2. One day we will understand all that confuses us now. Isaiah says when Christ comes, the eyes of those who see will no longer be closed, and their ears will be opened.
3. Our upside-down world will be turned right-side-up. Isaiah says that when Christ comes, the scoundrel will no longer be highly respected or the fool be called noble.
4. We must not be complacent when there is so much sin around us. Isaiah sharply chastises the women of Israel because they did not rise up against the evil of their times.
5. Righteousness results in peace, quietness, and confidence. Isaiah says if people turn to God, they will live in peaceful dwelling places and secure homes.

LOOKING UP *Help me, Lord, not to be casual about evil but to rise up in opposition wherever it is found. Give me wisdom to work daily against the evil that destroys Your creation.*

INEFFECTIVE

AUGUST 7

Isaiah 36-39

LOOKING BACK Famed spy Mata Hari was born on this day in 1876. Born Margaret Gertrude Zelle, she took the name Mata Hari (child of the dawn) when she began her stage career after an unhappy marriage. She became widely popular in Europe, pretending to be a Javanese dancer. Mata Hari's spectacular career as a dancer, courtesan, and spy brought her fame. She apparently became associated with the German spy network when her strange dances lost popularity. Arrested as a German spy (Agent H-21) in a Paris hotel in 1917, she was tried, convicted, and sentenced to death. Although her reputation was threatening, Mata Hari was really a very ineffective spy.

LOOKING IN *Sennacherib not only had a frightening reputation, he had the power to back it up. His army of 185,000 fierce warriors seemed invulnerable to Hezekiah. But after Judah's king prayed, God intervened and the Assyrian general suffered a strange and humiliating defeat. He was as ineffective against God's people as Mata Hari was against Germany's enemies. Never again could the Assyrians intimidate the people of Judah as they once had. The fifth century B.C. Greek historian Herodotus relates that the Assyrians suffered defeat because a plague of field mice destroyed their equipment. Hezekiah was the only ruler who withstood Sennacherib.*

LOOKING OUT

1. **Prayer, not panic, is the proper response to crisis. When Sennacherib threatened Judah, Hezekiah took the letter and spread it out before God in passionate prayer.**
2. **Even though God is fully aware of our problem, He wants us to approach Him for a solution. Hezekiah knew God knew, but he explains the situation to Him anyway.**
3. **We should have the right motive for our requested miracle. Hezekiah sought God's deliverance so the earth's kingdoms might know that God alone is real.**
4. **No matter what men may say, God always has the last word. Isaiah told Hezekiah that Sennacherib's great army would be defeated and the arrogant ruler taken down.**
5. **We must learn to rest in the Lord, because He can do what we cannot. An angel destroyed Sennacherib's vast army, and his own sons cut the arrogant ruler down.**

LOOKING UP *Help me, Lord, to take all my troubles to You, knowing that You can do what I cannot. Rather than panic when great troubles come, help me to rest in Your faithfulness.*

TURNING POINT

AUGUST 8

Isaiah 40-43

LOOKING BACK The pounding German army seemed invincible. However, on August 8, 1918, the Second Battle of Amiens changed all that. Two days after the Battle of the Marne ended, the British attacked Amiens with the objective of freeing the Amiens-Paris railway from bombardment by the Germans. In two hours of fighting, more than 16,000 German prisoners were captured and their forces turned back to the Hindenburg line. The battle is considered by many historians as the turning point of World War I due to its impact on the psyche of Germany. It was described by a German general as a "Black Day for Germany." The tide had turned.

LOOKING IN *The tide turns also in Isaiah's book as we reach chapter 40. The prophet spends the first 39 chapters pronouncing judgment on all the evil ones of our world. Judgment indeed is coming, but don't give up; mercy and redemption are also coming. The next 27 chapters of Isaiah focus on the redemptive process and the glorious future God has for all those who love Him. In chapter 40, Isaiah gives a message of comfort concerning God's forgiveness and infinite power. Chapter 42 says that God tells us: "Fear not...I will help you." Chapter 42 talks about a light for the nations. Finally, chapter 43 speaks of God's unfailing love and care.*

LOOKING OUT

1. **God covers all our sin and shame with His mercy. Isaiah's word picture portrays God folding the scroll double so no one can see the sins committed by His people.**
2. **God smooths out the rough places in our lives. Just as workers go before a king preparing his way, God goes before His people to make things easier for them.**
3. **God will have a witness with or without us. His glory will be seen on the earth. He invites us to be part of the revelation of His great plan for our universe.**
4. **God's Word will never pass away. The prophet notes that men come and go, but the eternal Word of God remains relevant for all times to all people.**
5. **God always treats His children tenderly. Those who follow God find He is the Good Shepherd Who gently leads His followers.**

LOOKING UP *Help me, Lord, not only to know Your wonderful character but to share it with those about me. Thank You for Your great love, forgiveness, and understanding.*

FEELINGS

AUGUST 9

Isaiah 44-48

August

LOOKING BACK Feelings were very high on this day in 1974 when Richard M. Nixon resigned the presidency of the United States. Nixon was facing almost certain impeachment for his involvement in the Watergate scandal. This scandal included a break-in at the Democratic national headquarters and other illegal activities by employees of Nixon's 1972 reelection committee. Nixon's attempts to cover up these crimes became a major part of the scandal. Feelings were high because Nixon was hated by many and loved by many. He had made a significant impact on America's foreign policy through his visit to China and by ending the Vietnam War.

LOOKING IN *Regardless of the feelings of those who loved or hated Nixon, the fact was he broke the law and had to go. Feelings are very real but should not determine the course of a nation or a life. Tragically, too often our commitments are based solely on feelings. That is sad, since feelings rise and fall like a roller coaster. Isaiah dealt with a similar problem. He spoke of God's great love for His people even when they felt as though He wasn't concerned for their welfare or had forgotten them in their distress. The prophet declares that God never forsakes those He passionately loves. Our faith must be decided by God's Word, not our whims.*

LOOKING OUT

1. Regardless of how we feel, we are very special people. God told Israel He had formed them in the womb. They were not to be afraid, because He had chosen them.
2. Regardless of how we feel, we will live, laugh, and love again. God told Israel that He would pour water on the thirsty land and streams on the dry ground.
3. Regardless of how we feel rejected, one day many will want to identify with us. God told His people that those who hated them would one day want to be called "Israel."
4. Regardless of how we feel, God has not forgotten us. God told His people that they were His servants whom He had made, and He could never forget them and their needs.
5. Regardless of how we feel, we are forgiven. God told Israel that He had swept away her offenses like a cloud and her sins like the morning mist. They were forgiven!

LOOKING UP *Help me, Lord, not to rely on my feelings but to lean totally on the wonderful promises in Your Word. Teach me more of Your Word so I will be more secure in You.*

VINDICATION

AUGUST 10

Isaiah 49-51

LOOKING BACK Herbert Hoover, one of the most maligned presidents the United States has known, was born on this day in 1874. Hoover was a brilliant organizer and administrator but had the misfortune of leading the nation during one of the blackest depressions in history. Though the depression was not his fault, Hoover was the man in charge, and the nation blamed him. His one term ended with a stunning defeat at the hands of the charismatic Franklin D. Roosevelt. After leaving the presidency, Hoover spent much time traveling, reading, speaking, and writing. Fortunately, Hoover lived long enough to see history exonerate his administration.

LOOKING IN *History does have a way of sorting things out. For that reason, Isaiah tells his nation they should look back to the history of Abraham to see the faithfulness of their God. In the bleakness of their present, Israel needs to hear that God will take them through and return them to joy. God is ever faithful to us no matter how bleak things look. In chapters 49 and 50, Isaiah tells God's people they have a mission beyond Israel to the whole world. Then, in chapters 51 and 52, Isaiah says that Israel is to be released and restored. He urges them to draw comfort from the past and look forward to a greater exodus. It is time to shake off grief and lethargy.*

LOOKING OUT

1. **In times of testing, we need to look at the lives of those who faithfully followed God. God told Israel to remember Abraham and how God had so uniquely blessed him.**
2. **We must not concentrate on the devastation around us but look to the Lord Who restores. Isaiah said God would make their deserts like Eden, with joy and gladness there.**
3. **We need to hold on because God is forever holding on to us. Isaiah reminded Israel that God's salvation lasts forever, and His righteousness would never fail them.**
4. **We need to stir up our faith because God is giving us the victory. Isaiah told Israel to awaken and clothe herself with strength because God would do again what He had done.**
5. **We must remember we are destined for victory, not defeat. The prophet reminded Israel that the ransomed of the Lord would return and enter Zion with singing.**

LOOKING UP *Help me, Lord, to remember how much You have helped others who have faced trials similar to mine. May I always remember that what You have done for them, You will do for me.*

FOREVER

AUGUST 11

Isaiah 52-57

LOOKING BACK The only man who served as president of the United States for a single day was born on this day in 1807. David R. Atchison, a Missouri legislator who served as president "pro tempore" of the Senate several times, served as president on Sunday, March 4, 1849. Zachary Taylor was to be sworn in on Monday, March 5, 1849, even though President James Polk's term had ended on March 3. Therefore, for a single day, Atchinson officially became the president of the United States. Obviously, nothing significant happened during Atchinson's brief tenure in office. He is remembered by few, and today his name is mostly just a footnote in history.

LOOKING IN *Fame and power are fleeting. In fact, almost all of what we regard as important will be a footnote in the history of eternity. Isaiah called his nation to turn away from that which is fleeting to that which lasts forever. He called the nation to salvation—prioritizing what is really important. Chapters 49 through 55 speak of the coming Messiah, a Servant Who will bring redemption to His people. Interestingly, Isaiah says the Servant will first suffer before His Kingdom comes. Chapters 54 and 55 speak of the expanding kingdom and salvation for all nations. Chapter 56 starts the last major section of Isaiah, speaking of Israel's shame and future glory.*

LOOKING OUT

1. **Salvation is open to all who want it. Isaiah records God's words, "Come, all you who are thirsty; come to the waters." God satisfies the hunger of our hearts.**
2. **Salvation is free but not cheap. The invitation is given to all, regardless. Money cannot buy what God has provided through the great cost of giving His only begotten Son.**
3. **Salvation is the only thing that can give man peace and joy. Isaiah asks, "Why spend money on what is not bread, and your labor on what does not satisfy?"**
4. **Salvation requires that we move at the point of conviction. Isaiah warns that we must seek the Lord while He may be found; call on Him while He is near.**
5. **Salvation dramatically changes our lives for the better. God's Word will produce what God intends for our lives. Sadness dissipates, and joy fills our hearts.**

LOOKING UP *Help me, Lord, always to appreciate the great price You paid for my salvation. Help me as I share Your great plan of salvation with others.*

SPECTACLE

AUGUST 12

Isaiah 58-62

LOOKING BACK Film pioneer Cecil B. DeMille was born on this day in 1881. He was a film showman extraordinaire, known for lavish screen spectacles. He produced more than 70 major films, which were noted more for their large scale than for subtle artistry. DeMille produced one of the earliest four-reel films, first used indoor lighting on an actor, and was the first to publicize the names of his stars. He also started the practice of sneak previews. One of his best-known films is the spectacular *Ten Commandments*, first made in 1923 and then remade in 1956. DeMille was awarded an Oscar in 1953. He died on January 21, 1969.

LOOKING IN *Israel's religious life was like one of DeMille's movie productions—a lavish spectacle. They fasted only to impress God and others and then wondered why God was ignoring them. The purpose of fasting was to seek to know God in a deeper experience. It was to be a time of confession, and when God's people sought a deeper walk with Him. Isaiah points out that this was not the reason for their fasting in his day. He calls the arrogant, religious "performers" back to real faith, saying that God would bless them if they would only forsake the "show" and do His will. Unfortunately, these arrogant leaders ignored the prophet.*

LOOKING OUT

1. **Just because people appear religious doesn't mean they are. Isaiah said the rebellious people talked a good game of faith but failed to live up to God's expectations.**
2. **Faith means doing what God wants, not what we want. The people fasted and prayed, but their religious exercises were just to cover up their selfish pursuits.**
3. **Fasting must not be an attempt to hold God hostage. Isaiah said the people fasted only to let their voices be heard on high, expecting to get whatever they wanted.**
4. **Faith is not only reaching out to God, but reaching out in love to those who need help. Isaiah said the fast God wants is for His people to become healers of the hurting.**
5. **In helping others, we help ourselves. God promises that those who reach out to heal the hurting will be greatly blessed by God. As we give, He gives back to us.**

LOOKING UP *Lord, help me to be a healer and helper of humanity, loving those You gave Your life to save. Always remind me that faith is what I do, not merely what I say.*

WALLS

AUGUST 13

Isaiah 63-66

August

LOOKING BACK Early in the morning, on this day in 1961, the East German government closed the border between the east and west sectors of Berlin with barbed wire fence. They wanted to discourage further population movement to the west. Telephone and postal services were interrupted, and later in the week, a concrete wall was built to strengthen the barrier between official crossing points. During the 27 years of its existence, the Berlin Wall symbolized ruthless government oppression. Many people died trying to cross it. Finally, after long and frustrating years, the brutal barrier was brought down. The wall was dismantled on November 9, 1989.

LOOKING IN *Walls do not last forever. Satan succeeded in building a wall between God and man. God sent His Son to break down that wall, and one day the dismantling will be completed. Isaiah looked forward to that time when the Prince of Peace would reign, and all the rebels against God would be brought to task. God has an answer to the woes of this world: new heavens and a new earth. Isaiah says that God will answer the prayer for His people in a way that exceeds their wildest dreams. But the answer will be two-edged: for those who are aligned against God there will be total destruction; for His faithful ones, life, joy, and peace beyond imagining.*

LOOKING OUT

1. **God's mercy is so great that before we even wanted Him, He was there for us. Isaiah says that God has revealed Himself to those who did not ask for Him.**
2. **We who know God must never take Him for granted. Isaiah noted that God had been merciful and loving to Israel, but the nation obstinately rejected Him.**
3. **Judgment will come on the rebellious, but God takes special care of those who love Him. Isaiah said that the people who seek God will find a resting place and joy.**
4. **When judgment comes, those who have served God will be protected and fed in the famine. God promises, "My servants will eat...my servants will rejoice."**
5. **God's plans for this earth are good. Isaiah looks forward to the day when the Lord rules and reigns. The past troubles will be forgotten as the Prince of Peace prevails.**

LOOKING UP *Help me, Lord, never to take Your love and mercy for granted. Keep me close to Your heart. Thank You for being my resting place and my place of joy.*

FOREORDAINED

AUGUST 14

Jeremiah 1-3

LOOKING BACK Elia, better known as Charles Lamb, was an English author famous for informal, personal essays and his highly individual and penetrating literary criticism. Lamb used the pen name, Elia, for many of his essays. Lamb's writing reveals much about him—his gentle and whimsical nature, his great capacity for friendship, and his warm humanity. Some essays recall his youth; others are character sketches of eccentric people whom Lamb liked. Behind Lamb's warmth and humor lay robust common sense. He scorned what he called "the nambypamby." On this day in 1801, Lamb wrote, "Sudden converts are superficial and transitory."

LOOKING IN *Charles Lamb was certainly right about converts. People who quickly decide to follow our Lord without much thought often fall away. However, those who have carefully considered the ramifications of obeying our Lord, and still choose to follow Him, likely stay firm in their faith. Jeremiah was not quick to answer God's call for his life, since he knew what it would entail. Once he did answer the call, there was no turning back. Nothing would stop him from speaking God's Word. Jeremiah was criticized, shamed, accused of treason, jailed, and came close to death many times, but he remained faithful.*

LOOKING OUT

1. **God equipped us for His service before we were born. God told a reluctant Jeremiah that even before he was born, God had set him apart to be Israel's prophet.**
2. **We must concentrate on God's direction rather than our weaknesses. God told Jeremiah not to say he was too young or inadequate. God would tell him what to say and do.**
3. **We can only speak God's words when we have had a personal encounter with Him. The Lord reached out and touched Jeremiah's mouth, ordaining him as a prophet.**
4. **Doing God's work involves both attacking evil and preaching righteousness. God told Jeremiah to uproot, tear down, destroy, overthrow, and then to build and plant.**
5. **Even though God sends us to do a hard work, He is always there to protect and provide. God told Jeremiah that many would fight against him, but they would not succeed.**

LOOKING UP *Help me, Lord, to respond to Your call on my life, knowing You will provide direction and support. May I always remember that before I was born You had a plan for me.*

WARNINGS

AUGUST 15

Jeremiah 4-6

LOOKING BACK Napoleon Bonaparte was born on this day in 1769. He had crowned himself emperor of France and was the greatest military genius of his time, creating an empire covering most of western and central Europe. Napoleon's ambition ultimately made him overextend his power. He was exiled from France to the tiny island of Elba, off the northwest coast of Italy. His wife and son were sent to his wife's father, the emperor of Austria. Napoleon never saw them again. He made a brief comeback but was exiled again. He had ignored warnings that times had changed and he was no longer what he once was. He died in exile on the island of St. Helena on May 5, 1821.

LOOKING IN *Like Napoleon, Israel continued to ignore warnings of disaster. Jeremiah spent his life trying to warn God's people, in spite of their refusal to hear. The Bible tells us more about the personal experiences of Jeremiah than any other prophet. His father's name was Hilkiah, a priest from Anathoth. Jeremiah was called to be a prophet in the thirteenth year of King Josiah and remained active under the Kings Jehoahaz-Shallum, Jehoiakim, Jehoiachin (also known as Jeconiah or Coniah), and Zedekiah. Jeremiah's preaching emphasized a high respect for those prophets whose warnings could have saved the people if they had only listened.*

LOOKING OUT

1. **We must be careful lest we lose our spiritual senses. Jeremiah charged that Israel had eyes but could not see and ears but could not hear.**
2. **We should love and respect our God, Who holds back the destructive forces that would destroy us. Jeremiah illustrates this idea by the boundary of the sea.**
3. **Sin keeps us poor. Jeremiah noted that the wrongdoings of God's people had shut off God's blessing and deprived His people of good.**
4. **We must be aware that there are enemies of God even in the church. Jeremiah noted that some who claimed to know God were merely putting up a front.**
5. **It is easy to detect the real believers because they are the ones who obey God's rules. Jeremiah outlined how devious false prophets function.**

LOOKING UP *Father, keep me finely attuned to You and Your Word. May I never lose my spiritual sensitivity to You or let it become dull through lethargy.*

FUTILITY

Jeremiah 7-10

LOOKING BACK Several years ago today, the "harmonic convergence" took place at 20 "sacred sites" around the world. Among these sites were Niagara Falls and the Grand Canyon. Occult believers gathered to meditate about peace and to ward off any impending doom. The harmonic convergence, projected from the ancient Mayan and Aztec calendars to begin on August 16, 1987, claimed to signal the beginning of a period of cleansing that would last until 1992. It was to be in preparation for alien intelligence to be confronted in the next century. Of course, this foolish "sacred" gathering was an exercise in futility and meaningless.

LOOKING IN *Throughout the centuries, man has foolishly turned to all kinds of strange ideas and gods to make life better. Tragically, he overlooks the one sure cure for the world's sickness—a return to the Creator. Jeremiah said that if we would walk in God's ways, it would go well with us. He constantly proclaimed God's judgment upon Judah and Jerusalem, and yet he was also a prophet of hope, proclaiming oracles of salvation. God forbade him to intercede for his people; still he interceded. God ordered him to live without marriage and family, and he had to stay away from the company of merrymakers and from houses of feasting. His was a hard ministry.*

LOOKING OUT

1. We must never succumb to the notion that we are so special we will escape God's judgment. Israel believed the Temple would never fall, but they were wrong.
2. We are judged by what we do, not just what we say, think, or feel. Jeremiah told Israel to change their ways and actions toward each other.
3. Our life outside the sanctuary must match our life inside God's house. Jeremiah says the people murder, commit adultery and perjury, then stand arrogantly before God.
4. We only hurt ourselves when we sin. God told Jeremiah, "Are they not rather harming themselves, to their own shame?" He then promised blessings if they repent.
5. Even when evil people do not listen, we must proclaim God's Word. God told Jeremiah that Israel would not hear, but it was his responsibility to faithfully warn.

LOOKING UP *Help me, Lord, to remember that You love me deeply, but You also demand righteousness of me. May my life outside the church match my behavior when I am inside it.*

DEMONSTRATION

AUGUST 17

Jeremiah 11-15

LOOKING BACK Robert Fulton began the first American steamboat trip between Albany and New York City on this day in 1807, on a boat later called the "Clermont." The trip took 32 hours to travel the 150 miles between the two New York cities. After years of promoting submarine warfare, Fulton finally designed and constructed his first steamboat. In 1803, he launched a steam-powered vessel in France, but his efforts stateside were ridiculed. Fulton's boat was dubbed "Fulton's Folly" by detractors until it made the successful trip from Albany to New York City. He gained a nation's respect when he proved by demonstration that steamboats could really work.

LOOKING IN *Jeremiah had been preaching, but few were listening. It was then that God told him to demonstrate his sermon by burying a linen belt in the crevice of a rock. Later, he retrieved the belt and used it as a powerful teaching tool. Few would forget the meaning of his illustrated sermon. Jeremiah is the second longest book of the Bible, next to the Psalms, and the only one of the Old Testament that tells us its origin. Jeremiah had dictated a first version to Baruch. The scroll was read first in public and again for state officials and the king. King Jehoiakim burned it piece by piece. Jeremiah then dictated a second enlarged edition of the first book.*

LOOKING OUT

1. How we live speaks louder than what we say. God instructs Jeremiah to act out a dramatic sermon, warning of judgment because actions speak louder than words.
2. God always lets us know where we have gone wrong to help us make it right. Jeremiah writes a long song outlining the cause of the coming captivity so the people can repent.
3. Pride puts us in harm's way. Jeremiah noted that Israel's arrogance had separated them from God. Because of this, God had to get their attention by permitting pain.
4. In spite of resolutions, a sinner cannot change his bad behavior. Jeremiah says those who are accustomed to doing evil cannot do good. God must change their character.
5. Sin drives us from the presence of God into dangerous and deadly places. Jeremiah noted that the gross sins of God's people had placed them in great peril.

LOOKING UP *Help me, Lord, to stay as far away from sin as I possibly can. I never want to be separated from You. Deal with those things in my character that displease You.*

NEUTRALITY

AUGUST 18

Jeremiah 16-20

LOOKING BACK President Woodrow Wilson made his passionate appeal for neutrality in World War I on this day in 1914. Two weeks before, he had issued his Proclamation of Neutrality, and now followed it up with a plea for Americans to remain impartial in thought and deed with respect to the war raging in Europe. Even when the Germans sank the British liner Lusitania in 1915, killing over 100 Americans, Wilson determined to stay neutral. By 1917, however, the Germans were attacking American ships, causing the passive president to finally enter the raging war. This was one of the hardest things that peace-loving Woodrow Wilson ever had to do.

LOOKING IN *When evil runs rampant, we must not stay neutral. Jeremiah called for his nation to take an aggressive stand against the raging evil, but they would not. Consequently, the prophet said God would withdraw His blessings and Israel would go into captivity. Jeremiah perceived, to his great sorrow and pain, that the sin of the people of Judah, like that of all nations, would bring about punishment. When he proclaimed this message and called for immediate repentance, he was arrested and nearly lynched as a traitor. Jeremiah survived the destruction of Jerusalem, and his prophecies became ones of comfort, restoration, and hope for a new moral order.*

LOOKING OUT

1. We save ourselves from much sorrow when we obey God. Jeremiah was told not to marry since the coming captivity would bring much sorrow and heartbreak.
2. Life becomes bleak when God withholds His blessings. God told Jeremiah that because of Israel's great sins, He would bring an end to their sounds of joy and gladness.
3. God permits pain to get our attention, not just hurt us. Jeremiah told the people the captivity was necessary so they could repent and be restored.
4. Heartbreak doesn't last forever; restoration will come. Even when pronouncing judgment, Jeremiah told Israel that God would bring them back to the land they loved.
5. Once we have repented, God begins to reveal Himself to us. He says, "This time I will teach them my power and might. Then they will know that my name is the Lord."

LOOKING UP *Help me, Lord, to know You better. Teach me Your power and Your might! May I always remember that at times You permit pain to get my attention.*

COMEUPPANCE

AUGUST 19

Jeremiah 21-24

LOOKING BACK In a plebiscite on this day in 1934, 89.9 percent of the German voters gave Adolf Hitler total power. Hitler was chancellor of the country but pushed for the additional office of president. This would place him in the incontestable supreme command of that country's destiny. The election paved the way for the obscene horror of the next few years as Hitler murdered, maimed, and plunged the world into a bloody war. Hitler was responsible for over six million Jews being exterminated in Nazi concentration camps. However, just 11 years later, this evil monster was brought down. He ended up a sick and pathetic suicide.

LOOKING IN *Powerful leaders often think they can break God's laws and get away with it. They are dead wrong. Jeremiah confronted the wicked King Jehoiakim, warning him that his atrocious sins would be called into account. After just 11 years, Jehoiakim was bound and taken to Babylon to die. The book of Jeremiah consists of four main sections. The first 25 chapters mostly record Jeremiah's haunting visions, oracles of judgment, and laments. Chapters 26 to 45 consist mostly of speeches by Jeremiah and stories about him. His prophecies against foreign nations make up the next six chapters. The last chapter is a historical appendix describing the fall of Jerusalem.*

LOOKING OUT

1. **Building one's life apart from God assures total defeat. Jeremiah tells the wicked Jehoiakim, "Woe to him who builds his palace by unrighteousness."**
2. **Taking advantage of the disadvantaged brings God's wrath. Jeremiah pronounces woe on Jehoiakim. His crimes: making people work for nothing and not paying employees.**
3. **Possessions do not make a man—compassion does. Jeremiah tells Jehoiakim that his magnificent palace doesn't make a king, but caring for the needy does.**
4. **Self-absorption and selfishness have a bitter end. Jeremiah tells the king his conduct will bring him down, and he will finally be buried in disgrace like a donkey.**
5. **No matter how much or how many the evil have around them, God brings them to judgment. Jeremiah tells the wicked king that he will soon give account for his sins.**

LOOKING UP *Help me, Lord, always to build my life around You and Your will for me. Forgive me of my sins. Help me to be unselfish in all areas of my life, caring for the less fortunate.*

ENEMIES

AUGUST 20

Jeremiah 25-28

LOOKING BACK Oliver Perry was born on this day in 1785. He became an American naval hero in the Battle of Lake Erie in 1812. President James Madison had not wanted the war, but Britain kept hijacking American seamen. Thus, in 1812, without much enthusiasm, Madison gave into the inevitable and declared war on Britain. After being promoted to master commandant, Perry received command of the Lake Erie Naval Force. He is best known for the Lake Erie battle and for saying, "We have met the enemy, and they are ours." Years later, Walt Kelly would corrupt that saying in his "Pogo" comic strip by paraphrasing, "We've met the enemy, and he is us."

LOOKING IN *Certainly Israel's greatest enemy was herself. Jeremiah railed against the nation's sin for decades, warning that captivity would surely come if they did not repent. The real enemy was not Nebuchadnezzar nor the overpowering Babylonian empire. Rather, it was the disobedient and destructive leaders who were leading the nation downward. Jeremiah recommended national surrender to Babylon's rule. He called Nebuchadnezzar, Judah's most hated enemy, the "servant of the Lord." Yet, the most aggressive oracles against Babylon are attributed to the prophet. Enemies challenged Jeremiah's prophetic honesty, but kings sought his advice.*

LOOKING OUT

1. **God's mercy is long, giving us many chances to repent. Jeremiah told Israel that for 23 years he had been preaching repentance, but the people continually refused to listen.**
2. **We have not gone too far or done too much. We still can be saved. Jeremiah said that in spite of their years of rebellion they could still avoid captivity by repenting.**
3. **God's Word is always very clear, letting us know what is right and wrong. Jeremiah clearly told Israel what they must cease doing to find salvation and preserve their land.**
4. **If we continue to rebel, God will even use His enemies to bring us to our senses. God called Nebuchadnezzar His servant, not because he was righteous but because he would be used to bring correction.**
5. **We are never left without hope, no matter how low we have gone. Jeremiah told the nation they would be in captivity for 70 years, but God would bring them back home again.**

LOOKING UP *Lord, today I want to thank You for Your great mercy and love that never leave us alone. Thank You that my discipline is never forever. You revive and restore me.*

TEAR-STAINED LETTER

AUGUST 21

Jeremiah 29-31

LOOKING BACK Quantrill's bloody raid on Lawrence, Kansas, took place on this day in 1863. He was the leader of a Confederate guerrilla band during the Civil War. Quantrill's troop was mustered into service in 1862 but continued to operate independently. The former school teacher was denied a commission for his barbaric approach to war. He and his men made raids against Kansas and Missouri residents who favored the Union. Quantrill and his men burned most of the Kansas town, killing 150 people. Frank James, Jesse James' brother, rode with the band that day. Later, William Clarke Quantrill, age 28, was killed during a raid in Kentucky.

LOOKING IN *William Clarke Quantrill was an evil and bloodthirsty man, not unlike Nebuchadnezzar of old. When Jeremiah called Nebuchadnezzar "God's servant," most of Judah was infuriated. However, the prophet was not speaking of the brutal ruler as a godly man but as the instrument God would use to discipline God's children. Just as Jeremiah and other prophets had foretold, Nebuchadnezzar did sweep in, destroy the city, raze the temple, and take hundreds into captivity. Those who had been kidnaped by the ruthless ruler were restless in Babylon and fomenting a rebellion. Jeremiah wrote them a tear-stained letter telling them to drop the plan.*

LOOKING OUT

1. God puts us where we are, though at times we don't like the location. Jeremiah reminded the captives in Babylon that God had taken them there, not Nebuchadnezzar.
2. We must make the best of our situation, where we are, with what we have. The prophet told the captives to build houses and plant gardens in the land of their suffering.
3. We are to become better, not bitter, in our present circumstance. Jeremiah wisely told the captives to marry, have sons and daughters, and to increase—not decrease—in number.
4. We are to pray for our enemies and do good to those who despitefully use us. Jeremiah instructed the captives to seek prosperity for their enemies in spite of oppression.
5. We must view submission as power, not humiliation. God promises to hear His people when they call, if they will just submit to Him.

LOOKING UP *Lord, even if sometimes I hear You say things that I don't really want to hear, help me submit to Your perfect will and way.*

DISMANTLING

AUGUST 22

Jeremiah 32-35

LOOKING BACK In the wake of the popular revolt that smashed the right-wing Soviet coup, a crowd of 10,000 Muscovites watched as cranes dismantled a 14-ton statue of Felix Dzerzhinsky on this day in 1991. Dzerzhinsky was the infamous Polish intellectual who had been tapped by Vladimir Lenin to organize the fledgling Soviet Union's secret police. The KGB developed from the Cheka, the secret police force Dzerzhinsky established. KGB means Committee for State Security. After trucks had hauled away the massive likeness of Dzerzhinsky, Moscow residents adorned the statue's pedestal and the nearby KGB headquarters with graffiti.

LOOKING IN *The smashing of Dzerzhinsky's statue reminds us again that evil and oppression do not last forever. Jeremiah foresaw that the oppressive evil of Israel would be dismantled by Nebuchadnezzar's Babylon. However, even though God would use this pagan ruler to bring discipline to Israel, Nebuchadnezzar would not escape his punishment. His kingdom, too, would be dismantled in disrespect. No earthly power or ruler is beyond God's judgment. The Bible's most aggressive oracles against Babylon and Nebuchadnezzar were spoken by Jeremiah. He told God's people that Judah's captivity would last 70 years.*

LOOKING OUT

1. **When we have second thoughts about God's direction, we need to go to Him for assurance. Jeremiah obeys by buying the Anathoth field but questions his decision. He prays.**
2. **God faithfully affirms His direction when we sincerely want to do His will. In response to Jeremiah's prayer, God answers, "Is anything too hard for me?"**
3. **Those who faithfully follow God have an inside track on what God is doing in our world. God tells Jeremiah all that He will permit Nebuchadnezzar to do to Jerusalem.**
4. **God's discipline is always therapeutic. God tells Jeremiah that He will give the Israeliltes singleness of heart and action so they will fear God and find good coming to them.**
5. **God's great love is everlasting, and there is nothing we can do to make Him stop loving us. God tells Jeremiah about His people: "I will never stop doing good to them."**

LOOKING UP *Help me, Lord, to do all You ask, though I might not understand why You require it of me. When I have second thoughts about Your commands may I come to You for assurance.*

INJUSTICE

AUGUST 23

Jeremiah 36-39

LOOKING BACK Nicola Sacco and Bartolomeo Vanzetti were executed on this day in 1927. Many believed then, and many still do, that it was one of the greatest miscarriages of justice in United States history. Sacco and Vanzetti were convicted of a shoe factory payroll robbery during which a guard had been killed. They maintained their innocence to the end, although no official would listen. It appears there was substantial evidence showing that both men were elsewhere at the time of the crime. On the 50th anniversary of their deaths, Governor Dukakis of Massachusetts proclaimed a memorial day for the men, saying that the trial was permeated by prejudice.

LOOKING IN *Injustice has plagued mankind ever since Cain killed Abel. Jeremiah lived during one of the most unjust eras in Israel's history. To make matters worse, Jehoiakim was a blatantly evil king whose rule of terror lasted 11 long years. In one of the most vivid chapters of the whole Bible, Jeremiah is banned from the Temple. He writes a prophetic message to the nation and its leaders. The Word is read publicly and then called to Jehoiakim's attention. When the scroll is read to the rebel king, he takes a knife and, piece by piece, slices it and contemptuously throws it into the fire. Jehoiakim may have burned the scroll, but not even his power could destroy the message.*

LOOKING OUT

1. **Even when we are in deep rebellion, God constantly seeks to reconcile us. Jeremiah wrote a plain message of repentance to the people and to King Jehoiakim.**
2. **Evil men may ban the messenger, but they never can succeed in banning the message. Even though Jeremiah was incarcerated, he sent his prophetic word by Baruch.**
3. **God's Word strikes fear in the hearts of those who love Him. Some of Jehoiakim's officials asked to hear Jeremiah's prophecy. When it was read, they quaked in fear.**
4. **Contemptuous rebels seek to destroy the message and the messengers, but God's Word prevails. Jehoiakim burned the scroll and ordered the arrest of Baruch and the prophet.**
5. **Those who are called by God will be faithful in spite of opposition and hardship. Though the scroll was destroyed, Jeremiah and Baruch produced another copy.**

LOOKING UP *Help me, Lord, to be faithful to Your calling despite opposition and difficulty. Though evil ones succeed in destroying my work, may I, like Jeremiah, build again what has been destroyed.*

INVASION

AUGUST 24

Jeremiah 40-45

LOOKING BACK British troops invaded Maryland and, on this day in 1814, burned the Capitol and other public buildings in Washington D.C. Only the heroic resistance at Fort McHenry kept the British from capturing Baltimore. Not only did the British burn several government buildings, but they also set the White House on fire. President James Madison and other high U.S. government officials fled to safety until British troops departed two days later. The British had been unaware of the strength of their position. American legend fondly remembers Dolley Madison fleeing from the burning White House with Stuart's portrait of George Washington under her arm.

LOOKING IN *The British invasion of Washington was nothing like Nebuchadnezzar's invasion of Jerusalem. Nebuchadnezzar had come to stay and destroy. Displaced Jews were rounded up and herded to Babylon. Jeremiah was chained and destined for Babylon until a sympathetic commander recognized him and set him free. Jeremiah then moved to Mizpah, the capital of Gedaliah, the newly appointed Jewish governor of Judah. When Gedaliah was assassinated, Jeremiah was deported to Egypt, against his will, by Jewish officers who had survived the catastrophes. In Egypt, he continued to prophesy against the Egyptians and his compatriots.*

LOOKING OUT

1. **When judgment falls, God always takes care of His own. Nebuchadnezzar had crushed Jerusalem, but Jeremiah was released when he was discovered among the captives.**
2. **God gives us favor in the eyes of the enemy when we are faithful to our Lord. The commander of Nebuchadnezzar's guard let Jeremiah choose his future home.**
3. **Godly men choose to identify with the suffering rather than find comfort for themselves. Jeremiah chose to stay with Judah's shattered remnant so he could comfort them.**
4. **God is careful to take care of the poor and helpless. Nebuchadnezzar appointed Gedaliah to be governor—a man who swore protection for the defeated people.**
5. **Good leadership in a nation brings prosperity. Gedaliah's rule was benevolent. Jeremiah reported that as a result, "they harvested an abundance of wine and summer fruit."**

LOOKING UP *Help me, Lord, not just to seek comfort for myself but sincerely to care for those who need help. Help me remember that no matter what troubles come on the world, I am safe in Your hands.*

CHANGE

AUGUST 25

Jeremiah 46-49

LOOKING BACK Paris, France, changed dramatically on this day in 1944. The 2nd French Armored Division entered Paris as dawn broke, bringing an end to the long and brutal German occupation. That afternoon, General Charles de Gaulle led a parade down the Champs Elysees in the City of Light. De Gaulle was the outstanding French patriot, soldier, and statesman of the 1900's who had led the French resistance against Germany all through the war. Though Hitler had ordered the destruction of Paris, German occupying-officer General Dietrich von Choltitz refused that order and, instead, wisely surrendered to French Major General Jacques Le Clerc.

LOOKING IN *Change is not always as dramatic or joyful as Paris experienced in 1944. However, it is very much a part of life. Change, even though it is sometimes unpleasant, can have a positive impact on us. Jeremiah uses a parable of the winemaker to instruct Moab about changes that would soon come to her. Israelites regarded the Moabites as close relatives. There were peaceful interchanges, as well as conflicts, between the Israelites and Moabites throughout history. The story of Ruth illustrates peaceful relations, while the episode of Ehud and Eglon illustrates conflict. Saul fought against the Moabites while David was a descendant of a Moabitess.*

LOOKING OUT

1. **Change can be good for us; it helps purify. Jeremiah tells Moab that she will be poured like wine from one vessel to another. Each pouring leaves the dregs behind.**
2. **God wants to perfect us until we are fit to be set before the King. Jeremiah uses the parable of wine-making to show how God perfects us until we are pleasing to Him.**
3. **God sends people into our lives who create discomfort so we can confront those things in us needing change. God tells Moab that the "pourers" are coming.**
4. **God moves us forward, not wanting us to go back to the old life. Jeremiah's wine-making parable speaks of the emptied jars being smashed, not to be used again.**
5. **There is even hope for the most wicked if they will fall at the Master's feet. God tells Moab that fortunes can be restored in the days to come if repentance occurs.**

LOOKING UP *Help me, Lord, not to resent unpleasant change but to recognize it as a chance to grow. May I not complain when You pour me from one circumstance to another.*

UNBELIEVABLE

AUGUST 26

Jeremiah 50-52

LOOKING BACK The "Father of Radio" was born on this day in 1873. During the early 1900's, Lee De Forest of the United States and certain other electrical engineers developed various devices called vacuum tubes, which could detect and amplify radio signals. Vacuum tubes led to the development of radio as we know it. In addition, De Forest invented the electron tube, radio knife for surgery, and photo electric cell. He also pioneered the creation of talking pictures and television, holding hundreds of patents. So unbelievable was the idea of wireless radio broadcasting that De Forest was actually accused of fraud and arrested for selling stock to underwrite his invention.

LOOKING IN *Many things seem unbelievable until they happen. When Jeremiah prophesied the destruction of Babylon, it seemed an unfathomable idea. Babylon was the most powerful nation on the face of the earth—the first world empire. Babylon was a capital city in ancient Mesopotamia (mostly modern Iraq) and is mentioned some 200 times in the Bible. At that time, it was the largest and most beautiful city in the Middle East. Jeremiah had his prophetic scroll read publicly and then dramatically sunk into the Euphrates River. No doubt many Babylonians laughed when Jeremiah's prophetic drama was played out. However, it wasn't long before it came true.*

LOOKING OUT

1. God is merciful even to those who disregard Him or hate Him. God warned Babylon of its judgment six full years before Nebuchadnezzar invaded Jerusalem.
2. God clearly outlines the consequences of our decisions long before we make them. Jeremiah carefully recorded all the evils that would befall the Babylonians if they continued in evil.
3. God's Word is open to all, not just a few. Jeremiah's warning scroll was given a public reading so all who lived in Babylon would know the truth.
4. God dramatically underlines His Word so it can't be easily forgotten. After Jeremiah's scroll was read, it was sunk publicly in the Euphrates as a bold warning.
5. God's Word always comes true. Babylon did not repent, and just as Jeremiah predicted, it was destroyed, never to rise again. With that, Jeremiah ended his preaching.

LOOKING UP *Help me, Lord, always to hear and heed Your Word, because I know all You say will come to pass. Thank You Lord because You care for all mankind and desire all to be saved.*

LAMENT

AUGUST 27

Lamentations 1-5

LOOKING BACK Larger than life, Lyndon Baines Johnson came bouncing into the world on this day in 1908. Johnson became president following the tragic assassination of John F. Kennedy. Johnson's most ardent desire was to be a great and greatly loved president. Born with a brash and expansive spirit of the Texas land which bred him, Johnson overwhelmed all around him. In spite of his good intentions, he was forced to leave office a bitter and frustrated man. The lingering Vietnam War was his undoing. On March 31, 1968, Johnson stunned the nation by announcing he would not run for reelection. Exhausted, ill, and disappointed, Johnson returned to die at his Texas ranch.

LOOKING IN *Jeremiah was exhausted and disappointed as he sat beside the broken-down walls of Jerusalem to sing his mournful lament. The people had not listened to him, and now the city lay in ruins. The prophet could only weep over the destruction. All five chapters of Lamentations are written in verse. The first four chapters are alphabetic acrostics. Each stanza (or three stanzas in chapter 3) begins with a letter of the Hebrew alphabet. The first four chapters relate the dreadful conditions brought about by the destruction and mourn the degradation of Jerusalem. The fifth chapter ends with a plea for God to forgive and restore Israel.*

LOOKING OUT

1. **Even though judgment is deserved, we must pray for mercy. Jeremiah knew the captivity would last 70 years, yet he pled with God for mercy and restoration.**
2. **God alone is the giver of joy. Jeremiah noted that joy had gone from his people's hearts and their dancing turned to mourning. Only in God's presence can we find joy.**
3. **Recognition of our sins is the first firm step to forgiveness. Jeremiah lamented that the crown had fallen from their heads because of the sin the nation committed.**
4. **In despair, we often wonder if God has forsaken us. Jeremiah knew differently, but still he lamented, "Why do you always forget us? Why do you forsake us so long?"**
5. **Restoration will come once we have completed the discipline God sets for us. Jeremiah cried out, "Restore us to yourself, O Lord, that we may return."**

LOOKING UP *Our nation, O Lord, deserves punishment, but please have mercy on us and restore us to Yourself. Forgive us of our great sins and help us correct our behavior.*

RESTORATION

AUGUST 28

Ezekiel 1-6

LOOKING BACK "Lemonade Lucy" was born on this day in 1831. Lucy Ware Hayes was the wife of Rutherford B. Hayes, 19th president of the United States. She was the first president's wife to have a college degree. She championed many of the leading moral causes of the day, supporting the abolition of slavery, prohibition of alcohol, and aid to the poor. She earned her nickname because she refused to serve alcohol in the White House and turned Sunday nights there into hymn sings. History has never quite decided on the quality of Rutherford B. Hayes' presidency. One thing is clear. Both Hayes and his wife were good people who restored integrity to the scandal-shocked nation.

LOOKING IN *Ezekiel came to the kingdom during the scandal-ridden years of Judah's last kings. He was taken captive at the fall of Jerusalem. Ezekiel lived among the conquered people explaining why they had been forced into captivity. He saw the nation's lack of integrity and insisted that only if they repented would God bring them back home. Ezekiel lived in his own house at Tel-Abib near the river Chebar, an irrigation canal that channeled the waters of the Euphrates River into the surrounding arid region. His call came in 593 B.C., the "thirtieth year." This probably indicates Ezekiel's age, although it could mean 30 years after the rediscovery of the book of the law.*

LOOKING OUT

1. We must be full of God's Word if we are to speak it. Ezekiel was told to eat the scroll before he spoke to Israel. He was to completely internalize God's Word.
2. God's call for repentance always starts with those who claim to know Him. Ezekiel was instructed to preach to Israel, not to people of obscure speech and different language.
3. We must be careful lest familiarity with religion deadens us to God's message. God told Ezekiel that those who did not know Him would be eager to hear, but Israel would not.
4. God gives us the strength and determination to fulfill His will. God said He would make Ezekiel's head harder than the hard-headed rebels who refused to heed God's Word.
5. When we begin to see sin as God sees it, we become angry. Ezekiel was lifted to God's viewpoint where he saw the open rebellion of God's people. He became angry.

LOOKING UP *Help me, Lord, to be full of Your Word that I might faithfully proclaim Your desires. Help me to realize You have planted me where I am. May I always be faithful in this place.*

AUGUST 29

FIRSTHAND

Ezekiel 7-10

LOOKING BACK Oliver Wendell Holmes was born on this day in 1809. An American writer who won fame for his essays and poems, Holmes was also a physician. His son, Oliver Wendell Holmes, Jr., became a famous associate justice of the Supreme Court. The senior Holmes was known for his keen mind and witty literary style. His enthusiasm and humor made him popular as a teacher and speaker. Holmes wrote many poems, including *Old Ironsides,* which protested the U.S. Navy's plan to destroy the "Constitution," a historic but unseaworthy frigate. The poem helped save the ship. Holmes once wisely wrote, "A moment's insight is sometimes worth a life's experience."

LOOKING IN *Ezekiel had a startling "moment's insight" when God paid an unexpected visit to him, giving the prophet instant understanding of how God's holiness had been offended. God's house had been desecrated and judgment was coming. These messages are not easy to understand because of their frequent use of symbolic imagery. We are not alone in struggling to understand Ezekiel. At one time, those under age 30 were not allowed to read chapters 1, and 40 through 48. Rabbi ben Hezekiah said he burned 300 jars of "midnight oil" in an attempt to harmonize the text. Ancient Jewish scholars believed difficulties of the book would be resolved when Elijah returned.*

LOOKING OUT

1. **God often comes to us at unexpected times. Ezekiel was at home with the elders when God suddenly appeared to show him an awful abomination.**
2. **God often comes to us in unexpected ways. God came to the prophet in the dramatic fashion of fire and metal, a unique presentation of Himself.**
3. **God often shows us unexpected things. Suddenly, Ezekiel was miraculously transported back to Jerusalem to see the evil idols the leaders had set up there.**
4. **God is holy and will not tolerate His house being defiled. Ezekiel is appalled at the blatant desecration of God's sacred temple.**
5. **Sin shuts off God's hearing. God tells the prophet that although the sinful people shout, He will refuse to hear them unless they repent.**

LOOKING UP *Help me, Lord, to keep the channel clear to You. May I always remember that sin shuts off Your hearing. Therefore, please forgive my sin and keep me from it.*

HORROR STORY

AUGUST 30

Ezekiel 11-15

LOOKING BACK The creator of Frankenstein was born on this day in 1797. Mary Wollstonecraft Shelly wrote the well-known horror story in response to a discussion by her husband and his friends. She was married to romantic poet Percy Bysshe Shelley and was the daughter of English philosopher William Godwin. In August 1811, the poet had eloped with 16-year-old Harriet Westbrook, the daughter of a former London coffee house owner. He abandoned her in 1814 and ran away with Mary Godwin. In addition to her famous novel *Frankenstein,* Mary Shelley is known for her work in editing and publishing her husband's unpublished work after his untimely death.

LOOKING IN *Israel, during Ezekiel's day, had its own personal horror story. Sin had forced the nation into captivity. Ezekiel's task was to explain why God had permitted the Babylonians to carry God's people away. He was the major interpreter of the Babylonian Exile. The prophet communicated God's clear message of repentance through word, song, and drama. Still the people would not listen. Their rebellion only compounded their problems and extended their pain. Ezekiel was a priest as well as a prophet. He stressed the importance of following religious law and strictly obeying religious forms and ceremonies. Ezekiel's ministry lasted from 593 to 572 or 571 B.C.*

LOOKING OUT

1. **Rebellion against God blinds us to reality. God told Ezekiel that His people had ears to hear and eyes to see, but their sin had blinded them and made them deaf.**
2. **God seeks every way possible to communicate with His rebellious children so they can be reconciled to Him. Ezekiel was instructed to act out a poignant and unforgettable parable.**
3. **Sometime God asks us to do things we don't fully understand. Ezekiel was told to pack his belongings and dig through a wall before he was given the full reason.**
4. **Only those who truly seek will find. Ezekiel acted out his drama, and when people asked why he was doing this, he told them God's message for the nation.**
5. **No matter how despairing the message, God always gives a glimmer of hope. Ezekiel dramatically foretold destruction but also said a remnant would be spared.**

LOOKING UP *Help me, Lord, to really hear You and see what You want for my life. I will obey You. May I always hunger and thirst after righteousness so I may be filled with You.*

NO EXCEPTIONS

AUGUST 31

Ezekiel 16-19

LOOKING BACK American writer William Saroyan was born on this day in 1908. Of Armenian descent, Saroyan was author of *The Human Comedy* and *The Time of Your Life*, a Pulitzer-winning play. He became known for loosely structured, impressionistic plays and stories that praise the common person's ability to live a full, happy life in a world of ugly reality. He once admonished, "In the time of your life, live, so that in that good time there shall be no ugliness or death for yourself or for any life your life touches." Just before he died, he told reporters, "Everybody has got to die, but I have always believed an exception would be made in my case. Now what?"

LOOKING IN *While Saroyan obviously knew that an exception would not be made in his death, the disobedient leaders of ancient Judah really believed they wouldn't face the same judgment as the northern ten tribes. They thought an exception would be made in their case. They were dead wrong, just as the prophets had warned. Ezekiel had the tough task of reminding the captive people where they had gone wrong so they could make things right. He carefully outlined the sins of his people and then listed God's expectations of true believers. Faith, Ezekiel noted, is far more than observing religious ceremonies. Real faith is living life as God directs us.*

LOOKING OUT

1. Sexual purity is a hallmark of a true believer. Ezekiel lists the marks of a godly man. Among the first is that he does not commit adultery by defiling his neighbor's wife.
2. Honesty is a hallmark of a true believer. Ezekiel notes that a righteous man does not oppress anyone but returns what he took in pledge for a loan.
3. Compassion is a hallmark of a true believer. Ezekiel notes that people of God give food to the hungry and provide clothing for the naked.
4. Fairness is a hallmark of a true believer. Ezekiel clearly says that one who loves God judges fairly between men and withholds his hand from doing wrong.
5. Obedience is a clear hallmark of a true believer. Ezekiel identifies a follower of God by saying he follows God's decrees and faithfully keeps His laws.

LOOKING UP *Help me, Lord, to exhibit all the hallmarks of a true believer. Make my light shine in a dark world. Help me to be pure, honest, compassionate, fair, and obedient.*

September

A Month of Five Important Jewish Holidays

Five Jewish holidays are celebrated in September or early October. They are Rosh Ha-Shanah, Tzom Gedaliah, Yom Kippur, Sukkot, and Simhat Torah.

Rosh Ha-Shanah, or New Year, usually begins in September, on the first day of the Hebrew month of Tishri, and lasts two days. Some Reform Jews celebrate it for one day.

Tzom Gedaliah is a day of fasting for the Jewish people mourning Gedaliah's assassination during the time of Jeremiah.

Yom Kippur is the Jewish day of atonement and the most important and sacred Jewish holy day. It falls in September or October, in the Jewish month of Tishri. It lasts from sunset on the ninth day of Tishri until three stars appear after the tenth day. It is a day of rejoicing. During this solemn religious festival, Jews pray for God's forgiveness, a good year, and long life.

Sukkot is a Jewish festival, lasting seven days, that begins on the 15th day of the Hebrew month of Tishri. The festival is also called the Feast of Tabernacles.

Simhat Torah is a Jewish festival of rejoicing in the Torah, or Law. It marks the end of the annual cycle of readings from the Torah that take place in the synagogue every Saturday morning. The cycle begins again on the first Saturday after Simhat Torah. The festival falls on the 23rd day of the Hebrew month of Tishri, usually occurring in September and October. Jews in Israel and Reform Jews observe the festival on the 22nd day of Tishri.

September is the ninth month of the year, according to the Gregorian calendar. It was the seventh month in the old Roman calendar, and its name comes from the Latin *septem*, meaning "seven." September later became the ninth month when the ancient Romans moved the beginning of their year from March 1 to January 1. September has had 29 days, 31 days, and, since the time of the Roman emperor Augustus, 30 days. Summer ends and autumn begins at the autumnal equinox, on September 22 or 23, in the northern half of the world. This month we finish the Old Testament by concluding Ezekiel and reading through the 12 Minor Prophets.

WAR

SEPTEMBER 1

Ezekiel 20-22

LOOKING BACK World War II began on this day in 1939. Lasting from that year until 1945, the war killed more people, destroyed more property, disrupted more lives, and probably had more far-reaching consequences than any other war in history. The exact number of people killed will never be known. Military deaths probably totaled about 17 million. Civilian deaths were even greater as a result of starvation, bombing raids, massacres, epidemics, and other war-related causes. It brought the downfall of Western Europe as the center of world power and led to the rise of the Soviet Union. World War II began when Germany invaded Poland on September 1, 1939.

LOOKING IN *Havoc and heartbreak always come when man disobeys God's Word and His will. Hitler's lust for power, combined with his burning hatred, spilled a little of hell out on humanity. Ezekiel warned his nation that their blatant disregard for God's Word and active aggression against the poor and powerless would result in untold agony. He said that God's judgment would sweep across the land like a forest fire. The sword of the Lord was drawn against Israel and was in the hand of the King of Babylon, who would destroy the capital cities of both Ammon and Judah. Five years after Jerusalem fell, Nebuchadnezzar attacked Ammon, just as Ezekiel had said.*

LOOKING OUT

1. We can prevent pain if we will learn from history. Ezekiel asks Israel if they will repeat the sins of their fathers or, more wisely, turn from the evil of the past.
2. It's useless to pray if we harbor sin in our hearts. God told His sinful people He would not permit them to inquire of Him. He only hears prayers from obedient children.
3. God is determined to perfect that which concerns us. Israel wanted to serve man-made gods. Our Lord replied, "What you have in mind will never happen."
4. Sin is sweet to the taste but bitter in the stomach. Ezekiel notes that after Israel had been sickened because of sin, they would loathe themselves for the evil they had done.
5. God saves us for His sake, not because we deserve it. God tells His people, "You will know that I am the Lord when I deal with you for my name's sake."

LOOKING UP *Help me, Lord, to learn from Scripture so I won't have to feel the pain of bitter experience. Cleanse my heart of any iniquity that my communication with You remain clear.*

CONFUSED

SEPTEMBER 2

Ezekiel 23-24

LOOKING BACK Britain and the American colonies dropped 11 days from their calendar on this day in 1751. Called the "Gregorian Correction," the British Calendar Act of 1751 proclaimed that the day following Wednesday, September 2, should become Thursday, September 14, 1752. When the calendar adjustment was announced to the public, there was rioting in the streets by those who felt cheated and who demanded the 11 days back. They sincerely thought part of their lives were taken away. The adjustment act also provided that New Year's Day (and the change of the year number) should fall on January 1 (instead of March 25) in 1752 and every year thereafter.

LOOKING IN *Even though 11 days were not really taken from a person's life by the British Calendar Act, many misunderstood. It is easy to get confused when the unfamiliar happens. Ezekiel was shattered when God told him his beloved wife would die. He could not understand why this was happening. It was especially hard on the prophet because God forbade him the customary forms of mourning. Ezekiel was to use his grief as an object lesson to Judah telling them that just as the desire of his eyes was taken from him, the desire of their eyes (the Temple) would be taken from them. The hurt would be so deep they wouldn't be able to cry.*

LOOKING OUT

1. God prepares us for the hard things we have to face. God told Ezekiel that his wife would die and that he would face a grief so deep that customary grieving would not alleviate the pain.
2. Bad things happen to good people. Ezekiel was a dedicated prophet of God yet had to face the loss of his beloved wife. Life is such that heartbreak comes to all.
3. There is a responsibility that goes beyond our pain. Even though Ezekiel suffered great loss, he still had to faithfully preach God's Word.
4. We must not waste our grief. God told Ezekiel to use his own experience with loss to explain the loss the nation would experience due to their refusal to repent.
5. God uses broken vessels for His glory. Ezekiel's life and experience became a living testimony to the nation. He was a sign to them that they might know God.

LOOKING UP *Help me, Lord, in spite of my hurt, to faithfully do Your will and Your work. May I always remember there is a responsibility that goes beyond my feelings.*

DANGER

SEPTEMBER 3

Ezekiel 25-28

LOOKING BACK Dressed as a sailor and carrying identification papers borrowed from a retired merchant seaman, Frederick Douglass escaped from slavery on this day in 1838. Born a slave, Douglass became the leading spokesman of African Americans in the 1800's. On the day of his escape, he boarded a train in Baltimore, Maryland, a slave state, and rode to Wilmington, Delaware, where he caught a steamboat to the free city of Philadelphia. He then transferred to a train headed for New York City, where he entered the protection of the Underground Railroad network. Douglass later became a great orator and one of the dynamic leaders of the anti-slavery struggle.

LOOKING IN *While Douglass escaped slavery and became a famed leader in history, Ezekiel said there would be no escape for four close neighbors of Judah. These hostile nations had rejoiced when the Israelites ran into trouble. Because of their angry attitude, Ammon, Moab, Edom, and Philistia would be destroyed. Many of them would go into slavery. Chapters 25 through 32 contain Ezekiel's prophecies against foreign nations. Although Ezekiel concentrated mainly on Israel, he and the other prophets were very conscious that God is the Lord of all the earth. There is no nation beyond the reach of His judgment, and He requires righteousness from all.*

LOOKING OUT

1. **Smirking when a spiritual leader falls brings God's displeasure. Ammon was sharply condemned to punishment by the Lord for delighting in Israel's failure and fall.**
2. **Denigrating God's people puts one in harm's way. Moab would come under attack from Babylon because of her attitude toward God's chosen.**
3. **Seeking revenge is dangerous business. Ezekiel pronounced doom on Edom since that nation took revenge on Judah for a perceived wrong.**
4. **Malice toward God's children brings swift and sure judgment. Philistia hated the Israelites, wishing to destroy them. God turned their wrath back on them.**
5. **Judgment's purpose is always to prove God's righteousness and draw people to Him. In each case, the pagan nations' judgments were given so they might know God.**

LOOKING UP *Help me, Lord, to be very careful what I say about Your servants and how I act toward them. May I always be loving to others and not be one who criticizes.*

HELPLESS

SEPTEMBER 4

Ezekiel 29-32

LOOKING BACK On this day in history, Adolf Hitler proclaimed, "No matter what happens, England will be destroyed, one way or another." Obviously, he was dead wrong. The brutal German dictator ruled Germany from 1933 to 1945, turning that country into a powerful war machine. He provoked World War II and then conquered most of Europe before he was defeated in 1945. He thought he was invincible but learned he was not. By April 1945, Hitler had become a broken man. His head, hands, and feet trembled, and he was tortured by stomach cramps. Deep in his besieged bunker, Hitler and Eva Braun, his mistress, killed themselves.

LOOKING IN *No matter how much power dictators have, they cannot fight God. Nebuchadnezzar is the classic example. He thought he was in charge, but Ezekiel says God was using him for His own purposes. From 605 to 562 B.C., Nebuchadnezzar II reigned as king of Babylon and ruler of the new Babylonian empire. His dominion covered much of the Middle East. Nebuchadnezzar was one of the most famous kings of the ancient world, best remembered for conquering the city of Jerusalem and for his great building projects. He probably built the Hanging Gardens of Babylon, one of the seven wonders of the ancient world.*

LOOKING OUT

1. **Many times we are unaware that God is using us. Nebuchadnezzar was not a servant of Jehovah and was totally unaware that he was being used by the Creator.**
2. **Many times it seems as though our labor for the Lord is in vain. Ezekiel records that Nebuchadnezzar got nothing for his attack on Tyre.**
3. **God always makes up for what we have missed. God determined to give Egypt to Nebuchadnezzar as a reward for what he had done.**
4. **All of our labor should be for the Lord. Ezekiel reports that God commends Nebuchadnezzar by saying he "did it for me."**
5. **God strengthens those who serve Him faithfully. The horn in Ezekiel's vision represents strength. Ezekiel notes that God makes Israel's horn grow.**

LOOKING UP *Thank You, Father, that You can use those who do not know You. This portion of Scripture reminds me that You can still move the hearts of kings.*

ENTERTAINMENT?

SEPTEMBER 5

Ezekiel 33-36

LOOKING BACK Legendary bandit Jesse James was born on this day in 1847. During the Civil War, he and his older brother, Frank, joined bands of killers and thieves led by Confederate sympathizers. After the war, they formed a new band with their cousins, the Youngers, and began to hold up trains, stagecoaches, and banks. In 1875, a bomb thrown into Jesse's mother's house killed his stepbrother, Archie Samuel, and injured his mother. Some believed detectives hurled the bomb and that James was being unjustly persecuted. On April 3, 1882, Robert Ford, a member of the James gang, shot 34-year-old Jesse in the back of the head to claim a $5,000 reward.

LOOKING IN *Crime is not entertainment! Jesse James was not a hero but a blood-thirsty killer. Tragically, many make light of what is deadly serious, thinking it is entertaining. That was the case in Ezekiel's day. When the prophet preached, the people came to hear him, not because they accepted or believed what he said, but because they considered it entertaining. In spite of all that had happened, the people were still not taking the prophet's words of warning seriously. God told Ezekiel that people were laughing behind his back. He warned that one day soon their laughter would turn to tears. Then they would know a prophet had been among them.*

LOOKING OUT

1. **When God asks us to speak, we must do so or else. God called Ezekiel to be a watchman. If he failed to warn, the blood of those punished would be on his hands.**
2. **Our responsibility is to speak regardless of the response. Ezekiel was held accountable only to speak. Those who listened were then responsible for their reaction.**
3. **God never delights in the destruction of the wicked. Ezekiel revealed the great heart of our loving Heavenly Father by saying God takes no pleasure in punishing.**
4. **Sin saps our strength. Ezekiel noted that Abraham was just one man, yet possessed the land. Even the whole nation couldn't do as much because sin had crippled them.**
5. **To hear and not do is sin. God told Ezekiel that people considered his sermons as mere entertainment. They heard the prophet's words but did not put them into practice.**

LOOKING UP *Help me, Lord, to not only hear Your Word but be careful to apply it to all areas of my life. May I always remember that sermons I hear are to be carefully considered and applied.*

NAMES

SEPTEMBER 6

Ezekiel 37-39

LOOKING BACK In 1991, on this day, Russian legislators voted to restore the name Saint Petersburg to the nation's second largest city. The city had been known as Leningrad for 67 years in honor of Vladimir I. Lenin, the Soviet Union's founder. Built by Peter the Great in 1703, the city has had three names in the 20th century. Russian leaders changed its German-sounding name to Petrograd in 1914 at the beginning of World War I, and Soviet Communist leaders changed its name to Leningrad in 1924, following their leader's death. St. Petersburg was the first Russian city built in imitation of western European cities such as London, Paris, and Vienna.

LOOKING IN *Names are important because they often identify character. Israel had been God's "chosen," but their determined rebellion belied that title. They had lost their reputation and good name in the world because of their sin. Ezekiel now said that reputation would be restored. The prophet noted that not only would Israel's good name be restored, but the people would be brought back from captivity to rebuild their devastated land. It seemed that at the time of this prophecy Ezekiel was only dreaming. However, history verifies that his words did come true. God's people returned to their homeland, proving God's care. God says what He means and means what He says.*

LOOKING OUT

1. Our lives are in a test tube, held up for the world to see. God told His people He would display His glory among the nations. They would see how God deals with Israel.
2. God's miracles are so dramatic it is clear they are the works of God. Our Lord said, "From that day forward the house of Israel will know that I am the Lord their God."
3. God makes it clear why He withholds blessings from us. Ezekiel's task was to let the captive people know they were in pain because they had been consistently unfaithful to God.
4. God always deals with us in the direction we are going. Ezekiel notes that God hid His face from His people due to their gross sin and uncleanness.
5. We are people in process making progress. While Israel was being disciplined for their sin, Ezekiel notes that God was restoring them to Himself and purifying His people.

LOOKING UP *Help me, Lord, to display Your lovingkindness in the way that I daily talk, act, and live. Each day let me grow more like You, fulfilling the vision You have for my life.*

PAINS

SEPTEMBER 7

Ezekiel 40-42

LOOKING BACK This is "Grandma Moses Day" in New York State. The famed American folk artist was born on this day in 1860. She didn't started painting until she was 78 years old, and only then because arthritis made it difficult for her to hold embroidery needles. Grandma Moses never had an art lesson. She painted simple but realistic scenes of rural life. Her colorful and lively pictures were based on memories of her own youth in the late 1800's. Critics praise her work for its freshness, innocence, and humanity. An art collector first discovered her paintings in the 1930's, catapulting the senior citizen to fame. Pain had given her fame and fortune.

LOOKING IN *Discomfort can force us into new and better positions, just as it did for Grandma Moses. Ezekiel is lifted up to get God's perspective on the pain of the captivity. He begins to see that God has permitted this difficult time in order to move His nation into a better position to fulfill all that the prophets had proclaimed concerning the coming Messiah. The prophet encourages Israel to hold on to hope. Chapters 40 through 48 portray Ezekiel's new Temple. Although, for the most part, these chapters make rather dull reading, they are, in a very real sense, the climax of the whole book. Ezekiel's vision had begun in Babylon but ends in a restored Jerusalem.*

LOOKING OUT

1. God never leaves us without His Word. Twenty-five years after the captivity and 14 years after the destruction of Jerusalem, God gives a special word to Ezekiel.
2. God lifts us above our present problems to see things as He views them. Ezekiel is taken in a vision to the land of Israel and set on a high hill to get God's perspective.
3. We need not despair no matter how desperate things look. Ezekiel saw buildings that looked like a ruined city. However, God had plans for this place.
4. God is always rebuilding what Satan has destroyed. Ezekiel sees a man whose appearance was like bronze measuring the ruined city for reconstruction.
5. God gives His Word to us so we can share it with others. God tells Ezekiel to inform Israel of what he sees. Thus, they could be encouraged during their days of despair.

LOOKING UP *Help me, Lord, to remember that no matter what is going on now, God has good plans for me. When I am down, help me look up to You rather than out on my problems.*

LEADERSHIP

Ezekiel 43-45

LOOKING BACK One of America's most controversial political leaders was assassinated on this day in 1935. Huey P. Long had been a farm boy with little formal education beyond high school, but he became governor of Louisiana and a United States senator. Long, nicknamed "the Kingfish," gained high office by calling for social reforms to benefit poor farmers and workers. He adopted the slogan "Every Man a King." This emphasis made him a strong threat to President Franklin Delano Roosevelt. However, Long was shot in the State Capitol in Baton Rouge by Carl A. Weiss, a physician. Members of Weiss' family were political enemies of Long.

LOOKING IN *Long's critics have called him a despicable demigod who used his offices for personal gain and raw power. Others claim he did much for his home state. Leaders such as Long have been given much. The prophet Ezekiel let such leaders know that God would hold them personally accountable for how they used the position and power handed to them. Ezekiel continued to preach until at least 571 B.C. His ministry can be divided into two phases: (1) 593-587, characterized by warnings of coming judgment on Judah and Jerusalem, and (2) 587-571, a period characterized by messages of great encouragement and hope for the future.*

LOOKING OUT

1. God holds leaders responsible for how they influence their followers. Ezekiel tells Israel's careless leaders, "You have gone far enough." They must start doing right.
2. God expects and insists on honesty in business and government. The princes of Israel are told emphatically they must start using honest scales and measures.
3. Leaders have a special obligation to God that comes before their obligation to followers. The princes of Israel are told they must bring a special gift to God in worship.
4. Followers are to participate in the ministry God has given to a leader. The princes of Israel were to make an offering, but all the people were to contribute to it.
5. All leaders are to set the pace for a nation's respect for God and worship of Him. The princes of Israel were to be moral examples and lead the nation in reverence for God.

LOOKING UP *Help me, Lord, to be the leader You expect me to be. Let me set the moral pace for my followers. May I always remember that You demand holiness in my life.*

LIFE

Ezekiel 46-48

LOOKING BACK Mao Tse-tung died on this day in 1976. He had led the long struggle that made China a Communist nation in 1949, becoming the ruler of China and one of the world's most powerful people. Mao made China a tightly controlled and oppressed society, controlling artistic, intellectual, military, industrial, and agricultural policies. Mao's face became familiar throughout the world. Pictures of him appeared everywhere in China. Young and old learned his slogans and studied his writings. His writings, particularly on guerrilla warfare and the role of peasants in communist revolutions, were studied and used by revolutionaries outside China.

LOOKING IN *Leaders like Mao rise to power by promising a better life to their people. But like Mao, they end up being more oppressive than predecessors. Quality of life can only come from the Creator of life. Ezekiel draws a vivid picture of a river of life flowing from the house of God. That river turns death to life and brings happiness to humanity. It's not known when, or how, Ezekiel died. An ancient Jewish tradition says he was put to death by his own people because of his preaching. A tomb in Kifl, south of ancient Babylon, is claimed to be that of Ezekiel. His influence on later Judaism was enormous. Some call him "the father of Judaism."*

LOOKING OUT

1. **Life always starts with the Creator. Ezekiel sees a river that starts at God's sanctuary. The Giver of Life has chosen to offer help to humanity from His sanctuary.**
2. **Grace grows greater the further we reach out to touch a world God loves. Ezekiel begins to follow the river, only to find the more it goes, the deeper and wider it flows.**
3. **Death turns to life when we give ourselves to God. All that has been touched by the water from the Temple blossoms and thrives. Trees grow beside this river of life.**
4. **The impossible becomes possible when God is in us. The life-giving river does the impossible; it turns the Dead Sea into a living ocean full of fish for mankind.**
5. **Our world will grow rich and free when we give ourselves to God. Trees of all kind grow by the river with their fruit for food and their leaves for healing.**

LOOKING UP *Thank You, Lord. You not only offer salvation but healing for our hurts. Help me, Lord, to be vitally involved in the healing of my world by introducing others to my Lord.*

GOOD MEN

SEPTEMBER 10

Daniel 1-3

LOOKING BACK "Gunsmoke," TV's longest running western, premiered on this day in 1955. When the show moved from radio to television, John Wayne was offered the role of Matt Dillon. He turned it down and recommended James Arness as the lead character. Other main regulars included Amanda Blake, Dennis Weaver, and Milburn Stone. "Gunsmoke" was incredibly popular, both as a half-hour and hour-long show. The weekly program was the number-one rated series for four seasons and a top ten hit for six seasons. The popularity of "Gunsmoke" had much to do with the fact that Marshall Dillon was a good man who could always be counted on.

LOOKING IN *Even in a perverse society, good men are usually greatly admired. Daniel was such a man. This young man of nobility was taken captive by Nebuchadnezzar, king of Babylon, and elevated to high rank in the Babylonian and Persian kingdoms. The Babylonians sought to remove all vestiges of Daniel's nationality and religion. For this reason, they sought to change the name of Daniel to Belteshazzar. Daniel was transported from Judah to Babylon in his early youth at the battle of Carchemish, 605 B.C. We don't know his precise age at the time. We do know he was trained in the arts, letters, and wisdom and loved God passionately.*

LOOKING OUT

1. God has us at the right place at just the right time. Even though Daniel would have preferred to be in Jerusalem, God had him in Babylon to minister to Nebuchadnezzar.
2. God gives us wisdom to deal with difficult people and situations. Daniel used "wisdom and tact" when he approached the commander of the king's guard.
3. Prayers open us to hear God's heart and direction. After Daniel had asked for time to interpret Nebuchadnezzar's dream, he asked his friends to join in prayer.
4. Praise must always be part of the prayer process. Daniel understood that his prayer was not complete until he praised God for answering his desperate plea.
5. When God gives us His Word, it makes us as bold as a lion. Daniel stood unafraid before the ruthless pagan king, because he knew God had filled his mouth with truth.

LOOKING UP *Help me, Lord, always to ask for Your wisdom when I am faced with difficult situations and people. May I always remember to praise You for Your loving care.*

CONTRASTS

SEPTEMBER 11

Daniel 4-6

LOOKING BACK David Herbert Lawrence was born on this day in 1885. This English writer delighted in shocking society through his works. For example, his frank discussion of sexual passion shocked many readers, and some of his novels were considered obscene. Lawrence's most famous novel, *Lady Chatterley's Lover*, published in 1928, was banned from publication in the United States until 1944, when a shortened version appeared. The complete novel was not published in the United States until 1959. Lawrence urged men and women to follow their instincts, not the norms of society. He is known for advocating hedonism.

LOOKING IN *Standing stark against the likes of Lawrence is the Jewish hero, Daniel. This remarkable individual lived in Babylon, from the end of the 600's B.C. to the late 500's B.C., and gave us the book of Daniel. In Jewish forms of the Bible, the book of Daniel is part of a collection called the Writings. Christian editions include it in a group called the Prophets. Daniel's book is divided into two parts. Chapters 1-6 contain six stories that deal with historical events over a period of almost 50 years in Babylon and emphasize Daniel's loyalty to his faith. Chapters 7-12 include stories of four visions. In captivity, God had not forgotten His own.*

LOOKING OUT

1. **Believers should be the best employees. Daniel was so faithful on his job that he rose to the top. King Darius planned to set him in authority over all the kingdom.**
2. **Jealousy and greed breed trouble and conflict. The satraps were jealous of the favor Daniel had and lusted after his power. They sought ways to destroy him.**
3. **Believers should so live that only false accusations can be made against them. Daniel's life was so circumspect that the satraps could not charge him with any wrongdoing.**
4. **God shuts the mouths of lions when our ways please Him. Even though thrown into a den of hungry lions, Daniel couldn't be touched.**
5. **Those who seek to destroy will themselves be destroyed. The satraps who planned Daniel's death were exposed and lost their lives because of their evil.**

LOOKING UP *Help me, Lord, to be the best employee possible, since I know this will please You. Thank You for reminding me that my work is "unto You."*

KINGDOMS

SEPTEMBER 12

Daniel 7-9

LOOKING BACK Nikita Khrushchev became the ruler of the Soviet Union on this day in 1953, preparing the way for his dictatorship. He would achieve that goal in 1958 and lead the Soviet Union until he was ousted in 1964. As Khrushchev rose through the ranks on his way to the top, a number of Communist Party officials became jealous of his growing power. However, he managed to remove them from their jobs. On March 27, 1958, Khrushchev replaced Bulganin as premier of the Soviet Union. Khrushchev became a strong dictator. As a dictator, he had little pity for weaker nations and his political enemies. He was greatly feared for many years but finally fell.

LOOKING IN *Daniel saw the rise and fall of great earthly kings and kingdoms. The second part of his book deals with future events and the end of time as we know it. The first six chapters contain remarkable stories of God's deliverance, reminding the exiles that God had not forgotten them in their troubles. Now, Daniel looks to the future for both Israel and the world at large. Chapter seven is a colorful preview of history as Daniel sees four beasts who represent the four coming empires. Chapter eight is a vision of the ram and the he-goat, focusing on the second and third empires. Chapter nine reveals Daniel's 70 weeks in the eternal plan of God.*

LOOKING OUT

1. **Kingdoms come and go, but God's Kingdom lasts forever. Daniel sees four massive world powers that are to come and fall before the end of time.**
2. **At times, it may seem that believers are losing their battle against evil. Daniel sees the fourth world power defeating the saints. History records the veracity of this prophecy.**
3. **When God joins our battles, we always win. Daniel sees in his vision that God's people are losing until the Ancient of Days steps in to help.**
4. **God has destined us to win, not lose. The kingdoms under the whole heaven will one day be handed over to the saints of God.**
5. **Some spiritual revelations are for private consumption, not for public proclamation. Daniel is troubled by what he sees but keeps the matter to himself.**

LOOKING UP *Thank You, Lord, for telling us time and again that the evil of this world will one day come to an end. I hold on to Your promises because You are truth.*

SHADOW

SEPTEMBER 13

Daniel 10-12

LOOKING BACK Physician Walter Reed was born on this day in 1851. He served as an army surgeon for 20 years and as a professor at the U.S. Army Medical College. Best known for his research on Yellow Fever, Reed's daring experiments proved the disease could be controlled. He also discovered how to control typhoid fever. During the Spanish-American War in 1898, Reed became chief of a commission to study the origin and spread of that disease in Army camps. His experiments showed that flies were the primary carriers of the infection and that dust and uncleanliness helped spread it. The Walter Reed Army Medical Center is named for him.

LOOKING IN *The shadow of a good man like Dr. Reed falls far into the future. Daniel's long shadow still affects our thinking centuries after he is gone. His prophecies of the end time are especially meaningful at this time in history. Daniel served Nebuchadnezzar and was in Babylon when the forces of Cyrus, the Persian, captured Babylon. Successively, Daniel was a high governmental official during the reigns of Cyrus and Cambyses. He served, during his old age, into the reign of Darius I, the son of Hystaspes. Daniel would probably have celebrated his 100th birthday during the reign of Darius. All through his life, Daniel remained faithful to God.*

LOOKING OUT

1. **Conflict against evil will intensify during the end time. Daniel has a vision of the last days in which he sees a powerful antichrist rising in opposition to believers.**
2. **Martyrdom will increase as the dark days grow darker. Daniel says God's people will instruct many, but for a time they will have to forfeit their lives for their faith.**
3. **Some believers will fall victim to sin in the last days, but God will use this time to purify them. Daniel says that those leaders who fall will be made spotless by our Lord.**
4. **God's calendar is firmly set and the judgment of evil will come. Daniel underlines the fact that the end will come at God's appointed time, holding man accountable.**
5. **In spite of his power, the antichrist will be brought down. Daniel ends his ominous prophecy by saying, "Yet he will come to his end, and no one will help him."**

LOOKING UP *Help me to remember, Lord, that You have time in Your hands, and one day evil will fall. May I remember that You take very special care of all those who remain faithful to You.*

UNFAITHFUL

SEPTEMBER 14

Hosea 1-6

LOOKING BACK "The Waltons," television's epitome of the ideal family, premiered on this day in 1972. During its nine-year run, the show spawned nearly a dozen spin-offs. The drama was based on writer Earl Hammer Jr.'s experiences growing up during the Great Depression in rural Virginia. It began as a TV movie, "The Homecoming," which was so well-received that it was turned into a weekly series covering the years 1933 to 1943. In spite of the difficulties of those depression years, "The Waltons" nearly always projected happiness and well-being. While the series was popular, its depiction of family life was highly idealized and—many thought—unrealistic.

LOOKING IN *Almost everyone wishes his family was like the Waltons, but that just isn't the way it is. The Bible is brutally honest about the problems many of its characters had in their marriages. Perhaps the most vivid example is the ill-fated union of Hosea and Gomer. Even God's prophets were not immune from betrayal, heartbreak, and separation. Hosea's marriage and family life dominate chapters 1 through 3 and surface from time to time in the remainder of the book. Primary interest is not in Hosea and his family, but in God and His family. Interpreters of Hosea must remember the material serves as symbolism of God's relationship to Israel.*

LOOKING OUT

1. **Marital problems bring out the worst in a person. Hosea is so hurt and angry with his wayward wife that he is brutal in his verbal abuse toward her.**
2. **Marital problems trap the children in the crossfire. Tragically, Hosea involves his innocent children angrily insisting, "Rebuke your mother, rebuke her..."**
3. **Marital problems drive people to destructive threats against each other. Hosea threatens to strip Gomer naked, turn her into a parched land, and slay her with thirst.**
4. **Marital unfaithfulness is so destructive that it requires tough love to correct it. Hosea cuts off his support to Gomer to force her to come to her senses.**
5. **Marriage requires that we do all we can to forgive and work through problems. In spite of his hurt, Hosea speaks of his great love for Gomer and hope for their future.**

LOOKING UP *Help me, Lord, to stay faithful and true to You and to the one You have given to me. May I always remember that adultery is not entertainment–it is disaster.*

PRESENCE

SEPTEMBER 15

Hosea 7-14

LOOKING BACK Greenpeace, the controversial environmental organization, was founded on this day in 1971. Committed to a green and peaceful world, the organization was started by 12 members of the "Don't Make a Wave" committee of Canada, when the boat *Phyllis Comeback* sailed to Alaska to protest U.S. nuclear testing. Some may disagree with its specific goals, but the organization's idea is good. Greenpeace's basic principle is "that determined individuals can alter the actions and purposes of even the overwhelming powerful by 'bearing witness'–drawing attention to an environmental abuse through their mere unwavering presence, whatever the risk."

LOOKING IN *Hosea was an unwanted presence in the courts of Israel's rulers, since he was always calling them to task for their unfaithfulness. His "bearing witness" made the sinners uncomfortable, but they could not still the voice of this passionate prophet. Yet they refused to repent. Hosea's ministry was in the northern kingdom of Israel from about 745 to the 730's or 720's B.C., during a period of great turmoil and uncertainty. The prophet had witnessed the repeated killings and successions of kings. Many people worshiped pagan gods. Hosea regarded such worship as unfaithfulness to God (spiritual adultery) and warned that evil would result.*

LOOKING OUT

1. **Selfishness breeds deception. Hosea says, "Israel was a spreading vine; he brought forth fruit for himself." This preoccupation with self led the nation to deception.**
2. **When people don't keep their word, all society suffers. Hosea says people had made promises they wouldn't keep. As a result, lawsuits grew like poisonous weeds.**
3. **When we return to God, we begin to see His enduring love. Hosea tells the people to sow righteousness, and then they will reap the fruit of God's unfailing love.**
4. **Sin blinds our eyes to reality. The prophet explains that they had planted wickedness, reaped evil, and eaten the fruit of deception. Sin always blinds our minds.**
5. **God wants us to lean on Him, not on our own strength or the help of others. Hosea says Israel would see defeat since they constantly refused to take God into their life.**

LOOKING UP *Help me, Lord, to stifle my selfishness and live expressing true love and care for others. May I always be wise enough to keep Your Word and live it out in my life.*

SEPTEMBER 16

SELF-SERVING

Joel 1-3

LOOKING BACK One of history's most malevolent persons died on this day in 1498. Tomas de Torquemada, as Inquisitor-General of Spain, ordered more than 10,000 people to be burned at the stake because they didn't agree with his religious views. He used the Inquisition for religious and political reasons, believing punishment of heretics and non-Christians—chiefly Jews and Muslims—was the only way to achieve political unity in Spain. Greatly feared and hated by millions, he persuaded Ferdinand and Isabella to rid Spain of Jews. More than a million families were driven from Spain during that time. The country never recovered from the resulting decline.

LOOKING IN *Many religious leaders in Joel's Israel were just as self-serving as Torquemada. For this reason the prophet proclaims that God's judgment has fallen on the nation. He says that the "natural" plague of locusts was really "supernatural." We know little of the personal life of the prophet. He probably lived in Jerusalem since he expresses an avid interest in the city. Joel's repeated references to Zion, his call to the people to assemble for worship, and his interest in the Temple rituals and sacrifices indicate this. Although the book has only 70 verses, some 20 references to and quotations from other prophets attest to his important prophetic position.*

LOOKING OUT

1. Sometimes natural disasters are really supernatural. Joel sees the seemingly natural devastating locust plague as a direct judgment of God on Israel.
2. Judgment doesn't let up until we have acknowledged our wrong. Joel talks of the waves of locusts coming one after another and admonishes the people that this is a wake-up call.
3. Our reaction to pain should be careful soul-searching and repentance. Joel tells the leaders to put on sackcloth and ashes in humble repentance.
4. God always responds in love, acceptance, and forgiveness when we repent. Joel defines the character of God by saying He is gracious and compassionate.
5. God can, and will, restore the wasted years when we come to him. Joel says the Lord will restore to Israel the years the locust had eaten.

LOOKING UP *Help me, Lord, to search my heart so I can make sure all sin is purged and my life pleases You. May I always remember that You do restore the years the locusts have eaten.*

RIGHTEOUSNESS

Amos 1-5

LOOKING BACK The Battle of Antietam, the bloodiest day of the American Civil War, occurred on this day in 1862. The brutal confrontation was sparked when the Confederacy hoped to gain European recognition by winning a victory in Union territory. To accomplish this objective, General Robert E. Lee invaded Maryland, taking up a position at Sharpsburg, a town on Antietam Creek. Union forces soon attacked. Lee's force of about 40,000 men suffered heavy losses and had to retreat to Virginia. When the battle was over, nearly 25,000 men were killed or wounded. Because Lee had retreated, the North called Antietam a Union victory.

LOOKING IN *Death and destruction always occur when there is injustice. Amos cried out against injustice in ancient Israel. Just as the American Civil War was fought over the issue of slavery, Amos said sweeping death and destruction would come to his nation if gross social evils were not corrected. Amos was the first prophet to have his sayings collected into a single work. Also, he expressed for the first time in prophetic literature the idea that there is one God for all humanity, for both Israel and the other nations. Amos was a native of the southern kingdom of Judah and was active at the shrine of Bethel in the northern kingdom of Israel.*

LOOKING OUT

1. **Life can only come from the Source of Life. God encourages the people by saying, "Seek me and live." Life apart from God will end in sure destruction.**
2. **We can only be safe if we get out of the path of God's judgment. Amos reminds Israel that God is sweeping through like a fire that no one can quench.**
3. **Righteous living requires that we hate evil, love good, and maintain justice. Amos angrily accuses the leaders of condoning sin and taking advantage of the powerless.**
4. **God will judge all sin, not just those sins we detest. Amos says the religious leaders look forward to the "Day of the Lord," not knowing they will suffer judgment.**
5. **Religious form without substance is repulsive to God. Amos announces that God hates their acts of worship because they are insincere.**

LOOKING UP *Help me, Lord, to love good, hate evil, and be just in all my dealings. May I always live in the light of Your coming, knowing I will give account of my life.*

LOST

SEPTEMBER 18

Amos 6-9

LOOKING BACK On September 18, 1793, President George Washington laid the Capitol cornerstone, in Washington D.C., with a Masonic ceremony. A year earlier, the government had held a contest for a Capitol design. William Thornton, an American doctor and amateur architect, submitted the winning entry. The cornerstone laying was the first and last time the engraved silver-plated stone was seen. During the extension of the east front of the Capitol in 1958, an unsuccessful effort was made to find it. In spite of all searches with our modern technology and equipment, this very important piece of American history remains lost.

LOOKING IN *Amos said that a cornerstone of Israel's faith had also been lost. That cornerstone was God's command to take care of the poor and vulnerable. In their consuming greed, the nation had neglected this cardinal fact of faith. Amos' preaching so infuriated the leadership that they tried to kill the prophet. Amaziah was especially anxious to shut Amos up. However, the prophet had God's authority for his words and could not be silenced. Amaziah would die in exile. The invading army would abuse Amaziah's wife, kill his children, and seize his land. It is an awesome thing to oppose God's message or try to do away with those God sends to warn His people.*

LOOKING OUT

1. **Satan always tries to stop what God is doing. Amos preached God's Word to Israel, upsetting the evil one. Satan inspired Amaziah to oppose Amos.**
2. **Opposition to God's Word and work sometimes comes from unexpected places. Amaziah, a priest, should have known better than to fight Amos.**
3. **One who speaks God's Word often finds himself *persona non grata*. Amaziah tried to chase Amos from the country because he didn't like the prophet's message.**
4. **If God has called us, criticism won't stop us. Amos stood firm in his conviction. He knew he was following God's specific orders.**
5. **Critics of God's spokesmen stand on dangerous ground. Amaziah would pay dearly for his attempt to sabotage God's message.**

LOOKING UP *Lord, help me to be wise enough not to criticize those whom You have called. May I live so close to You that I am able to quickly recognize those You have anointed.*

DEVASTATION

SEPTEMBER 19

Obadiah 1

LOOKING BACK Devastating Mexico City earthquakes shook the world's largest city on this day in 1985. Mexico City is the chief city in one of the world's most populous urban centers. More than eight million people live in Mexico City, while about 15 million live in the city's metropolitan area. Nearly 10,000 persons perished in the earthquakes that registered 8.1 and 7.5, respectively, on the Richter scale. Damage to buildings was estimated at more than $1 billion, and 100,000 homes were destroyed or severely damaged. People from many countries converged on Mexico City to assist the earthquake victims. This was one of the worst disasters in Mexico's history.

LOOKING IN *Obadiah traveled to Edom to warn the people that God would bring devastation on them because of their active hostility against Israel. The Edomites were very proud people and didn't believe they could ever be threatened because of their secure position. Edom covered the area southeast and southwest of the Dead Sea, on opposite sides of the Arabah. The name Edom derives from a Semitic root which means "red" or "ruddy" and characterizes the red sandstone terrain of much of the area. The Edomites lived high in the crags of those rocks, which made them hard to attack. However, their position would not prevent God's punishment.*

LOOKING OUT

1. **Pride is deceptive. Obadiah notes that the pride of the Edomites had caused them to believe no one could ever touch them. They thought they could do as they pleased.**
2. **We never get so high that we can't be brought down. Obadiah says even though the Edomites live high in the clefts of the rocks, it will not help them.**
3. **We cannot stand aloof from heartbreak and escape unscathed. Obadiah accuses the Edomites of standing idly by as hostile enemies pillaged God's people.**
4. **To refuse to help someone in trouble is actually aiding and abetting the criminal. Obadiah condemns Edom because they refused to help when they could.**
5. **What we have done to others will be done to us. Obadiah informs the Edomites that God is watching carefully what they have done to His people and will repay them in kind.**

LOOKING UP *Help me, Lord, not just to voice my concerns for those in trouble but move to help them. Keep me humble lest pride destroy me as it did the Edomites.*

PREJUDICE

SEPTEMBER 20

Jonah 1-4

LOOKING BACK Avid reformer and writer Upton Sinclair was born on this day in 1878. He was famous as an enthusiastic supporter of socialism. Sinclair's best-known novel, *The Jungle,* was a powerful naturalistic exposure of the wretched sanitary and working conditions in the meat-packing industry. It led to the passage of America's first pure food laws. Sinclair also wrote several nonfiction books exposing what he saw as the corruption that capitalism created in various areas of American life. Sinclair authored *The Cup of Fury,* which attacked alcoholism. He helped organize the American Civil Liberties Union and the League for Industrial Democracy.

LOOKING IN *Unlike Sinclair, Jonah was a reluctant reformer. God called him to preach to Israel's bitter enemies, the Assyrians. Determined to escape this assignment, Jonah fled. However, God's long arm reached out to arrest the disobedient prophet, bringing him to his knees. In the last chapter of Jonah, God contrasts Jonah's sympathy for the plant with his lack of sympathy for Nineveh. According to most interpretations, the story contrasts the narrow concerns of Jonah with the universal concerns of God. The story calls on all of us to reject narrow nationalism and return to our mission of preaching God's forgiveness and mercy to all people.*

LOOKING OUT

1. You can run, but you can't hide. Jonah didn't like the assignment God gave him, so he ran. However, God dogged the footsteps of the disobedient prophet.
2. Our disobedience imperils others. Jonah's disobedience not only put his life in danger but also threatened the lives of those innocents on board the storm-tossed ship.
3. God does not compel us to go; He just makes us willing to go. God left Jonah in the belly of the fish for three agonizing days–long enough to make him willing.
4. No matter how wicked they have been, when people truly repent, God forgives and restores. Nineveh was the capital of the brutal Assyrian empire, but God forgave them.
5. God wants our hearts to be broken with the things that break His heart. Jonah complained because Nineveh wasn't destroyed. God dealt tenderly with the hard-hearted prophet.

LOOKING UP *Help my heart, Lord, to be broken with the things that break Your heart. Deal with any prejudices I have. I know those attitudes do not please You.*

EDUCATION

Micah 1-7

LOOKING BACK H.G. Wells was born on this day in 1866. The English novelist and historian drew on his lower middle class background in some of his finest novels. His training as a scientist is reflected in his imaginative science fiction stories. *The Time Machine* describes the adventures of a man who can transport himself into the future. Wells wrote about an invasion from Mars in *The War of the Worlds* and described a fictional utopia in *The Shape of Things to Come*. He also wrote *The Outline of History*, a story of the development of the human race. Wells once observed, "Human history becomes more and more a race between education and catastrophe."

LOOKING IN *The prophets spent their lives trying to help their nation avoid catastrophe by educating God's people. When these preachers of righteousness were heeded, things went well. When people ignored the prophets' words, catastrophe resulted. Micah was one of those prophets who tried to educate God's people. Micah lived about 700 B.C., during the reign of King Hezekiah of Judah. The first part of his book contains prophecies of punishment against Samaria and Jerusalem for the corruption of their leaders. The second part contains judgments focusing on the broken relationship between God and Israel and hopeful prophecies of God reestablishing His people.*

LOOKING OUT

1. **Those who hurt us the most are those from whom we expect it the least. Micah warns Israel, "A man's enemies are the members of his own household."**
2. **We may be knocked down, but we are never knocked out. Micah says, "Though I have fallen, I will rise. Though I sit in darkness, the Lord will be my light."**
3. **Knowing God's character helps us hold on in hard times. Micah understands that God is good, and one day the sorrows of the present will be past. He holds on.**
4. **Even though the day is dark, expect miracles. God's promise to His people is, "As in the days when you came out of Egypt, I will show you my wonders."**
5. **The love of God is greater far than tongue or pen could ever tell. Micah asks, "Who is a God like you, who pardons sins and forgives the transgression of the remnant...?"**

LOOKING UP *Help me, Lord, to know You better. In doing so, I will rest easier through difficult times. When I am deeply hurt by those near me, may I be quick to forgive.*

RIDES

SEPTEMBER 22

Nahum 1-3

LOOKING BACK Paul Revere is not the only American patriot who made a famous ride into history. Courageous Tacy Richardson made her dangerous ride on this day in 1777. On her favorite horse, Fearnaught, the 23-year-old woman galloped several perilous miles from her family farm to warn General George Washington of the approaching British troops led by General William Howe. As it turned out, the British crossing of the Schuylkill at Gordon's Ford was a feint to deceive Washington. It worked, causing Washington to withdraw his troops to Pottstown, clearing the way for General Howe to take over Washington's headquarters.

LOOKING IN *Nahum also made a courageous spiritual ride deep into enemy territory. He went there to warn Nineveh of impending destruction. Though the city had repented when Jonah preached there decades earlier, this time there would be no opportunity for salvation. The Assyrians had gone too far and done too much to God's people. They would not escape the wrath of a just God. Nahum's description of the city is so vivid that some believe he actually lived to witness Nineveh's fall. His striking images of God's wrath, along with images of God's refuge and safety, lend great power and immediacy to the prophet's dynamic words.*

LOOKING OUT

1. **Salvation is an ongoing experience. Nineveh had been spared destruction during Jonah's time. Now the nation faces destruction because they have forgotten God.**
2. **God deals with us in the direction we are going. Nahum says the Lord is good to those that trust Him but relentlessly pursues His foes into the darkness.**
3. **In spite of the darkness, we should rejoice that justice will be done. Nahum tells Israel, "No more will the wicked invade you; they will be completely destroyed."**
4. **The darkness of evil dissipates when the light of God's Son shines fully. Nahum says Nineveh is like locusts that fly away when the sun appears, never to be found.**
5. **There is a line over which we must not cross, or we are forever lost. Nahum offers no hope of redemption for wicked Assyria, who had sinned away her day of grace.**

LOOKING UP *Help me, Lord, to let my light shine so the darkness of evil will flee away. Thank You that justice will finally be done in our world, and the wicked will be punished.*

QUESTIONS

Habakkuk 1-3

LOOKING BACK President Ferdinand Marcos of the Philippines proclaimed martial law on this day in 1972. He claimed a severe threat of communism was taking over the Asian nation. Marcos served as president of the Philippines from 1965 to 1986. In 1973, the Philippines adopted a constitution that gave him broad powers as both president and prime minister. In 1978, Marcos took the title of prime minister while remaining as president. Marcos and his party were accused of widespread election fraud in a presidential election held in February, 1986. Anger was so great that he was forced to leave the country after widespread protests broke out against him.

LOOKING IN *Throughout Marcos' 21-year-reign, there were many questions about abuse of power. Often, he was viewed as a ruthless ruler who circumvented the freedom of citizens and became incredibly wealthy at their expense. During those hard years many wondered if they would ever get out from under his heel of oppression. Habakkuk also had many questions about the corrupt leadership of his nation. How long would a holy God put up with this evil? When God told him the Babylonians were coming to discipline His people, Habakkuk was shocked. How could God use a more wicked nation than Israel to discipline His people?*

LOOKING OUT

1. **At times, all of us feel that we speak but God doesn't listen. Habakkuk cries out, "How long, O Lord, must I call for help, but you do not listen?"**
2. **At times, we don't like or understand God's answers to our prayers. God tells Habakkuk that He will punish Israel, but the prophet doesn't approve of God's method.**
3. **God's timing is always right, even though it doesn't agree with our timing. God tells the prophet that the vision may seem long in coming, but it will arrive right on time.**
4. **No matter how bad things appear, God is still in control of our world. Habakkuk acknowledges, "But the Lord is in his holy temple; let all the earth be silent before him."**
5. **We must throw ourselves on God in trust, when we don't understand. The prophet says though all outward signs are dark, he will still trust in the Lord.**

LOOKING UP *Help me, Lord, to throw myself on You in trust regardless of the state of affairs around me. Many of Your ways I don't understand, but I do remember that You always know best.*

SELFISH

SEPTEMBER 24

Zephaniah 1-3

LOOKING BACK "Black Friday" was on this day in 1869. Financiers Jay Gould and James Fisk had caused the price of gold to rise sharply by buying large amounts of it in New York City. They planned to sell their gold for a big profit. The rise in gold prices caused a financial panic. To end the panic, President Ulysses S. Grant ordered the U.S. Treasury to sell $4 million of the nation's gold reserves. The sale caused the price of gold to fall sharply. Many people who had speculated on the rising price lost heavily, but Gould and Fisk made about $11 million. They had been warned of the Treasury's intentions and greedily moved to cash in on the panic.

LOOKING IN *Zephaniah told Israel there would come a "Black Friday." That would be "the day of the Lord," a time of great judgment for all those who had greedily taken advantage of the vulnerable and disobeyed God's Word. Zephaniah drew a sharp line between those who were being responsible with their lives and those who lived arrogantly and selfishly. The prophet predicted that a faithful few would be spared God's anger and be preserved in Jerusalem and in the rest of Judah. God would gather them there, and they would willingly accept His rule. The book of Zephaniah, only three chapters in length, looks toward the punishment of all sinful nations.*

LOOKING OUT

1. **Righteousness should be our number one goal. Zephaniah pleads with his backslidden people to turn from their sins and seek God's righteousness.**
2. **Humility must become a very high priority for us. Zephaniah calls for God's people to seek humility. In doing so, they place themselves under God's direction.**
3. **When we are under God's direction, we have His protection. Zephaniah speaks of coming judgment, but those who love God will stand strong under the stress.**
4. **Regardless of what the arrogant now say, the meek will inherit the earth. Zephaniah says the proud will be taken away. God will give what they leave to His followers.**
5. **Judgment Day will be a time of great rejoicing for those who love God. Those who live for God need not fear the day when God calls all of humanity into account.**

LOOKING UP *Help me, Lord, to passionately pursue righteousness and humility. I only want to serve You. May I always remember that when I stay in Your will, I am under Your protection.*

CHANGE

Haggai 1-2

LOOKING BACK Writer William Faulkner was born on this day in 1897. He ranks among the leading authors in American literature by changing the style and structure of the American novel. Many early critics of Faulkner denounced his books for their emphasis on violence and abnormality. *Sanctuary*, a story involving rape and murder, was most severely criticized. Later, the critics recognized that Faulkner had been criticizing the faults in society by showing them in contrast to what he called the "eternal verities." Faulkner said it is the writer's duty to remind readers of universal values such as love, honor, pity, pride, compassion, and sacrifice.

LOOKING IN *Haggai changed the style and structure of prophecy with his unique approach. Sharp-tongued and very direct, Haggai preached that the rebuilt Temple would signify the return of God's favor to the Jewish people and would bring them better times. He called upon the priests to purify certain religious activities. The old prophet addressed Zerubbabel, the Persian-appointed governor of Judah, about a glorious future age when God would destroy foreign kingdoms. Then, he said, a king, a descendant of the great King David, would reign. Haggai lived in Jerusalem about 520 B.C. The Jews had just returned from exile in Babylon.*

LOOKING OUT

1. We must get—and keep—our priorities straight. God said the Israelites excused their inactivity by saying it wasn't a good time for building. God begged to differ with them.
2. Misplaced priorities rob us of finances and fulfillment. Haggai challenged the people to consider their actions and see why they were broke, unfed, and unhappy.
3. God blesses us when we respond by being responsible. Israel's leaders listened to Haggai and responded positively to them. God began to release what He had withheld.
4. If we go with God, our future can be far greater than our past. Haggai encouraged the people by saying God's blessings on the second Temple would far exceed the first.
5. God can so use us that we impress positively all we touch. God promised Zerubbabel he would be a signet ring–a seal of God's authority and healing.

LOOKING UP *Lord, help me live so close to You that I touch everyone with Your love and tenderness. Help me keep my priorities straight, giving You first place in my life.*

PREOCCUPATION

SEPTEMBER 26

Zechariah 1-4

LOOKING BACK T.S. Eliot was born September 26, 1888, in St. Louis, Missouri. He ranks among the most important poets of the 1900's, departing radically from the techniques and subject matter of pre-World War I poetry. His poetry, along with his critical works, helped to reshape modern literature. Eliot studied at Harvard, the Sorbonne in Paris, and Oxford. While he was working as a bank clerk in England, Eliot's poems came to the attention of Ezra Pound, who encouraged Eliot and helped him with his poetry. Eliot lamented the preoccupation of his era by saying, "There never was a time so completely parochial, so shut off from the past."

LOOKING IN *Zechariah was also deeply disturbed about the preoccupation of his time. In 538 B.C., Cyrus the Great, emperor of the Persian Empire, had issued an edict allowing the Jews in Babylon to return to Jerusalem. Over the next two decades, many exiles took advantage of Persian leniency, returned home, and began to reestablish life in Jerusalem or Judah. They were to rebuild the Temple, but the work stopped due to opposition from those who had not gone into exile and from the local officials. Zechariah and Haggai told them they were wasting their resources on their own pursuits. God would not bless them until they got their priorities straight.*

LOOKING OUT

1. **God speaks in ways that we cannot easily forget. Zechariah receives a dramatic and dazzling vision of a man among the myrtle trees.**
2. **Many miss what is really important. In Zechariah's vision, all the world is at rest, unaware of the dynamic spiritual powers at work.**
3. **Justice always seems slow in coming. The angel in Zechariah's vision wondered how long God would withhold favor from Israel.**
4. **We should relax. God is still in control no matter how things appear. God speaks kind and comforting words to the questioning angel.**
5. **God has great plans for His children. Zechariah begins to understand that though things are not good at the present, God promises a bright future for His children.**

LOOKING UP *Thank You, Lord, for speaking so clearly to me that I cannot miss Your message. Help me always to be quick to obey Your commands and do Your will.*

PATROL

SEPTEMBER 27

Zechariah 5-8

LOOKING BACK On this day in 1964, the Warren Commission Report on the Kennedy assassination was issued. The long and detailed account assured Americans that Lee Harvey Oswald acted alone in the assassination of President John F. Kennedy on November 22, 1963. Congress reopened the investigation, and in 1979, the House Select Committee on Assassinations issued a report stating a conspiracy was most likely involved, although no trail of a conspiracy could be established. Since then, a spate of books has been published offering various theories as to who was responsible for Kennedy's death. The fact is no one really knows for sure.

LOOKING IN *Zechariah says God never has to wonder who does what or what happens to whom. He "patrols" the earth and no matter how it appears, God is still very much in charge. Therefore, we must be careful to act responsibly. Zechariah elaborates on a plan to rebuild a Temple and reestablish a community for the Israelites returning from exile. In the first section, a series of visions and oracles helps the Israelites understand and accept the new form of government by high priest and governor that the Persian authorities have permitted. The second section focuses on the struggles of the Jews after the Persian Empire experienced rebellions in Babylon and Egypt.*

LOOKING OUT

1. **God patrols the whole earth and remains firmly in charge. Zechariah's vision of the four chariots is like his first vision, saying God keeps watch over all the world.**
2. **We work, but it is Christ Who builds the church. In his vision, Zechariah sees the coming Messiah as the One Who builds the Temple of God.**
3. **Jesus is not only our High Priest but also the King of our life. Zechariah's vision proclaims the coming Messiah as the One Who brings together the roles of priest and king.**
4. **We receive help from unexpected places and people when we work in cooperation with God. Zechariah tells Israel that faraway people will help in rebuilding.**
5. **All of God's promises are fulfilled for those who diligently obey. Zechariah knows God's blessings are directly tied to how well we respond to His Word.**

LOOKING UP *Help me, Lord, to make You the King of my life, not just the One Who has forgiven my sins. Thank You for sending me help from unexpected places when I am in crisis.*

HOPE

SEPTEMBER 28

Zechariah 9-11

LOOKING BACK Confucius, the most influential and respected philosopher in Chinese history, was born on this day in 551 B.C. From about 100 B.C. to the revolution of 1911, the ideas of Confucius served as the single strongest influence on Chinese society. Millions of people in China, Japan, Korea, and Vietnam honor Confucius as others honor founders of religions. However, Confucianism has no organization or clergy. It does not teach a belief in a deity or the existence of life after death. Rather, it stresses moral and political ideas. It emphasizes respect for ancestors and governmental authority and teaches that rulers must govern according to high moral standards.

LOOKING IN *Unlike Confucianism, the Bible offers hope, not only in this life but in the life to come. Zechariah lets his people know they are "prisoners of hope" and, as such, have a great responsibility as God's "chosen" ones. The message of Zechariah may be summarized under two headings: prosperity and purification. Simply put, God promised the people of Judah and Jerusalem prosperity if they purified themselves from sin. This message is found in the first six chapters of the book of Zechariah. Those chapters are written in the form of eight visions, with two messages of exhortation. The later chapters deal with purification and holiness.*

LOOKING OUT

1. **No matter how dark the present, we can rejoice because God has a good future for us. Zechariah tells his discouraged nation that God will send the Messiah to them.**
2. **Sometimes we miss God's gifts because our expectations are not based on His Word. Many missed the Messiah because they were ignorant of God's Word.**
3. **Past patterns of bad behavior can be broken and new life given. Zechariah tells us that we are not prisoners of our past but are now "prisoners of hope."**
4. **God gives back to us far more than the devil has stolen. Zechariah gives God's promise: "I announce that I will restore twice as much to you."**
5. **When we read "the back of the book," we see that we win. Zechariah speaks of judgment and hard times on the disobedient, but the righteous will flourish.**

LOOKING UP *Help me, Lord, to always remember You have good plans for me. Thank You for giving me hope. Help me to always let my expectations be in accordance with Your Word.*

MESSIAH

SEPTEMBER 29

Zechariah 12-14

LOOKING BACK The first public knowledge of England's famed Scotland Yard occurred on this day in 1829. When the new officers appeared, there was jeering, abuse, and disapproval from political opponents. The Greater London Metropolitan Police had been established by an act of Parliament at the request of Home Secretary Sir Robert Peel, after whom the London police officers became known as "bobbies." Scotland Yard, the site of the first headquarters near Charing Cross, soon became the official name of the force. Public sentiment against Scotland Yard soon turned from disapproval to great confidence.

LOOKING IN *Zechariah predicted that Israel's Messiah would also be met with jeering, abuse, and disapproval when He first appeared. However, the prophet proclaimed the day would come, when all men everywhere would bow down to Him. These chapters picture God strengthening His people for a great battle against the nations. But in the midst of triumph there is national mourning for "him whom they have pierced." Many scholars see this as repentance for the crucifixion of our Lord and as the nation's turning to Christ. The final chapter pictures the last great battle against evil. God Himself will appear, ushering in perpetual day for his children.*

LOOKING OUT

1. **When we recognize Jesus as the Messiah, a fountain is opened to cleanse us from sin. Zechariah says the people will one day recognize our Lord as Lord.**
2. **When Jesus comes into our hearts, there is room for none other but Him. Zechariah says that when Israel accepts the Messiah, all other idols will be banished.**
3. **When Christ comes into our hearts, we listen to none but those teachers who passionately love Him. False teachers no longer can sway one who is in love with the Lord.**
4. **When Christ comes, all impurities are taken from us. When Jesus becomes Lord of our world, all evil influences will be purged and righteousness restored.**
5. **Even though He has been rejected by many, one day every knee will bow to the Lordship of Jesus Christ. One day all men everywhere will accept the Messiah.**

LOOKING UP *Lord, help me to be faithful to the very end. I long for the day all the world will bow at Your feet. In the meantime, help me to work my best and be all You want of me.*

CHAOS

SEPTEMBER 30

Malachi 1-4

LOOKING BACK Rioting broke out on this day in 1962 when James Meredith became the first Black to enroll in the all-White University of Mississippi. He tried to register at the school in the fall, accompanied by federal marshals. Police and other state officials repeatedly barred his entrance. A large protest group that gathered on the campus rioted against Meredith and the marshals. Two people were killed. But Meredith succeeded in registering, and federal troops stayed on the campus to protect him until he graduated in 1963. In 1966, Meredith led a march in the South to encourage Blacks to vote. In Mississippi, a sniper shot Meredith, but he recovered.

LOOKING IN *Death and destruction result when God's laws are violated. Malachi knows Israel's social and religious sins. He warns that they cannot be blessed until they repent and return to God. He presents his case in seven arguments. Malachi means, "my messenger," or "my angel." Some people in ancient Israel believed that an angel wrote this book because of the name. We know nothing about Malachi other than what we are told in this book. He is not mentioned anywhere else in the Old or New Testament. The purpose of Malachi was to assure the people that God still loved them, but He demanded honor, respect, and faithfulness from them.*

LOOKING OUT

1. **God wants our very best, not our useless leftovers. Malachi chides the Israelites for their offerings of blemished sacrifices to God.**
2. **We are to offer God's advice, not our own ideas. Malachi tells the religious counselors that their lips should flow with the Word of God, not their own opinions.**
3. **God hates divorce, but not the divorced. Malachi shames the Israelites because they are divorcing the wives of their youth to marry younger pagan women.**
4. **How we deal with God financially opens or shuts the windows of heaven. Malachi begs the people to tithe. He says God will bless them beyond measure for their obedience.**
5. **The more we know Christ, the fewer fears we have. Malachi says of Him, the "Sun of Righteousness" rises with healing in His wings.**

LOOKING UP *Help me, Lord, to let You have full leadership of my life, and may I always give You my very best. May I be faithful with the resources You have so graciously given me.*

OCTOBER

A Busy Month for the Earth's Janitors

Sparrows and other "seedeaters" can be considered the earth's janitors during this bountiful month of October, cleaning up the earth before the onset of winter. This is the month when the fields and meadows are rich with weed seeds. Sparrows, mice, and other "seedeaters" grow fat, eating the millions of weed seeds that might otherwise damage the next year's crop. In the North Temperate Zone, the first frost usually occurs in October. Farmers finish harvesting most crops as the weather begins to change. October's cool weather is most usually interrupted by several days of warm, hazy sunshine. Leaves change to brilliant crimson, russet, and gold. Wild asters, goldenrod, and fringed gentians bloom. The frost kills many insects. Most birds have left for the South, but sparrows are fond of October.

October is the 10th month of the year according to the Gregorian calendar. Its name comes from the Latin word for eight. October was the 8th month in the early Roman calendar. It later became the 10th month when the ancient Romans moved the beginning of the year from March 1 to January 1. October has had 31 days since the time of the Roman emperor Augustus. In the Jewish calendar, our month of October is actually part of the Jewish months of Tishri and Marcheshvan. Plowing and grain planting take place in Israel during this time of the year. The "first rains" mentioned in Deuteronomy also occur in Israel during the latter part of our October.

When the Jews returned from Babylonian Exile, they brought with them the names of the Babylonian calendar, at the same time counting the new year from the spring. Although the rabbis returned to an autumnal new year, Judaism retains these Babylonian names.They are: Nisan (March-April); Iyyar (April-May); Sivan (May-June); Tammuz (June-July); Ab (July-August); Elul (August-September); Tishri (September-October); Marcheshvan (October-November); Chislev (November-December); Tebeth (December-January); Shebat (January-February); Adar (February-March). During this month of October, we start reading the New Testament, moving from the Gospel of Matthew through John 10.

CONTROL

OCTOBER 1

Matthew 1-4

LOOKING BACK Babe Ruth called his famous shot on this day in 1932. In the fifth inning of game three of the World Series, with a count of two balls and two strikes and with hostile Cub fans shouting at him, Babe Ruth pointed to the center-field bleachers in Chicago's Wrigley Field. He followed up by hitting a soaring home run high above the very spot to which he had gestured. With that homer, Ruth squashed the Cubs' hopes of winning the game, and the Yankees went on to sweep the series. For more than a half century, controversy has raged as to whether Ruth really did call the shot or just made some gesture. Even some of the eyewitnesses disagree on the matter.

LOOKING IN *No one can disagree with the fact that Jesus called all the shots during the wilderness temptation. Satan threw all he had at our Lord, but Jesus never lost control of the situation. He proved Himself Lord of grinding temptation. Matthew first records this remarkable confrontation between Satan and our Lord. Matthew was a tax collector whom Jesus called to be an apostle. He is the same person Mark calls Levi, and thus the son of Alphaeus. James, the son of Alphaeus, is also listed among the apostles. This would indicate that both Matthew and his (half) brother were in close association with Jesus.*

LOOKING OUT

1. At times, it is God's will for us to be in places where we will be severely tested. The Holy Spirit led Jesus into the barren desert to be tempted by the devil.
2. Temptation always calls us to yield to the drives of the flesh. Jesus was desperately hungry when Satan challenged Him to turn the stones into bread.
3. Temptation prods us to waste our energy defending ourselves, our position, or our authority. Satan challenged Jesus to prove His Messiahship by a death-defying stunt.
4. Temptation lures us to paper the house while the house is on fire. The devil tempted Jesus to accept the power and prestige of this world rather than live for eternity.
5. God's Word defeats the devil's devices. Jesus always used the Scripture in its proper context to overcome the vicious attacks of the evil one.

LOOKING UP *Help me, Lord, to be true to You when I face temptation, knowing it will strengthen my faith. May I hide God's Word in my heart so that I might not fail or fall during these times.*

MANDATE

OCTOBER 2

Matthew 5-7

LOOKING BACK Hindu holy man and political leader Mohandas Gandhi was born on this day in 1869. He helped free India from British control by a unique method of nonviolent resistance. Gandhi is honored by the people of India as the father of their nation, which was granted independence in 1947. On January 13, 1948, at the age of 78, Gandhi began his last fast, hoping to end bloodshed among Hindu, Muslim, and other groups. Their leaders did pledge to stop fighting, and Gandhi broke his fast. Twelve days later, while on his way to a prayer meeting, Gandhi was assassinated by a Hindu fanatic who opposed his program of tolerance for all creeds and religions.

LOOKING IN *Even though he was a Hindu, Gandhi greatly admired Jesus. In fact, the Indian leader's favorite song was "When I Survey the Wondrous Cross." One of the main reasons Gandhi admired Jesus was because of His famous "Sermon on the Mount." In this remarkable sermon, our Lord outlines the constitution of His Kingdom. He starts with the astounding study on how to be happy. His words are completely contrary to all the world teaches or our carnal natures dictate. This sermon is the first and longest of the five sections in which Matthew gathers together the Lord's teachings. Here Jesus shows His followers how they ought to live in this world.*

LOOKING OUT

1. **Happiness is never what the world thinks. Jesus outlines the basis of true happiness in the Beatitudes. They run counter to what our modern culture teaches.**
2. **Our effectiveness for Christ is destroyed if we become corrupted with the world. Salt loses its "saltiness" when mixed with foreign elements.**
3. **There are no "secret-service" Christians. We are to be cities set on a hill that can be clearly seen by all. We are to be lights in this darkened world.**
4. **God's Word is eternal; it never changes. Jesus said that heaven and earth would pass away before the least part of God's Word would be nullified.**
5. **Those who live and teach God's Word are held in high esteem. Jesus said those who practice and share God's Word are called great in the Kingdom of Heaven.**

LOOKING UP *Help me, Lord, to live purely before You so I might become all You desire me to be. Give me strength to always be bold for You, never compromising my testimony.*

CONFUSION

Matthew 8-11

LOOKING BACK On this day in 1960, the Andy Griffith show premiered on television. It ran weekly for many seasons and is still viewed on reruns throughout the world. In fact, some 2,000 members of the "Andy Griffith Rerun Watchers Club" celebrate with festivities every year on this date. The stars of the show have gone on to other things, but many still see them in the gentle roles they portrayed so well. One reason the show is still popular is that it imagines a world of kindness, gentleness, and goodness. We love to laugh at Barney Fife and enjoy loveable Opie. Andy and Aunt Bea round out the cast, assuring that all is well and things always work out.

LOOKING IN *The real world is very much unlike television sitcoms. This is a world of hurt, anger, bloodshed, and turmoil. John the Baptist had no illusions about this evil world. His preaching got him into a lot of trouble, and he ended up in Herod's prison. Awaiting his fate, John became depressed. When his disciples visited, John asked them to go to Jesus to see if He was really the Messiah. Our Lord sent back assurance to the discouraged prophet and then gave him a wonderful compliment. John's practice of baptizing wasn't new; washings had long been part of Jewish piety. Gentile converts to Judaism washed themselves as a form of ceremonial cleansing.*

LOOKING OUT

1. **Hard times can drive us to doubt. John the Baptist had preached Christ's coming, but his present circumstances shook his faith. Jesus gave him assurance.**
2. **A ministry can be judged by its results. Jesus told John's disciples to report to John that prophesies in the Word were now coming to pass.**
3. **We must not question how God runs His business. Jesus told John's disciples to relay the message, "Happy is the person who is not offended in me."**
4. **All things point to Christ. Jesus said that John the Baptist and the prophets were good, but their mission was to prepare the way for the promised Messiah.**
5. **Wisdom is proved by her actions. Jesus noted that results make it very apparent whether we have moved in wisdom or foolishness.**

LOOKING UP *Father, forgive me for the times I have questioned the way You run Your business. Help me always to trust You, though I don't understand all that is happening.*

NEW AGE

OCTOBER 4

Matthew 12-13

LOOKING BACK A whole new age was ushered in on this day in 1957, when the Soviet Union launched Sputnik I. Actually, "Sputnik" was the name of a series of unmanned satellites launched by the Soviet Union. Sputnik I was the first artificial earth satellite, and it began the space age. It circled the earth once every 96 minutes at a speed of 18,000 mph, until it fell to the earth on January 4, 1958. The Soviet Union launched nine much larger Sputniks, from November 1957 to March 1961. The earliest of these carried the first space traveler, a dog named Laika. Sputnik I's launch also heated up the Cold War, promoting fear of the U.S.S.R.'s advanced technology.

LOOKING IN *Jesus launched a whole new age when He rocketed into Israel's religious life. He challenged the ideas and smugness of the arrogant religious leaders of the day who had so long distorted God's Word, putting God's people in bondage. The largest group of leaders feeling threatened was the Pharisees. They were masters at self-promotion and became livid when anyone dared disagree with their "exalted" ideas. Jesus immediately ran into conflict with these pompous religious leaders when His teachings countered their man-made ideas of holiness. They denigrated His miracles by claiming they were of Satan.*

LOOKING OUT

1. God used miracles to attract attention to Christ's deity. Jesus healed a demon-possessed man, causing the crowd to ask, "Could this be the Son of David (Messiah)?"
2. Preconceived ideas can keep us from truth and distort our thinking. The Pharisees were so angry at Jesus' teaching that they tried to explain the miracle away.
3. Error must be confronted with truth. Jesus knew the wicked hearts of the Pharisees and confronted them with, "Every kingdom divided against itself will be ruined."
4. We must be careful never to attribute God's work to that of the evil one. Jesus cautioned the critical Pharisees, saying it is dangerous to speak against the work of the Holy Spirit.
5. We don't have to listen long before we know what is in the heart of the speaker. Jesus said, "For out of the overflow of the heart the mouth speaks."

LOOKING UP *Help me, Lord, to be very careful in judging spiritual matters lest I offend God's precious Spirit. Give me wisdom always to confront error with Your truth.*

"UNBELIEVED"

OCTOBER 5

Matthew 14-16

LOOKING BACK "The Father of the Space Age" was born on this day in 1882. Largely ignored or ridiculed during his lifetime because of his dreams of rocket travel, Robert Hutchings Goddard's achievements in the field of rocketry were finally fully appreciated after his death. In 1919, his classic report was published in which he described the kind of rocket flight necessary to reach the moon. The article was met with such skeptical comments by the press that Goddard avoided further publicity. Rather, he continued his work in relative anonymity; designing, building, and launching the world's first liquid-propellant rocket in 1926.

LOOKING IN *Religious leaders of Jesus' day ridiculed Him and chose not to believe His messages. Even Peter audaciously rebuked Jesus because he didn't like what the Lord proclaimed. Only after His Lord's death and resurrection did Peter and the skeptics understand the Lord's words. From the first, Jesus's teachings brought Him into conflict with the Pharisees. Tradition, for them, was binding. They preferred the oral teachings of the rabbis over the written Word of God. Jesus never hesitated to denounce tradition whenever it watered down or undermined Scriptural principles. The conflict grew until the angry Pharisees demanded Christ's death.*

LOOKING OUT

1. Our loving Heavenly Father always prepares us for the future. Jesus started to share with His disciples how He would be killed by His enemies and then raised back to life.
2. Using human reasoning in spiritual matters deters God's work. Jesus sharply rebuked Peter because the big fisherman was not acting like a child of the kingdom.
3. When Christ bids us come, He bids us come and die. Jesus told His disciples that if they were to follow Him, it would mean personal denial and a cruel cross.
4. He is no fool who gives what he cannot keep to gain what he cannot lose. Jesus asked, "What good will it be for a man if he gains the whole world, yet forfeits his soul?"
5. Faith is not just what one thinks, feels, believes, or speaks—it's what one does. Jesus said that at the end of the age God will reward each man for what he has done.

LOOKING UP *Help me, Lord, to be a "doer" of Your will and Word, not just one who talks the talk. Make me ever willing to give my all for You and Your work.*

DANGEROUS

OCTOBER 6

Matthew 17-20

October

LOOKING BACK Egyptian president and Nobel Peace Prize recipient Anwar El-Sadat was killed by assassins in Cairo on this day in 1981. When Sadat was gunned down, he had been reviewing a military parade commemorating the 1973 Egyptian-Israeli War. At least eight other persons were reported killed in the attack. Sadat was bitterly hated by extremists because of the peace he brokered with Israel. In 1978, Middle East leaders met with President Carter at Camp David, Maryland, to discuss ways to bring peace to their war-torn region. Sadat and Israel's Prime Minister Menachem Begin reached an agreement that eventually led to a peace treaty.

LOOKING IN *Bringing peace between warring parties is never easy, and sometimes even dangerous. Yet, we are to seek reconciliation, not recrimination. Jesus gives us a difficult, but brilliant, approach for attempting reconciliation. This section of Matthew's Gospel contains our Lord's fourth teaching on Kingdom principles. He tells His disciples that His Kingdom works on different standards than those of the world. Status-seeking is out. Also, it is not "survival of the fittest" but caring for our weaker brothers and sisters that matters. Unlimited forgiveness is expected from those whom God has so graciously forgiven. Forgiveness is never easy but always necessary.*

LOOKING OUT

1. Our Lord desires that we reconcile with those who offend us rather than ignoring them or becoming bitter against them. He offers a formula for reconciliation.
2. One-on-one confrontation is the first step to reconciliation. When our brother or sister offends us, we are to go to them alone and talk openly about the offense.
3. If a stubborn, offending brother or sister refuses reconciliation, we are to take one or two others with us for a second loving and honest confrontation.
4. If an angry, offending brother or sister still refuses reconciliation, we are to explain the problem to the church so believers can assist in bringing peace between us.
5. If all of these reconciliation efforts fail, we are to consider the offender a disobedient person who has opted in rebellion to disobey God and His Word.

LOOKING UP *Help me, Lord, to always follow Your formula for reconciliation, no matter how uncomfortable it is. Forgive me for those times I have stubbornly refused to obey You.*

FRAUD

OCTOBER 7

Matthew 21-22

LOOKING BACK English bibliophile and literary forger James Thomas Wise was born on this day in 1859. He was considered one of England's most distinguished experts in bibliography until it was revealed that he also was a forger. This master criminal had fooled experts for many years. Wise had forged dozens of "first editions" and "unique" publications over a period of more than 20 years. Many of these items had been sold at high prices to collectors and libraries, but he was finally exposed. Some of his forgeries even purported to predate the real first editions. Wise's health broke when the 1934 exposure came, and he soon died in disgrace.

LOOKING IN *When Jesus cleansed the Temple, He exposed the money-changers for what they really were. They were not there to help the worshipers, as they claimed, but were frauds. They only wanted to rip off those who had come to pray. The dealers operated in the outer court of the Temple, the Court of the Gentiles. Jews from abroad were not allowed to use their own currency to pay the annual Temple dues. These greedy money-changers fixed an unreasonably high rate of exchange, taking advantage of the vulnerable. Jesus overturned their tables and drove them from the Temple, making healing and help available to those who needed it.*

LOOKING OUT

1. **God sets divine appointments for us. As Jesus approached Jerusalem, He instructed His disciples to keep such an appointment with the owner of a donkey.**
2. **Jesus is the "Prince of Peace," not the "King of War." Jesus chose an animal of peace to ride on Palm Sunday rather than a horse—an animal of war.**
3. **We must seek God's approval because human applause is deceptive. The same crowd that proclaimed Jesus as King would cry, "Crucify Him," just a few days later.**
4. **Satan always seeks to circumvent God's plan for His house. The church is to be a place of prayer, not a house of merchandise. Jesus cleared the Temple of money-grabbers.**
5. **When human selfishness is pushed aside, miracles occur. Once the Temple was cleansed of the money-grabbers, the blind and the lame could enter to be healed.**

LOOKING UP *Help me, Lord, to seek Your approval, not the applause of men. Use me in Your healing work. May I always remember that You set divine appointments for me.*

TALENTS

Matthew 23-25

LOOKING BACK Flying ace Eddie Rickenbacker was born on this day in 1890. He was the leading United States fighter pilot in World War I, shooting down 22 enemy planes and four balloons. Rickenbacker was a greatly talented man who was also a famed professional automobile racer, winning an international reputation. During World War II, Rickenbacker was a civilian inspector of American air bases abroad. On one inspection trip in 1942, his plane was forced down in the Pacific Ocean. Rickenbacker and six others survived on rubber rafts for 24 days before being rescued. In this crisis, the famed ace had to use all his talents to survive.

LOOKING IN *Not everyone has the talents of an Eddie Rickenbacker. However, all have been given a measure of "giftedness." Jesus outlined the responsibility we all have in using what God has invested in us. Our Lord said that those who refuse to use it, lose it, and their very souls! Jesus gave this important teaching while in Jerusalem. It was Spring, and people from far and near were crowding into the busy city for Passover. Lodging in the city was not easily available, so Jesus and His friends stayed at nearby Bethany. Each day, they walked the two miles into Jerusalem, over the shoulder of the Mount of Olives and down through the thick grove of trees.*

LOOKING OUT

1. **Every person has been given talent for a special purpose. Jesus told the parable of the talents to emphasize our responsibility and God's expectations of us.**
2. **Every person must discover his "giftedness" and use it to the limit of his ability. The man in the parable gave his workers talents but did not leave them specific instructions.**
3. **Even though it seems long in coming, there will be a day we must give an account of how we have used what God has given. The rich man returned "after a long time."**
4. **When we are faithful with the few responsibilities we have been given, God trusts us with more. The two faithful workers were rewarded and promoted.**
5. **It is evil to refuse to use what God has given us. The man who buried his talent is called wicked and cast into outer darkness. God expects a return on His investment in us.**

LOOKING UP *Help me, Lord, to discover my special "giftedness" and use it to the best of my ability. May I use what You have given me so I will hear You say, "Thou good and faithful servant..."*

CHANGE

OCTOBER 9

Matthew 26-28

LOOKING BACK Clarence Saunders changed America's way of life on this day in 1917. He was awarded a patent for a self-service method of operating a food store—the first supermarket. Early supermarkets sold only food, offered few services, and displayed merchandise in shipping containers. Now, supermarkets still sell a variety of food products, but many also stock general merchandise such as auto supplies, cleaning products, cooking utensils, and greeting cards. Some have banking and post office facilities and offer such services as menu-planning and baby-sitting. There are now over 30,000 supermarkets in the United States alone.

LOOKING IN *Jesus dramatically changed the whole face of faith when He gave His disciples the "Great Commission" just before He ascended into heaven. The new "age of evangelism" started with this commission. No longer were people to be passive in their beliefs but to actively and aggressively share the wonderful news of salvation. This commission also notes that witnessing is more than merely sharing one's testimony. Rather, it is making disciples of all people everywhere. Matthew, the most Jewish of all the Gospels, closes with a word from the Lord that throws His Kingdom open to people of every nation and all generations.*

LOOKING OUT

1. Faith is a decision. In spite of the overwhelming evidence of the resurrection, Matthew records, "When they saw him, they worshiped him; but some doubted."
2. Witnessing is far more than just telling our story. Jesus commissioned us to "go and make disciples of all nations." We must also mentor those to whom we give testimony.
3. We must make a clear public proclamation of our faith. Water baptism is publicly identifying with Christ and serving notice that we intend to be His disciples.
4. Obedience is a learned behavior. Jesus said we are to teach all followers of Him to obey everything He has commanded. Obedience doesn't come naturally.
5. No matter what we face or where we are, Christ will always sustain us. Jesus' last words to us were: "And surely I am with you always, to the very end of the age."

LOOKING UP *Help me, Lord, to accept the "Great Commission" as my personal commission from You. Thank You for counting me worthy to work for You.*

FAST MOVING

OCTOBER 10

Mark 1-3

LOOKING BACK Vice-President Spiro Agnew resigned on this day in 1973, becoming the first person in that position to resign while under criminal investigation. The only other vice-president to resign was John C. Calhoun, who left the office in 1832 after being chosen to fill a U.S. Senate seat from South Carolina. Agnew's resignation was part of the events occurring in the United States during the Watergate affair. Watergate was the biggest political scandal in U.S. history. It included various illegal activities designed to help President Richard M. Nixon win reelection in 1972, and resulted in Nixon's resignation 10 months after Agnew was forced to quit.

LOOKING IN *Mark's Gospel, like the events during Watergate, is fast-moving. While Matthew is formal and stately, Mark is bursting with life and full of action. Mark wrote his Gospel for Gentile Christians. He explained Jewish customs in detail for the benefit of readers unfamiliar with Judaism, and translated several Aramaic expressions for a Greek-speaking audience. His Gospel also contained many terms borrowed from Latin and written in Greek. Tradition places Mark in Rome, preserving the words of Peter for Roman Christians. According to tradition, Peter was martyred in Rome during the Neronian persecution.*

LOOKING OUT

1. **Prayer results in great spiritual power. Jesus always knew the Father's will because He communicated with Him on a daily basis.**
2. **Our Lord is deeply touched by our pain. The leper's awful plight filled our Lord with great compassion. He moved to relieve the sorrow and shame.**
3. **Cure is always the will of the Father. Jesus told the leper, "I am willing, be clean." Our Lord wants us to be well and whole.**
4. **God's miracles in our lives are powerful testimonies to others. Jesus told the lepers to go to the priests and show them so they would see and believe.**
5. **Disobedience hinders God's work. The leper's enthusiasm outweighed his obedience, hampering Christ's ministry. Because the leper disobeyed, Jesus could not enter the town.**

LOOKING UP *Lord, make me sensitive to the pain of others. Like You, may I always reach out to help the hurting. I know this pleases the Father.*

FICTION?

OCTOBER 11

Mark 4-5

LOOKING BACK When it comes to history, it is hard at times to separate fiction from fact, since writers can distort truth. Episcopal clergyman and traveling bookseller Mason Locke Weems was born on this day in 1759. He is best remembered for the fictitious stories he presented as historical fact. Among his best-known "fables" is the story of George Washington chopping down the cherry tree with a hatchet. Parson Weems' fictionalized histories delighted many readers who accepted them as true. They became immensely popular and were bestsellers for many years. Weems also wrote biographies of other leading Americans and several moral tracts.

LOOKING IN *Many skeptics would like to relegate the story of Jesus calming the storm to the arena of fictionalized history. However, this can't be done for there simply were too many witnesses to the event. The Sea of Galilee is really a freshwater lake nestled in the hills of northern Palestine. Its surface is nearly 700 feet below the level of the Mediterranean, some thirty miles to the west. Fed chiefly by the Jordan River, which originates in the foothills of the Lebanon Mountains, the Sea of Galilee is 13 miles long from north to south and eight miles wide. Its location makes it subject to sudden and violent storms, which are usually of short duration.*

LOOKING OUT

1. **Our Lord's commands do not depend on circumstances. Jesus told His disciples to take Him to the other side of the lake despite threatening weather conditions.**
2. **God never promises the absence of storms but assures safety during the stress. A storm appeared suddenly on the shallow lake, threatening the lives of the weary sailors.**
3. **When Christ speaks, the storms and stresses of this life abate. Jesus stood in the sinking boat and commanded the storm to stop. It obeyed the Master's voice.**
4. **Not only are we rescued by Christ's miracles, but others are saved. Mark records there were other boats along with theirs. They were also saved when the storm ceased.**
5. **We would have less stress if we would listen to the Lord's commands. Jesus had told the disciples to go across the lake, not to go out in the middle and drown.**

LOOKING UP *Help me, Lord, to trust You more, knowing that You can, and will, still the storms of my life. May I always remember that You have promised me safe passage in spite of the storms.*

DESTINY

OCTOBER 12

Mark 6-7

LOOKING BACK This is dubbed as "Destiny Day" by many who claim that Columbus discovered the New World on October 12. They are wrong; the real day of discovery was actually October 13. According to modern historians, Dutch sailor Piet de Stuini persuaded Columbus to change the ship's log to make it appear that October 12 was the date of the New World landing. Historians now think that Columbus altered the date for very practical reasons. He felt the 13th might have caused superstitious fear in other sailors or potential investors for later voyages. The change of dates was discovered and revealed years later by a history study group.

LOOKING IN *While some might be willing to change the facts for convenience or "practical" reasons, our Lord refused to bow to this kind of pressure. That refusal often got Him in trouble with those who vehemently opposed His message. This became most evident when our Lord visited His hometown synagogue in Nazareth. His uncompromising preaching was received with cold cynicism. There were desperate people who needed healing, but the negative environment prevented the Master from touching many of them. Mark says our Lord was amazed at their lack of faith. Tragically, the hometown folk missed the greatest opportunity ever offered them.*

LOOKING OUT

1. **Those who see Jesus as only a human teacher miss out. In Nazareth, the people only saw Jesus as a hometown boy who somehow dazzled people with His magic.**
2. **We are often offended by the things we don't understand. The people of Nazareth could not understand our Lord's power. Their reaction was to be angry with Him.**
3. **A negative environment is not conducive to faith. Mark reports that Jesus could only do a few miracles in Nazareth because of their resentment and unbelief.**
4. **To enter ministry is to learn to live by faith. Jesus sent His disciples out two by two, telling them to go in expectation of God's daily provision for them.**
5. **We are to shake off resentment against those who reject us and our message. Jesus told His disciples to shake the dust off their feet when they left a place of rejection.**

LOOKING UP *Help me, Lord, to create a pleasant and positive environment so faith can flourish. Forgive me for the times I have spread my doubt.*

TRANSFIGURED

OCTOBER 13

Mark 8-9

LOOKING BACK A woman who was transfigured from an ordinary housewife to a legend was born on this day in 1754. Mary Ludwig, better known as Molly Pitcher, traveled with her husband to fight in the Revolutionary War. She received half-rations in the Continental Army in return for cooking, washing, sewing, and doing other work. During the battle of Monmouth, her husband fell from a heatstroke. She took his place, helping his crew fire the cannon. For this action, she gained the nickname "Molly Pitcher," representative of all women who fought valiantly. Today, a monument honoring her, graces her burial plot in Carlisle, Pennsylvania.

LOOKING IN *Jesus was transfigured but not in the same sense as Molly Pitcher. The event took place shortly after the confession at Caesarea Philippi, the first passion prediction, and a discourse on the cost of discipleship. Jesus took Peter, James, and John to a mountain where the transfiguration occurred. Our Lord's personal appearance and that of His garments were changed. Moses and Elijah appeared and talked with Jesus. Remarkably, Peter, James, and John recognized the Old Testament characters though they had no previous personal description of them. The three disciples were so profoundly moved they could never doubt that Jesus was indeed the Messiah.*

LOOKING OUT

1. **God reveals Himself to those who stay close. Peter, James, and John were in the inner circle. Jesus invited them to accompany Him to the Mount of Transfiguration.**
2. **God fulfills our dreams even if it takes eternity to do so. Moses finally made it into the Promised Land. He and Elijah met on the mountain with the transfigured Christ.**
3. **Often we talk when we should be listening. Peter, awed by the transfigured Lord, blurts out, "Let's put up three shelters-one for you, one for Moses, and one for Elijah."**
4. **There is a time to keep silent and a time to share great spiritual moments. Jesus told the disciples not to tell of the transfiguration until after He was raised from the dead.**
5. **Often God's great work in our world is not seen until later. When the disciples asked about Elijah's return, Jesus said he had already come in the form of John the Baptist.**

LOOKING UP *Lord, help me stay very close to You that I might witness Your majesty, power, and presence. Make me wise enough to keep from speaking when I should be listening.*

SACRIFICE

OCTOBER 14

Mark 10-11

LOOKING BACK People will respond to a call for sacrifice. That became clear when John F. Kennedy proposed the Peace Corps on this day in 1960. Speaking impromptu, the presidential candidate asked several thousand students, "How many of you who are going to be doctors are willing to spend your days in Ghana? How many of you (technicians and engineers) are willing to work in the Foreign Service?" The response was so favorable that just 19 days later, Kennedy formally proposed establishing a Peace Corps. It became a reality in 1961. The idea of an "army" to work for peace was first suggested by the American philosopher William James in 1904.

LOOKING IN *One area where people need to respond in sacrifice is marriage. Jesus addressed marriage and divorce when the Pharisees tested Him with a legal question. Even though their question was not sincere, our Lord let it be known how God feels about the marriage union. God hates divorce, but He doesn't hate the divorced. The rabbis disagreed about divorce. Some allowed it for anything that displeased the husband, while others permitted divorce only on the grounds of unfaithfulness. Jesus went back to God's purpose for man and woman at the very beginning. That is the ideal. Moses' edict on divorce fell far short of God's desire for the family.*

LOOKING OUT

1. It's tragic to know the rules without knowing the Ruler. The Pharisees knew the laws of divorce but failed to recognize the One Who gave these laws to mankind.
2. God's laws were given to protect, not prosecute. God's laws on divorce were given to protect the sanctity of marriage, children, and the vulnerable spouse.
3. The one cause for divorce is "hardness of the heart." Any hurt or offense in marriage can be forgiven, but only if both parties are willing to lovingly work things out.
4. God builds the walls of marriage high so those inside will stay there, and those outside the marriage union cannot get inside; thus, the prohibition on easy divorce.
5. God desires that we have one mate and one God for life. Jesus said that marriage partners are to put each other first before all others and consider themselves one flesh.

LOOKING UP *Help me, Lord, to keep my marriage strong by obeying Your Word and following Your will. Help me to reach out in love to those who have been shattered by divorce.*

CRITICS

OCTOBER 15

Mark 12-13

LOOKING BACK German philosopher and classical scholar Friedrich Nietzsche was born on this day in 1844. He deeply influenced many philosophers, artists, and psychologists of the 1900's. Nietzsche also was a favorite of Adolf Hitler, who especially liked Nietzsche's contempt for the weak and his expectation of the ultimate triumph of a superman. Hitler fanned the flames of hell when he put into practice that horrendous philosophy. Nietzsche was also a severe critic of religion, especially Christianity. He proclaimed that "God is dead," and, consequently, religion could no longer serve as the foundation for societies' moral values.

LOOKING IN *Nietzsche wasn't the first critic of our Lord's teaching. The Pharisees and Sadducees tried their best to trick Jesus into making some fatal mistake so they could accuse Him of blasphemy, discredit Him, and force His death. However, at every turn, their evil purpose was thwarted. The Pharisees were the most numerous of the various Jewish parties, although Josephus stated that they numbered only about 6,000. They controlled the synagogues and exercised great control over the general population. The Sadducees were the aristocrats of the time. They were the party of the rich and the high priestly families, in charge of the Temple and its services.*

LOOKING OUT

1. **We should live so that even our enemies know we are people of righteousness. The enemies of Jesus had to admit, "Teacher, we know you are a man of integrity."**
2. **Truth is not a nose of wax to be molded differently for every person. The enemies of Jesus knew His teachings favored no one but were in accordance with the truth.**
3. **God can give us supernatural wisdom to confound our enemies. Jesus amazed His critics with His answer to their trick question about whether they should pay taxes.**
4. **Ignorance of the Bible precipitates ignorant questions. The Sadducees left red-faced when Jesus pointed out their obvious lack of knowledge of God's Word.**
5. **We must be careful to listen closely to our Lord's words. They reveal deep truth. Jesus noted that God's words about Himself reveal the truth of eternal life.**

LOOKING UP *Help me, Lord, to live such a good life so that those who hate me will see my integrity. Make me strong in the truth, standing firmly in Your Word.*

EXTRAVAGANCE

OCTOBER 16

Mark 14-16

LOOKING BACK Marie Antoinette, the beautiful queen of France, died on the guillotine on this day in 1793. Her frivolity and extravagance helped undermine the monarchy and bring about the bloody French Revolution. She was lively and lavish, and the stiff formalities of court life bored her, causing her to amuse herself with fancy balls, theatricals, and gambling. She urged dismissal of able officials who tried to reduce royal spending. Marie became unpopular and was blamed for the corruption of the French court. She lavished money on court favorites and paid no attention to France's financial crisis. Her selfishness finally brought her down.

LOOKING IN *Extravagance is not always bad; it does have its place. The woman who anointed Jesus with expensive perfume is an example of wise extravagance. As the Passover festival approached, events moved swiftly to a climax. Perhaps intuitively sensing the tragedy ahead, Mary poured out the precious perfume in a lavish, extravagant gesture of affection. The cost for the ointment was enormous (a working man earned one denarius a day). This luxury import was worth nearly a year's wages. Mary deeply loved our Lord and took that occasion to show her affection. It was a unique opportunity that earned her eternal recognition.*

LOOKING OUT

1. **Jesus goes to unexpected places to meet unlikely people. Our Lord is at the home of Simon the leper, an outcast of society. It is a surprising place for Him to be.**
2. **Love gifts to our Lord seldom make sense to practical-minded observers. The woman's elaborate gift of sacred expensive perfume raised eyebrows.**
3. **There are special moments in which we can express great love. We must take those times when they come, or they are lost forever. This was such a time in our Lord's life.**
4. **Our Lord takes special note of the great sacrifice made by those who love Him. Jesus said the woman who anointed Him would never be forgotten.**
5. **Great expressions of worship either inspire others or irritate them. Judas immediately went to the chief priests and set up the mechanism to betray our Lord.**

LOOKING UP *Help me, Lord, to somehow express my deepest love for You in a special, sacrificial way. May I always give You my very best-those things that are dearest to me.*

PARENTING

OCTOBER 17

Luke 1-2

LOOKING BACK Jupiter Hammon, America's first published Black poet, was born on this day in 1711. Every year, the anniversary of his birth is celebrated as Black Poetry Day. Hammon was born into slavery, probably in Long Island, New York, and was taught to read. As a trusted servant, he was allowed to use his master's library. On Christmas Day, 1760, his 88-line broadside poem, "An Evening Thought," was published. Hammon was 49 years old when this was achieved. He lived another 30 years, gaining fame as an excellent poet. Hammon was only able to reach his potential because a parent figure cared enough to teach him to read and to nurture him.

LOOKING IN *Good parenting is absolutely necessary if children are to reach their potential. The Bible talks much about the responsibilities and privileges of parenting. Luke's record of the early years of our Lord gives us more insight into how the Father feels about parenting. God did not place His only begotten Son into just any home. Mary and Joseph were especially chosen by God to be the earthly parents of the most important child this world would ever know. Luke gives us the fullest life-story of Jesus that we possess. This Gospel is the first part of a two-part history of Christian beginnings. Acts, the second part, tells the growth of the early church.*

LOOKING OUT

1. **God values righteous parents. The Heavenly Father placed His only begotten Son in a home that regularly respected and worshiped Him.**
2. **God values caring parents. Joseph and Mary were deeply concerned when they learned that Jesus was not with the group. They immediately returned to Jerusalem to find Him.**
3. **God values responsible parents who demand responsibility from their children. Mary confronted Jesus with the question, "Why have you treated us like this?"**
4. **God values believing parents. Joseph and Mary did not understand all that Jesus said to them, but they believed His "spiritual" explanation.**
5. **God values faithful parents. Joseph and Mary faithfully finished raising Jesus, helping the Son of God to grow in stature and wisdom.**

LOOKING UP *Lord, help me to be the parent you desire me to be. Give me wisdom that I might train up my children in the way they should go. Help me to be a godly example to them.*

JUDGMENT

OCTOBER 18

Luke 3-4

LOOKING BACK The first session of the German war crimes trials started in Berlin on this day in 1945, with indictments against 24 former Nazi leaders. Later sessions were held at Nuremberg. The trials exposed the monstrous evils inflicted by Nazi Germany. The Nuremberg part took place from 1945 to 1949. During the more than 10 months that the first trials lasted, one defendant committed suicide and another was excused because of his physical and mental condition. Judgment came on October 1, 1946. Twelve Nazi leaders were sentenced to death by hanging, three faced life imprisonment, four had lesser prison terms, and three were acquitted.

LOOKING IN *John the Baptist warned of coming judgment if his hearers did not repent. When various respondents asked what they should do, John outlined what repentance meant to them, and to us. John was probably raised in a Jewish community in the Judean wilderness. Pious Jews fled to these wilderness communities to escape the sinfulness they saw in their nation. John appeared in Judea, proclaiming Christ's coming and baptizing people into a new, purified community. After John's death, many of his followers joined Jesus. Still others made up a movement that continued after his death. Paul found a group of John's followers in Ephesus in the A.D. 50's.*

LOOKING OUT

1. **Repentance is more than merely saying, "I'm sorry." John the Baptist warned hearers to avoid God's wrath by producing fruit in keeping with repentance.**
2. **Real repentance causes people to turn from selfishness to sharing. John told his hearers that the man with two coats should give one to the person who had none.**
3. **Real repentance causes businessmen to act with honesty. John told the tax collectors they were not to exact more than what the government required of them.**
4. **Real repentance causes people to behave morally, be careful what they say about others, and be content with their pay. John demanded a high standard for soldiers.**
5. **Real men of God always point to the Savior rather than hog the spotlight for themselves. John the Baptist refused to accept accolades but pointed to the coming Christ.**

LOOKING UP *Help me, Lord, to exhibit the true signs of repentance in my life and always point to You. Teach me to be honest in all my dealings with my family, in my business, and with my finances.*

LOVE

OCTOBER 19

Luke 5-7

LOOKING BACK Martha Wayles Skelton Jefferson was born on this day in 1748. She was the much-loved wife of President Thomas Jefferson. He had married Martha, a widow, in 1772. According to legend, Jefferson's love of music helped him win his reluctant bride. Two rival suitors came to call one day but left without a word when they saw the couple playing a duet on the harpsichord and violin. Jefferson and Skelton married and settled at Monticello, where they had one son and five daughters, but only two children lived to maturity. Mrs. Jefferson died after only 10 years of marriage. Jefferson reared his two daughters. He never remarried.

LOOKING IN *Jesus talked much about love. However, His demands for love exceed what we normally think. He insists that we love our enemies and do good to those who are not good to us. To love as Christ loved is a great challenge, but it is demanded of all those who faithfully follow Him. This section of Luke contains a shorter version of the famed Sermon on the Mount. Jesus probably taught these truths on several different occasions. Here He speaks directly to His disciples within the hearing of the crowds, who were amazed at both Jesus' teaching and the authority with which He taught. His words challenge and change the lives of His followers.*

LOOKING OUT

1. Love is far more than a feeling. Jesus said we are to love our enemies. We can't feel good about them, but we can express love in our attitudes and actions toward them.
2. Whatever bad we give out comes back to us in full force. Jesus said those who judge will be judged, and those who condemn will be condemned.
3. Whatever good we give out will come back to us in greater measure. Forgiveness is ours if we forgive. Blessings pour out on us when we are generous.
4. When we teach, we must be sure that what we say has been given to us by the Teacher. Jesus said the blind cannot lead the blind, or both will fall into the ditch.
5. Our primary agenda should be to take care of our own sins rather than ranting about the sins of others. Jesus said to remove the two-by-four from our eye first.

LOOKING UP *Help me, Lord, to give of my love and resources just as You have done so graciously. May I always remember that God has not called me to judge others but to follow Him.*

PROMISE

OCTOBER 20

Luke 8-9

LOOKING BACK On this day in 1944, General Douglas MacArthur fulfilled a promise he had made when forced to leave the Philippines on March 11, 1942. When the Japanese invasion pushed the American troops out of that Asian nation, MacArthur fervently promised, "I shall return." He did just that, landing four divisions on the east coast of the Philippines. The famed general began his dramatic invasion of the Philippines on Leyte, a small island in the 7,000-island chain. U.S. aircraft dropped hundreds of tons of bombs to prepare the way. That overwhelming fire power forced the Japanese to give up the island nation they had so brutally conquered.

LOOKING IN *Jesus also keeps a promise He made even though it seems impossible for Him to do so. Jairus, a ruler of the synagogue, has a desperately ill daughter. Jesus assures him that she would be okay. Then, on the way to her, Jesus is interrupted by a hemorrhaging woman. The woman tries not to advertise her presence because under Jewish Law she is considered polluted and untouchable. She reaches out to touch Jesus. He feels the difference between a casual touch and a desperate reach. The incident must have encouraged Jairus. The fact that Jairus came to Jesus shows that not all religious leaders were opposed to our Lord. Jesus kept His promise to Jairus.*

LOOKING OUT

1. **Great need has a way of erasing discussions of doctrinal differences. Jairus was a ruler of the synagogue but never questioned Jesus' doctrine when his daughter was dying.**
2. **Miracles often occur when we allow ourselves to be interrupted. Jesus was on his way to an urgent meeting but stopped to heal the woman with the issue of blood.**
3. **We must press through to get the healing touch from the Lord. The woman with the issue of blood was so desperate she pushed through the throng to Jesus.**
4. **It's never too late when our Lord is involved. Servants arrived with the bad news that Jairus' daughter was dead. However, they did not know our Lord's involvement.**
5. **Our Lord, Who created the human body, is certainly able to repair and restore it. Jairus' daughter was healed as our Lord took her by the hand and commanded, "Arise!"**

LOOKING UP *Help me, Lord, never to give up no matter how dark the night. I have You in every situation. Thank You that You have power over the most desperate situations.*

PRAYER

OCTOBER 21

Luke 10-11

LOOKING BACK Poet Samuel Taylor Coleridge was born on this day in 1772. His poem, "The Rime of the Ancient Mariner" is one of the greatest in English literature, and all his major poems are among the most original. About 1800, Coleridge's health began to fail. He had begun taking opium to relieve the pain of rheumatism, spending his last years under a doctor's care, largely to control his opium addiction. Coleridge claimed that his unfinished famous poem, "Kubla Khan," was inspired by an opium dream. Perhaps he was right, since the poem is very difficult to understand, as was another work, "Christabel," an unfinished narrative of medieval times.

LOOKING IN *Unlike Coleridge's poems, our Lord's directives are easy to understand. This is especially true with His fascinating discourse on prayer. His disciples had asked Him to teach them to pray. The pattern Jesus set forth is simple yet profound, serving as our guide to praying. Matthew has a longer form of the Lord's Prayer. Jesus is not supplying a form of words but is giving us a pattern of prayer. He teaches us to come to God simply and talk to Him as we would to our own father. We share our concerns and confidently tell our needs. The disciples knew the power Christ had in prayer and wanted to share in the secret.*

LOOKING OUT

1. Prayer is a learned activity. Powerful praying does not come naturally. The disciples asked the Lord to teach them to pray, since they had witnessed its dynamic results.
2. Powerful praying always starts with praise. Jesus taught us to begin our petition with, "Father, hallowed be your name." Praise reminds us of God's greatness and goodness.
3. Powerful praying involves more than things we want. Jesus taught us to pray, "Thy Kingdom come." This moves us beyond selfishness to the larger realm of God's will.
4. Powerful praying is also very practical. Jesus told us to pray for daily provision and forgiveness of sin. We are forgiven in the same measure that we extend forgiveness.
5. Powerful praying recognizes one's own propensity for sin. Jesus told us to pray, "And lead us not into temptation." All of us have a vulnerability.

LOOKING UP *Teach me to pray, Lord, according to Your will and in the way You taught the disciples to pray. May my first response to difficulty be to come to You in prayer.*

WORRY

OCTOBER 22

Luke 12-13

LOOKING BACK The world was supposed to end on this day in 1844. William Miller, a Baptist minister in Low Hampton, New York, was one of many students of the Bible who have tried to predict the date for the coming of Christ. For years, Miller studied the prophecies recorded in the Old Testament book of Daniel and the New Testament book of Revelation. After many calculations, he announced in 1831 that the Second Advent would occur on this day in 1844. Thousands of people believed him, and some sold their possessions. His followers waited in vain for the coming of Christ and the end of the world. They worried needlessly.

LOOKING IN *Worry cannot add to life, but it surely can take away a lot of joy. Jesus addressed the worry problem by saying we are to live in trust, not anxiety. He not only told us what we should not do but gave us clear instructions on how we are to break the worry habit. We would be wise to heed. These chapters of Luke contain a collection of Jesus' teachings about the future and the way future events should affect life here and now. The consequences of following a short-sighted materialistic philosophy will prove disastrous in the end. Jesus also addressed the misconception that disasters only happen to those who are the worst of sinners.*

LOOKING OUT

1. **To worry is to insult our God. Jesus spoke much about the futility and destructive power of worry. He commanded us not to be so concerned about those who pass away.**
2. **The way to fight worry is to look around God's world and see His faithful provision. Jesus told us to consider the ravens who do not sow or reap, yet God takes care of them.**
3. **Worry does nothing to solve the problems we face. Jesus said we cannot add a single hour to our life through worry. If we can't do that, then why spend the time worrying?**
4. **Those who follow Christ must develop other priorities than those of the world. Pagans seek temporal things while believers should seek God's Kingdom first and foremost.**
5. **God wants us to build a fence against our fear and learn to live in trust. Jesus said not to be afraid and to divest ourselves of those things that bind us to fear.**

LOOKING UP *Help me, Lord, to break the destructive habit of worry and learn to live by totally trusting You. May I always remember that to worry is to insult my God.*

EFFORT

OCTOBER 23

Luke 14-16

LOOKING BACK American swimming champion Gertrude Ederle was born on this day in 1906. She was the first woman to swim the treacherous English Channel. Born in New York City, Ederle swam from Capre Gris-nez, France, to Dover, England, on August 26, 1926, when she was just 19 years old. At the same time, she broke the previous world record by swimming the 35-mile distance in 14 hours and 31 minutes. During her swimming career, Ederle broke many other records and was a gold medal winner at the 1924 summer Olympic games. From 1921 to 1925, Ederle set 29 U.S. and world records for swimming races, ranging from the 50-yard to the half-mile race.

LOOKING IN *Gertrude Ederle's swimming feats were amazing but also grueling. Anytime one attempts to do something significant, there is a huge price to pay. The more important the goal, the more difficult the endeavor. This is especially true concerning the most important thing in the world: following God. Jesus clearly outlines the cost of discipleship for those who consider following Him. It is not a walk in the park but a fight to the finish. In our Lord's story about counting the cost, Jesus makes the point that no one can follow Him unless he is prepared for all that implies. We must remember the world is a battleground, not a playground.*

LOOKING OUT

1. **Following Christ means loving Him more than anyone or anything. The love of our Lord causes all other loves to pale in comparison.**
2. **Following Christ means sacrifice. When Christ bids us come, He bids us come and die. There is a cross to carry and a price to pay.**
3. **Following Christ means counting the cost. Jesus encourages His followers to think things through carefully before committing to discipleship.**
4. **Following Christ means staying pure. Jesus said salt is good, but it must remain pure to be used. Corrupted salt is worth nothing and will be cast aside.**
5. **Following Christ means hearing Him. We must not listen to the voices of the world but attune ourselves to His voice alone. Jesus said, "My sheep know my voice."**

LOOKING UP *Lord, I do want to be Your disciple regardless of the cost. Please help me to be faithful and true to You in hard times as well as good times.*

PEACE

OCTOBER 24

Luke 17-18

October

LOOKING BACK The United Nations was started on this day in 1945, with two main goals: peace and human dignity. This world body was begun shortly after World War II. As the horrible war drew to an end, the nations that opposed Germany, Italy, and Japan decided that such a conflict must never be permitted to happen again. Representatives of those nations met in San Francisco in April of 1945 to work out a plan for an organization to help keep world peace. This plan was described in a document called the "Charter of the United Nations." In June 1945, 50 nations signed the charter as U.N. members. Now, over 100 other nations have joined.

LOOKING IN *Man's struggle for peace is always challenging, due to man's evil nature. Real peace is only possible if we take the "Prince of Peace" (Jesus Christ) into our hearts. Then, we determine to live by His precepts. In this section of Luke, Jesus tells us more about prayer through two unforgettable parables. The first portrays the unjust judge. The intent is not to say God is unjust but to encourage persistence in prayer. The second story involves a Pharisee and a sinner praying. The Pharisee prays simply to give himself a pat on the back. It's the "worthless" tax collector who is heard because he comes clean before God.*

LOOKING OUT

1. We are held responsible if we push people into temptations. Jesus said things that cause sin abound, but "Woe to the person through whom they come."
2. We must be very careful never to condone sin; it destroys those God loves. Jesus cautions that we must watch ourselves lest we encourage unrighteousness.
3. We must always deal with others in the direction they are going. Those who repent are to be forgiven quickly, while those who sin are to be rebuked.
4. Our willingness to forgive must never have limits. Jesus said we are to forgive even when another sins against us seven times in a day and comes back to ask our forgiveness.
5. Following Jesus is joyful but has great responsibilities. We must not anticipate rewards and accolades for just doing what is expected.

LOOKING UP *Help me, Lord, to be loving, forgiving, and responsible as Your faithful follower. May I joyfully take up my task for You, not working because I expect blessing but because I love You.*

LIFE-CHANGER

OCTOBER 25

Luke 19-20

LOOKING BACK Controversial artist Pablo Picasso was born on this day in 1881. Called by many the greatest artist of the 20th century, Picasso dominated the art world for decades. His art was very influential among artists of his time as well as later artists. Although best known for his paintings, Picasso produced sculptures, drawings, prints, and ceramics. He was highly imaginative and original, borrowing from historical examples and creating new styles. Picasso not only created enduring works of art but also expanded our definition of what art could be. He once commented, "I am only a public entertainer who has understood his time."

LOOKING IN *Jesus understood His time, but He was not an entertainer. He was a "life-changer." This was never so clear as with the incident of Zacchaeus. The little, hated tax collector had no hope of redemption, much less acceptance. In one wonderful moment, our Lord changed that. Zacchaeus was not only accepted but made part of God's family. In those days, the tax collector was a political office created by the Romans to help collect taxes in the provinces. Actually, the title "tax collector" is more correct than the older term "publican" in referring to the lowest rank in the structure. Zacchaeus is called a "chief among the publicans."*

LOOKING OUT

1. Often behind the facade of prosperity and happiness lies a longing for something that really satisfies. Zacchaeus was wealthy and powerful but unfulfilled.
2. Guilt and shame often keep us away from the very thing that would save us. Zacchaeus, feeling unworthy to meet Jesus, climbed a tree to see Him pass by.
3. Our Lord reaches out to all who are hungry in heart. Jesus invited Zacchaeus not only to meet Him but to spend time learning what it meant to follow Him.
4. God sees beyond the facade to the heart that really wants to know Him. All the people criticized our Lord for associating with Zacchaeus, but God knew his hunger.
5. Real conversion means a total change of direction and a desire to make things right. Zacchaeus determined to pay back four times the amount he had stolen.

LOOKING UP *Help me, Lord, neither to be appalled nor awed by appearances but to see the hunger of the heart. May I remember that even the most calloused of individuals may hunger for You.*

STUBBORN

OCTOBER 26

Luke 21-22

LOOKING BACK This is "Mule Day," the anniversary of the first importation of Spanish jacks to the United States on this day in 1785. Mules are said to have been bred in this country by George Washington, from the pair given by King Charles III of Spain. The mule is a domesticated, hybrid animal that results from crossing a mare (female horse) and a jack (male donkey). Mules were once popular work animals throughout the world. They can remain strong under much harsh treatment and work but perform better when treated with kindness. The phrase, "stubborn as a mule," entered our lexicon because of their cantankerous nature.

LOOKING IN *Peter certainly was "stubborn as a mule." He insisted that even if all others denied the Lord, he would remain true. Jesus knew that while Peter's intent was good, he would crumble in the time of trial. Our Lord told Peter that he would fall but also rise again. Four names are used in the New Testament to refer to the big fisherman. They are: the Hebrew name "Simeon" (in the book of Acts); the Greek equivalent "Simon" (nearly fifty times in the Gospels and Acts); "Cephas," most frequently used by Paul and occurring only once outside his writings; and "Peter." The names "Cephas" and "Peter" both mean "rock."*

LOOKING OUT

1. **The closer we get to Christ, the more Satan seeks to challenge us. Jesus told Peter, a member of the inner circle, "Simon, Simon, Satan has asked to sift you as wheat."**
2. **No matter how much we are attacked by the evil one, Jesus is there with His rod of protection to help us. Jesus told Peter, "But I have prayed for you."**
3. **After we have failed, we can better strengthen others. Jesus knew Peter would fall, but that failure would humble him, making him more compassionate and understanding.**
4. **Real prayer is determining to follow God's will. Jesus agonized in the garden, not wanting to face the cross. However, He stayed in prayer until He submitted to God's will.**
5. **When our burdens get too hard to bear, our loving God sends help to comfort us. An angel appeared to Christ in the garden to strengthen Him during His agony.**

LOOKING UP *Help me, Lord, to remain humble, knowing that I am not as strong as I sometimes think. Help me remember that real prayer is submitting to Your will, not wanting my own way.*

DARING

OCTOBER 27

Luke 23-24

LOOKING BACK Theodore Roosevelt, one of the most daring presidents, was born on this day in 1858. He was the youngest man ever to become president of the United States, taking the office at age 42. Roosevelt had been vice-president for only six months when President William McKinley was assassinated in September, 1901. Roosevelt won wide popularity, and millions of Americans affectionately called him "Teddy" or "T.R." In 1904, the voters elected him to a full-term as president. Roosevelt was the first president to ride in an automobile, submerge in a submarine, and fly in an airplane. He was famous for his bold and daring lifestyle.

LOOKING IN *Peter was also bold and daring. Often brash and sometimes rude, this big fisherman loved our Lord passionately and wanted to find out truth for himself. When strange rumors filled the air about the resurrection of Jesus, Peter rushed to the tomb while other disciples waited. Peter was born in Bethsaida, a town in Palestine on the east bank of the River Jordan. Andrew, his brother, and the apostle Philip also came from Bethsaida. Peter later moved to the nearby town of Capernaum on the bank of the Sea of Galilee, where he became a fisherman. He was warm, generous, stubborn, and impulsive. Peter was married and may have had children.*

LOOKING OUT

1. **Crisis often forces us to take an unpopular stand. Joseph of Arimathea had not consented to the decision and action of the council. He buried our Lord in his own tomb.**
2. **Jesus is not a dead religious leader but the living Son of God. The angels asked the women, "Why do you look for the living among the dead? He is not here; he has risen."**
3. **Sometimes only in looking back can we understand the present. The angels reminded the women of what Jesus said before His death. Suddenly, it all made perfect sense.**
4. **The great miracles of God are hard for the human mind to understand. The disciples thought the women reporting Christ's resurrection were speaking nonsense.**
5. **True truth-seekers don't just listen but move to find out for themselves. Peter had a hard time believing Jesus was alive but ran to the tomb to discover if it were true.**

LOOKING UP *Help me Lord, not to just listen to those who speak of Your miracles, but to find out for myself. May I always passionately seek a closer walk with You.*

CHRIST

OCTOBER 28

John 1-2

LOOKING BACK After three years of hard work, the Statue of Liberty was dedicated on this day in 1886. The majestic copper sculpture towers above Liberty Island at the entrance to New York Harbor in Upper New York Bay and is one of the largest statues ever built. It was given by the people of France in 1884 as an expression of friendship and to express the ideal of liberty shared by both peoples. Emma Lazarus' famed words are inscribed on its pedestal, "Give me your tired, your poor, Your huddled masses yearning to breathe free, The wretched refuse of your teeming shore. Send these, the homeless, tempest-tost to me. I lift my lamp beside the golden door!"

LOOKING IN *Many immigrants have found safety and solace in America. However, others have experienced burning prejudice. There is an active movement to close the borders and let foreigners know they are not welcome. This attitude seems to deny the words stated on the statue. God never says one thing but means another. When He invites"whosoever will" to come, that excludes no one. John now picks up his pen to add to the glorious Gospel story. He tells us that salvation is not an afterthought of the Father. John lets us know that Jesus, the only begotten Son of God, existed before time began. He is our most perfect and complete expression of the person of God.*

LOOKING OUT

1. **Our Lord's life did not begin at Bethlehem but is everlasting. John says, "In the beginning was the Word, and the Word was with God, and the Word was God."**
2. **Life can only be found in our Lord, because He is life. John notes, "Through him all things were made; without him nothing was made that has been made."**
3. **God poured Himself into human flesh because He would not let man die in darkness. John adds, "The true light that gives light to every man was coming into the world."**
4. **Sin so blinds us that we cannot see the obvious. John says, "He was in the world, and though the world was made by him, the world did not recognize him."**
5. **In accepting Christ, we join the universe's elite. John says, "Yet to all who received him, to those who believed in his name, he gave the right to become children of God..."**

LOOKING UP *Help me, Lord, to know more about Your eternal character and Your great love for us. Thank You for giving me the right and the power to become Your child.*

CRASH

OCTOBER 29

John 3-5

LOOKING BACK The stock market crashed on this day in 1929, just four days after President Herbert Hoover proclaimed, "The fundamental business of this country...is on a sound and prosperous basis." Billions of dollars were lost on that single day. The boom was over. More than 16 billion shares of stock were dumped and vast fortunes lost. Frightened investors ordered their brokers to sell at whatever price. The resulting "Great Depression," which lasted until about 1939, involved North America, Europe, and other industrialized countries. In 1932, one out of four U.S. workers was unemployed.

LOOKING IN *Often, we move along in life ignoring warnings just as leaders did before the stock market crash of 1929. This is not a new problem. The woman at the well had obviously done this in her many relationships. She went through a series of five husbands and one live-in boyfriend. Jesus appeared and offered her "living water" that would quench her thirst for lasting love. No wonder the woman was surprised at the encounter! For 700 years, religious and racial prejudice had separated the Jews and Samaritans. Add to this the contempt found in the Jewish prayer of that time which stated, "Blessed are thou, Lord,...Who hast not made me a woman."*

LOOKING OUT

1. Those who love Christ refuse to get caught up in unholy competition. Jesus left for Galilee rather than be pitted by some in rivalry with John the Baptist.
2. Divine appointments often come in unexpected places. Jesus, weary and thirsty, sits down by the well as a Samaritan woman comes to draw water.
3. Divine appointments are often with unexpected people. The Samaritan woman was an outcast in her own society. She drew water when other women were not present.
4. When conviction comes, we often try to divert it with a religious question. The Samaritan woman tried to draw Jesus into theological debate, not wanting to address her sin.
5. Once we encounter Christ, we cannot help but talk about Him. The Samaritan woman tasted the "living water" and immediately ran back into town to share the good news.

LOOKING UP *Help me, Lord, to see today as a time for divine appointments in unlikely places with unexpected people. May I be very sensitive to the way You lead.*

QUESTIONS

OCTOBER 30

John 6-7

LOOKING BACK Stephen S. Wise and Abba Hillel Silver noted the tragic results of prejudice on this day in 1945. They said, "Had the doors of Palestine been kept open, hundreds of thousands of Jews, now dead, might have been alive today." In the early 1930's, over 100,000 Jewish refugees came to Palestine from Nazi Germany and Poland. This alarmed many. An organized general uprising almost paralyzed Palestine. In 1939, the British drastically limited Jewish immigration. While Hitler was murdering millions of Jews, there was no place for them to escape. The world finally woke up to its responsibility, but by that time, it was too late for millions.

LOOKING IN *Prejudice always seeks to destroy regardless of its object. Jesus came face to face with blind prejudice in the episode of the woman caught in the act of adultery. Even though two persons were involved in this act, only one was brought before the self-righteous authorities. The lawyers tried to trap Jesus with their contemptible example of the law's violation. They intended to push Jesus into contradicting Mosaic law or violating Roman law since Jews were not permitted to carry out the death sentence. Jesus violated neither. He did not condemn or condone the woman's conduct. Rather, our loving Lord gave her a second chance.*

LOOKING OUT

1. **Where was the man? The woman had been caught in the very act of adultery, but only she was brought forward for condemnation. Man's justice is always biased.**
2. **Where was their love? Religious leaders are supposed to be those who reach out in love to the lost. These accusers only wanted to use and abuse the adulterous woman.**
3. **What did Jesus write on the ground? We do not have the answer to this, but perhaps He wrote the sins of the accusers who soon felt condemnation for their condemning.**
4. **What did Jesus tell the woman? He forgave her, restored her dignity, and offered her the opportunity to "go and sin no more." Jesus came to restore the lost.**
5. **What would she do? She was probably a prostitute, since the accusers knew exactly where to find her. Now our loving God would provide her with a new livelihood.**

LOOKING UP *Help me, Lord, never to be condemning but always involved in redeeming. Let me work with You, restoring those who have lost their dignity through disobedience and sin.*

KNOWING

OCTOBER 31

John 8-10

LOOKING BACK Famed singer and actress Ethel Waters was born on this day in 1896. Married when she was 13, Waters began her singing career at the urging of friends. She gained recognition as a singer of both blues and popular songs and starred in several Broadway musicals. Born in Chester, Pennsylvania, Waters started singing in nightclubs and in vaudeville when she was just 17 years old. One of her most memorable statements was, "God don't sponsor no flops." In her later years, she often appeared with Billy Graham and became famous for her rendition of the gospel song, "His Eye Is On the Sparrow." Her popular autobiography carries that same title.

LOOKING IN *Jesus epitomized the love and care of our Heavenly Father. John uses various word pictures to describe our Lord. One of the most powerful is that of the Good Shepherd Who cares for, and shares with, His sheep. Just as the sheep are totally dependent on the Shepherd, so we rely on Christ. The shepherd was a familiar figure in Palestine. He spent much of His life with the flock. His own sheep knew and responded to his voice. He led them to fresh grazing pastures, guarding them from the wild animals that posed great danger. In the Old Testament, God is called the Shepherd of His people, while in the New, Jesus is Shepherd of the church.*

LOOKING OUT

1. When we know Jesus Christ, we know His voice. Intimacy with Jesus assures that we will hear Him when He speaks to us. He said, "My sheep know my voice."
2. When we know Christ, we will not follow a false shepherd. No matter how charismatic someone is, he will not be able to lead the true believer away from the Good Shepherd.
3. When we know Christ, we will be satisfied. Jesus says His sheep will "come in and go out, and find pasture." That is, they will be fully satisfied.
4. When we know Christ, we discover His great love for us. Jesus notes that only those who follow Him are really aware of how much the Heavenly Father loves them.
5. When we know Christ, we begin to recognize His sovereignty. Jesus notes that He has the ability to lay down His life and take it up any moment He desires.

LOOKING UP *Thank You, Lord, for Your wonderful love. Help me always to stay close to the Good Shepherd Who knows me intimately yet loves me greatly.*

NOVEMBER..........

A Month Retaining its Name because of Modesty

November has only retained its name because of the modesty of one of Rome's most fascinating caesars. It is the 11th month of the year, and takes its name from *novem*, the Latin word for nine. In the early Roman calendar, November was the ninth month. Because July was named for Julius Caesar and August for Augustus Caesar, the Roman Senate offered to name the 11th month for Tiberius Caesar. His full name was Tiberius Claudius Nero, and he was the emperor of Rome during the life of Jesus. Tiberius modestly refused the senate's offer saying, "What will you do if you have thirteen emperors?"

The Anglo-Saxons referred to November as "the wind month" and sometimes "the blood month," probably because during this period they killed animals for their winter meat. November comes between autumn and winter. In the North Temperate regions, during this month the trees are bare, and the dead leaves on the earth have lost the brilliant color they had in October. Soft snow seldom hides the bareness of the fields, but the grays and browns of the landscapes are sometimes relieved by delightful days of hazy sunshine. Many outdoor activities in the North come to a halt in November. The crops have been stored or shipped to processing plants and mills.

Near the end of November, the people of the United States celebrate Thanksgiving Day. In Canada, where the colder climate forces farmers to harvest crops earlier, Thanksgiving is celebrated in October. Election Day in the United States always falls on the first Tuesday after the first Monday in November. Originally, there were 30 days in November, then 29, then 31; but from the time of Augustus, it has had 30 days. During November, we will read the Gospel of John, Acts, Romans, 1 Corinthians, and the first nine chapters of 2 Corinthians.

UNCONVINCED

John 11-12

LOOKING BACK Elaborate and giant kites will be flown today in Santiago, Sacatepequez, a village about 20 miles from Guatemala City. Kites are the oldest form of aircraft. They probably originated in China more than 2,000 years ago. Many years ago, the townspeople of Santiago, Sacatepequez, were told by a magician that a secret way to get rid of evil spirits was by flying kites. He said the evil spirits were frightened by the noise of the wind against paper. Since that time long ago, the kite festival has been held at the cemetery every year on November 1 or 2. The villagers claim that "to this day no one knows of bad spirits roaming the streets of town."

LOOKING IN *It is surprising what some choose to believe. Tragically, many people prefer to believe in superstition and lies rather than truth. This is not a new problem. In our Lord's day, many people saw the miracles He performed and heard the words He preached. They even knew the messages the prophets had spoken about the coming Messiah. Yet, they insisted on holding on to their old traditions rather than accepting our Lord as Savior. They were so threatened by His teachings they tried to kill Him. It's amazing that all saw the great miracles of our Lord, but some still refused to believe. While belief has great power, so does unbelief.*

LOOKING OUT

1. Miracles are spectacular, but they fail to convince everyone. Even though many saw the miracles Christ performed, not all believed in Him.
2. Often, in holding onto the old, we miss the new. Some, who saw Jesus and His work, still didn't want the old establishment shaken.
3. Our tendency to preserve position and influence can make us miss God's best. The Pharisees tried to stop Jesus, because it meant they would lose their power.
4. Even the evil devices of the enemy play into the hands of our good God. Caiphas unwittingly prophesied accurately concerning our Lord fulfilling Scripture.
5. At times, God keeps us guessing until His perfect time comes. Jesus deliberately kept out of sight until it was the Father's time for Him to appear.

LOOKING UP *Lord, may I never get so caught up in the miracles that I neglect Your message. Help me to always discern the way You move in my life and in the world.*

STRENGTH

NOVEMBER 2

John 13-14

LOOKING BACK Some say the weakest United States president was born on this day in 1865. Warren G. Harding was an easy-going man who learned too late that leadership demands strength. Harding's administration was first damaged by the short, severe depression of 1921. Within two years, the Teapot Dome oil scandal erupted, along with other graft in governmental agencies. Harding probably became aware of this widespread corruption in the summer of 1923. His anxiety about it may have hastened his death. Historians rank Harding as one of the weakest–if not the weakest–presidents. He failed because he was weak-willed and a poor judge of character.

LOOKING IN *Greatness demands strength, and greatness is very different from what the world applauds. Jesus showed us what real strength is. The occasion is the Last Supper. The disciples have been arguing over who is the greatest. In a stunning display, Jesus gives them the answer by taking the servant's towel and basin to wash their feet. The Master is well aware of Who He is and His purpose. A shocked Simon Peter objects to the action of the Lord but is reminded that if he wants to be part of Christ's Kingdom he must accept the concept that leadership demands servanthood. Apparently, our Lord's action further infuriates Judas.*

LOOKING OUT

1. **Love is best expressed in serving, not in being served. Jesus humbly takes the towel and basin to clarify just how deeply He loves His disciples.**
2. **When we are secure, position is not important. Jesus knew Who He was. Therefore, He was very comfortable serving. Only the insecure are reluctant to serve.**
3. **Often we don't understand what God is doing until much later. The disciples would realize later what Christ had done in this unique display of His Lordship.**
4. **Our lives are to imitate the life of our Lord. Jesus told His followers they were to do as He had just done. To be Christian means to be like Christ.**
5. **It is not enough to know, we must do! Jesus said His followers would only be blessed if they did as He had done. God blesses the obedient to reinforce that behavior.**

LOOKING UP *Lord, help me swallow my pride and take the servant's towel and basin. Forgive me, for in my great pride I prefer the prophet's mantle over the servant's towel.*

SPIRIT

NOVEMBER 3

John 15-17

LOOKING BACK William Cullen Bryant, the first great American poet, was born on this day in 1794. Bryant's poems are noted for their dignified style, exact descriptions of nature, and appeal to the emotions. In 1811, Bryant wrote a major part of his most famous poem, "Thanatopsis." Bryant's father submitted it to a Boston magazine. At first, the editors refused to believe that any American could have written such brilliant verses. The magazine published "Thanatopsis," and the poem quickly established Bryant as a leading poet. In 1821, Bryant added an introduction and also a final stanza, which begins with the line, "So live, that when thy summons comes..."

LOOKING IN *"Thanatopsis" admonishes us to live daily so that when death comes there will be no regrets. It was intended to remind us how fragile and short life is. In the business of everyday life, it is easy to lose perspective. A much better way to keep a proper view of things is with the Holy Spirit as our guide and helper. Jesus tells His disciples that He is going away but He will not leave them without comfort. The Holy Spirit would come to convict men of the truth and lead them into a deeper understanding of it. Only later, on the dramatic Day of Pentecost, would they begin to understand the meaning of these strange words.*

LOOKING OUT

1. **The Holy Spirit convicts. Convincing us of our sin makes possible the first step to our salvation-confession. Conviction is not to make us feel bad but to point us to Christ.**
2. **The Holy Spirit lets us know God's great goodness to us. We are not doomed to destruction but can be saved by God's love.**
3. **The Holy Spirit delivers from judgment. God's Spirit assures us that Christ took the full penalty for our sin. We need not live under condemnation.**
4. **The Holy Spirit guides us into all truth. We need not fear getting sidetracked when we faithfully follow God's Spirit. He keeps us on track and our eyes on Christ.**
5. **The Holy Spirit always speaks of Jesus. The centerpiece of all theology is Jesus Christ. The Spirit focuses on Jesus, not Himself.**

LOOKING UP *Thank You, Lord, for sending the Holy Spirit Who faithfully sets forth the truth of the Gospel in clear light.*

SURPRISE

NOVEMBER 4

John 18-19

LOOKING BACK One of the world's greatest surprises came on this day in 1922. King Tut's tomb was finally discovered at Luxor, Egypt, revealing fabulous riches buried for centuries. Archaeologist Howard Carter had searched for Tutankhamen's tomb for 10 years. He finally discovered that its entrance had been hidden by debris resulting from diggings at the entrance of the nearby tomb of King Ramses VI. Tutankhamen's four-room tomb contained more than 5,000 objects, including many beautifully carved and gold-covered items. A magnificent lifelike gold mask of Tutankhamen covered the head and shoulders of the royal mummy.

LOOKING IN *The disciples were also in for a great surprise. They had expected Jesus to set up an earthly kingdom. Their hopes were dashed with the betrayal and crucifixion. John's account of the events offers details omitted by other Gospel writers. For example, he names the slave whose ear Peter severed (Malchus). Also, John tells us about the weather, the charcoal fire, Jewish religious scruples over entering the Roman's house, exchanges between Jesus and Pilate, and the terrible apostasy of God's people declaring they have no king but Caesar. Though they were shocked, a greater surprise awaited them on resurrection morning.*

LOOKING OUT

1. **Man proposes but God disposes. The crucifiers honestly thought they were in charge. What they didn't realize is they were following God's script.**
2. **God will have a witness regardless of man's opposition. In spite of the Jewish officials' objection, Pilate's sign proclaimed Christ for Who He really was.**
3. **Regardless of our personal pain, we must care for those God has placed around us. Jesus turns to John asking that he take care of His mother.**
4. **Fear of man keeps us from God's best. Joseph of Arimathea had followed the Lord secretly, missing God's best because of his fear.**
5. **Crisis reveals who we really are. Joseph and Nicodemus, both secret followers of our Lord, were exposed by the events of the cross.**

LOOKING UP *Thank You, Lord, that though the dark hours following the crucifixion caused all hell to rejoice, Satan's victory was short-lived. You are the resurrection and the life.*

SIGHTINGS

NOVEMBER 5

John 20-21

LOOKING BACK On this day in 1991, media mogul Robert Maxwell died after falling from his yacht, the "Lady Ghislaine." His body was found floating 20 miles away near the Canary Islands. Maxwell's demise was very mysterious, adding more controversy to his already controversial and intriguing larger-than-life story. Was it murder, suicide, or an accident? The truth has never been sorted out, because when he died, his vast empire was found to be in significant financial despair. Born into a poor farm family in Czechoslovakia, Maxwell ended his life a billionaire with a financially troubled media empire that stretched around the world.

LOOKING IN *Unlike the events surrounding Maxwell's death, the demise of our Lord is well-documented. Not only is His death recorded for history, but also His resurrection. Some historians say Christ's resurrection is the best documented event in history. Hundreds saw Jesus after He was raised. Only John tells us how Jesus came to seven of them as they were fishing. John was there. He remembers how many fish they caught, and their surprise and relief at finding the net intact. He remembers how Jesus gave Peter the chance to cancel out his three-fold denial with the three-times-repeated question, "Do you love me?" He remembers and affirms the resurrection.*

LOOKING OUT

1. Jesus appears to the unlikely, letting them know His great love. Mary Magdalene, a woman of questionable character whom Jesus saved, saw Him first.
2. Jesus appears to the unfaithful, letting them know He forgives them. Even though all the disciples had deserted Jesus, He lovingly came to them.
3. Jesus appears to the unbelieving, letting them know they can trust Him. Thomas refused to believe until Jesus showed Himself to the doubting skeptic.
4. When Jesus appears and speaks to us, all our doubts and voices fade. Thomas' demands for proof were no longer needed when Jesus came.
5. We are saved to serve, not to float through life enjoying our status. Jesus clearly instructed His followers they were to take the good news to all the earth.

LOOKING UP *Thank You, Lord, that in spite of my failures, You never leave me. Help me to be faithful to You in my worship and service.*

KNOWING

Acts 1-3

LOOKING BACK "Meet the Press" started on this day in 1947. It holds the distinction of being the oldest program on television. Television journalism developed quickly after World War II, and many radio newscasters moved into TV news. The success of "Meet the Press"sparked other journalistic programs with nightly newscasts starting in 1948. In the 1950's, TV began to increase its coverage of public affairs. Today, there are scores of journalism programs ranging all the way from the lurid tabloid, to magazine formats, to discussions of serious issues by leading authorities. Whole cable networks are devoted to news and its impact on our daily life.

LOOKING IN *The "need to know" drives the news industry. That need is not new. In the early church, there was a great need to know what was happening to new believers. God used Luke to write a journalistic account of the acts of the Holy Spirit, reporting to believers everywhere that God was at work, and they were part of a great move of God in the world. The book of Acts covers a period of some 30 years, from the birth of the church on the Day of Pentecost to the close of Paul's imprisonment at Rome. It describes the spread of Christianity and how our Lord satisfies the longings of the heart. It might also be called "The Acts of the Holy Spirit."*

LOOKING OUT

1. **Worship involves more than emotional experiences; it involves learning God's Word. The new converts devoted their time to the apostles' teaching.**
2. **Worship involves fellowship with others of like-precious faith. The new converts regularly spent time with other believers to grow in faith.**
3. **Worship involves celebrating communion. The early believers continually celebrated the Lord's Supper as a reminder of Christ's sacrificial death for sins.**
4. **Worship involves prayer. The early church members learned that communication with God is a key aspect of worship. If we know Him, we talk to Him.**
5. **Worship involves unselfishness with one's resources. The early Christians were generous in sharing their possessions, time, and finances with others.**

LOOKING UP *Thank You, Lord, for shaking me out of my old lifestyles so I can start a new adventure in the Spirit. Help me to make a dramatic difference in my world.*

CONFLICT

Acts 4-5

LOOKING BACK French philosopher Albert Camus was born on this date in 1913. He was a journalist, essayist, philosopher, novelist, and playwright who won the 1957 Nobel Prize for literature. His writing transcends its setting, because it deals with moral problems of universal importance. Camus said, "The struggle to reach the top is itself enough to fulfill the heart of man." Camus was concerned with the freedom and responsibility of the individual, the alienation of the individual from society, and the difficulty of facing life without the comfort of believing in God or in absolute moral standards. He was killed in an automobile accident in 1960.

LOOKING IN *While Camus was right about many things, he was wrong to say the struggle to reach the top is enough to fulfill the heart of man. Nothing can fulfill man except a relationship with God that challenges and changes him. The lame man at the Gate Beautiful had struggled physically all his life and still was a beggar. However, one day he met the Master through Peter and John, and his whole life changed. The angry Sanhedrin heard Peter preach a scathing message of rebuke. In response, they insisted the apostles be arrested. When the church prayed, even the bars of iron could not hold the apostles. It became obvious a power higher than man's was involved.*

LOOKING OUT

1. **God's blessings arouse jealousy in the disobedient. The high priest and his associates were filled with jealousy because of the miracles the apostles performed.**
2. **God comes to us in our darkest hours. In jail, the disciples were visited by an angel during the night hours. The encounter would have deep impact on the church.**
3. **We're to teach all the counsel of God. The angel clearly tells the apostles to "speak all the words of this life." We can't pick and choose what we share.**
4. **Man cannot keep in what God wants out. The authorities could lock up the disciples; but in response to prayer, God sends an angel to set them free.**
5. **When God's laws conflict with those of man, we must obey God. The apostles were told not to preach, but God had told them differently.**

LOOKING UP *Help me, Lord, to listen to You rather than seek the approval of the crowd. Give me the strength to do Your will when what You ask conflicts with the wishes of man.*

PREDICTION

NOVEMBER 8

Acts 6-7

LOOKING BACK It is scheduled to return again in 2061. Halley's Comet comes approximately every 76 years and is named after its discoverer, Edmund Halley. The English astronomer studied the paths of comets. Before he made his investigations, most people believed comets appeared by chance and traveled through space in no set path. Born on this date in 1656, Halley discovered his comet in 1682, and first conceived its periodicity. He accurately wrote, "I may venture to foretell this comet will return again in 1758." There have been 28 recorded appearances of Halley's comet since 240 B.C. Halley died long before he saw his prophecy come to pass.

LOOKING IN *Halley could make his accurate prediction since he knew God created the world to operate on a precise schedule. Just as the laws of nature are set and can be counted on, Abraham knew that God's Word was also sound and reliable. Therefore, he could leave his home without clear instructions where to go. All he knew was that God had told Him to go and would one day tell him where. This trusting attitude made Abraham our symbol of faith. Stephen, the church's first martyr, recalled the remarkable life of Abraham and God's dealing with His people. He did this to lead up to the fulfillment of prophecy and promise in Jesus Christ.*

LOOKING OUT

1. **You don't have to get better before you get saved. God called Abraham while he was still in Mesopotamia, apparently unconcerned about his future or relationship with Jehovah.**
2. **Faith is stepping out when you don't have all the facts. Abraham was told to leave but not where to go. Faith is always spelled R-I-S-K.**
3. **Faith is knowing that God will make His will known in His time. Abraham knew God's character and was assured that God would tell him his destination.**
4. **God's promises are not dependent on our prospects. Abraham and Sarah had absolutely no possibility of having a child, yet God promised a son.**
5. **God shares His secrets with His friends. Because Abraham lived close to the Creator, God revealed to Abraham the future of his descendants in stunning detail.**

LOOKING UP *Thank You, Lord, for giving me faith, though at times what You ask me to do is frightening. I will trust You and wait for Your instructions on the way I am to take.*

ASTOUNDED

NOVEMBER 9

Acts 8-9

LOOKING BACK Reverend Leonard Grimes turned his sermons into shoe leather. In Leesburg Virginia, in 1815, Grimes was born on this day to parents who were free. He grew to despise slavery. As a free Black man living in Washington D.C., Grimes became active in assisting fugitive slaves to escape, though it cost him his freedom. He was caught and imprisoned in Richmond, Virginia. After his imprisonment, Grimes founded and became the first minister of the Twelfth Street Baptist Church in Boston, Massachusetts, where he served until his death in 1874. Pastor Grimes wisely believed that faith is far more than merely claiming to be a Christian—it is what we do!

LOOKING IN *The very name, "The Book of Acts" suggests that faith is more than what one thinks or feels. Here we are introduced to many Spirit-filled people who made a deep impact on our world. Philip witnessed to the Ethiopian, who carried the message of the Gospel back to Africa. Saul of Tarsus was converted. He would forever change the world through his dynamic life and testimony. Dorcas also was one who did far more than merely claim to be a Christian. Her work was so effective that when she died, the whole community, being very upset, sought Peter to see if he could do something about the situation. He could—and did.*

LOOKING OUT

1. **A life well-lived is a life of serving. She had such an impact that all the saints wanted Dorcas to live. She had wisely spent her life helping others.**
2. **We're to minister to the poor and powerless. Dorcas was commended because she was always helping the poor.**
3. **Prayer is humbly seeking God's will. Peter fell to his knees, asking God's direction and healing for Dorcas. He willingly submitted to God's choice in the matter.**
4. **Prayer makes us bold to believe for the impossible. God gave Peter a gift of faith. Though Dorcas was dead, she came back to life through his prayer.**
5. **Faith in Christ breaks down raw and ugly prejudice. Peter, a good Jew, was now staying at an untouchable tanner's house, a place normally avoided.**

LOOKING UP *Help me, Lord, to live a life worth saving. May I not only believe in Christ but live my faith in practical expressions of love to others.*

FOUND

NOVEMBER 10

Acts 10-12

LOOKING BACK The man who opened up more of the world's surface than anyone else in history owed his success to a burning faith, a medicine chest, and unfailing good manners. Wherever David Livingstone traveled in unexplored Africa, he always treated the Africans with love and courtesy. Livingstone was born in Scotland and received a medical degree from the University of Glasgow. It was on this day, in 1871, that journalist Henry Stanley finally found Dr. Livingstone at Ujiji, Africa. Livingstone had been missing for two years. When the two met, Stanley uttered those often quoted, immortal words, "Dr. Livingstone, I presume."

LOOKING IN *Although Livingstone was world-famous, he was also most humble. He saw himself merely as God's servant. When a reporter once asked how he could sacrifice a lucrative medical practice to become a missionary, Livingstone replied, "If a commission by an earthly king is considered an honor, how can a commission by a Heavenly King be considered a sacrifice?" King Herod had just the opposite attitude. This pampered son of a famous family was quarrelsome and arrogant. It would be these negative qualities that would bring him down in horror. His arrogance would be cut short. He was struck down with a loathsome intestinal disease.*

LOOKING OUT

1. **Pride will bring us down. Herod, scion of the family ruling Palestine, was arrogant and surly. He died in pain. Pride heads the list of the seven sins God hates.**
2. **Flattery is deadly. The people hated Herod, but since they needed his food, they flattered him. The foolish and arrogant king believed their false praise.**
3. **It is dangerous not to acknowledge God. The angel of the Lord struck Herod down because he took all the praise. Moses reminded us that God will share His glory with no man.**
4. **Regardless of government, the Gospel goes forth. Rulers come and go, but truth marches on, winning more to Christ. The gates of hell will not prevail against the church.**
5. **God trains us for large tasks by giving us smaller ones. Paul was being prepared for his later work by being given a simple assignment of taking relief to the Judean Christians.**

LOOKING UP *Thank You, Lord, that whether a government is benevolent, belligerent, or benign toward the Gospel, Your Word will prosper. Help me to faithfully proclaim it.*

ZAPPED

NOVEMBER 11

Acts 13-15

LOOKING BACK He lived for combat. George S. Patton was born on this day in 1885. Ambitious and flamboyant, Patton served in Mexico, Europe, and North Africa. Known as "Old Blood and Guts," Patton received world attention and official censure in 1943 for slapping a hospitalized shell-shocked soldier. While a full general, Patton was relieved of his command in 1945. He had been extremely critical of leadership in public statements. Patton died at Heidelberg, Germany, on December 21, 1945, of injuries received in an automobile accident. Movies have been made about him and books written, because he was totally consumed with the mission of war.

LOOKING IN *Consumed with a mission is not always bad. Paul the apostle was also passionate about his mission. However, he ministered life rather than death. Acts 13 begins what has been called "The Acts of Paul," because he is now the dominant character in this history of the early church. Paul's work in bringing Christianity to Gentiles shows his tremendous energy and dedication. He is often called the "Apostle to the Gentiles." Immediately after Paul's conversion, he went to an area of Arabia that is now in Jordan and then to Syria and Cilicia. We know little about Paul's life as a missionary during the next 15 years. Then we learn more about this great man.*

LOOKING OUT

1. **Ministry starts where we are. Paul and Barnabas began their remarkable missionary endeavors by proclaiming God's Word in the Jewish synagogue.**
2. **The ministry is more grind than glory. John Mark soon left Paul and Barnabas because demands were too tough.**
3. **Satan always has those who try to keep sincere seekers away. Elymus tried to turn Sergius Paulus from faith in Jesus Christ.**
4. **The devil and his kids are no match for God's anointed. Paul struck Elymus blind, shocking all those who saw it. It's best not to mess with God's anointed.**
5. **God always satisfies the hungry of heart. The proconsul believed because God had proven His power and truth. An experience always overcomes an argument.**

LOOKING UP *Lord, help me to have the power to witness of Your Word and work in my life. May I never be intimidated by those who wish to stop the work You are doing.*

PROFESSIONAL

NOVEMBER 12

Acts 16-18

LOOKING BACK William "Pudge" Heffelfinger became the first professional football player on this day in 1892. Football originated in the United States. It began to develop during the mid-1800's, growing out of soccer and rugby, two kicking games that were developed in England. Heffelfinger was paid $25 for expenses and a cash bonus of $500. It was the cash bonus that made him a professional. Scoring the winning touchdown for the Allegheny Athletic Association, Heffelfinger's team beat the Pittsburgh Athletic Club, 4-0. Since then, professional football players have been part of our culture, and most usually, are grossly overpaid in today's sports-crazed society.

LOOKING IN *In today's reading, Paul becomes the first "professional" missionary to the Gentiles. At times he receives pay for his work, while at other times he works as a tentmaker to support his missionary efforts. Regardless of compensation, Paul is totally dedicated to sharing the Gospel that had changed his life. He and Barnabas do all they can to witness to their own people but are firmly rejected. Rather than giving up, Paul turns to the Gentiles who begin to eagerly accept Jesus Christ. The most productive period of Paul's career begins shortly before A.D. 50. Acts describes Paul's three missionary journeys during this period.*

LOOKING OUT

1. **Consistency is the key to successful witness. Paul went to the synagogue every Sabbath to testify of his faith in Jesus Christ.**
2. **To be effective in witness, we must have singleness of purpose. At this time, Paul specifically targeted his Jewish peers, trying to move them to faith.**
3. **When one rejects our message, we should move on to another who might be more open. The Jews rejected Paul's ministry, but that didn't stop him or his work.**
4. **When one door of opportunity is closed, God will open another for us. Paul, rejected by the Jews, now turns his full attention to winning the Gentiles to the Lord.**
5. **God assures us of His protection when we need it. Paul is moving into dangerous territory. God speaks to him in a vision assuring Paul he is in His care.**

LOOKING UP *Lord, give me a passion to share my faith with others. Thank You that You will help me to be faithful regardless of how my testimony is received.*

STRIKE

NOVEMBER 13

Acts 19-20

LOOKING BACK The first known sit-down strike occurred on this day in 1933 at the Hormel Packing Company. There are various kinds of strikes. A sit-down strike occurs when workers stop but don't leave their place of employment. An authorized strike is one agreed upon by the union. Also, there are wildcat strikes, called by workers without official union support; walkouts, where workers leave their jobs; sympathy strikes, when one union supports another striking union; jurisdictional strikes, when rival unions claim exclusive right to do certain work; and secondary strikes, where workers try to force employers to stop doing business with other struck businesses.

LOOKING IN *Strike tactics in the United States and other industrial countries have been relatively peaceful for many years. But fights, loss of life, and destruction of property were common in the 1800's and early 1900's. Rebellion can quickly escalate into violence and destruction. The people of Ephesus learned this when Demetrius stirred up rebellion against Paul's preaching. The Gospel was endangering the business of the idol-makers in Ephesus. In order to stir up opposition against the Christians, the craftsmen appealed to the civil pride of the city. It wasn't long before the protest got out of hand. A wise city clerk helped bring things under control.*

LOOKING OUT

1. When the god of this world is challenged, all hell breaks loose. Demetrius fomented a riot by mentioning how much money would be lost if the apostles were permitted to preach.
2. When we challenge old superstitions, anger often flares. The people of Ephesus got into an uproar when the validity of the Greek goddess Artemis was challenged.
3. Rebellion is contagious. The mob atmosphere spread. Soon the whole city of Ephesus was upset because Demetrius had started his rebellion against God.
4. Sometimes keeping silent is our best defense against false accusations. Paul wanted to speak, but other believers around him advised Paul to remain silent.
5. Reason can calm ruffled feathers. The wise city clerk of Ephesus reminded the people of the very real threat that their rebellion could be misunderstood by Roman rulers.

LOOKING UP *Thank You, Lord, that regardless of how the evil one rants and raves, You are always there to protect and guide me. Help me not to be intimidated by his tactics.*

COMMUNICATION

NOVEMBER 14

Acts 21-23

LOOKING BACK Renowned poet William Cowper was also one of the great English letter writers. A shy, gentle man, he suffered frequent attacks of spiritual despair. Perhaps that is what inspired him to write the famous hymn, "There is a Fountain Filled With Blood." This song was part of *Olney Hymns* produced by Cowper and his pastor, John Newton. The classic collection of songs included Newton's hymn, "Amazing Grace." Cowper possessed a wonderful sense of humor. On this day in 1782, he published a merry secular ballad entitled, "The History of John Gilpin, Showing How He Went Further Than He Intended, and Came Home Safe Again."

LOOKING IN *Paul perhaps "went further than he had intended" when he tried to accommodate critics who misunderstood his ministry to the Gentiles. However, the apostle's willingness to take the Jewish vow shows how much he sought peace, not division, among the early church membership. Garbled tales had reached the Jewish Christians in Jerusalem concerning Paul. Some of those rumors said that he had been teaching Jews to abandon circumcision and the law. Many had wrongly assumed he had brought Gentiles into the inner Temple, a clear violation of law. Paul made every effort to quell the rumors and show respect for his Jewish brothers.*

LOOKING OUT

1. **No matter how big we get, we should still submit to authority. Paul willingly and humbly placed himself under church leadership.**
2. **Good communication is constructive. After Paul had explained what God was doing, church leaders rejoiced in all that was happening.**
3. **Misinformation breeds confusion and contention. Jewish Christians misunderstood Paul's divine calling and ministry to the Gentiles.**
4. **At times, we have to sacrifice to bring peace. Even though it was not required, Paul submitted to the Jewish vow to alleviate tension.**
5. **A good man wants peace more than he wants his own way. To ensure peace, Paul, without complaining, submitted to the leader's request.**

LOOKING UP *Help me, Lord, to seek peace where there is conflict. Make me wise enough to avoid dissension and division, without sacrificing truth and principles.*

DECEIT

NOVEMBER 15

Acts 24-26

LOOKING BACK This is "George Spelvin Day." November 15 is believed to be the anniversary of George Spelvin's theatrical birth in Charles A. Gardiner's play, *Karl the Peddler*. This 1886 production was the first time a fictitious name was used in a play program to hide the fact that an actor is performing in more than one role. Since then, the name George Spelvin, or its female equivalent (Georgina, Georgette, etc.), has stood for theatrical deceit. Since that first presentation, the fictitious George Spelvin is said to have appeared in over 10,000 Broadway performances. In English theater, the equivalent to George Spelvin is Walter Plinge.

LOOKING IN *Jewish leaders opposed to the early church had to resort to all kinds of deceit to try to stop the rapid growth of Christianity. Ananias, the Jewish high priest from A.D. 47 to A.D. 58, engaged a lawyer named Tertullus to bring false charges against the apostles, but it didn't work. Ananias wanted to appease Roman authorities and representatives. This is what probably prompted him to take such a personal interest in destroying Paul. History reveals that because of Ananias' pro-Roman sentiments, he was brutally assassinated by anti-Roman Jewish revolutionaries at the outbreak of the first great Jewish revolt against Rome, in the year A.D. 66.*

LOOKING OUT

1. **Evil men will go to great lengths to discredit God's work. Ananias and the elders were so determined to destroy Paul that they endured hardship just to accuse him.**
2. **When you're right, all you have to do is tell the truth. Tertulus "buttered up" Felix with flattery and lies, while all Paul did was present the facts.**
3. **Preaching righteousness strikes fear in unbelievers. Felix was terrified when Paul talked of self-control and judgment, since it pointed out the leader's fatal flaw.**
4. **Indecision is a decision. Felix was obviously convicted by what he heard, but he put off making an immediate decision.**
5. **When we are in God's hands, we don't have to buy our way out of trouble. Paul knew God would take care of him and refused to pay the bribe wanted.**

LOOKING UP *Thank You, Lord, because truth sets me free from many anxieties. I rest in You for Your constant protection and provision.*

DEVASTATION

NOVEMBER 16

Acts 27-28

LOOKING BACK General William T. Sherman started his devastating "march to the sea" on this day in 1864. Sherman was a leading Union general in the American Civil War who became most famous for the march across Georgia and for another through the Carolinas in 1865. On these marches, Sherman's troops destroyed much of the South's military and economic resources. He captured Atlanta, burning most of it. He then began his "march to the sea," where his troops stripped barns, fields, and some houses. Sherman hoped that the terrible destruction would break the South's will to continue fighting. The march ended at Savannah, Georgia, near the ocean.

LOOKING IN *Satan did all he could to discourage Paul from continuing his mission. One devastation after another hit the determined apostle. No sooner had the apostle been saved from shipwreck than a snake sank its fiery fangs into his arm. It is not known what kind of snake struck Paul on the island of Malta. Apparently, it was a deadly variety. The islanders were sure Paul would die within minutes. They reasoned that the gods were out to get him even though he had escaped the sea. When he didn't die, the islanders assumed Paul was superhuman. He used the occasion to tell them about Jesus. Salvation came to the island.*

LOOKING OUT

1. **God always keeps His promises no matter how dark things appear. God had promised that no lives would be lost in the shipwreck, and they weren't.**
2. **Satan always continues his attack. Paul escaped death at sea, but then the poisonous snake bit him as he gathered firewood.**
3. **We can shake Satan's attacks off without harm. Paul confidently and defiantly shook off the viper into the fire. The poisonous bite did not harm him.**
4. **God always turns the negative to the positive. Satan tried to kill Paul, but God turned the tables on the enemy by sending a revival to the remote island.**
5. **God provides for the minister through those receiving the ministry. The blessed islanders gladly provided Paul's needed supplies.**

LOOKING UP *Thank You, Lord, that although the evil one attacks, he cannot destroy what You protect. Keep me confident of Your protection as I work for You.*

CHARGES

NOVEMBER 17

Romans 1-3

LOOKING BACK On this day in 1734, colonial printer and journalist John Peter Zenger was arrested and charged with libel because he had criticized British Governor William Cosby in his newspaper. He published the New York Weekly Journal. The British arrested Zenger and tried him in 1735 for criminal libel. Zenger's lawyers were disbarred, and he was left almost defenseless. Finally, Alexander Hamilton, a famous Philadelphia lawyer, took his case and persuaded a jury to find Zenger "not guilty." Hamilton argued that Zenger had printed the truth, and that truth is not libelous. This was the first major victory for freedom of the press in the colonies.

LOOKING IN *Paul the apostle was accused of all kinds of things because of his testimony for Christ. Arrested, tried, and convicted, Paul kept on preaching the truth until he was finally executed. Paul's great love for Christ manifested itself not only in his life but also in his writings. The book of Romans is Paul's great doctrinal epistle, presenting the case for the Gospel. Romans is Paul's longest and most systematic letter. The main theme of the first 11 chapters is that Jews and Gentiles are equally in need of salvation and both have access to salvation through faith in Jesus Christ. In the five remaining chapters, Paul discusses problems in Christian living.*

LOOKING OUT

1. **Sin has infected us all. Paul notes Gentiles and Jews are alike, for all have been stained and enslaved by sin. All of humanity needs the salvation Jesus offers.**
2. **Telling what is wrong doesn't make it right. Paul notes that while the law was good, it failed because it could only point out evil, not change it.**
3. **It is not what we have done, but Who we know. Salvation is by faith in Christ alone. We are made righteous by a personal relationship with our Lord.**
4. **Faith is a flower that blooms for all. Paul said this righteousness comes to all who believe in Jesus Christ. God is no respecter of persons.**
5. **Justice demanded the death of Christ. Sin could not go unpunished; it had to be dealt with. Therefore, God sent His only begotten Son.**

LOOKING UP *Thank you, Lord, for the law which pointed out the problem. Thank You even more for Jesus Christ, Who provided the solution for my sin by His vicarious death on the cross.*

DOCTRINE

NOVEMBER 18

Romans 4-5

LOOKING BACK Louis Jacques Mande Dagurre, French tax collector, theater scene painter, physicist, and inventor was born on this day in 1789. Dagurre is best remembered for his invention of the daguerreotype photographic process. It was one of the earliest ways to permit a photographic image to be chemically fixed to provide a permanent picture. The process was presented to the French Academy of Science on January 8, 1839. Daguerreotype portraits were tremendously popular during the 1840's and 1850's. The daguerreotype was eventually replaced by other processes but was the start of man's ability to communicate clearly through pictures.

LOOKING IN *Just as the daguerreotype let men see nature as it really was, not only as artists depicted it, so the Law defined sin. However, while the Law could sharply define the difference between right and wrong, it could do nothing to correct the situation. The book of Romans says this is where Jesus comes in. God sent His Son so that we could be free from sin and death. Romans is the sixth book of the New Testament. It's a letter from the apostle Paul to the Christians in Rome, probably written from Corinth, Greece, about A.D. 56. The epistle was a letter of introduction, preparing the way for a visit Paul intended to make on his way to do missionary work in Spain.*

LOOKING OUT

1. Sin is hereditary and contagious. Paul makes the point that Adam's sin corrupted the whole race. All who are born are now infected by it.
2. Death became necessary because of sin. If there were no death to stop an exceedingly evil person, this world would be a cesspool–hell itself.
3. The Law made it possible for us to identify sin because it points out what displeases God. Sin existed before the law but was not defined until after the law was given.
4. Salvation and life come only by decision. While sin affects all, salvation is reserved only for those who trust in Christ and turn from their wicked ways.
5. God's grace grows faster than man's evil. We must not be discouraged. Paul says, "But where sin increased, grace increased all the more..."

LOOKING UP *Thank You, Father, that You have forgiven my sins. I am so grateful You not only told me where I was wrong but have provided a way of salvation.*

ELOQUENCE

NOVEMBER 19

Romans 6-8

LOOKING BACK Abraham Lincoln didn't think much of the speech he gave on this day in 1863. In fact, noted orator Edward Everett had spoken for two hours, while the address President Lincoln gave lasted less than two minutes. Later, one newspaper criticized Lincoln by saying the speech was an insult to all those who had lost their lives on that spot. The occasion of Lincoln's speech was the dedication of 17 acres of a battlefield at Gettysburg that had been set aside as a national cemetery. Today, the Gettysburg Address by Lincoln is considered one of the most eloquent speeches ever delivered in the English language. The critical newspaper editor was dead wrong.

LOOKING IN *Eloquence is not measured by a great number of words; it is determined by content of thought. Romans eight is one of the most eloquent dissertations known. Earlier, Paul had pointed out that God's forgiveness is big enough to deal with any amount of human sin. Now he states we are guilt-free if we have given our hearts to the Lord. Chapter eight starts with "no condemnation" and ends with "no separation." Paul reminds us the Holy Spirit is alive and active within us. He gives us the ability to pray and understand God's ways. The Holy Spirit's presence convinces us we really are God's children in spite of what the evil one says.*

LOOKING OUT

1. **There is a vast difference between conviction and condemnation. The Holy Spirit doesn't point out our sin to embarrass us but to bring us to Jesus.**
2. **We can measure a man by how he thinks. Paul states that the good man will always have the mind of Christ. All other thinking is corrupt.**
3. **Praying in the Spirit gives us power. Only the Holy Spirit gives us power, and only the Holy Spirit knows God's will. As He prompts prayers, answers come.**
4. **Tough times are never terminal for the believer. Paul understood that all things work together for good because God is always in control.**
5. **We are totally secure in Christ. Nothing on this earth or in the spiritual world can separate us from our loving Christ. We can rest in His protection and care.**

LOOKING UP *Precious Holy Spirit, fill my life with Your presence. May I always permit You to pray through me and use me as You desire. Let me ever lift up Jesus.*

SALVATION

Romans 9-11

LOOKING BACK Born at Marshfield, Missouri, on this day in 1889, Edwin Powell Hubble's name has long outlived him. Hubble was the astronomer who discovered and developed the concept of an expanding universe. He was the first to demonstrate that the universe contains star systems other than our galaxy, the Milky Way. His contribution has been called "the most spectacular astronomical discovery of the 20th century." As a tribute, the Hubble Space Telescope, deployed from the U.S. Space Shuttle Discovery, was named for him. The Hubble Space Telescope, with a 240-centimeter mirror, allows man to see farther into space than ever before.

LOOKING IN *While Hubble's discoveries may be "the most spectacular astronomical discovery of the 20th century," they can't compare to the thrill of finding Christ. Paul clearly outlines what it takes to be saved and mourns for those who have rejected Christ. He says God still has good things ahead for the Jews. All can be saved. Romans is the most significant theological letter ever written. Augustine of Hippo, the most influential of the church fathers, was converted upon reading it. Martin Luther was studying Romans when he learned that faith alone justifies us before God. John Wesley was converted while reading Luther's introduction to Romans.*

LOOKING OUT

1. It's not enough to be religious; we must know God. Paul stated that his people's zeal was intense but misdirected. They had missed the Messiah.
2. Spiritual arrogance breeds apostasy. Paul reminds us that the misdirected often seek to establish their own righteousness, not God's.
3. There are two steps to salvation–confession and positioning. We must confess that Jesus is able to help us, and then make Him the living center of our life.
4. We are expected to tell the good news of Christ. Paul said the lost cannot know about God unless they are told. We have an awesome responsibility to share our witness.
5. Faith is fed by God's Word. Romans notes that faith comes from hearing the message from the Word of God. The more we hear God's Word, the greater our faith.

LOOKING UP *Thank You, Lord, for saving my soul. Please give me the wisdom and the way to communicate my faith to those who are lost. Help me to be concerned for them as You are for me.*

RELATIONSHIPS

NOVEMBER 21

Romans 12-14

LOOKING BACK She was known by many as the "Witch of Wall Street." Hetty Green, the richest woman in the world at the time of her death, was born on this day in 1835 at New Bedford, Maine. Henrietta Howland Robinson Green had inherited some $6 million of her money from her father but parlayed it into an incredible fortune of $100 million through shrewd investments and careful management. She spent little on personal comforts. Hetty was miserly and difficult, thus earning her title. Hetty lived in cheap boardinghouses; wore ancient, tattered, and faded clothes; and rode around town in a carriage that had once been used as a henhouse.

LOOKING IN *Hetty Green died rich but bereft of friends. She had invested her life in things that didn't last. Paul told the Romans they needed to work on their relationships as part of their faith in Christ. The petty arguments over small differences were to stop, and peace was to be pursued by the church. This final section of Romans is a summons to practical obedience to God. Paul says Christians should live transformed lives and demonstrate this in good stewardship of their spiritual gifts, in fulfilling their obligations to the state, in making love supreme, and in seeking to nurture others in the fellowship of the church, being particularly careful to bear with and edify the weak.*

LOOKING OUT

1. Accept each other. Paul admonished the Romans to accept those whose faith was weak, without comment, rather than putting them down because they lacked maturity.
2. Allow for each other. Paul told us not to look down on those who are different than we are, for God accepts them. If God takes them in, who are we to keep them out?
3. Respect each other. We all come from different experiences, and many of our religious expressions have much to do with the culture from which we come.
4. Remove the roadblocks. Often religious people set up rules that keep others away. Paul said we are to make faith appealing to the outsider.
5. Some things are better left unsaid. Rather than argue differences, Paul advises, "Whatever you believe about these things keep between yourself and God."

LOOKING UP *Help me, Lord, never to be part of division and dissension. Help me to bring the church together in spiritual unity rather than split it in angry differences.*

VIOLENCE

NOVEMBER 22

Romans 15-16

LOOKING BACK "Stop the Violence Day" is observed annually on this day. It is the sad anniversary of President John F. Kennedy's assassination. Begun in 1990, this special day operates on the premise, "If we can stop the violence for one day, we can stop the violence every day, one day at a time." During this time, the media is asked to encourage the public to display white ribbons and drive with their headlights on as a show of peace. Through the years on this day, some peace rallies have been held, with television and radio stations often observing a moment of silence in honor of the year's victims of violence. Sadly, this effort has had little effect in stopping violence.

LOOKING IN *Violence and broken relationships are spiritual problems and can only be solved through spiritual solutions. Paul admonishes the Romans to get along, as an expression of their faith in Jesus Christ. All of us are prone to selfishness. Therefore, we must have Christ's help to overcome it. In the conclusion of this remarkable letter to the Romans, Paul summarizes his ministry and his plans for the future. He requests the readers' prayers and commends Phoebe. After sending greetings to individual Christians, Paul ends Romans with praise for God "to the only wise God through Jesus Christ be glory for endless ages! Amen."*

LOOKING OUT

1. **The strong are to help the weak. We must not be arrogant, for all of us are at different points in our journey. The more mature among us are to lead.**
2. **We must not be self-centered. Paul warns that believers are not to please themselves but serve the Lord and others, just as Christ took the towel and basin.**
3. **God's Word strengthens and lifts us. Paul notes that we should always desire God's Word. Scripture gives enormous strength and encouragement.**
4. **Our unity glorifies God. Paul prayed for a spirit of unity. He desired that with one heart all might bring glory to our Lord.**
5. **Accepting others brings praise to God. Too often, we major on minor differences and bring division. Paul told us to accept others in Christ.**

LOOKING UP *Thank You, Lord, for doctrine. Help me to keep Your doctrine free of the litter of personal and cultural preferences.*

KILLERS

NOVEMBER 23

1 Corinthians 1-3

LOOKING BACK Famed killer Billy the Kid was born on this date in 1859. "The Kid," as he was known, was a failure at everything legal. He escaped from jail at age 21 while under the sentence of hanging. Recaptured at Stinking Springs, New Mexico and returned to jail, he again escaped, only to be shot through the heart by pursuing Lincoln County Sheriff Pat Garrett at Fort Sumner, New Mexico, during the night of July 14, 1881. Billy's real name was Henry McCarty. He was said to have been born in New York City. He shot a man to death during a quarrel and became a fugitive, using the name William H. Bonney. He would soon be known as Billy the Kid.

LOOKING IN *Paul spoke of another kind of killer in his Corinthian letter. These were believers killing the church because they had divided into quarreling groups, insisting their leader was better than others. Paul warns that true leaders are servants. Both Corinthian letters are written to members of the church Paul established in Corinth, Greece. Paul wrote the first letter from Ephesus, in what is now Turkey, about A.D. 54. In the first half of the letter, he discusses problems reported to him orally, especially the problem of divisions in the church. In the rest of the letter, Paul discusses questions the Corinthians had raised in a letter they wrote to Paul.*

LOOKING OUT

1. **There are no stars in the kingdom, only servants. Paul condemned the Corinthians for exalting man over God. Jesus set the principle of servant leadership.**
2. **We labor at our various tasks, but God gives the increase. Paul says that like the farmer we plow and plant, yet only God can cause what is planted to grow.**
3. **We will be rewarded in proportion to our effort. Those who labor hard and faithfully will be given great rewards. Those who labor little will be paid accordingly.**
4. **We are all being grown and built by God. Paul uses two vivid word pictures to remind us that God is the Master Cultivator and Constructor of our lives.**
5. **We must not be careless with how and what we teach and preach. Doctrine is very important. We must build properly on the right foundation.**

LOOKING UP *Help me, Lord, to have a good and tender spirit. Forgive me for the times I have acted ugly and not properly portrayed what it is to be a follower of You.*

LAWSUITS

NOVEMBER 24

1 Corinthians 4-6

LOOKING BACK During the Civil War, the decisive Battle of Chattanooga, Tennessee occurred on this date in 1863. Union General Ulysses S. Grant launched this famed battle which shook the arrogant confidence of the Confederacy. Falsely secure in the knowledge that his troops were in an impregnable position on Lookout Mountain, Confederate General Braxton Bragg and his army were overrun by the Union Forces. Bragg himself barely escaped capture. The Battle of Chattanooga is famous for the Union Army's spectacular advance up a heavily fortified slope into the teeth of enemy guns. It was a turning point in the bloody war between the states.

LOOKING IN *The Corinthians had a similar arrogance that nearly brought them ruin. Paul had to correct this highly successful church because their actions were wrong. One major issue was the constant quarreling that led to one lawsuit after another. In addition to Jerusalem, Antioch of Syria, and Ephesus, Corinth was one of four prominent centers in the New Testament account of the early church. Paul's first extended ministry in one city was at Corinth. His three longest letters are associated with Corinth. First and Second Corinthians were written to Corinth. Aquila, Priscilla, Silas, Timothy, Apollos, and Titus were all in Corinth.*

LOOKING OUT

1. When wronged, our first appeal should not be to the courts. Since believers are to judge the world one day, present conflicts should be arbitrated by believers.
2. Conflict resolution helps prepare us for the day we will judge angels. The way we handle these issues trains us for our future roles which are bigger than we think.
3. Wisdom doesn't come from earthly position, power, or prestige. Paul tells the church to select good judges based on their spiritual wisdom, not earthly knowledge.
4. Continued conflicts tell us much about ourselves and our maturity level in Christ. Paul says the quarrels prove the Corinthians are immature.
5. If we want to make heaven, there is a crowd we must avoid. Paul listed those who would never have eternal life and those who would drag us down.

LOOKING UP *Thank You, Lord, that no matter how evil I have been, there is forgiveness and restoration in You. I rejoice in the fact that You have made me Your child.*

HOLD IT!

NOVEMBER 25

1 Corinthians 7-8

LOOKING BACK One of the world's richest and most giving men was born on this date in 1835 in Dunfermline, Scotland. Andrew Carnegie was an American financier, philanthropist, and benefactor of more that 2,500 libraries, concert halls, and other educational facilities. Carnegie Hall, Carnegie Foundation, and the Carnegie Endowment for International Peace are among his gifts. Carnegie sincerely believed that wealthy individuals should use their fortunes to aid people and society. He opposed charity but believed in helping others to help themselves, chiefly by providing educational opportunities. Carnegie wrote, "The man who dies rich, dies disgraced."

LOOKING IN *Carnegie knew that happiness does not reside in a change of financial status or circumstances. It is internal, and one has to fulfill his divine calling to really be joyful. Paul encouraged the Corinthians to stop thinking like the world and to settle down to the place God assigned them. Corinth was a cosmopolitan city composed of people from varying cultural backgrounds. They enjoyed both the pleasures of the Isthmian games and the wealth the visitors brought to the city. While their ships were being carried across the isthmus, sailors came to the city to spend money. Even in an age of sexual immorality, Corinth was known for its licentious lifestyle.*

LOOKING OUT

1. Marriage is more than self-fulfillment. With marriage, the believer becomes responsible for his or her mate's welfare and comfort.
2. We must get into a position where we are less tempted. Paul tells those who can't act appropriately to get married rather than burn with lust.
3. We are not to manipulate others. Paul said that if an unbeliever wanted to depart a marriage, let him or her go rather than try to control the unbeliever's behavior.
4. God wants us to stay where we are. Happiness does not reside in another position. Each of us has been assigned a place in life by God, Who wants us where we are.
5. Obedience is the key to pleasing God. It is important that we do all God asks and stay where we are assigned until God chooses to change our position.

LOOKING UP *Forgive me, Lord, for listening to the world that tells me I will be happier if I change my circumstances. Help me remember that my real joy lies in being where You want me.*

SELFLESS

NOVEMBER 26

1 Corinthians 9-11

LOOKING BACK Today marks the anniversary of the first United States holiday set by presidential proclamation. President George Washington proclaimed this day in 1789 as "Thanksgiving Day." Both houses of Congress, by their joint committee, had requested him "to recommend a day of public thanksgiving and prayer, to be observed by acknowledging with grateful hearts the many and signal favors of Almighty God, especially by affording them an opportunity to peaceably establish a form of government for their safety and happiness." For many years, the country had no regular national Thanksgiving Day until Abraham Lincoln established it in 1863.

LOOKING IN *Thanksgiving and praise are designated to move us beyond self-centeredness to acknowledge the wonderful provision and protection of our God. Paul admonished the Corinthians to start thinking beyond their own selfish desires to the needs and feelings of others. Real faith always looks beyond itself. It cares and shares. Believers are to be different from the rest of the world. While most others are self-centered, the true believer must be God-centered and put the welfare of others before his own. This exemplifies the mind of Christ. James reminds us that pure religion is to care for the helpless and to stay pure from the world's contamination.*

LOOKING OUT

1. **There are things that we can do but shouldn't. Even though some things are permitted, Paul tells the church that these might be lawful but not beneficial.**
2. **We should constantly denounce selfishness. The great apostle admonishes the Corinthians not to seek their own good but the good of others.**
3. **We must respect another's conscience. Cultural differences forbid some things that are allowed elsewhere. We must recognize that principle in our actions toward others.**
4. **Everything we do should be for God's glory. In a selfish world, we stand out because our goals are far different than those aims of society.**
5. **All our actions are to bring others to Christ. Paul structured his behavior and lifestyle so that others might find salvation.**

LOOKING UP *Help me, Lord, to be aware of how others see my walk with You. Let me live so close to You that I will be a good testimony.*

GIFTS

NOVEMBER 27

1 Corinthians 12-14

LOOKING BACK Stratford-on-Avon is a quiet English market town, famous as the birthplace of William Shakespeare, and one of the oldest towns in England. Reverend Francis Gastrell made the mistake of cutting down a sacred tree there, and on this day in 1759, the town corporation expelled him from the community. Gastrell had lived in Shakespeare's home and tired of admirers of the bard swarming over his property to look at the 150-year-old mulberry tree. The tree had been planted by Shakespeare. When it was cut down, the townspeople were so enraged they demanded the vicar to leave. He did, "amid ragings and cursings of its people."

LOOKING IN *It's amazing that people can get so upset over things that are temporal and ignore the spiritual. Paul encouraged the Corinthians to seek spiritual things over the temporary. God has made wonderful gifts available to enhance our walk with Him and to help us accomplish our assignments. The Corinthians believed that spectacular religious expressions showed a man's spiritual status. God had given the church many remarkable gifts. Paul doesn't underestimate these gifts but does bring the church back into proper balance in their expression. The gifts were given to edify the church, not to enhance the reputation of the one who had the gift.*

LOOKING OUT

1. **There is a treasure-trove of gifts available to us. Paul admonished the church to become aware of spiritual gifts and to seek them for the benefit of the entire church.**
2. **All gifts of God lift up Jesus Christ. The best way to separate truth from error is to discover who is lifted up. The Holy Spirit speaks of Christ, not Himself.**
3. **We are all different but in one way the same. While we all have different abilities, anointings, and assignments, we have the same Holy Spirit.**
4. **The gifts of the Holy Spirit are for the common good, not ego-boosting. God's gifts are to strengthen and assist all the church, not to bolster one person's reputation.**
5. **God chooses who gets what. While we desire the best gifts, the Holy Spirit wisely decides who to anoint for what task. We must trust His choices.**

LOOKING UP *Thank You, Lord, that supernatural assistance is available to us through the gifts of the Holy Spirit. Fill me with Your Spirit that I might be more effective for You.*

GIVING

1 Corinthians 15-16

LOOKING BACK John Bunyan was born on this date in 1628. He was the famed English preacher who spent many years in jail for his testimony and preaching. Best known for his classic work, *Pilgrim's Progress,* Bunyan came to know the Lord through the influence of his dedicated wife. He became convinced he had led a bad life and joined a nonconformist church in Bedford. Soon he began to preach there. Bunyan was arrested for preaching without a license and was jailed in 1660. He spent most of the next 12 years in prison, was released, and then rearrested in 1675. During the last prison term, Bunyan penned his greatest work, *Pilgrim's Progress.*

LOOKING IN *Like John Bunyan, Paul was no stranger to persecution for his preaching. Like the gifted English preacher, Paul never gave up. In his stirring letter to the Corinthians, Paul admonishes them to seek spiritual gifts that would assist them as they went through the fire. Closing his first letter to the Corinthians, Paul takes up some practical matters. He instructs them on how they are to handle their offerings. He writes that he is looking forward to an extended visit with them. Paul also takes time to give them news and instructions about various individuals they know and then closes with greetings from the Asian churches.*

LOOKING OUT

1. **God expects consistent giving. Paul told the church to set aside a time weekly to receive the tithes and offerings. Giving teaches us to be unselfish and loving.**
2. **God expects equal sacrifice, not equal gifts. God's method of investment in His Kingdom is fair. We are to give according to our incomes.**
3. **God expects accountability from those who handle the offerings. Paul set up a careful plan so that those who gave were assured their offerings were used properly.**
4. **All our actions must be prompted by love. Paul said we are to be on guard, stand firm, and have courage and love. He reminded the Corinthians that love is the greater grace.**
5. **"Giving" people deserve recognition. Paul took time to appreciate those who cared for his needs. In recognizing generosity, Paul encouraged others to learn the grace of giving.**

LOOKING UP *Lord, help me to remember that worship involves all of my life. It is how I live and how I give. May all of my actions be motivated and guided by love.*

NEW LIFE

NOVEMBER 29

2 Corinthians 1-4

LOOKING BACK Czechoslovakia began a new life as a nation on this day in 1989. Forty-one years of one-party communist rule ended with the nation's parliament voting unanimously to repeal the constitutional clauses giving the party power. The vote came at the end of a 12-day revolution sparked by the beating of protestors. Although the communist party remained in power, the tide of reform led to its ouster by the Civic Forum, headed by playwright Vaclav Havel. Demands were made for free elections with equal rights for all parties, a mixed economy, and support for foreign investments. In the first free election since World War II, Havel became president.

LOOKING IN *Saul of Tarsus was given a new life on the Damascus road. At an early age, Paul had entered the synagogue day school where he learned to read and write by copying Scripture. He eventually went to Jerusalem to study under the famous rabbi, Gamaliel. When he met Christ on the road to Damascus, Paul's whole life was changed and his ministry set. Paul didn't hesitate to remind the churches that he possessed apostolic authority from the Lord. He stated that his appointment was from God and that he preached the authentic gospel because he received it by dramatic revelation. His call was recognized by the leaders of the Jerusalem church.*

LOOKING OUT

1. God's great mercy offsets any trials we might face. Paul was so thrilled God had called him that he ignored all difficulties.
2. Ministry must be open and straightforward. Paul says that he is always careful to "tell it like it is" and not practice any kind of deception in his preaching.
3. Sin blinds us to reality. The Gospel is only hidden from those who refuse to believe. Satan has succeeded in blinding their eyes to truth.
4. Our weakness emphasizes God's strength. Paul says his humanness shows the all-surpassing power of God. All that is done is accomplished by the mercy and grace of God.
5. We may be knocked down, but we are never knocked out. Paul assures us that difficulties do come, but we are not defeated by them.

LOOKING UP *Help me, Lord, to be so caught up with the great mercy of God that I overlook any hardships and trials of ministry. Thank You that You have called me into Your work.*

MAGNANIMOUS

2 Corinthians 5-9

LOOKING BACK Winston Churchill was born on this day in 1874. Often called, "the man of the century," Churchill became one of the greatest statesmen in world history. He reached the height of his fame as the heroic Prime Minister of Great Britain during World War II. Churchill offered his people only "blood, toil, tears, and sweat" as they struggled to keep their freedom. Early in World War II, Great Britain stood alone against Nazi Germany. The British people refused to give in despite the tremendous odds against them. Churchill's personal courage, the magic of his words, and his faith in victory inspired the British to "their finest hour."

LOOKING IN *After the War that ended Nazi horror, Churchill generously refused to take credit for what he had done. He said, "It was the nation that had the lion heart. I had the luck to be called upon to give the roar." It was this type of magnanimous attitude that Paul encouraged in the Corinthians. He spent a great deal of time telling the church they needed to be generous in their attitudes and in giving. This generous spirit is a sign of spiritual maturity and is a great testimony to others. Practical instructions rub shoulders here with spiritual principles. Christian giving is a loving response to the self-giving of our Lord Jesus Christ. We should give cheerfully and often.*

LOOKING OUT

1. Loving people give out of their need, not just their abundance. It is easy for those who have a lot to give, but Paul commends the Macedonians for giving out of their little.
2. Spiritually mature people are generous. Paul wanted the Corinthians to excel in giving as they did in other things, proving their maturity in Jesus Christ.
3. Our giving exposes the sincerity of our faith. If we love our Lord, we will love His work. Paul tested the Corinthians by challenging them to give generously to God.
4. God wants us to give willingly. Giving, Paul noted, is a great privilege and honor, not a tiresome burden. God loves a cheerful giver.
5. God desires equality. Our plenty is to supply for needs of others; their plenty is to meet our needs. One day we might need the help of others just as they need ours now.

LOOKING UP *Lord, help me to discard fear that can keep me from generosity to You and Your work. May I fully trust in You as Provider and obey quickly when You impress me to give.*

DECEMBER..........

A Misnamed Month for Gifts and Giving

It's called "the frosty month," but that is misleading. While winter does begin in December in the northern half of the world, it doesn't officially start until December 21 or 22. Thus, most of December is usually warmer than other winter months. On the first day of winter, the sun reaches the solstice, when it appears to have gone farthest south. In the Northern Hemisphere, it is the shortest day of the year, and the longest day in the southern half of the world. December is the 12th and last month of the year according to the Gregorian calendar. It was the 10th month in the early Roman calendar taking its name from the Latin word *decem*, which means 10. It became the 12th month in a later Roman calendar. In 46 B.C., Julius Caesar added two days to December, which before had only 29 days.

The latter part of December has long been a holiday season. Christmas is the chief holiday of the month. Some in New England observe December 21 as Forefathers' Day in honor of the landing of the Pilgrims at Plymouth on December 21, 1620. People in several European countries celebrate December 6 as the Feast of Saint Nicholas. After Christmas Day on December 25, some churches observe the Feast of Saint Stephen on December 26, the Feast of Saint John the Evangelist on December 27, and Holy Innocents' Day on December 28. Boxing Day is observed in Britain, Australia, New Zealand, and Canada. This includes giving money and other gifts to charitable institutions, needy individuals, and people in service jobs. The holiday's exact origin is unknown. It may have begun with the lords and ladies of England, who presented Christmas gifts in boxes to their servants on December 26. Or it may have begun with priests, who opened the church's alms (charity) boxes on the day after Christmas and distributed the contents to the poor.

During December, in the Northern Hemisphere, most birds have gone to warmer climates. But many animals are active. Mink, ermine, beavers, and foxes grow beautiful coats of fur. Nature finishes preparing for the long winter ahead. Many people make feeding places for birds and squirrels. This month, we finish reading God's Word and prepare to start through it again on January 1. We study the Pauline epistles, the general epistles, and end with the magnificent book of Revelation that points to a new world under the leadership of our Lord Jesus Christ.

IDEALS

2 Corinthians 10-13

LOOKING BACK On this day in 1955, Rosa Parks, a Black woman from Montgomery, Alabama, was arrested after refusing to give up her seat on a city bus, testing the city's racial segregation laws. That incident sparked the Civil Rights Movement which brought Martin Luther King, Jr. to the forefront. For 382 days, from December 5, 1955 to December 20, 1956, thousands of Blacks refused to ride Montgomery's buses. Their boycott ended when the U.S. Supreme Court declared segregated seating on city buses unconstitutional. The boycott's success encouraged other mass protests demanding civil rights for Blacks, and it exposed the tragedy of segregation.

LOOKING IN *One of segregation's greatest tragedies is that it, like sin, strips dignity from all of us. God's Word speaks much about this matter. Paul ends his writings to the Corinthians by urging them to give dignity, respect, and love to each other. He notes that God wants His children to be men and women of peace and love, not people promoting conflict and confusion. We are to reflect the character of our Lord, Who loves and accepts all who come to Him. This is not always easy, but it is necessary. Paul looks forward to this third visit with the Corinthians. When he comes he doesn't want to encounter bickering, splinter groups, and general disorder among them.*

LOOKING OUT

1. **We are to examine ourselves, not the weaknesses of others. There is plenty in our own lives that needs attention.**
2. **Our goal is to be like Jesus. To be a disciple of our Lord means that we strive to be Christ-like. Our aim is for perfection; our model is the Lord Jesus Christ.**
3. **Unity is precious to God. Paul admonished the Corinthians to strive to be of one mind in Christ. Keeping the peace among us is hard but necessary business.**
4. **Peace is hard to come by but is absolutely necessary. God wants His children to be peacemakers and peace keepers.**
5. **Respect and love for others marks us as God's children. We are lovingly and respectfully to greet others in Christ.**

LOOKING UP *Help me, Lord, always to aim for the highest goals of Christian living, expressing love for God and others daily. Make me more patient with others.*

HEART

DECEMBER 2

Galatians 1-6

LOOKING BACK Barney C. Clark became the first recipient of an artificial heart on this day in 1982. A surgical team led by William C. DeVries of the University of Utah implanted a mechanical device as the first permanent artificial heart. The device used, an air-powered Jarvik-7 heart, was designed by American physician Robert K. Jarvik. The operation was performed on the 61-year-old Clark at Utah Medical Center in Salt Lake City. Near death at the time of the operation, Clark survived almost 112 days after the implantation. He died on March 23, 1983. This medical breakthrough would have many positive effects for heart treatment in the years that followed.

LOOKING IN *While physical hearts can be transplanted, there is no physician who can change the sinful human heart. That ability is our Lord's alone. He can perform a spiritual heart transplant, taking our old nature and making it new. In Galatians, Paul contrasts the two natures of man–flesh and Spirit. He does this in a brilliant word picture involving fruit. Paul says there is the fruit of the flesh and the fruit of the Spirit. He then describes what that fruit is. We are admonished to sow to please the Spirit rather than to please the flesh.Whatever we sow will grow. We can be different, but it is a work of God's Spirit. Good things happen when we accept Christ.*

LOOKING OUT

1. **The only way to live above sin is to walk in the Spirit. If we live by the Spirit, we won't fulfill the desires of the flesh. If we ignore God's Spirit, corruption results.**
2. **Living without God brings out the worst in us. Paul listed the horrendous acts of the sinful nature which produce rotten fruit in all of us.**
3. **God's Spirit in us makes us loving, joyful, and peaceful. These qualities grow naturally from the Spirit-filled life but are not found in a life of sin.**
4. **God's Spirit makes us patient, kind, and good. Walking with our Lord assures that we will develop His character.**
5. **God's Spirit makes us faithful, gentle, and self-controlled. What we can't do on our own, the Holy Spirit does in us.**

LOOKING UP *Lord, fill me with Your Holy Spirit so that I might produce good fruit in my life. Help me to become less selfish and more like my loving Lord.*

PORTRAIT

DECEMBER 3

Ephesians 1-6

LOOKING BACK He never finished it, but it still made him famous. American artist Gilbert Charles Stuart was born on this day in 1755. He achieved fame for his unfinished portrait of George Washington, probably the best-known portrait in America. In early 1793, Stuart was heavily in debt. He planned to make money by painting Washington's portrait. Actually, Washington sat for three different Stuart portraits in 1795 and 1796. The "Vaughan" type, a bust portrait, shows Washington's head and upper body. "Lansdowne" is a full-length portrait of Washington as statesman, and "Atheneum" is the familiar unfinished oval of Washington's head.

LOOKING IN *Paul's task in Ephesians was to paint an accurate and finished portrait of the Christian life. He tells the Ephesians that faith must be acted out in real life. How a believer treats his family, business associates, employers, and fellow Christians speaks volumes as to his belief. If Christians understand their calling in Christ, then proper conduct will follow naturally. The first half of Ephesians describes the hope for the unification of all of God's creation in Christ and in the church. The second half urges Christians to live in a manner worthy of this calling. Paul wrote Ephesians while in prison, possibly in Rome, about A.D. 60.*

LOOKING OUT

1. **Careful living pleases Christ. Paul notes that we are to be careful how we live and take advantage of every opportunity to share.**
2. **We are to be controlled by no other spirit than that of Christ. Paul emphasizes that our Lord wants us to be filled with His Holy Spirit.**
3. **We are to be grateful in our worship. God's Word instructs us to consistently sing praises to our Lord and be thankful for what He has done.**
4. **Submission is not only for wives. Paul tells us we all, regardless of our status in life, must submit unselfishly to each other in Christian love.**
5. **Our families should reflect our faith. Husbands are to love their wives as Christ sacrificially loved the church, and wives are to respect their husbands.**

LOOKING UP *Lord, make me very practical in my faith as I tool out my Christianity in everyday life. May it affect my family, business, work, recreation, and friendships.*

POSITIVE

DECEMBER 4

Philippians 1-4

LOOKING BACK America's first thanksgiving took place on this day in 1619 at Berkeley Plantation, Virginia. It was entirely religious and did not involve feasting. A group of 38 English settlers arrived at Berkeley Plantation, on the James River, near what is now Charles City, Virginia. Their charter required that the day of arrival be observed yearly as a day of thanksgiving to God. For many years, the country had no regular national Thanksgiving Day. Sarah Josepha Hale, the editor of *Godey's Lady's Book*, worked many years to promote the idea of a national Thanksgiving Day. Then President Lincoln set aside "a day of thanksgiving and praise to our beneficent Father."

LOOKING IN *Giving thanks builds our faith and helps us stay positive. Paul's letter to the Philippians is filled with thanksgiving for all God has done. Paul also says that if we serve Christ, nothing in our future can ultimately harm us. The apostle is writing this letter from prison. In spite of the negative circumstances, Philippians is a warm, personal, and positive letter. Paul writes to thank the church at Philippi for the gift he has recently received while in prison. He informs them of his circumstances and of Timothy's and Epaphroditus' travel plans. Philippians is sheer positive power. Paul doesn't complain but looks to the future with great gratitude.*

LOOKING OUT

1. **Hard times can be the best of times. Paul doesn't complain but notes that his hardships have inspired others to accomplish greater works for God.**
2. **Rather than be suspicious of others' ministries, we need to be thankful the Gospel is being preached. Paul refuses to be dragged into a spirit of criticism.**
3. **Nothing can defeat us when we only want to please God. Paul states emphatically his desire that in life or death he would please Christ.**
4. **Our future is secure in Christ regardless of what happens. Paul rightly observes that if we live, we continue to please our Lord. If we die, we gain.**
5. **Regardless of what happens, Paul says we are to conduct ourselves in a manner worthy of the Gospel of Christ. Circumstances must never dictate our behavior.**

LOOKING UP *Lord, please help me to always have a positive attitude no matter the circumstances. Forgive me for the many times I have failed in this area.*

SUBMISSION

DECEMBER 5

Colossians 1-4

LOOKING BACK On this day in 1876, Ulysses S. Grant publicly apologized for his failures as president. In a speech to Congress, Grant claimed the mistakes he made while in office were due to his inexperience. His errors, he said, were "errors of judgment, not intent." While Grant's personal integrity was never formally questioned, he was closely associated with many government scandals which became public during his presidency. He unwittingly aided Jay Gould in an attempt to corner the gold market and in the Credit Mobilier affair. Many of the president's friends defrauded the government, forever tainting the reputation of President Grant.

LOOKING IN *As president, Grant learned it's very easy to get caught up in the evil around us or to give tacit approval to it. Paul warned the Colossians to be careful in their behavior lest their testimony be tainted. Satan always seeks to discredit us to compromise our witness. We must stay spiritually alert. Colossians is mainly a warning against combining Christianity with a worldly "philosophy" that involves Jewish observances. The author argued that faith in Jesus is completely sufficient, and that nothing need be added to it. Paul wrote this letter to the Christians in Colossae (in what is now western Turkey).*

LOOKING OUT

1. **Submission is not hard for those who are clothed with kindness. Real leadership is done with a servant's heart, just as our Lord took the towel and basin.**
2. **Husbands are to be kind, not harsh, with their wives. Words create worlds of hostility or hope. Harsh words destroy relationships and grieve our Lord.**
3. **Obeying parents brings glory to God. Paul notes that a child's submission to the parents' authority pleases the Lord.**
4. **Employees are to work for their bosses as they would for Christ. Paul observes that those who do this will be abundantly rewarded.**
5. **Employers are to be fair with their employees. Paul states that God looks with disfavor on those who take advantage of their workers.**

LOOKING UP *Lord, help me to remember that sermons are not to be high-sounding words spoken in the sanctuary on a Sunday morning. Rather, those words must be put into practical practice.*

PREPARED

DECEMBER 6

1 Thessalonians 1-5

LOOKING BACK Halifax, Nova Scotia, was nearly wiped out on this date in 1917. A devastating explosion killed 1,654 people when the Norwegian ship "Imo" plowed into the French munitions ship "Mont Blanc." The Norwegian ship was loaded with supplies for war-torn Europe, and the "Mont Blanc" carried 4,000 tons of TNT, 2,300 tons of picric acid, 61 tons of other explosives, and a deck of highly flammable benzene, which ignited and touched off the explosion. A tidal wave caused by the explosion washed much of the city away. At that time, Halifax was serving as the headquarters of Allied convoys sailing between North America and Europe.

LOOKING IN *Tragedies such as happened in Halifax conjure up images of judgment day, mentioned much in the Bible. In 1 Thessalonians, Paul addressed the coming of the Lord, which would precede such a day, telling us we should be prepared. Thessalonica was the largest city in Macedonia. Paul, Silas, and Timothy evangelized the city against the strong opposition of the Jews. Their stay was short, but they were successful in establishing a church. There was not time to give much instruction to the new converts. Questions arose as to some aspects of the Gospel and of the conduct demanded of believers. Paul wrote this letter to address these issues.*

LOOKING OUT

1. We are to show respect for spiritual leaders. Paul tells the Thessalonians that God holds them (and us) responsible for work, for attitudes.
2. God wants us to work, not just lie around waiting for His coming. Paul sharply rebukes the irresponsible and warns those who were idle to get back to work.
3. Joy and gratitude should be hallmarks of our faith. Paul tells the Thessalonians they are to rejoice in all things regardless of the hard times faced.
4. We are to respect spiritual things and not make light of them. Paul admonishes us not to treat prophecy with contempt.
5. God wants us to be pure in body, soul, and spirit. As faithful believers, every part of our being should be dedicated to our precious Lord.

LOOKING UP *Help me, Lord, to always live in the light of Your second coming. May I be prepared for that great day, and may my life exhibit what it means to follow You daily.*

MISTAKE

DECEMBER 7

2 Thessalonians 1-3

LOOKING BACK In a little over an hour, the course of the world changed. On this date in 1941, at 7:55 A.M., nearly 200 Japanese aircraft attacked Pearl Harbor, leaving almost 3,000 people dead. Nearly the entire U.S. Pacific Fleet was anchored there, and few ships escaped damage, while 200 U.S. aircraft on the ground were destroyed. The attack on Pearl Harbor brought about immediate U.S. entry into the hell of World War II. History now shows us there had been many warnings that a Japanese attack was imminent. However, for whatever reasons, the United States' government authorities continued to ignore them. That decision was a disastrous and costly mistake.

LOOKING IN *Paul had warned the Thessalonians that Jesus would return, bringing judgment to the world. While they didn't ignore his warnings, some misinterpreted them. They assumed Christ would return right away. While they exulted in their new relationship to God, they apparently didn't take seriously the demands of Christian teaching. Some had come to believe that "the coming of our Lord" was at hand, or had even begun. These had given up working for their living. Perhaps they held the view that the Lord's coming was so close there was no point in working. Paul wrote to settle them down a little, while not restraining their enthusiasm.*

LOOKING OUT

1. **If we suffer with Christ, we will reign with Him. The great apostle, who had suffered so much himself, said that enduring hardship counts us worthy of the Kingdom.**
2. **Those who persecute God's kids will one day be paid back for their evil deeds. Paul noted that God keeps careful records of those who harm His children.**
3. **Relief from our suffering does not always come in our time. We must be patient, for one day our God will make all things right.**
4. **While we do not understand all that happens to us, we should pray that we will be found worthy of His calling. We must remember that God is still in charge.**
5. **Our single aim must be to bring glory to our Lord by the way we act and react. Paul said we can do this according to the grace of God in us.**

LOOKING UP *Help me, Lord, to hold on in spite of difficult things I face. May I remember that You have gone before me and will bring me through this trial.*

VALUES

DECEMBER 8

1 Timothy 1-6

LOOKING BACK William Crapo Durant, known as the "godfather of the automobile industry," was born on this day in 1861. The founder of General Motors developed the idea that success in the auto industry lay in bringing together a combination of car manufacturers who offered a variety of models. He also outlined the principles of mass production, low costs, wide distribution, and increased profits. In addition, Durant founded the Chevrolet Motor Company. He lost, regained, and again lost control of GM, after which he founded Durant Motors. He went bankrupt in the Depression and operated a Flint, Michigan, bowling alley in the last working years of his life.

LOOKING IN *Durant illustrates that life has many bends and twists. If we let circumstances dictate our emotions, we will be depressed and distressed. Paul wrote to Timothy saying God gives power to live above circumstances. Timothy was probably born in Lystra, in Asia Minor. His father was Greek, his mother Jewish, but he had become a Christian. He is thought to have converted to Christianity when Paul made his first missionary journey and talked with him. Timothy joined Paul on his second journey. References in the New Testament indicate that Timothy remained Paul's trusted friend until Paul's death.*

LOOKING OUT

1. **"Know it alls" really know nothing. Paul tells the young preacher that false teachers pretend to be wise but, in actuality, are very foolish.**
2. **"Know it alls" are more interested in argument than godliness. Paul admonishes Timothy that it is unhealthy to promote controversies.**
3. **The goal of godliness is goodness, not gold. Pastors must understand that contentment with what God has given us is demanded by our Lord.**
4. **Money is to be used, not worshiped. Paul sadly recounts that many have destroyed themselves by pursuing money rather than God.**
5. **Our goals should be very clear. Paul specifically outlines what these goals are to be: righteousness, godliness, faith, love, endurance, and gentleness.**

LOOKING UP *Help me, Lord, to remember that all of us are called to reflect the nature of our Lord and to function in His church. How we act and react reflects Who we love.*

DETERMINATION

DECEMBER 9

2 Timothy 1-4

LOOKING BACK Winston Churchill had bulldog tenacity and the determination of a mule. He reached the height of his fame as the heroic Prime Minister of Great Britain during World War II. Churchill offered his people only "blood, toil, tears, and sweat" as they struggled to keep their freedom. Early in World War II, Great Britain stood alone against Nazi Germany. In spite of this, the Brits refused to give in, although the odds against them were tremendous. Churchill's personal courage, the magic of his words, and his faith in victory inspired the British to "their finest hour." On this day in 1944, Churchill said, "My guiding principle is, 'No peace without victory.'"

LOOKING IN *Paul had the same type of tenacity and determination. This last letter to Timothy is the last one he would write before giving his life for the Gospel. Paul wrote this letter from his jail cell during his second imprisonment in Rome. He was awaiting trial for his faith. It is clear that he felt he would not be released. Timothy had been the apostle's representative in the city of Ephesus for some time. Paul wrote stirring words of encouragement and instruction to his young disciple. Paul longed to see Timothy and asked him to come to Rome for a visit. It is generally believed that Timothy went. There is no fear in this last letter, only a sense of victory.*

LOOKING OUT

1. **Faith is like a fire–it must be kept alive. Paul told Timothy to stir up the gift God had given him. There were still great things to be done for God.**
2. **God's Spirit makes us bold, loving, and controlled. Paul reminded his "son in the faith" that we have not been given the spirit of fear, but of God's power.**
3. **We're God's, not because we're good, but because of His great purpose and plan. Because of God's wonderful love, we are part of a divine drama.**
4. **Christ came to heal our blindness. Paul told the young preacher the purpose of life could now be seen and that we would live forever with Him.**
5. **Faith is a treasure to keep carefully guarded. God's gift of salvation is the most priceless thing we will ever possess. Paul was now ready to meet his Master.**

LOOKING UP *Father, You who have given me so much, please give me one thing more: a grateful heart. Thank You that You will always be with me.*

RESPECT

DECEMBER 10

Titus 1-3

LOOKING BACK One of America's greatest poets was so reclusive and mysterious that little is known about her life. Emily Dickinson was born on this date in 1830 at Amherst, Massachusetts. Neither she nor her poems were known to more than a few. Seven of her poems were published during her life, but after her death, her sister, Lacinia, discovered almost 2,000 others written on the backs of envelopes and on other scraps of paper locked in her bureau. They were published gradually over the next 50 years, beginning in 1890. Today, she is noted as one of the most original poets. She and Walt Whitman are considered the two most gifted poets in American literature.

LOOKING IN *Like Emily Dickinson, not much is known about Titus either. We do know he was the Gentile companion of Paul and recipient of the New Testament letter bearing his name. Though Acts doesn't mention Titus, he was quite involved in Paul's missionary activities, and his book teaches us much about the church. Paul apparently was released after his first Roman imprisonment and made additional journeys, unrecorded in Acts. One of the missionary expeditions took him and Titus to Crete, where Titus remained behind to oversee and administer the church. According to ancient church tradition, Titus was the first bishop of Crete.*

LOOKING OUT

1. **To be respected, we must be respectful. Paul told Titus that the older men who walked with the Lord should be held in high esteem by the church.**
2. **We never get too old to be effective. Paul instructed the older women in the church to use their experiences to help the younger ladies.**
3. **Our families must be a priority. Paul encouraged mothers to deeply love their husbands and children. The family was God's idea from the beginning of mankind.**
4. **Being an example is our best witness. Paul told Titus that in everything involving their lives, believers were to be examples of their faith.**
5. **The way we work gives powerful testimony. Christian workers must give their very best to employers as a witness. They work as unto the Lord.**

LOOKING UP *Help me always to remember, Lord, that the way I behave either brings credit or discredit to the faith and to Your precious name. Help me to be a good example of a believer.*

ABDICATION

DECEMBER 11

Philemon 1

LOOKING BACK England's King Edward VIII abdicated his throne on this day in 1936 to marry, as he said, "the woman I love." She turned out to be the twice-divorced American, Wallis Warfield Simpson, who had captured the heart of the king months before he stepped down. While many viewed Edward's abdication as wonderfully "romantic," others saw it as a gross evasion of responsibility, sending him and his wife to virtual exile. After his controversial abdication, Edward was created Duke of Windsor by his brother-successor, George VI. The Duke of Windsor died in Paris, May 28, 1972, but was buried in England, near Windsor Castle.

LOOKING IN *Abdication of responsibility is not an option for believers. Paul wrote to Philemon reminding him he should not abdicate his responsibility as a follower of Christ. Although Philemon had been hurt by the runaway slave, Onesimus, he was to forgive the one who had fled and stolen from him. The reason: Onesimus was no longer a slave, but a brother. Philemon had a judicial right to punish severely or even kill Onesimus. Paul's short and masterful epistle of some 355 Greek words challenged Philemon to apply Christian love in dealing with Onesimus. Some scholars even say Paul's approach eventually prompted the end of slavery.*

LOOKING OUT

1. **Our faith should be in Christ, not a creed. Paul affirmed that Philemon had placed his faith in Jesus Christ, not just a code of ethics.**
2. **Our faith must extend itself in love for God's kids. Paul commends Philemon for actively showing his love for other believers.**
3. **Our faith is to be shared. Paul acknowledged that Philemon did not just talk faith; he lived it out by sharing what he had with those in need.**
4. **Our faith should be deepened and matured. Paul sincerely wanted his friend Philemon's faith to come to a full understanding of God.**
5. **Our faith brings great joy to God. Paul was overjoyed because Philemon's faith was strong and his testimony sure.**

LOOKING UP *Lord, help me to be loving and forgiving even though I have been deeply hurt. Keep me from holding a grudge lest I be unforgiving and miss Your great mercy.*

LIGHT

DECEMBER 12

Hebrews 1-2

LOOKING BACK Joseph Hayne Rainey was sworn in as a member of the United States House of Representatives on this day in 1870. Just five years after the end of the Civil War, fought to end slavery, Rainey became the first Black to serve in the House. Rainey was from South Carolina, and for nine years he filled the Congressional seat of Benjamin Franklin Whittemore, which had been declared vacant. The enslavement of Blacks in the American Colonies had begun during the 1600's. By 1860, the slave states had about four million slaves. The slaves made up nearly a third of the South's population. Vermont was the first state in the U.S. to forbid involuntary slavery.

LOOKING IN *Even though the United States had a long way to go to erase prejudice against the Blacks, Rainey's election to the House of Representatives was a small light at the end of a dark tunnel. The terrible inequities of this world do darken our existence. However, Hebrews says there is a light at the end of this long, dark tunnel. This present darkness will not last forever. One day all things will be subject to God, making the world far different than it is now. Although Hebrews is called an epistle (letter), it is really a type of religious essay. Its author is unknown, and it was probably written during the persecution of Christians by Rome under the Emperor Domitian.*

LOOKING OUT

1. **Faith demands constant attention. The writer of Hebrews says we are to pay careful attention lest we drift away from the faith.**
2. **God's gifts are at His will, not our want. Hebrews makes the point that the gifts of the Holy Spirit are distributed to the church at God's will.**
3. **This present darkness is not forever. All things and all people will eventually become subject to God.**
4. **Suffering produces growth. Surprisingly, Hebrews says that even Jesus, God's Son, had to learn obedience through the things which He suffered.**
5. **Christ lowered Himself that we might be exalted. The Bible declares that He took on the frail garment of flesh to identify with His creation.**

LOOKING UP *Help me, Lord, to prepare for the day we will rule and reign with You. Teach me submission to Your will. Help me to be a good servant to You.*

CENTER

DECEMBER 13

Hebrews 3-4

LOOKING BACK A few months after the Civil War ended, Phillips Brooks traveled to the Holy Land. On Christmas Eve in 1865, the Philadelphia clergyman rode a horse five miles south from Jerusalem to Bethlehem. As he stood atop a hill overlooking the sleepy village, he saw the mouth of the cave where the Shepherds may have rested that first Christmas night. The beautiful scene left a deep impression on the young pastor. Three years later, Brooks would write the song that made him famous: "O Little Town of Bethlehem." Brooks was born on this day in 1835 in Boston, Massachusetts. He died in the same city 58 years later.

LOOKING IN *Just as Christ is the center of Christmas, we must also make Him the center of our lives. Hebrews admonishes us to center our thinking on Jesus, responding to His faithful discipline. He is making us into a trophy of His grace. In three ways, the author of Hebrews tries to help his readers remain faithful as Christians, despite persecution. First, he praises the greatness of Christianity, mainly by showing that it is superior, in his view, to Judaism. Second, he presents Jesus as an example of being perfected through suffering. Third, he warns of the spiritual consequences to Christians of abandoning their faith.*

LOOKING OUT

1. **Making Christ the center of our thinking assures a good life. Hebrews says we are always to fix our thoughts on Him.**
2. **We are people in process making progress. Hebrews notes that we are God's house being built according to His plans and purposes.**
3. **Whether we become bitter or better is up to us. God's Word warns that we must not harden our hearts when the Lord corrects us.**
4. **Those refusing God's correction will never find peace. Hebrews' writer says that God had determined to never give rest to the disobedient.**
5. **We are to help others in their faith. Hebrews admonishes us that our role is to encourage believers to avoid sin and to stay close to Christ.**

LOOKING UP *Thank You, Lord, for Your great miracles in my life. May I never take them for granted or relegate them to mere "coincidences."*

GROWTH

DECEMBER 14

Hebrews 5-7

LOOKING BACK Today, as the Christmas season intensifies, we will probably hear the carol, "Hark the Herald Angels Sing." One musical expert calls this song one of the four most popular hymns in the English language. The words came from the prolific pen of Charles Wesley, who, with his brother John, founded the Methodist church. During his lifetime, Charles wrote over 6,500 hymns, many of which are still sung. Charles authored this carol around 1739, a year after his conversion. The Wesleys were not only well-known for their rigid theology, but also for their excellent work habits. They faithfully fulfilled their callings in spite of all hardships.

LOOKING IN *God expects his servants to work hard at their faith. He has invested His most priceless possession in us that we might have eternal life. Therefore, He expects us not only to appreciate the gift of His Son but also to fulfill the calling He has given us. The writer of Hebrews makes this very clear. Since the author is not named in the book itself, many have speculated as to who the author was. Luke, Clement of Rome, Priscilla, Barnabas, Apollos, or a Hellenist like Stephen have all been suggested. Origen, an early church father, was probably more correct when he said that only God knew who wrote Hebrews.*

LOOKING OUT

1. **Faith is like riding a bicycle–you either go on or you go off. We must move forward in our faith by maturing in our relationship with Christ.**
2. **After receiving so much of God's grace, we must never fall back. Hebrews says that once enlightened, we are forever responsible.**
3. **Our sin hurts our Lord. Even now, Hebrews says, our sin has an effect on our Lord. It puts Christ on the cross again, subjecting Him to public disgrace.**
4. **God always expects a return on His investment. Just as a farmer expects to reap his crops, God wants fruit from us. We will give an account of how we have used our resources.**
5. **Those who follow Christ must never be lazy. Christianity is a life of action, not just an experience of thoughtful contemplation.**

LOOKING UP *Help me, Lord, to grow daily in You and Your Word. Let me put the foolish and childish things behind me that I might become all You desire me to be.*

PERSEVERANCE

DECEMBER 15

Hebrews 8-10

LOOKING BACK Among the many carols that will be sung today is one originally entitled "Adeste Fidelis." Best known as "O Come All Ye Faithful," the song speaks of perseverance. It was penned in 1750 by John Francis Wade, who made his living as an artist doing calligraphy and copying manuscripts by hand. Wade was a Roman Catholic and wrote the song in Latin. He originally inserted it into a hymnal that he was copying for an English-speaking church in Portugal. Thirty-five years later, the song was sent to a Portuguese chapel in London, England, where a well-known singing group started performing it, and its popularity spread around the world.

LOOKING IN *God's people are not only to be known for their faith but also for their faithfulness. We are to persevere in spite of opposition or circumstances. Hebrews tells us to draw near to the Lord, hold unswerving to the faith, prod others to love and good works, and not give up meeting regularly with other believers in worship. Many have speculated that Hebrews was originally a sermon preached to a church in Rome and later sent to a church outside of Rome, perhaps experiencing similar circumstances. In this case, Hebrews 1-12 would represent the original sermon, and Hebrews 13 would represent the brief note attached for the second congregation.*

LOOKING OUT

1. We have the right and responsibility to enter God's presence. The writer of Hebrews tells us that Christ made the way for us to draw near to Him.
2. In spite of all discouragements, we are to hold firmly to hope. Hebrews notes that God will do what He has promised He would do.
3. God wants us to help others along the path of faith. Hebrews admonishes that we are to spur one another on toward love and good deeds.
4. We must be faithful in our attendance to God's house. The writer of this book says we need the fellowship and strength of our fellow believers.
5. We must be faithful because it is a dreadful thing to fall into the hands of the living God. Our God is to be revered. He is not our buddy; He is our God!

LOOKING UP *Thank You, Lord, that the way is open so we can come right into God's presence. May I always express deep reverence for You in the way I think, talk, and act.*

ANGELS

DECEMBER 16

Hebrews 11-13

LOOKING BACK Today, Christmas carols fill the air. Among the most loved song of this sacred season is the beautiful, "Angels From the Realms of Glory." This carol was not written by a clergyman or worship leader. Rather, it was penned by a controversial newspaper editor. James Montgomery was imprisoned twice for his steaming editorials against slavery and for the rights of the poor. These incarcerations never dimmed his spirit or stopped his determined compassion. Montgomery wrote his "angel" carol as an editorial in his newspaper on Christmas Eve, 1861. By the time of his death, this remarkable newspaperman had penned over 400 hymns.

LOOKING IN *Angels continue to be a fascinating topic for songs, stories, and television series. On occasion, God does send angels to this earth as His messengers. The writer of Hebrews warns that we must be careful how we entertain strangers because they just might be angels. The term "angel" is derived from the Greek word "angelos" which means "messenger." "Angelos" and the Hebrew equivalent, "malak," are the two most common terms used to describe these beings. When an angel appears, his task is to convey the message or do the will of the God Who sent him. Since the focus is on the message, the Bible rarely describes the messenger in detail.*

LOOKING OUT

1. **Love is an ongoing decision. Hebrews insists that we keep on loving and forgiving each other as brothers and sisters in Christ.**
2. **We can be "touched by an angel." Hebrews makes it clear that God does send His messengers to us on occasion. Therefore, we must be careful always to be hospitable.**
3. **We are to feel the hurt of those who are hurting. God wants us to identify fully with all the suffering saints, offering them comfort and help.**
4. **Marriage must be kept pure and holy. The writer of Hebrews insists that adultery and immorality must never be part of the believer's life.**
5. **Satisfaction with where we are and what we have pleases our Lord. Hebrews also says it keeps us from dangerous ambitions.**

LOOKING UP *Lord, help me to be faithful to You in all of my life experiences. May my home, marriage, use of money, and social life please You.*

ISSUES

DECEMBER 17

James 1-5

LOOKING BACK Today, you will probably hear the strains of a haunting Christmas carol that has been around a long time: "It Came Upon the Midnight Clear." Edmund Hamilton Sears penned this carol in 1849 to address severe social problems. The California Gold Rush was underway, along with many social upheavals. The Industrial Revolution was altering the nation's economy. The job market was rapidly changing, causing many jobs to become obsolete. Tensions were building that in just a few years would erupt into the tragic Civil War. It was in this turbulent setting that Sears, in his carol, begged believers to exercise peace on earth, good will toward men.

LOOKING IN *Sears' passionate plea of 150 years ago is as relevant today as it was then. Men of faith are to make a difference in their world, working peace and promoting good will. Real faith must result in changed behavior. James states emphatically that faith is far more than mental assent or idle contemplation. This great epistle encourages believers to do far more than hear the Word–they must live it! The letter is one of exhortation for practical Christianity. The author states principles of conduct and frequently provides poignant illustrations. His concerns are clearly more practical and less abstract than those of any other New Testament writer.*

LOOKING OUT

1. **We need a fast ear and a slow tongue. God's Word says that to answer a matter before we hear it is shame and folly.**
2. **Anger should be held in check. While anger is a natural emotion, it does not produce the righteousness God requires.**
3. **Moral filth must be plowed out and God's Word planted in our hearts. James says that this action will result in peace and joy.**
4. **We must not merely hear God's Word but put it into practice. Like soap, God's Word must be applied to be effective.**
5. **Real religion is loving Christ and caring for those He cares for. James tells us that Christ wants us to help and protect the vulnerable.**

LOOKING UP *Lord, help me to be very practical in my faith. Help me to be aware of the great needs around me. Give me strength as I move to make a difference.*

TRIUMPH

1 Peter 1-5

LOOKING BACK Today, you will probably hear Henry Wadsworth Longfellow's haunting carol written during the depths of the bloody Civil War. In 1863, he penned, "I heard the bells on Christmas day, their old familiar carols play, and loud and sweet their words repeat of peace on earth good will to men." He pondered the message and sadly added, "And in despair I bowed my head, There is no peace on earth, 'I said, 'For hate is strong and mocks the song of peace on earth good will to men.'" But then his faith rose, "Then pealed the bells more loud and deep. 'God is not dead nor doth He sleep. The wrong shall fail, the right prevail with peace on earth, good will to men.'"

LOOKING IN *Like Longfellow, when we look around at our war-torn world, we are often tempted to think that evil triumphs. However, that is just an illusion. Peter wrote his letter to persecuted Christians to encourage them to follow Christ's example when subjected to suffering. Their pain would not last forever. He assured them that one day evil would fall and truth triumph. Peter addressed his epistle to churches of the provinces in northern Asia Minor (modern Turkey). The readers were converted Jews and Gentiles suffering persecution. Peter told them to hope in God's ultimate deliverance and hence remain steadfast during their persecutions.*

LOOKING OUT

1. **We are to follow in the steps of our Lord. Peter says that Jesus came not only to die for our sins but also to show us how to live.**
2. **Regardless of accusations against Him, Jesus committed no sin. God's Word notes that accusations against us do not make the charges true.**
3. **When accusations are leveled against us, we must not retaliate or threaten. Peter reminds us that Jesus set the example.**
4. **When we are accused, we need not defend ourselves but place our fate in the hands of God. This is what Jesus did. His followers are to do the same.**
5. **Sometimes we have to take the blame even though we are not guilty. Jesus was innocent but took the sins of the world on Himself.**

LOOKING UP *Forgive me, Father, for the many times I have not reacted to insults and hurts in the way You instructed. Help me to follow Christ as my example when these things happen.*

AGAIN

2 Peter 1-3

LOOKING BACK Today, you will probably hear the most famous Christmas carol of all time. It was spurred by a crisis. There was bad news that Christmas Eve in 1818. Father Joseph Mohr learned that the church organ was broken and couldn't be fixed in time for the Mass late that evening. To help the situation, Mohr hastily penned a simple poem inspired by a new baby's birth that same day. He arrived at the church that evening, placed the poem in the hands of his organist, Franz Gruber, and asked him to compose a tune. Gruber was frustrated because the organ was broken. Mohr thrust a guitar in his hand, and Gruber began to strum a tune. "Silent Night" was born.

LOOKING IN *"Silent Night" is loved because it so beautifully describes the tenderness of Jesus' first coming to this earth. Peter says that just as our Lord came on that first Christmas, He will return the second time. However, this time He will not come as a baby, but as the Lord of lords and King of kings. Peter looks forward to that glorious day, encouraging all believers to know that Jesus will come as the Father had promised. Peter says there will always be those who scoff at the idea of Christ's return–the more as time passes. But we have God's Word on the issue. God's delays are out of mercy, not weakness. We must live in the light of that second coming.*

LOOKING OUT

1. **God's Word helps us keep our thinking straight. Peter wrote to the churches in Asia to stimulate their wholesome thinking.**
2. **We should not be surprised that so many discount Christ's coming. Peter told us that scoffers would appear in the last days.**
3. **God doesn't reckon time as we do. Since a thousand years is as a day, and a day as a thousand years, Jesus may have been away only about two days.**
4. **God will not be rushed to send His Son back to wrap up time. He wants all people everywhere to have the opportunity to know Him.**
5. **Jesus will return! In light of this, Peter reminds us we must live responsible and wholesome lives to be ready when He appears.**

LOOKING UP *Help me, Lord, to live carefully and prayerfully in the light of Your return. While I am waiting, help me share Your great good news with all those around me.*

JOY

DECEMBER 20

1 John 1-5

LOOKING BACK "Joy to the World," a carol you will probably hear today, was written out of frustration. As a teenager, Isaac Watts was frustrated with the archaic tunes and mediocre lyrics of religious music. His father, tired of hearing his son's complaints, challenged young Isaac to do better. At 18, Watts presented his first hymn to the congregation of his church. It was an immediate hit. Every week for the next two years, Isaac Watts produced a new song. "Joy to the World" is one of Watt's most loved carols. It was inspired from Psalm 98, and the tune was probably provided by George Frederick Handel, the composer of "The Messiah." He and Watts were friends.

LOOKING IN *Watts was right to put a lot of joy into the music about our Lord. The greatest joy we can know in this world is that God sent His Son to die for us that we might live. Watts' carol celebrates that fact. John, the beloved disciple, also celebrated that we can not only know that God sent His Son but also know for sure that we are saved. John's three letters provide us with a window on an early Christian church, its problems, and its developing doctrine. First John seems to be a treatise written to the church community. Although longest of the three letters, 1 John is called an epistle (letter), but it is really a kind of theological essay.*

LOOKING OUT

1. **Obedience is the hallmark of a real Christian. John says we know that we know Christ because we do what is right.**
2. **Love of others is a believer's identifying mark. John reports that we can know we have passed from death to life because we love.**
3. **We know that we know Christ if we love in action, not just in words. John states that Christians act out their faith in compassion.**
4. **We know that we know God because of His Spirit. John says the Holy Spirit gives us sure witness to our salvation.**
5. **We know we know Him because of His Word. John says he wrote this entire epistle to assure believers of their salvation.**

LOOKING UP *Thank You, Father, that I don't have to wonder if I am saved. You have given me many ways to know that I know You. Keep me from sin and true to You.*

ANTICHRISTS

DECEMBER 21

2 John 1

December

LOOKING BACK Two very different men were born on this date some 75 years apart. Benjamin Disraeli, the famed prime minister of England, was born in 1804. Disraeli was a champion for the poor and oppressed, leading his nation to many positive reforms. Seventy-five years later, one of the most feared and evil leaders the world had known was born at Gori, Georgia. His real name was Yosif Vissarionovich Djugashvili. In 1913, he adopted the name "Stalin" from a Russian word that means "man of steel." He became responsible for the deaths of nearly 10 million people.

LOOKING IN *John told the church there are two very different kinds of people in the world. First, there are believers, but then there are also antichrists who seek to destroy faith. We must learn to recognize both and treat them accordingly. The Bible's only use of the term "antichrist," is in John's epistles. His first letter spoke of the antichrist who is the great enemy of God and, in particular, antichrists who precede that great enemy. These antichrists were human teachers who had left the church. Such antichrists deny the incarnation and Christ's deity. In 2 John, the antichrists are identified as deceivers who teach that Jesus Christ did not come in the flesh.*

LOOKING OUT

1. **There is a special camaraderie among those who know the Lord. John had a special love for the chosen lady to whom he addressed this letter.**
2. **Grace, mercy, and peace are reserved for those who serve God. John says that these come because of our Lord's sacrifice.**
3. **Antichrists are in the world, and they seek to deceive us. John notes that we should not be surprised by their presence or intent.**
4. **Obedience and love are inseparable. John says that if we love God, we will keep His commandments and do His will.**
5. **Great joy comes to those who help others grow in truth. John said his joy was made complete in Christian fellowship.**

LOOKING UP *Lord, help me to be alert to the devil's determination to deceive. May I never aid and abet the activity of those who deny Your divinity and Lordship.*

HOSPITALITY

DECEMBER 22

3 John 1

LOOKING BACK James Edward Oglethorpe cared for the "down-and-outers." As a member of the English Parliament, he became interested in the plight of the poor. He sought to help those incarcerated in debtors' prisons by establishing an American colony. Oglethorpe received a charter from King George II, and in 1733, he and 114 colonists arrived in America to establish their settlement where the city of Savannah, Georgia, stands today. He governed wisely for nine years but was finally forced to return to England, being very much in debt because of his loans to colonists. This good and compassionate man was born on this date in 1696.

LOOKING IN *Those who care for others are highly acclaimed in Scripture. In 3 John, the apostle commends the faithfulness of Gaius. This generous man had opened his heart and home to those preaching the Gospel. Caring and sharing is godly. Gaius was a common name, and it is not likely that this Gaius is the same as any others mentioned in Scripture. If tradition is anything to go by, he may have been a leader of the church at Pergamum. What matters more is that Gaius lived in the truth and lived it out in his daily life. His words, his deeds, his character were all consistent. His conduct is much different than that of Diotrephes, who John also mentions.*

LOOKING OUT

1. **The family of God should support other members of the family who proclaim the Gospel. John emphatically insists that we must stand together.**
2. **When we support a ministry, we become a partner of that ministry. John says we share in the blessings of the work we support.**
3. **A good reputation follows a conscientious walk with God. John notes that a blameless walk results from commitment to Christ.**
4. **Believers should stand firm against hypocrites diluting the mission of the church. John tells us that those who oppose Christ are to be exposed.**
5. **Our role model must be Christ. John says that we are not to imitate the way of the world but follow hard after Jesus Christ.**

LOOKING UP *Help me, Lord, always to support and assist those who are preaching the Gospel of Christ. May I be hospitable to those You send my way.*

JUDGMENT

DECEMBER 23

Jude 1

LOOKING BACK Hideki Tojo, the prime minister of Japan who had whipped the nation into war frenzy, was executed on this date in 1948. Military officers began to hold political office in Japan during the 1930's. By 1936, they had control of the government. General Hideki Tojo, as premier of Japan was the driving force behind the raid on Pearl Harbor that brought the United States into World War II. After Japan's surrender in August, 1945, Tojo was arrested as a war criminal, tried by a military tribunal, and sentenced to death on November 12, 1948. He, along with six other rabid Japanese leaders, died by hanging at Sugamo Prison in Tokyo.

LOOKING IN *As the Japanese people learned, it does matter to whom we listen. Jude knew the power of persuasion exercised by false teachers who tried to turn believers from the truth. He wrote his urgent letter to warn Christians they must not entertain views of those who opposed Christ. Jude is a letter of exhortation to the "called" and "beloved."He tells them to "contend for the faith which was once delivered unto the saints." Simultaneously, it is a direct attack against the opponents of the gospel. Following his negative description of the opponents, Jude concludes by urging his readers to have attitudes and lifestyles different from the opponents.*

LOOKING OUT

1. **Christians need to beware of false teachers infiltrating the church. Jude says these "corrupters" of the Gospel are not to be condoned or tolerated.**
2. **Godless people can be detected by their beliefs. Jude notes that our words and actions speak volumes about where we stand.**
3. **Believers should be merciful to unbelievers. Mercy is the hallmark of our Lord and should be part of our Christian character.**
4. **Those who trust in Christ will be presented to the Father faultless. Jude says that through faith we are the righteousness of Christ.**
5. **The judgment of God on unbelievers is certain. Jude underlines what all Scripture says about the coming judgment of the world.**

LOOKING UP *Teach me, Lord, to be wise in my associations. Help me never to compromise the truth or stray the least from Your path. Thank You for guiding me.*

LORD

DECEMBER 24

Revelation 1-3

LOOKING BACK Ironically, it was on Christmas Eve in 1942 that German rocket engineer Wernher von Braun launched the first surface-to-surface guided missile. Within two years of that date, buzz bombs, a form of guided missile, were used by Germany against Great Britain. They had been made possible by von Braun's invention. Christmas Eve is hailed as a period of peace, yet one of man's deadliest inventions was birthed on that night. However, in fairness, von Braun's discovery also paved the way for our space travel. He directed the teams that built the various rockets that sent the first American into space and landed the first astronauts on the moon.

LOOKING IN *Like von Braun's rocket invention, most things can be used for either good or evil. Jesus, the Prince of Peace, whose birth we celebrate this season, will come into our life to help us choose that which helps and heals rather than debilitates and destroys. The first chapters of Revelation tell of Christ's coming, this time not as a helpless babe in a manger but as the "King of kings and Lord of lords." Like other apocalyptic literature, Revelation is addressed to people undergoing persecution. It encourages them to withstand the persecution by predicting the approaching end of the world, when God will rescue them by destroying the powers of evil.*

LOOKING OUT

1. **Jesus Christ was alive long before Bethlehem. The white hair in John's dramatic vision symbolizes our Lord's eternal existence.**
2. **Jesus Christ has all insight. John describes our Lord as having "eyes like blazing fire." This symbolizes the omniscience of our Lord.**
3. **Jesus Christ conquers all. John reports Christ has "feet like bronze glowing in a furnace." This indicates that Jesus will trample all of God's enemies.**
4. **Jesus Christ answers all the cries of mankind. John says He has a "voice like the sound of rushing waters." This indicates our Lord's universality.**
5. **Jesus Christ is perfect in judgment. John sees the two-edged sword coming out of our Lord's mouth. This symbolizes His righteous judgment.**

LOOKING UP *Thank You, Lord, for being all powerful and conquering evil. Help me to live in readiness for Your second coming.*

GLORY

DECEMBER 25

Revelation 4-5

LOOKING BACK The first mention of December 25 as the birth date of Jesus occurred in A.D. 336 in an early Roman calendar. The celebration of this day as Jesus' birth date was probably influenced by pagan festivals held at that time. The ancient Romans held year-end celebrations to honor Saturn, their harvest god, and Mithras, the god of light. Various peoples in northern Europe held festivals in mid-December to celebrate the end of the harvest season. As part of all these celebrations, the people prepared special foods, decorated their homes with greenery, and joined in singing and gift-giving. These customs gradually became part of the Christmas celebration.

LOOKING IN *While some have resisted observing Christ's birth on December 25 because of the association with pagan celebrations, others see this as simply making Christian what was once pagan. They point out that this is exactly what Jesus does to us when we accept Him as our Savior. Jesus' birth was fulfillment of God's great plan for this sin-cursed world. That plan is still being carried out. In Revelation, John is given a preview of what God had in mind for us and this world. Swept up in the awesome presence of God, John has trouble communicating what he sees in human language. Therefore, he uses marvelous word pictures.*

LOOKING OUT

1. **God wants us to know His great plans for us. John is invited into heaven to learn God's destiny for our world.**
2. **God's glory is so marvelous it defies description. John struggles with how to communicate the greatness of God. There are no words to describe what he sees.**
3. **God's power is beyond man's comprehension. John is awestruck as he sees all heaven shake with lightning and thunder.**
4. **God's holiness is awesome. John reports it is so great that the hosts of heaven constantly sing of His holiness and power.**
5. **One day, we will joyfully lay our crowns at His feet. John says that the twenty-four elders precede us in this honor.**

LOOKING UP *Lord, help me to give You glory with my life and lips. Thank You that You have found me worthy to be called by Your name and do Your work.*

HORSEMEN

DECEMBER 26

Revelation 6-8

LOOKING BACK Two very different designations are given for today, December 26. The first is positive while the second is not. In several countries, this day is known as "Boxing Day." Formerly, it was the time when Christmas gift boxes were traditionally given "to those who serve, such as the postman, the lamplighter, the dustman, and all other functionaries who render services to the public at large, without receiving payment therefore from any individual." The negative designation for December 26 is "National Whiner's Day." It is a day dedicated to whiners, especially those who return Christmas gifts and are dissatisfied with their life.

LOOKING IN *From the beginning, men have set aside time and dedicated days for many things, good and bad. However, there is one day that God Himself has designated, and it is still to come. That awesome time is "Judgment Day." In Revelation, John talks about this time when God will make all wrongs right. The expression "Day of Judgment" appears several times in the Bible as a frightful day of dread connected with God's wrath. God's Word says this day can only be overcome through faith in Christ. Closely connected with the second coming of Christ, it is a part of the end-time events connected with the close of human history.*

LOOKING OUT

1. **Good always overcomes evil. John sees that while evil is a savage and destroying "beast," God's "Lamb" will finally abolish it forever.**
2. **Raging war will precede evil's final demise. John talks about the great white horse whose Rider is armed with a bow, symbolizing a final war.**
3. **Revolution and civil strife will come before our Lord's return. The red horse of Revelation stands for unprecedented unrest at the end time.**
4. **Famines will ravage the world in the final conflict against evil. The black horse symbolizes world-wide hunger that will strike the wicked world.**
5. **Pestilence and massive deaths will come before evil is finally destroyed. The pale horse symbolizes a tragedy greater than any known in human history.**

LOOKING UP *Lord, may I never forget how very awful evil is. Thank You that it will not forever rule on our earth.*

CONTROL

DECEMBER 27

Revelation 9-11

LOOKING BACK French chemist-bacteriologist Louis Pasteur was born on this day in 1822. His contributions to chemistry, medicine, and industry have greatly benefited humanity. Pasteur's discovery that diseases are spread by bacteria has saved countless lives. Although already famous at age 26, he started probing the mysteries of bacteriology. Others saw bacteria before Pasteur, but he was the first to show that living things come only from living things. Scientists at that time believed in spontaneous generation–life coming from things not alive, such as dirt. Pasteur proved that although bacteria lived almost everywhere, their spread could be controlled.

LOOKING IN *Pasteur's discoveries laid the foundation for the miracle of modern medicine. For the first time, man saw that many diseases could be contained and cured. Just as Pasteur uncovered the cause of many diseases and pointed toward their cure, God's Word says the disease of sin will one day be contained and cured. Revelation points to the glorious world to come (a world of "no more death or mourning or crying or pain"), at the reappearing of the crucified and risen Jesus. This now enthroned Lord will return to conclude world history with the destruction of God's enemies, the final salvation of His own people, and the creation of a new heaven and earth.*

LOOKING OUT

1. All that evil has built will go to God and His children. John says that this world's kingdoms will become the Kingdoms of our Christ.
2. God's justice seems long in coming, but it is sure. Revelation notes that the elders will rejoice because Christ has begun to reign.
3. No one escapes God's judgment. John reminds us that all of mankind, living and dead, will appear before God to give an account.
4. Judgment day for the believer is a glorious time. John says that the faithful will be given their rewards on the awesome day of God's judgment.
5. Those who have despoiled this earth will be despoiled. John assures us that one day God will right all the past wrongs done by the evil one.

LOOKING UP *Keep me true, Lord, to Your Word. Help me to be prepared for the final Judgment Day. Thank You that I need not dread that time but look forward to it.*

INNOCENTS

Revelation 12-14

LOOKING BACK "Holy Innocents Day" or "Childermas," is observed by many Christians on December 28. This time commemorates the massacre of the children in Bethlehem, ordered by King Herod when he heard that Christ was born. Evil Herod felt his precarious throne was threatened and determined to kill the new "king." Early and medieval accounts claimed that as many as 144,000 children under two years of age were murdered by the mad king. However, more recent scholars have revised that figure, saying Bethlehem was a small town when Christ was born. They now estimate the number of children killed to be between six and 20.

LOOKING IN *Throughout the centuries, "innocents" have been routinely murdered by evil people. John the Revelator knew the church was birthed in great pain. First, Jesus suffered intensely, and then His church felt the pangs of persecution. John noted that this pain would not last forever. God has a great and wonderful plan for His children. We are to hold on firmly to our faith. John lets us know that the murder of the "innocents" will one day be avenged. John's situation when he wrote Revelation was one of suffering. He was a "fellow partaker in the tribulation." He was exiled on the lonely Isle of Patmos, not knowing whether he would be released or executed.*

LOOKING OUT

1. **The church was born in pain. John sees that Christ's first coming, and the church's birth, involved much suffering and hardship.**
2. **There is an eternal enemy of the church. Satan, standing angrily against God, always seeks to kill Christ and the church.**
3. **Just as the Father protected His only begotten Son from the evil one, John says we are daily spared from Satan's fury.**
4. **The conflict between good and evil did not originate on earth but in heaven. John recounts the fall of Satan from heaven because of his pride.**
5. **Christ's victorious death, along with our testimony, brings Satan down. Revelation recounts that the victory has already been won on Calvary!**

LOOKING UP *Help me to remember, Lord, that although Satan is strong and powerful–his attacks fierce–his time is short. Thank You that he is a defeated foe.*

MASSACRE

DECEMBER 29

Revelation 15-16

LOOKING BACK On this day in 1890, a band of about 350 Lakota Sioux sought by the Army surrendered to the U.S. Army near Wounded Knee Creek in South Dakota. The band, consisting of about 120 men and 230 women and children, were followers of the Ghost Dance religion, which taught that God would restore the Indian world to the way it was before Whites arrived. Army leaders feared the religion would lead to an Indian uprising. About 470 troops surrounded the Lakota band. As the troops began to disarm the band the next day, someone—whether an Indian or a soldier is uncertain—fired a shot. The troops then fired on the Lakota, killing some 300 of them.

LOOKING IN *Evil is horrible whether it is expressed personally, corporately, or nationally. Revelation vividly exposes how awful evil is. John says that when Satan and his minions are finally put down, all of the universe will rejoice. Heaven will burst into triumphant song because the originator of pain and sorrow will have been destroyed. These chapters of Revelation tell us the great disasters of human history are warnings of the final "Day of Judgment." The plagues John describes here vividly recall those which fell on Egypt at the time of the exodus. John tells believers not to fear since they are protected by their God.*

LOOKING OUT

1. **God's justice is always fair. Man often punishes unfairly, but God never does. John tells us our God is fair in dealing out discipline.**
2. **God's justice is always right. Revelation admits that while human justice is often miscarried, God's judgment is never undeserved.**
3. **Sin causes us to bite the hand that feeds us. John says that evil men will not repent but curse the One Who could alleviate their pain and suffering.**
4. **Sin never makes sense. Rather than coming to their senses through pain, John sees the evil ones rebelling even more.**
5. **When God's judgment comes, it will be swift and sure. John admonishes followers of Jesus to be ready for the judgment day.**

LOOKING UP *Thank You, Father, that You have provided a way for me to escape the just judgments of God. Help me to clearly communicate this escape route to all others.*

CONFUSED

DECEMBER 30

Revelation 17-19

LOOKING BACK Canadian author Stephen Leacock was born on this day in 1869. Although Leacock is the most popular humorist in Canadian literature, he also wrote serious works and was a distinguished professor of economics and political science. Most of his humorous works poke good-natured fun at everyday people and events by treating them with mock seriousness. Leacock's best-known book is "Sunshine Sketches of a Little Town," a charming portrait of life in a small town based on Orillia, Ontario. He is often quoted for his words about one of his characters: "He flung himself upon his horse and rode off madly in all directions."

LOOKING IN *Leacock's description could very well be said of Satan, when he is finally defeated by our Lord. The evil one will be so totally confused that he will attempt to "ride off madly in all directions at once." Yet it won't do him any good. Satan will finally be defeated by the One he rebelled against eons ago. Chapters 18 and 19 tell of the fall of Babylon, long the symbol of evil. The Old Testament prophets had so often denounced the literal Babylon that it became a byword for human pride and vainglory. John says God's people will be vindicated. Justice will be done. John says Babylon's fall is so certain that it can be said to have happened already.*

LOOKING OUT

1. **The whole universe will rejoice when evil is finally subdued. John sees all heaven burst out in shouting because evil and the evil one are fallen.**
2. **When evil is forever stilled, all will see that its power was just an illusion. John reminds us that all salvation, glory, and power belong to God.**
3. **One day, we will be part of a magnificent wedding in heaven. John reveals that Christ and His church will celebrate at a glorious supper.**
4. **Only One is worthy of our worship: our living Lord Jesus Christ! The angel refused to let John bow down to him.**
5. **All of God's Word revolves around Jesus Christ. John says the testimony of Jesus is the "spirit of all prophecy" throughout history.**

LOOKING UP *Lord, increase my faith as I look forward to the time when all evil crumbles. I rejoice in Your strength that gives me victory in this present evil world and hope for a bright tomorrow.*

CHANGE

DECEMBER 31

Revelation 20-22

LOOKING BACK A strange activity takes place in Japan every year on this date. In the evening, groups of "Namahage" men disguised as devils make door-to-door visits, growling, "Any good-for-nothing-fellow hereabout?" Their object is to give sluggards an opportunity to change their ways and become diligent. Otherwise, according to legend, they will be punished by devils. Many Japanese people say they are not devout worshipers and do not have strong religious beliefs. However, nearly everyone in Japanese society engages in some religious practice or ritual based on the two major religious traditions in Japan: Shinto and Buddhism.

LOOKING IN *The final book of the Bible tells us that one day there will be a final ferreting out of all the world's "good-for-nothings." However, at that time their opportunity to change will have passed. Judgment Day has come. Evil is eradicated. Satan is overthrown. All must account for their lives. God introduces His new world. With everything evil gone and death destroyed, the new age is like none known before. Our new lives are one long unclouded wedding day for all who know God. It is the happiest, most joyful time imaginable. There is now no sorrow, no pain, no parting, no night–because our God is always there.*

LOOKING OUT

1. **Satan will finally be under God's firm control. John sees that the evil one will be bound for a thousand years, helpless and alone.**
2. **Martyrs have a special place in the Kingdom. John reports that those who have suffered for Christ will reign forever with Him.**
3. **All must firmly reject the evil one. John notes that after being bound, Satan is released for a season to tempt all who had not resisted him.**
4. **There is a general resurrection where everyone must stand before God. John lets us know that all of us must give an account for what we have done.**
5. **There will be a finality to sin and strife. John confidently asserts that Satan and his followers are thrown into the lake of fire, burning forever.**

LOOKING UP *Lord, my final prayer for this year is to thank You for saving and sustaining me. As we enter the new year, may I be ever more faithful in following You.*

DID YOU KNOW?

There are Lost Books of the Bible

Although we don't have them, the Bible mentions many books we would find fascinating. Joshua and Samuel tell of the Book of Jashar. It probably consisted of poems on events in Israel's history, collected during the time of David or Solomon.

The War of the Lord is noted in Numbers. This book was likely a collection of poems which relate the conquest of the land during the time of Moses and Joshua. As the title of the book suggests, the Lord was responsible for the success of the conquest because He was their commander-in-chief.

Shemaiah the Prophet is just one of the many books noted in Chronicles. Others are the Book of Samuel the Seer, Nathan the Prophet, Gad the Seer, The Prophecy of Ahijah the Shilonite, and Visions of Iddo the Seer Against Jeroboam the Son of Nebat.

Some Other Fascinating Facts

There are far more than ten Commandments in the Bible. Actually, there is a total of 613 specific commandments in the Law of Moses. Most of these are contained in the Book of Leviticus.

Early Bibles were handwritten on scrolls, containing no punctuation, verses, or chapters. These were added later to facilitate reading. "Center words" made sure nothing was omitted. If a specific word didn't show up, the scribe had left something out.

Though dogs are mentioned in the Bible two dozen times, cats are not referred to at all. The only place a cat is mentioned is once in the Apocrypha, which appears in the Letter of Jeremiah.

Did You Know?

The earliest Roman writer to mention Jesus was a governor in Asia Minor named Pliny. He wrote to the emperor Trajan in 112 A.D., describing the trials of Christians, noting: "They had been accustomed to meet before daybreak, and to recite a hymn antiphonally to Christ, as to a god." Some years later, the Roman historian Tacitus wrote that the name *Christians* "derives from Christus, who was condemned by Pontius Pilate during the reign of Tiberius."

Perhaps the most intriguing historical reference to Jesus comes from the Jewish historian Josephus. In his first-century Jewish Antiquities, he wrote: "About this time there lived Jesus, a wise man, if indeed one ought to call him a man. For he was one who wrought surprising feats and was a teacher of such people as accept truth gladly. He won over many Jews and many Greeks. He was the Messiah." Josephus then went on to record Christ's resurrection, saying God had prophesied this event. He added, "And the tribe of Christians, so called after him, has still to this day not disappeared."

Early Christians were persecuted severely by the Roman government. They began to use the fish as both a secret code and anti-Roman symbol. This sign often identified the places of worship for believers and served as a means of noting those who followed Jesus Christ. The fish appears often in Rome's catacombs, the burial places for the early Christians.

The fish became Christianity's symbol because each of the letters in the Greek word for fish, *ichthus*, are the same as those in the phrase *Iesous Christos Theou Huios Soter*. Translated into English, the phrase means "Jesus Christ, of God the Son, Savior." Jesus also said His followers were "fishers of men."

BIBLE STATISTICS

	Old Testament	New Testament
Longest book	Psalms	Luke
Shortest book	**Obadiah**	**3 John**
Longest chapter	Psalm 119	Matthew 26
Shortest chapter	**Psalm 17**	**Revelation 15**
Longest verse	Esther 8:9	Revelation 20:4
Shortest verse	**1 Chronicles 1:25**	**John 11:35**
Middle book	Proverbs	2 Thessalonians
Middle chapter	**Job 29**	**Romans 13-14**
Middle verse	2 Chronicles 20:13	Acts 7:7
Middle chapter of the Bible	**Psalm 117**	
Middle verse of the Bible	Psalm 118:8	
Most mentioned mortal	**David (1,118 times)**	